Settlement Folk

SETTLEMENT FOLK

*Social Thought and the American
Settlement Movement, 1885–1930*

Mina Carson

The University of Chicago Press
Chicago and London

Mina Carson is assistant professor of history at Oregon
State University.

The University of Chicago Press, Chicago 60637
The University of Chicago Press, Ltd., London

© 1990 by The University of Chicago
All rights reserved. Published 1990
Printed in the United States of America

99 98 97 96 95 94 93 92 91 90   54321

Library of Congress Cataloging-in-Publication Data

Carson, Mina Julia.
    Settlement folk : social thought and the American settlement
movement, 1885–1930 / Mina Carson.
        p.   cm.
    ISBN 0-226-09501-0 (alk. paper)
    1. Social settlements—United States—History—20th century.
2. Social settlements—United States—History—19th century.
I. Title.
HV4194.C37   1990
362.5'57'097309041—dc20   89-20319
                                                       CIP

∞ The paper used in this publication meets the minimum
requirements of the American National Standard for Information
Sciences—Permanence of Paper for Printed Library Materials,
ANSI Z39.48-1984.

To Robert, Helen, Laura, and Sally, with love and gratitude

Contents

Preface

We are beginning to enjoy the fruits of a resurgence of interest in the Anglo-American settlement house movement. The centenary of the first settlement ventures in England and America, the maturation of women's history, an ever-increasing sophistication in the study of urban development and institutions, and perhaps the current struggle to re-draw a workable social agenda have all contributed to a renewed focus on a remarkable and long-lived social movement.[1]

Contemporary historiography of the settlement impulse must be dated from Allen F. Davis's groundbreaking *Spearheads for Reform* (1967), which located the settlement houses at the eye of urban pro-gressive reform at the turn of the century. The 1960s saw the floodtide of the great civil rights movement and, under Lyndon Baines Johnson and a Democratic Congress, a new federal commitment of human and material resources to lingering and exacerbated social problems, par-ticularly in American cities. It was time for a work like Davis's, both celebratory and shrewdly critical of a voluntarist movement that reached out to enlist public energies in tackling a sweeping agenda of social ills. Davis acknowledged—and I too acknowledge—a debt to those historians, including Walter Bremner, Clarke Chambers, and Roy Lubove, who had already boldly marked out the social welfare ideas and initiatives of an industrializing America as subjects urgently in need of their brand of critical, creative study and analysis.

In a canny and immensely useful article a few years ago, Clarke Chambers assessed the state of "welfare history" and charted some future directions.[2] In the course of suggesting that welfare historians have kept a surprising distance from the "bottom up" perspective of the "new social history," Chambers pointed out a partial exception: advo-cates of the "social control" model of social welfare history, who have argued that the most important constant in modern American welfare initiatives has been their broad disciplinary function, addressed vari-ously to "controlling" subpopulations and maintaining a certain eco-nomic status quo. Yet through all the subtle shadings of their arguments, Chambers maintained, even the social control historians did not truly address the roles of the poor in the social welfare equation. (Indeed, the thrust of some of their arguments militates against acknowledging a genuine power struggle, much less a collaboration, between the "actors" and the "acted upon.") Though I agree with Chambers's general assessment, I suggest that the social control debate played a critical role in sketching alternative ethical and political vantage points from which to evaluate the successes and failures of liberal American social welfare programs. The social control debate also helped keep welfare history alive, complex, and healthily angry during the transitional years of the 1970s.

The ground of American social debate, and by extension its historiography, has shifted sharply in the 1980s, with the first effective political challenge to the liberal consensus on public responsibility for social welfare that jelled in the mid-1930s. Prevailing social assumptions and attendant federal policies of the long, long New Deal, barely jostled by previous conservative presidencies, splintered in the 1980s. Whatever one's private reactions to these developments, it would be hard to deny that the teaching and writing of American social and cultural history have been fundamentally, and probably creatively, shaken up. At the same time United States historiography, locked in a dialectic with these external lurches into an undiscernible future, has manifested an exciting diversity and a tendency to reappropriate older methods and concerns for fertile melding with the new. In particular, a newly omnivorous "cultural history" now takes account of, among other things, twenty years of hard labor in "bottom up" history to offer new readings of the interplay of elites and masses, groups and individuals, popular culture and formative intellectual paradigms, lives and ideas. Previous historiographic categories are jogged loose and clatter to the ground.

This new cultural history is where I want to locate my own history of the settlement ideology. Ever since I can remember, I have been fascinated and disturbed by the phenomenon of social conscience: its various origins, motives, elaborations, perversions. For a child, and teenager, of the American sixties this is an unsurprising obsession, I think. Thus my interest in the settlement movement was from the beginning centered not on those the settlement workers proposed to engage themselves with, but on the settlement workers themselves: bold, energetic, idealistic, yet conventional, acting out a kind of heroism made possible by what some today might call their naïveté about social relations in an industrial society.

Settlement Folk is, as its title suggests, a group or corporate biography of the primary actors in a peculiarly rich and suggestive episode in the interplay of ideas and experience. In fact, in its complex and almost overdetermined Victorian origins the settlement movement was *predicated* on the notion that ideas untested by experience are "life"-less, hollow, useless. Like earlier welfare historians, I may be judged by some as willing implicitly to dismiss the idiosyncratic and potent personhood of the settlement "neighbors"—the settlement workers' intended beneficiaries—by focusing primarily on what Chambers calls the "movers and shakers" of this social welfare experiment. However, I needed to focus on *one* story, and the story I chose is the settlements' central role in appropriating and repeatedly *re*articulating certain Victorian values: trying those values this way and that, testing, rationalizing, and refining them in the light of hard experience and so at last preparing them to play new roles in a "modernized" social welfare paradigm. As I traced the settlement impulse backward, then forward, I learned that its history is a variation on the important theme of the survival of the old at the heart of the new—in this case with the ironic twist that the old values in a sense *programmed* the new even as they seemed overcome by change. This is a book about how the settlement workers *thought* they could be of service to those they sought to serve, how they themselves might be affected, and how those ideas changed and remained the same over the first forty-five years of this vigorous, plurally significant movement.

By "primary actors" I mean those with the biggest speaking parts. Just as most of the poor—or in the settlers' polite terminology, the "neighbors"—remain silent in this study, so do most of the myriad lesser-known settlement leaders and foot soldiers. A number of historians have recently, and rightly, begun to question how representative was the widely recognized liberalism of the most prominent settlement leaders: Jane Addams, Lillian Wald, Vida Scudder, Graham Taylor, Robert Woods, John Elliott, and a few more.[3] In tracing the evolution of the settlement ideology, I have chosen to concentrate on the most articulate leaders for several reasons. First, they were the ones who in fact outlined settlement ideology in the most authoritative forms and forums. These women and men were repeatedly, both tacitly and overtly (through election to various leadership positions in the movement), recognized by their colleagues as leaders and spokesmen. Second, these people have left the fullest records, both professionally and personally; it is *possible,* frankly, to trace their careers and their ideas over a long period, to note continuity and change in the ways they interacted with their peers, their public, and their opponents. Finally, these individuals not only were recognized as leaders by their settlement colleagues, but moved freely and influentially in social, political, and intellectual circles beyond the settlement houses. Given my interest in the ways settlement ideology reflected and influenced broader social thought, it made sense to study the ideas and careers of those people who played palpable roles in the evolution of American social and intellectual life. These women and men certainly did not represent the ideas and beliefs of all settlement workers—I have tried to note significant conflicts not just with their neighbors, their "followers," and members of the public but among the leaders themselves—but there is ample reason to take them seriously not just as mouthpieces for a movement but as American voices in their own right.

Beyond my gratitude to, and humility before, those historians I've mentioned above, as well as all the others whose broad shoulders bear the weight of so many succeeding students, I have more immediate debts. First, to the staffs of the libraries and repositories where I spent so many hours: the Chicago Historical Society, the Special Collections department of the University of Chicago Library, the Rare Book and Manuscript Library of Columbia University, the Houghton and Widener Libraries at Harvard University, the Manuscript Collection at the University of Illinois at Chicago Circle (where I spent several charmed weeks in the summer-warm second floor of the old Hull-House mansion poring over the Jane Addams Memorial Collection), the Social Welfare History Archives at the University of Minnesota, the Minnesota Historical Society, the New York Public Library, the Newberry Library, the Schlesinger Library at Radcliffe College, and the Sophia Smith Collection at Smith College. These blessedly quiet, orderly places allowed me to serve my apprenticeship as a working historian, and I am always amazed by the seemingly unflappable courtesy of archivists and librarians toward their obsessed, harried, and sometimes not thoroughly considerate clientele.

The Charles Warren Center of Harvard University generously funded three research trips for the dissertation from which this book developed. Friends and colleagues listened patiently as I played around with my ideas about the settlements and innumerable ancillary topics. Virginia deJohn Anderson, Michael Baenan, Eve Kornfeld, Jennifer Laurendeau, and Charles McGovern among my graduate-school peers probably weathered the most frequent and sustained onslaughts. Helena Wall read and commented shrewdly and generously on everything I showed her and in myriad other ways boosted me through the long haul. Her philosophy of graduate studies seemed to be that this too is life. That helped. Robin McKinley's interest and example kept before me the vision of a guild of writers beyond the academy dedicated to craft, no matter what the genre. C. C. Piepho challenged me, put up with me, taught me how to use a computer, and forced me to justify my work by demonstrating its connection to people living as well as defunct. He even offered to read it.

Administrators and colleagues at Northeast Missouri State University made it possible for me to keep the settlements pot simmering while I performed my other academic duties. Particular appreciation goes to Darrell Krueger and James Lyons for making available the time and institutional research support I needed to finish this project. Thanks too to Moureen Coulter and Marc Gallicchio, who read and commented on parts of the final manuscript. Among colleagues at other universities I'd like to acknowledge the generously shared comments and ideas of Clarke Chambers, Ruth Crocker, Ellen Fitzpatrick, Joseph Kett, Lucy Knight, Seth Koven, Daniel Levine, Mary Lynn McCree, Jon Roberts, and Barbara Sicherman.

I've waited ten years to acknowledge my continuing gratitude to, and for, my family by dedicating this book to them. It's not enough, but it's what I can do. And to Beth, who gracefully survived the final roller coaster ride of this project—the next one?

A final paragraph is reserved for my mentors, though I'm not sure how I can do justice to their unfailing support. James Turner has been my teacher and friend for fifteen years. He has spent more hours reading, listening to, commenting on, and gently redirecting my notions about history than any other individual. Anything useful about this book is partly his. Donald Fleming saw me not only through graduate school—not at every juncture the easiest task—but, as is his selfless practice, far beyond. Armed with felt-tipped pens that deal out question marks and exclamation points sparsely but tellingly, Donald sets breathtakingly high standards for his students and tells them calmly that they're equal to the challenge. In his own stunning writing, his incomparable lectures, and those cryptic marginal notes, he started hares I'll be chasing for years.

Prologue: The English Background

In 1884 the Anglican clergyman Samuel Barnett and a group of young Oxford men "planted" the first settlement, Toynbee Hall, in the East End of London. The idea of "personal service" to the poor inspired their venture. The settlement founders believed that the friendly visiting of the Charity Organisation Society and the East End clergy was not enough to break down class barriers and establish genuine, uplifting interaction between rich and poor. In residing among the poor, they would become neighbors and friends, sharing the concerns of the district and the cultural advantages of their fortunate birth and education. As they brought art, music, literature, and moral idealism to the East Londoners, they would be giving, in the words of one sympathizer, "not money, but themselves."[1] In return, the settlement residents would gain the opportunity to splice their lives more tightly to the social organism. They would gain fuller lives not by denying their social position, but by reconceiving it.

Only a decade after the founding of Toynbee Hall, the history and personalities of the first settlement had taken on the status of legend. The legend stints the complexity but does not exaggerate the remarkable coherence of the cultural origins of the settlement idea. Entwining the ideological genealogy of the movement was a web of personal and intellectual associations, from Carlyle, Ruskin, and the Christian Socialists to the founders of the charity organization movement and the philosophical idealists and Broad Church activists of mid-Victorian Oxford. The roots of the American settlement movement lay in that transatlantic tangle of apostolic relationships among men and women as well as ideas.

The problem of poverty in Victorian Britain was cast in resonantly *moral* and *personal* terms. Many nineteenth-century English writers saw poverty and misery as symptoms of a failure to transmit and realize common values. By the 1860s it seemed clear to these observers that the

I

Poor Law and the welter of private philanthropic efforts were not only inadequate but misguided. "Indiscriminate almsgiving"—the catch phrase of the charity reformers—further degraded the poor by rewarding mendicancy, which robbed them of independence and self-respect. Chaotic and impulsive charity was equally debilitating to the beneficent classes. Feeling purged of further obligation to their fellowmen, the well-to-do continued to enrich themselves at the expense of their own souls. It is not surprising that the most popular solutions to the problem of poverty would turn on the transformation of the characters not only of the poor but also of the rich.[2]

Intellectually, the centrality of *character* in Victorian social reform thought was tightly bound up with a revolt against utilitarianism. Thomas Carlyle raised the first resounding cry against the materialism and spiritual sterility of modern society, and he found its redemption in a cult of character—more specifically, a cult of the hero. Carlyle proposed to burn away the atomistic self-seeking of the industrial order with a new faith in the organic unity of mankind. "Men cannot live isolated," he exhorted the Victorians; "we *are* all bound together, for mutual good or else for mutual misery, as living nerves in the same body. No highest man can disunite himself from any lowest."[3] True social reform would be spearheaded by a new, "working" aristocracy of talent and inner nobility or, as he wrote in *Chartism* (1839), a "corporation of the Best, of the Bravest," not afraid to exercise leadership, to "teach and spiritually guide" the people.[4] While Carlyle was no democrat in the usual sense, his spiritual aristocracy was open to all who could somehow make themselves worthy. "If Hero mean *sincere* man," he asked, "why may not every one of us be a Hero?"[5] His evocation of the exalted, self-forged inner qualities of the hero captured the Victorian imagination.

John Ruskin found in Carlyle a formulation of the antiutilitarianism he himself arrived at through meditating on the social function of art and the artist. Carlyle spoke through Ruskin's assertion that "great art is pre-eminently and finally the expression of the spirits of great men."[6] In a good society, artists or craftsmen worked with freedom and purity of expression to embody in art the "social and political virtues" of their nation, for the pleasure and inspiration of all the people. Ruskin's aesthetic revulsion against the artistic products of a mechanized era broadened in the 1860s into an indictment of the economic philosophy they reflected. "THERE IS NO WEALTH BUT LIFE," he thundered.[7] A product's value should be determined not by its market price, but by its ability to sustain or enhance human life. Nor should labor be measured by its cash value; it should be considered an expression of the human spirit, as Carlyle had enjoined. Ruskin evoked a society in which *all* laborers would emulate his idealized medieval craftsman, creating objects of natural and unadorned beauty rather than slaving at the meaningless, routinized tasks of the factory. The practical expression of Ruskin's passion for craft was the arts-and-crafts movement carried on by William Morris and others. Through workshops and classes open to all, Ruskin hoped to show his contemporaries that art could be the social medium through which Everyman aspired to Carlylean heroism.

A new spirituality was to be central to both Carlyle's and Ruskin's visions of the new society, yet each stood at the periphery of orthodox Christian belief. They represented in the English-speaking world that multiform effort of the nineteenth century to adapt religion to modern life by exalting an idealized *human* spirit as an appropriate object of reverence, and by allowing the individual to offer a standard of personal morality as a substitute for religious ritual in manifesting assent to the primacy of nonmaterial values. But at the same time vital reform movements arose *within* the churches, sparked not only by the new criticism and the new science but also by the urgency of social relief and reform in industrial England. A number of Anglicans, most but not all of liberal or Broad Church sympathies, moved beyond traditional church philanthropy to formulate a theological imperative for social action. Frederick Denison Maurice was the most influential of the church's social philosophers. Maurice too found himself repelled by Benthamism as a young man; breaking from his father's Unitarianism in 1831, he became a minister in the Church of England in 1834. For a long time his visionary theology was his only politics, but in the late 1840s he finally lent his growing prestige to a new, anti-Chartist social reform vision.[8] His intellectual leadership of the Christian Socialist movement in the early 1850s rested on a potent theological case for a universal church, binding the nation together under Christ as "Head and King of the race." A specifically Christian social ethics, infused with sacrifice and brotherhood, would replace selfish individualism with social and economic cooperation. To many believers, Maurice and his followers held out a timely application of religion to the modern world.[9]

The ideas of John Ruskin and the Christian Socialists found an extraordinary conjunction in the thought and work of Octavia Hill, the daughter and granddaughter of noted educational and sanitary reformers. Hill exemplifies in retrospect the ways the Victorian reformers' faith in the socially beneficent influence of character and personality was founded and replicated in their own lives. Forced by her father's bankruptcy to go to work at fourteen, Octavia became the manager of one of the Christian Socialists' cooperative workrooms for the poor; shortly thereafter, through her association with Maurice and the "band of brothers," she met John Ruskin. She was deeply attracted to Ruskin as a man and a thinker, and she correctly discerned important continuities between his and Maurice's essentially conservative visions of the good society.[10]

In the early 1860s, as Ruskin poured his new social ideas into *Unto This Last* and *Sesame and Lilies,* Hill began to turn over in her mind a scheme for reformed housing for the poor predicated on the same beneficent tutelage of the poor by the well-to-do that she had found so gratifying in her work with the Christian Socialists. By then a close family friend, Ruskin agreed to help her financially as she purchased several run-down tenements and converted them into model flats for poor tenants. By enforcing the prompt payment of rent she would teach the poor responsibility; by investing part of the rent money in improvements requested by the tenants she would teach them pride in their dwellings; by encouraging sewing circles and play groups she would fertilize neighborly interdependence and intimacy. As her holdings grew she employed landlord's agents, genteel ladies and gentlemen who would act as friends and examples to the poor; she envisioned thus "a return of the old fellowship between rich and poor."[11] Her benign vision of urban order and discipline, resting on a feudalistic bondage of wealthy and poor, echoed Carlyle's assertion that "we *are* all bound together" as well as Maurice's visionary theology of unity under Christ. In 1869, four years after the inception of her housing experiment, Hill's method received an important endorsement when the Charity Organisation Society was formed out of the remnants of several previous initiatives in combating urban poverty—or, as its partisans had it, "pauperism."

To weed out the beggars from the "deserving poor," the COS would systematically coordinate existing agencies so that each "case" (the first modern use of this concept) received a single judicious assessment and the truly needy might be referred to the most appropriate source for aid. As in Hill's housing scheme, the key to the COS plan was the proposed army of "friendly visitors" responsible for initial investigations and follow-up visits.[12] Sir Charles Trevelyan, one of the founders, explained that the COS's chief aim was "to knit all classes together in the bonds of mutual help and goodwill."[13]

Predictably, the COS met resistance from the start, not only from the poor but also from philanthropists and observers who were repelled by its apparent cold-bloodedness in dealing with the indigent.[14] One of the few districts in which ideal coordination was briefly achieved was Marylebone, Octavia Hill's home and command post for her own philanthropic ventures. Not only was Hill an ardent supporter of the COS idea, she had an important local ally, W. H. Fremantle, the rector of Saint Mary's Church in Bryanstone Square, a graduate of Balliol College, Oxford. A liberal churchman, he believed that the key to social reform was an invigorated and truly national Church of England, dedicated not to saving individuals "out of the world," but to saving the world itself.[15]

It was in Fremantle's enthusiastic young curate, Samuel Augustus Barnett, a gentle, pious rebel against his wealthy Bristol family's Toryism, that these two strong individuals found the apostle who would merge their theological and philanthropic lessons and carry their religion of "personal service" into a bold, positive experiment in dissolving class barriers and asserting the brotherhood of man in the grim slums of industrial England. In 1873 Barnett and his bride, Henrietta Rowland, one of Hill's agents, were assigned to Saint Jude's parish in Whitechapel. Over the next decade, as they reckoned with the spiritual blight and intractable poverty of East London, the Barnetts began to question the adequacy of the charity organization philosophy they had learned from Octavia Hill.[16]

The Barnett's quarrel with charity organization was not with what it did, but with what it did *not* do. As Barnett faced his "grief of impotence" in failing to convert his poor parishioners, he came at last to the conviction that "the walls of degrading and crippling environment hid from many the light of truth."[17] By the 1880s the Barnetts were publicly advocating state responsibility not only for poor relief, but also old-age pensions, improved housing, and public libraries and galleries.

"Practicable socialism" was their name for this moderate program of public welfare. As the rhetoric of social change heated up in the early 1880s, Barnett distinguished himself from more radical spokesmen in his unshakable belief that social regeneration would proceed "one by one"—through the dedication of the fortunate to the spiritual well-being of their poorer brethren. Money would never be enough. The rich owed the poor their *real* "wealth": the "knowledge, the character, the happiness which are the gift of God to this age."[18]

Even before Barnett and others began organizing recruiting trips to the Oxford colleges to lure some of the most eligible of England's wealthy to East London, several young university men had found their way to the industrial districts and had independently drawn the same conclusions as Fremantle, Hill, and the Barnetts.[19] Edward Denison, a young Oxford graduate influenced by Carlyle, took rooms in Stepney to live and teach among the poor as an urgent, inescapable duty. "I should be a thief and a murderer if I withheld what I so evidently owe." Dying young in 1870, widely eulogized, Denison became a cynosure of the new social work.[20] A few years later another impassioned volunteer, Arnold Toynbee of Balliol College, Oxford, directly inspired the first generation of settlement residents; his own premature death gave the Barnetts' settlement its name. Personally recruited to Balliol by its awe-inspiring master Benjamin Jowett, Toynbee became a living legend at Oxford; one contemporary remembered: "Everything about him, his personal appearance, his bearing, his language, combined to invest him with an air of indescribable distinction."[21] As Toynbee began making trips to workingmen's clubs in the East End, speaking, listening, striving to know the "working classes" and infect his fellow students with the same urgency, he came under the powerful influence of Thomas Hill Green, the idealist philosopher at Balliol who made a credo of public service, resting on the moral imperative to pursue the social good over individual gratification. From Green Toynbee would borrow an elaborated framework of religion as social morality and an ethic of positive freedom that, like the ideas of Carlyle, Ruskin, and the Christian Socialists, rejected utilitarianism.[22] Though Toynbee's ideas were moderate and derivative, his moral passion ignited his peers. In the year before his death at thirty-one in 1883, he distilled the cri de coeur of the conscience-stricken middle classes into a final plea to the workers: "You have . . . to forgive us, for we have wronged you; we have sinned against you grievously . . . ; but if you will forgive us—nay, whether you will forgive us or not—we will serve you, we will devote our lives to your service, and we cannot do more. . . . We are willing to give up something much dearer than fame and social position. We are willing to give up the life we came from, the life with books and with those we love."[23]

Though Toynbee's death provided one of the final goads to the settlement experiment, his style was rather more extreme, even melodramatic, than Barnett might have been comfortable with. While he exemplified the chivalry of self-sacrifice by the privileged, his suggestion that the students would give up "books and . . . those we love" misconstrued Barnett's vision of regeneration through friendship across class barriers. What the rich had to offer was *precisely* their books—the uplifting power of literature and art—and the normality and richness of the lives *they* were fortunate enough to live "with those we love."

At the time of the Toynbee Hall organizational meeting in January 1884, Barnett had been visiting the university for years, to talk with the young men in his shambling, low-key manner about the pleasures of social service. While not charismatic like Toynbee, Barnett had with his quiet zeal already cultivated a small following eager to fall in with his new scheme for a permanent settlement in East London.[24] Money and volunteers appeared in profusion. The new joint-stock association bought a site beside Saint Jude's and built an imposing neo-Tudor building. Barnett became warden. The new residents—fourteen in the first year, from both Oxford and Cambridge—paid room and board and were to engage in social service in their free time.[25]

The settlement appeal, which went out over industrial England and within a very few years was heard across the Atlantic, was couched in the resonant terms of mid-Victorian discourse on the relation between the individual and society. It represented one culmination of that strain of nineteenth-century British culture that rejected Manchester economics and Benthamite utilitarianism in favor of an organic polity in which each individual conceived his or her life and work in relation to the whole. This concept of social organicism figured heavily in the philanthropic predecessors to the settlements. It was a complex, double-edged idea. On the one hand, it was part of an assertion of human brotherhood and spiritual equality: one aspect of the beneficent humanitarianism of the nineteenth century, pointing toward increasing political and social democracy. On the other hand, the organic metaphor offered a kind of license to philanthropists and politicians to exercise far-reaching social control over those large and threatening segments of society outside the pale of the moral law and social codes that nominally governed the behavior of the middle and upper classes. As industrialization fed the sprawling growth of the cities, reformers felt a heightened sense of urgency to check and reverse the "antisocial" tendencies of this marginal population. The attraction of localism and direct personal contact in social work was partly their apparent efficiency in imposing social discipline.[26]

The settlement idea drew on both of these inseparable impulses in nineteenth-century social work. As two American settlement leaders observed in the 1920s, "The English settlement expressed a certain feudal tradition and asserted profound inequalities among citizens in the very act of traversing them."[27] The English pioneers occasionally availed themselves of the easy analogy. Barnett beckoned the Oxford students to constitute East London's "leisured class," who would "see that the laws are carried out and generally keep the social life going," while Henry Scott Holland of Oxford House said bluntly, "Come and be the squires of East London."[28]

Although the use of feudal imagery for an urban industrial society was chiefly an English conceit, in America too the settlement idea would represent a reaction against the fragmenting effects of a new social order. Like the English students who moved into Toynbee Hall, the American settlement pioneers had been prepared for the call to a new kind of social service by the pontifical literature that made its way across the Atlantic, from Carlyle and Ruskin through the Christian Socialists and the Arnolds, father and son, down to the social literature of their own day. The Americans too responded to the rhetoric of "character" and the eulogies of the settlement pioneers that celebrated their personal qualities as enthusiastically as their ideas. In the United States as in England, the settlements served another function for the wellborn than the ostensible one of "educating" them in the realities of poverty. The settlement resident was offered a chance simultaneously to *be* and to *do*: to represent in his or her person the "highest life of his day," as Barnett put it, and to share that life in active and concrete ways with the less fortunate.

Thus in the United States as well as in England, the settlement movement was Janus faced. The settlement idea drew heavily on the cultural values of high Victorianism that enthroned "personal service" as the epitome of philanthropy. At the same time, by promoting social and economic research and by tying investigation to reform and knowledge to action, the settlement workers would help construct a new paradigm of social welfare based on specially trained professionals with the skills and knowledge to offer effective social services in a technocratic society.

The tensions that arose as the first cohort of settlement leaders tried to honor the past while charting the future were unavoidable. These tensions were perpetuated by the settlement doctrine that elevated method and process over concrete goals and thus dictated elasticity and flexibility. From the beginning, the settlements' single institutional goal was the infinite expansion of their method: breaking down class barriers through individual friendships between rich and poor. Paradoxically, it was this emphasis on goalless *process,* epitomized by that favorite Victorian activity, character building, that propelled the settlements most surely into the future. The settlements helped preserve old values by adapting them to a new world; they themselves survived because their form was by doctrine infinitely malleable and responsive to circumstances. In the United States, the Victorian cult of character found new theoretical incarnations in the twentieth century. The settlement workers' emphasis on activity and engagement as the primary means to enrich their own lives and those of their adopted neighbors made them natural carriers of the pragmatic approach to social and educational reform based on new theories of personality formation and social interaction propounded by academics like John Dewey, Charles Horton Cooley, and Simon N. Patten. The persistence of the social concerns of philosophical idealism in the work of the prominent American pragmatists found a real-world expression in the ideological evolution of the settlement movement. By the 1920s the settlements had domesticated several other modern manifestations of the continuing vitality of the old concept of "character building": a heightened emphasis on group work with young people and the habit clinics and child guidance concept of the mental hygiene movement. The Victorian understanding of the duty of individuals to promote the well-being of their fellowmen, and the religion of character as the measure of personal "wealth," remained at the core of the "new" social welfare ideology of the twentieth century.

1

The Transit to America: Liberal Christianity and the Liberal Arts

The settlement idea crossed the Atlantic with remarkable speed, part of the brisk trade in tourists and ideas that characterized cultural relations between England and America in the late nineteenth century. Finding themselves in an urban industrial society, Americans sought new language and concepts to control and express their perceptions of change. A shared language and culture turned them to England for inspiration just as the English were rediscovering the United States as an instructive and amusing field for social observation. Educated Americans were steeped in the literature of Victorian England. While a few escaped from a jarring American present by identifying with a mythic Anglo-Saxon past, others were inducted into romantic protest against the ugliness of industrial society through the writings of Carlyle, Ruskin, Dickens, Matthew Arnold, and Charles Kingsley. Transatlantic travel became easier and more common for prosperous Americans, and their pilgrimages to the glories of the English past brought them face to face with the ferment of the English present, roiled by social problems and conditions peculiarly reminiscent of the evolving American scene. As addicted as the English to voluntary organization, the Americans borrowed English forms to achieve similar objectives. The SPCA and the COS were two recent British imports sponsored by American philanthropists. In the late 1880s and early 1890s, the Americans likewise appropriated the settlement idea, though in its transplantation to America, the movement underwent subtle but important sea changes.[1]

Certain tensions in American society and culture prepared the ground for the settlement's hearty reception. In the 1880s a number of Protestant theologians began to push their churches to grapple in new ways with urban social problems by accepting the concept of human brotherhood under Christ as a mandate for social service. They promoted this idea in the language of social organicism popularized by a few influential self-denominated social scientists. These churchmen found an audience among the educated middle class, whose self-conceptions had been challenged by the changing post–Civil War economy. An increasingly bureaucratic society demanded a new kind of literacy and offered new careers to those prepared to seize opportunities. Institutions of higher learning proliferated, and their collective enrollment multiplied by five between 1860 and 1900. The land-grant colleges and the new universities that incorporated professional and technical departments vied with the liberal arts colleges for students and educational legitimacy. The liberal arts curriculum was attacked and defended as a repository of knowledge and culture and a training ground for American youth. The debate that rumbled through the 1880s into the new century carried the burden of more amorphous questions concerning the fate and validity of genteel culture, and the genteel individual, in a technocratic society. As the liberal arts colleges advertised their efforts to cultivate "Christian character" in their students, their graduates, particularly the women, struggled with the question of exactly what it was they had been prepared to *do*. As in England, the American settlements, largely staffed by young college graduates, offered a social sanctuary to the Victorian concept of character as an autonomous social force. But the settlements would also provide a platform and testing ground for new social scientific concepts of social structure and the dynamics of social change, as well as a field of action for individuals trained in the functions and services of the new society.

In the United States as in England, the clergy's response to the social conditions of the 1880s provided a goad, a rhetoric, and an interpretive framework to many middle-class people confronting the "social problem" or the "social question": the constellation of ills generated by unregulated economic growth and unprecedented immigration into the cities. The American counterpart of English Christian Socialism was commonly called "social Christianity," "applied Christianity," or later, the "Social Gospel." To the modern Protestant commitment to social service that had grown from the concerns of the Benevolent Empire of the early nineteenth century, the Social Gospel added a critique of the social and economic system that generated conflict and poverty.[2] Though the Social Gospelers were theologically diverse, for many of the ministers and laypeople most active in founding the American settlement movement, the liberal tendency in post–Civil War Protestant theology offered a persuasive and comfortable intellectual underpinning for social service. Liberalism, or the "new theology," successfully reconciled religious observance with an acceptance of Darwinism, historicism, and scientific empiricism and thus forged a Protestantism that "fit" into a new Western intellectual universe.[3]

The harsh tenets of Calvinism had been under attack for decades. The liberals gratefully acknowledged the groundbreaking theology of Horace Bushnell, who suggested in *Christian Nurture* (1847) that conversion was not the work of a moment wrought upon a hapless sinner but ideally the gradual result of a lifetime of beneficent Christian influences in the home. At the heart of his personal approach to religion was a quasi-transcendental belief in the indwelling of God's spirit in the individual.[4] This legacy was reinforced for the post–Civil War liberals by their reading of Frederick Denison Maurice and another Anglican cleric, Frederick W. Robertson, who wrote compellingly of the personal accessibility of Christ and his mission to humanity in illuminating the "natural" relationship between God and man: "Man is God's child and the sin of man consists in perpetually living as if it were false."[5]

William Jewett Tucker of Andover Theological Seminary was drawn to the ministry just after the Civil War by "certain moral and spiritual values which . . . had little recognition within the sphere of organized religion." As minister of the Madison Square Church before being called to Andover, he had labored to awaken the social conscience of New York businessmen and professionals.[6] Another prominent liberal and Bushnell's biographer, Theodore T. Munger of New Haven, exhorted the rising generation to a virile morality. In a popular book of inspirational essays first published in 1880, Munger stressed the "essential oneness of man with God," the "manliness" and earnestness demanded by true faith, and the seat of practical faith in the conscience. Citing Coleridge, Thomas Arnold, Maurice, Robertson, and the questionable example of Ralph Waldo Emerson, he recommended a close study of the character and personality of Jesus Christ the *man*.[7]

Munger and other early liberals rarely specified the real-world behaviors that fulfilled the prescription of moral thought and conduct. But in the mid-1880s a social agenda began to take shape.[8] As they adjusted doctrine and practice to modern science and social needs, a number of liberals embraced the heuristic aids and useful language of nascent American social science. Abetted by lay sympathizers in philanthropy, government, and the universities, these churchmen helped to popularize an image of the social sciences as experimental, scientific disciplines whose ultimate aim was ethical and subjectivist social reform. While Lester Frank Ward adumbrated his concept of "dynamic sociology," repudiating Herbert Spencer's concept of social evolution as the product of uncontrollable forces, thoughtful religious progressives bent the idea of the "social organism" to their own visions of purposeful change.[9]

In 1883 a group of Andover theologians began to spread the Social Gospel in a new journal, the *Andover Review*. The editors proposed to "connect theology with life" and "point out the path to unity of religious belief." Over the next decade the journal explored the connections among liberal theology, social science, and human welfare. William Jewett Tucker struck the keynote by calling for a new evangelism aimed at the flood of immigrants bringing "habits of irreligion and immorality" to American cities. Praising Octavia Hill's London housing work, he declared that America too needed an urban ministry to make "every tenement house . . . a parish." He deplored the "natural theology" built on the false premise that Christ culled souls from the world as Darwinian nature culled lives. This theology of selective spiritual fitness must be replaced by a universal gospel centered on Christ's embracing love of mankind. The ways of nature were *not* the ways of salvation.[10]

While these theologians locked Darwinian science out of the spiritual realm, they opened the gates to the suggestive concepts of social science. John Graham Brooks, who would leave the Unitarian ministry in 1891 to devote his time to labor reform, hailed the inspirational power of a non-Spencerian interpretation of the "social organism" in dealing with specific social problems. The analogy of human society as a biological body worked through the power of sympathetic imagination, which allowed pain in one limb to signal the need for relief to the rest of the organism. Enlightened Christians would reject the equation of private interest with the public good and prepare to make sacrifices in the best interests of the social whole.[11]

Brooks was a longtime member of the American Social Science Association and its president from 1903 to 1905.[12] Other clergymen also hailed the mutually beneficial relationship between Christian ethics and social science. The Reverend Henry C. Potter, Episcopal bishop of New York, suggested that housing and sanitary reform must be motivated by the "power of personal sympathy" and the Christian ethic of personal responsibility. He too praised Octavia Hill for having "transfused the spirit of scientific reform with the spell of self-sacrificing and Christ-like enthusiasm."[13] Francis Greenwood Peabody, a Unitarian clergyman and professor of divinity at Harvard, called for an "inductive ethics" of social reform: "the power of the Christian ideal, the sense of the organic life

of man, the discovery of personal happiness in the service of the community, . . . this wondrous dynamic . . . has slowly penetrated the
Christian world and is finding now its systematic and scientific
expression."[14]

By the mid-1880s many American colleges and universities offered
haphazard instruction in what was then called "social science," usually
under the older rubrics of political economy, history, and jurisprudence.[15] At Harvard, Peabody's first "social ethics" course in 1880
spawned an academic department that served both divinity students and
undergraduates and later sponsored exhibitions and a series of
monographs.[16] A few years later, Tucker developed an elective program
in social economics at Andover. Influenced by the social and economic
history of Freeman, Stubbs, and J. R. Green, Tucker organized his
courses around the evolution of society's treatment of three marginal
groups: labor, the "criminal classes," and the poor and disabled. Besides the "new historians," Tucker's reading list included Spencer,
Marx's *Capital,* Toynbee on the Industrial Revolution, John Stuart Mill,
the economic historian Thorold Rogers, Henry George, and the economist Richard T. Ely. His Andover courses marked Tucker's rejection of
charity organization and other reforms in traditional philanthropy in
favor of bolder social changes to bring about "economic justice."[17]

Before accepting the Dartmouth College presidency in 1893, Tucker
forged one more link between religion and social reform by sponsoring a settlement house in Boston, headed by one of his most responsive
students, Robert Woods. Another Congregational seminarian, Graham
Taylor, took a similar route from social Christianity to settlement work;
in 1894 he founded Chicago Commons in conjunction with a new
Department of Christian Sociology at the Chicago Theological Seminary.

Taylor converted to the Social Gospel during his tumultuous ministry
of the Fourth Congregational Church of Hartford during the 1880s. The
troubled Fourth Church, in the center of the now industrial city, had
been left to its indifferent neighbors as more prosperous residents fled
to the outskirts and took their pastors with them. Taylor reached out to
his poor and alienated parishioners with adult Bible classes, prayer
meetings, and home visits. His proposals for a citywide evangelical
effort met with hostility from his fellow Congregational ministers, heirs
to Bushnell's legacy but liberal in theology alone. Taylor persisted.
Inspired by the methods of Dwight L. Moody, the YMCA and YWCA, and
the Salvation Army, Taylor initially used revival meetings combined with

personal appeals to combat drink and prostitution and bring people into the church. Looking for contacts and inspiration beyond Hartford, by the mid-1880s he was familiar with the work of Josiah Strong, Washington Gladden, Lyman Abbott, and Richard T. Ely.[18]

In 1888 Taylor's pastoral successes were recognized with his election as professor of practical theology at the seminary, still theologically conservative but responding now to currents of social change. He determined to use the Fourth Church as a "laboratory" for his students' "field work . . . in religious education and pastoral evangelism."[19] Though he was aware of Peabody's and Tucker's work, Taylor developed his own curriculum. Like Tucker, he drew from an eclectic range of sources, beginning with the growing literature of social Christianity. Taylor was one of the first American readers of Canon Fremantle's *World as the Subject of Redemption*. Among American Social Gospel leaders he relied chiefly on Washington Gladden, Josiah Strong, and John Graham Brooks. He found himself drawn to liberal theology and gratefully accepted a gift from Bushnell's widow of a dozen copies of *Christian Nurture* for his students. To prepare them for pastoral social work, Taylor read widely in the literature of both religious and secular charities, including the COS, the YMCA, foreign missions, and the work of Dr. Joseph Chalmers and Octavia Hill. He was intrigued by the new ideas on the interaction of heredity and environment in determining social behavior, such as the Reverend Oscar McCulloch's *The Tribe of Ishmael* and, later, Richard Louis Dugdale's *The Jukes*.[20]

This motley selection fed several evolving notions. Taylor's pastoral work had made him question the assumption that a person's social behavior was determined by moral character, and he suggested in his inaugural seminary address that a combination of heredity and environment shaped one's spiritual and social destinies. Besides reflecting his characteristic distaste for intellectual fine-tuning, the address signified Taylor's conviction that the church had a clear duty to reckon with social issues. Accepting the Christian Socialist idea of the "unity of the human race" under Christ, Taylor combed the Bible for evidence and found Paul's statement, "God who made the world hath made of one blood all nations of men."[21]

A number of social scientists enthusiastically witnessed this wedding of Christian ethics to social scientific inquiry and applications. In those fin de siècle years of transition in the structure and content of academic disciplines, the *process* of change was multidimensional, intermittent, and untidy. There were two major shifts in the organization and conceptualization of the social sciences: one, the professionalization or "academicization" of the social sciences—their gradual absorption into the universities and the identification of a distinct content and methodology for each major discipline; two, the erection of standards of research and analysis that gradually challenged the earlier teleological assumption that the primary and direct object of empirical social investigation was social reform. These two aspects of change were confluent at many points; yet in the lives of certain key individuals, professionalization was perfectly compatible with a continued commitment to social reform. Indeed, the record is muddied even after 1900 by several universities' sponsorship of emerging schools of social work that employed a number of nonacademic social reformers.[22]

By the mid-1880s the identification of social science and social welfare had a twenty-year tradition in the United States. In 1865 a collection of academics, reformers, philanthropists, public officials, and members of the legal and medical professions founded the American Social Science Association. These self-styled "social scientists" came together to draw out the lessons of the government's successes in wartime mobilization and the Sanitary Commission's exemplary work in rationalizing health and welfare. The members scoffed at William Graham Sumner's Cassandran warnings against government intervention in economic and social life. They publicized the work of state welfare agencies and private organizations such as the American COS. As Thomas Haskell, the ASSA's most penetrating historian, notes, "No distinction was made between inquiry and reform."[23]

The ASSA's demise in 1909 followed its failure to retain the loyalty and commitment of the most creative academic social scientists, who chose instead to support discrete professional organizations in history, economics, sociology, and political science. In the short run, however, the ASSA set the stage for the interaction of social Christianity and the new German-influenced social scientific thought of the 1880s and 1890s. Over a longer period, American social reform movements (including the settlements) and the ideology of social work would continue to be influenced at key points by academics equally committed to social change and to the professional demands of their own disciplines.

While Peabody, Tucker, and Taylor created a meeting ground for social theory and social action in the seminaries, the formidably energetic Richard T. Ely became the foremost exemplar of the academic dedicated to social reform. A scholarship student at Dartmouth and Columbia, Ely won a graduate fellowship to study philosophy in Ger-

many. He was soon rerouted to economics and converted to the historical method and ethical bias of Karl Knies at Heidelberg.[24] In 1885,
as a young instructor at Johns Hopkins, he joined a few other German-
trained economists, including Henry C. Adams, Simon Patten, and
E. R. A. Seligman, in founding the American Economic Association, a
professional group representing "a protest against the system of laissez-
faire" and a forum for new economic theories. Ely's reformist vision for
the AEA was repudiated by the membership within two years; though
most American economists were ready to stop beating the dead horse
of laissez-faire, few would endorse Ely's proposition that the state was
an "educational and ethical agency whose positive aid is an indispensable condition of human progress."[25]

In *Social Aspects of Christianity* (1889) and *Socialism* (1895), Ely
pictured society as an organism whose human units could function in
concert only when they were actuated by the spirit of Christian cooperation. In the mid-1880s he supported the controversial Knights of
Labor for espousing a cooperative vision of human brotherhood rather
than a divisive theory of class warfare, and he defended socialism's
"necessary and beneficial" repudiation of the "Cain's curse" of philosophical individualism.[26] Ely promoted sociological study in the seminaries, and he preached in churches and religious gatherings that Christianity, social service, and social science all served the same end: "Love
to man is philanthropy," he wrote, "and the science which deals with
this part of the gospel is called sociology. The two are inseparable."[27]
Both in the churches and notably in his Chautauqua appearances, Ely
reached an audience of women as well as men—particularly notable
given his practical message of Christian service.

Like the American churchmen who harked back to the English Christian Socialists, Ely was inspired by the strain of English religious life that
jibed with German economic thought in rejecting laissez-faire. Like
Graham Taylor, Ely was deeply affected by Fremantle's *World as the
Subject of Redemption;* he promoted the book at every chance and
arranged for an American edition in 1895, which made its way back to
England and finally reached a large audience.[28]

In their constant recourse to social organicism and the brotherhood
of man, these Protestant clergymen and their academic allies tacitly
rejected the idea of irreconcilable social cleavages under the present
order. Their confidence in the motive power of Christian love and
cooperation reinforced the American preference for voluntarism over
legal coercion in social welfare. The possibility of social unity rested

ultimately upon individuals' willingness to convert to Christian social ideals; the Social Gospelers endorsed a gradualist, meliorist vision of social change. Though Social Christianity has often been seen as a bulwark of the status quo, it was a multifaceted, shifting movement, and a number of "moderates" ultimately joined the radicals in supporting certain forms of labor action and social protest.[29] What distinguished the Social Gospel of the 1890s from earlier forms of church activism was precisely its assumption that social injustice contributed to poverty, vice, and urban social dislocation. If this recognition did not lead to radical social analysis, it did signify a willingness to challenge prevailing social ethics.

Further, for many of its adherents Social Christianity embodied more than a social critique fueled by religious idealism. The liberals' task had been to fashion a Christian faith that would appeal to an educated and skeptical urban audience. Social Christianity taught that the core of religion was ethics, a timely and uncontroversial emphasis that revitalized organized Protestantism for a small but significant sector of its traditional constituency.[30] In focusing on the individual's moral obligations to society, the liberal Social Gospelers could draw upon language and ideas as resonant to nineteenth-century Americans as they were to the English. A major test of good ("Christian") character was ethical behavior. "Christian" became, in effect, synonymous with "ethical," and what each lost in specificity it gained in suggestive force.

The genuine piety of the Social Gospel movement coexisted in the late nineteenth century with a decline in religious belief, though not observance, and the increasing social acceptability of genteel doubt.[31] One of the most significant testimonials to the growing power of ethics as an autonomous quasi-religious force is the rise of the Ethical Culture movement in both America and England from the mid-1870s on. Ethical Culture was created by a disillusioned rabbinical candidate, Felix Adler, a graduate of Columbia and Heidelberg who was spurned by his father's temple after preaching a maiden sermon on social ethics. On 15 May 1876 he inaugurated the Ethical Culture movement with a speech at Carnegie Hall calling for a new "religion" that sought the "common ground where we may all grasp hands as brothers united in mankind's common cause."[32] The movement grew rapidly, formalized as societies sponsoring lectures, schools, and ultimately settlements in the cities where it took root. Ethical Culture set out to achieve precisely what the Protestant liberals were hedging against: excising the supernatural from religious idealism and replacing it with a purely humanistic ethics.[33]

In England, where the idea of religion as the handmaiden of social reform was gaining strength within segments of the Church of England and among nonconformists, a handful of aggressive American "missionaries" easily gained a hearing. In its first report in 1886 the London Ethical Society stated that "the claims of morality" were based on "the rational nature of man as a member of an organic spiritual community."[34] For its first two years the society held its Sunday evening lectures at Toynbee Hall, an appropriate site for the promotion of Ethical Culture's activist, instrumentalist concept of ethics and social morality.[35] As the English settlements welcomed Ethical Culture, several of the American Ethical Culture leaders helped to launch the settlement movement in the United States.

Social science and social ethics found a meeting place not only in the churches but also in colleges and universities. After 1880 American higher education was characterized by a tremendous growth in enrollment (from 30,000 in 1860 to 250,000 in 1900), the rise of the university, and an intensive reevaluation of the aims and curriculum of the traditional liberal arts college. The growing pains of American higher education generated a set of debates beginning in the 1880s and extending into the new century. As higher premiums were placed on professional and technical education, as well as graduate programs emphasizing specialized research, defenders of the undergraduate liberal arts curriculum increasingly fell back on the moral and personal benefits of a liberal education. No other course of study, they asserted, so effectively developed a young person's character.[36]

The bewildering variety of academic options reopened the ever-popular and vexatious question of the pedagogical purpose of undergraduate education. In 1871, when President Charles W. Eliot introduced the elective principle into the Harvard undergraduate curriculum, he abandoned the "faculty psychology," which had prescribed a balanced "classical" curriculum to develop the universal faculties of the human mind, in favor of a philosophy of intellectual individualism.[37] He defended the moral as well as intellectual soundness of allowing undergraduates an unprecedented amount of choice. The purpose of the university should be to "train young men to self-control and self-reliance through liberty."[38]

The example of the Harvard "system," though extreme, coupled with the vindication of scientific education by the technical and agricultural schools, greatly advanced the de facto flexibility of American undergraduate education. Paradoxically, these years also witnessed a new vitality in the collegiate ideal, though in a different guise and with different justifications than in the antebellum period. The ideal of the balanced classical curriculum was gradually replaced by the ideal of the "well-rounded man," a product of the entire collegiate "experience." An autonomous student culture was encouraged rather than deplored, and the college became a little world with its own newspapers and literary journals, organizations, patriotic rituals, and a full calendar of lectures, concerts, and social events—and of course intercollegiate athletics.[39] As the educators loosened their disciplinary grip on their students, they touted these developments as the outward manifestations of a richer *inner* education, a more appropriate preparation for the challenges of the modern world.[40]

Even a modernized liberal arts curriculum, boasting laboratory sciences, social sciences, and a deemphasis on Greek and Latin, met with some worldly skepticism. To the question, Does college training pay? one alumnus responded in 1890 that it was not the content but the general intellectual discipline of a college education that prepared a man to enter the world of business.[41] President Daniel Coit Gilman of Johns Hopkins argued that a liberal education cultivated certain "intellectual powers" crucial to modern life.[42] His advocacy of the continuing relevance of a "liberal education" resembled Matthew Arnold's passionate defense of "sweetness and light": the evangelical quest to make "the best that has been thought and known in the world" available to all in the interest of progress toward human perfection. Gilman too feared a cultural decline brought on by the clamor of material concerns for society's energies. This endorsement of the humanistic value of culture—culture for its own sake, in effect—held a compelling place in late Victorian thought.[43] It took on particular urgency in the American collegiate setting, because there was more at stake than "culture for its own sake." Not only were the colleges and universities the natural repository of liberal culture, to many they seemed the *only* remaining locus for the preservation and propagation of that refinement fostered by familiarity with the Western cultural tradition. As the colleges opened their doors to a wider segment of society, the collegiate mission became the social as well as cultural indoctrination of these new applicants for the credentials of gentility. The colleges took on by default the obligation of perpetuating *two* vital elements in the self-definition of the middle classes: cultural literacy, and the less tangible constellation of attitudes and attributes most frequently denominated "character."[44]

Most advocates of liberal education specified the moral value of undergraduate education. One defender of Harvard's elective system insisted that "it uplifts character as no other training can." The earmark of
the uplifted character was "manliness," a quality the author could define only through its manifestations: "a greater ease in uprightness, a
quicker response to studious appeal, a deeper seriousness, . . . an
increase of courtesy, a growing disregard of coarseness and vice, a
decay of the boyish fancy that it is girlish to show enthusiasm."[45]

Others also cited the cultivation of character—the making of "a possible man into an actual man"—as the college's distinctive contribution
to higher education.[46] John E. Bradley, the president of Illinois College,
claimed that the college's highest purpose was to produce "trained and
symmetrical manhood" through an intellectual discipline that would
"inform the mind" and "invigorate the will." Again, the capstone of a
symmetrical education was character. "By character we mean integrity,
moral uprightness; we mean spiritual uplift—the reaching out of the
soul towards God. We also mean that quality in a man which begets
confidence and respect." Not just the course of study, but also physical
training and competition and an atmosphere of simple social democracy worked together in the college to develop the inner man and his
outer presence.

Finally there was the professor, the "living teacher," as President
Bradley stated, "more important than the textbook or the apparatus
which he uses." The primary attribute of the good instructor was "manhood." Invoking Thomas Arnold of Rugby, Bradley urged that the colleges seek not only excellent scholarship but also the professor's ability
to "impress moral and social ideals" upon his students—to exemplify
"manly spirit and gentlemanly demeanor."[47] Charles F. Thwing of Western Reserve University likewise suggested the paramount importance of
the teacher's personality in shaping the character of college youth.[48]
Thwing also tapped the Arnoldian language popularized by Thomas
Hughes (an early Christian Socialist) in calling for "an aggressive Christian manhood and manliness" in professors, who owed the obligation
of moral influence "to the entire college constituency and to the nation."[49]

A graduate of Harvard College (1876) and Andover Theological Seminary (1879), Thwing was president of Western Reserve during thirty
years of spectacular growth from 1890 to 1921, and the most prolific
advocate of the Victorian idea of the college as a school of Christian
character for Christian living. Deeply influenced by his training at Con-

gregationalist Andover, Thwing argued that "the Christian attitude is that of the most vigorous morality, the broadest philanthropy, and the wisest charity; in that it represents the noblest motives, the purest sentiment, and the most aggressive righteousness."[50] In liberal fashion, Thwing found the essence of Christianity not in dogma but in morality, infused into secular life in ways that led to intellectual and social progress. His Victorian vision of the college as the training ground of the nation's Christian leadership foreshadowed the progressive idea of the university as the intellectual engine of social reform.

If college education ideally fostered a "manly" Christianity in young men, what could it do for young women? This question was bound up with the issues surrounding the insistent movement of middle-class women into public life and the public economy. Experience soon refuted the chief arguments of early opponents of women's higher education: that women were intellectually incapable of college work and that the strain of college life would damage their naturally delicate health. The most useful service of alarmists like Dr. Edward Clarke, author of *Sex in Education* (1873), was to force college authorities, particularly at the new women's colleges (Vassar, Smith, Wells, Wellesley, Bryn Mawr, and Mount Holyoke) to provide good food and accommodations and encourage physical health through exercise.[51] The prophets of degeneracy did not deter increasing numbers of women from enrolling and succeeding in women's colleges and seminaries as well as coeducational colleges and universities. In 1890 women made up over 35 percent of collegiate enrollment, and the percentage relative to men continued to rise until the 1930s. Because this influx of women into colleges and universities preceded any consensual rationalization for educating women, questions concerning the content and purpose of their education received confused and splintered responses.[52]

In 1905 a woman officer of the University of California stated baldly: "The strongest argument in favor of educating women is that it prepares them to be wiser and better mothers."[53] But this time-honored argument for developing women's intellects was challenged by an alarming statistical trend that surfaced at the turn of the century: college-educated women seemed to marry later than their noncollege peers, if they married at all. A later marriage age reduced the fertility of these women and led to mutterings of "race suicide" that weakened the force of enlightened motherhood as an argument for educating women.[54]

Among college graduates who delayed or eschewed marriage for paid work, an overwhelming number became teachers.[55] A much smaller number pursued further study to become doctors, lawyers, university teachers, and scientists; others managed to carve out careers in literature and publishing, business, government, and the administration of arts and philanthropy.[56] But imposing difficulties continued to stand in the way of a woman's free career choice. Discouragement from prospective employers, teachers, friends, family, and popular culture would often have been magnified by a young woman's internal doubts, fears, and guilt. In the changing culture of the 1880s and 1890s, the educators' own persistent confusion and conflict over educational goals for their women students was critical. The young woman in doubt about her future had no recourse to a generally accepted set of guidelines and boundaries.

The purported aim of a man's college education was to strengthen the character as well as the mind: to develop in him a "manly" Christianity, which he would take into his secular calling. For slightly different reasons, similar emphasis on the educated woman's ideal personal attributes emerged from the discordant discussion of the college's role in preparing her for her proper social function. This concord on what a woman should *be* softened the conflict and anxiety over what she should *do*. As the champions of women's education refined their arguments, a new rhetorical ideal of womanhood emerged that combined the affective and the intellectual, private influence and public responsibility, individual aspiration and internalized restraint. A change was rung on the "cult of true womanhood." Once again it was asserted that the woman bore a special burden in the progress and refinement of civilization, but she was to be prepared not by shielding her from the harsh realities of public life, but by educating her about them.

Discussion of the educational needs and goals of women often centered on the formal curriculum. As college women stubbornly continued to elect the same subjects as men, and to succeed in them, educators shifted the grounds of debate by asking whether women were being prepared for their future lives and careers.[57] As one educator admitted, "the destiny of the girl who goes to college is carefully concealed from her," so it was impossible to frame a universal response.[58] Three strands of argument developed. The most popular rested on the assertion that "general culture" made better wives and mothers. At its most vigorous and open ended, this view led from a new vision of companionate marriage to an acceptance that women were playing larger roles in the economy and society and needed as much as men the intellectual discipline now associated with a liberal arts education, no matter what its specific content.[59] A second argument held that even if they ultimately married, most college women would at some point be self-supporting and ought to prepare themselves for this possibility in college.[60] A third line of argument combined the social and civic idealism of the first with the instrumentalism of the second. The strongest argument for women to study the sciences was offered not by egalitarians hoping to boost more women into research positions, but by those who claimed that women occupied a special sphere in both public and private life. A grounding in biology and chemistry could only enhance the housekeeping skills of the future wife and mother.[61] It is not surprising that home economics emerged as a full-blown academic discipline at the turn of the century. Its advocates stressed its legitimate scientific underpinnings as well as its applicability to the future lives of most women students.[62]

But perhaps the part of the formal curriculum that received the lion's share of attention for its relevance to women's educational needs was the social sciences. Not only did social science address domestic relations, it was useful in those areas of community life in which women were increasingly active: philanthropy and voluntary social work. Kate Holladay Claghorn argued that in the past, the woman's "instinct and natural emotion" had been considered sufficient qualification for charity work, but contemporary social life was too sophisticated and even potentially "dangerous" for such a "primitive" approach. College training could complement the woman's instinctive attraction to charity work: "Modern methods of history, of economics, of sociology, tend to the appreciation of the human being as a most complex subject of study [and] observation."[63]

President Thwing also urged the special claims of modern charity work on women graduates: "College women are *women*: they have tenderness and sympathy; college women are *college* women: they have a clear understanding of the origin of distressing poverty, and should have a method for dealing properly with these dreadful problems."[64] Thwing's blithe confidence in the average graduate's diagnostic and therapeutic skills was not unusual in the heady early days of American academic sociology. Equally significant was his easy assumption that an appropriate college education could only enhance the fitness of the womanly nature for social service. Educators who defended the curriculum's adaptability to women's special needs unwittingly bolstered this equation of womanly activities with womanly attributes, a notion that became embedded in the rhetoric of the new American philanthropy that fused social science to the Social Gospel.

The Reverend Samuel W. Dike, an Andover theologian and an early family sociologist, made the connection explicit. Higher education should promote a progressive and sexually determined "differentiation of function" to further the organic "solidarity of the social life." Through the study of sociology, women's interest in the "place of the family in the social order, and of women in the family" could grow to embrace the more complex relations of the larger society. The world called for the service of women "of a higher order of culture," trained not only in literature and the sciences, but in the practical problems of modern society. Writing in 1892, Dike pointed to rural and urban missionary work, "scientific social surveys," university extension, and the university settlements as appropriate endeavors for educated women.[65]

Although Dike pictured a social order in which educated women would move freely from domestic cares to public social service, his vision implicitly constricted women's occupational roles by tying them to a predetermined range of "natural" interests and aptitudes.[66] He shared the common belief that women's affective faculties dominated the rational, with this "natural" tendency strengthened by a conventional upbringing. By advocating an education designed to complement and strengthen the emotional nature of women by channeling it toward social service in the selfless and nurturing vein of motherhood, Dike carried to one logical conclusion the contention of women's educators that college training was equally valuable to domestic and professional "careers." He spoke for those educators, Social Gospelers, and philanthropists who saw an irresistible logic in bending the formal curriculum, particularly in the new social sciences, to the ideal of womanly service.[67]

It is tempting to construe this vision of a special curriculum for women as a setback to the struggle for women's equal educational opportunity. Indeed, by the early twentieth century these arguments for a separate female *intellectual* sphere were buttressing movements *away from* coeducation, most notably at the University of Chicago.[68] It is easy, too, to locate the roots of this idea in certain contradictions in the rhetoric and structure of women's higher education from its beginning. Despite their resistance to curricular innovations that would tacitly acknowledge intellectual differences between women and men, the women's colleges responded to the widespread fear that education would produce "mannish" women by deliberately creating an atmosphere designed to protect and cultivate the womanly character, deportment, tastes, and ideals of their students. The ideal of womanly service was present from the beginning; their graduates were to be apostles of culture in home and community life. Their formal studies, even if not deliberately "feminized," would abet this purpose. Greek and Latin, history, science, and modern literature were components of that broader culture, their mastery a means of developing mental and moral discipline and their content constituting that Western cultural heritage idealized by Matthew Arnold as "the best that has been thought and known in the world."

Despite the rhetorical recognition of the "special needs" of women students, however, it was in linking curriculum and collegiate environment that the ideals of women's education in the late nineteenth century most resembled those put forward in defense of liberal education for men. Liberal studies in a morally uplifting atmosphere would develop both mind and character, fitting the individual for service to the broader society. In the social and intellectual ferment of the late 1880s and 1890s, the "service ideal" became androgynous. It was certainly significant that the new ideal of educated womanhood could not shake off older strains of biological and cultural determinism and "exceptionalism." But it is equally noteworthy that young women shielded by the assurance that they were filling "womanly" roles could now freely enter certain sectors of public life; and further, that young men armed with the moral justification of "Christian manliness" could work on an equal footing with women in social and philanthropic endeavors.

2
American Founders

By 1890 settlement houses had been established in Boston, New York, and Chicago, by people working independently yet claiming the same ideological parentage. Despite differences in their religious, geographic, and social backgrounds, the American founders shared the ideas and values that nourished the settlement idea. They also shared certain personal qualities. Besides the competence, charisma, and energy needed to pull an institution into existence, they shared a willingness, or a need, to break out of prescribed roles and place themselves in a personally satisfying relationship to their society. They were genteel and optimistic rebels, seizing the religious and ethical currency of their culture to parlay personal restlessness and discomfort into publicly justifiable action.

In her carefully crafted autobiography, *Twenty Years at Hull-House* (1910), Jane Addams gave little inspirational credit to Toynbee Hall and the other English settlements. Instead she charmed her readers with her childhood daydream of dwelling someday in "a large house . . . right in the midst of horrid little houses."[1] In fact the English settlement idea would have been familiar to many Americans by 1890. Toynbee Hall had begun to attract even visitors more interested in monuments than in social movements. Several of the American founders first encountered the settlement idea as tourists rather than pilgrims.

Robert Woods had a clear assignment when he sailed to England in May 1890. A recent graduate of Andover Theological Seminary, Woods had been handpicked by Professor Tucker to take charge of his projected social settlement in Boston. Packing notebooks and letters of introduction, Woods embarked for a six-month stay at Toynbee Hall to observe what he called in a subsequent book "English social movements."[2]

Attracted by its growing reputation as a center of social Christianity, Woods had gravitated to Andover after an indifferent undergraduate career at Amherst. Though deeply religious, he did not seriously think of ordination; at this time he had a notion that he would be a journalist.

That he chose a seminary program for his advanced studies reveals something about Woods as well as about the options in American graduate education in social science at the time. Woods was the son of Scotch-Irish immigrants who settled in Pittsburgh. His father, a successful small businessman, established a comfortable suburban home and became a pillar of the Presbyterian church. He died when Robert was fifteen. Catherine Hall Woods encouraged her sons to go on to college, and Robert chose Amherst on the recommendation of a classics teacher.[3]

Amherst College in the 1880s fed Woods's gregariousness and challenged his unformed intellect. He spent more time in his first year memorizing names and faces in the college directory than doing his coursework. Brought up to shun alcohol and "secret societies," he resisted joining a fraternity until his senior year. Instead he throve on card parties, long hikes with friends, intense and rambling midnight discussions. Though in retrospect he regretted the aloofness of the Amherst faculty, he did fall under the potent influence of the philosophy professor Charles E. Garman, who forced Woods to question the doctrinal Calvinism of his childhood. He remembered Garman's course as "a series of protracted meetings in the full light of modern day, in which every student, by means of modern instances and in terms of the present crisis, was brought face to face with the issues of God and humanity, of freedom and immortality." President Julius Hawley Seelye, also a Christian philosopher, imparted a tone of moral earnestness to the college. "He declared," recalled Woods, "that no career could be of higher service to the nation than that of the educated man who should go among the people and in largeness of mind and heart join with them in working out the labor problem." The Amherst faculty members chose an odd but touching way to recognize moral as well as intellectual education by voting to graduate Woods and two of his classmates cum laude despite their lackluster academic records.[4]

"Am resolved to try to make it as happy and bright as my college life," Woods jotted after his first day at Andover.[5] He arrived during the "heresy trial" of 1886, precipitated by the Board of Visitors' action against William Jewett Tucker and the other editors of the *Andover Review,* allegedly guilty of "heterodoxy" and betrayal of the Andover creed. (Ultimately all the accused were exonerated, though one case dragged on for six years.) The spectacular opening phases in an improvised "courtroom" in a Boston hotel thrust theological issues into the public eye, and the professors' vindication constituted, in effect, the genteel burial of "orthodox" Calvinism and a license to those with liberal leanings to interpret creedal boundaries "intelligently."[6] The trial and controversy stimulated Woods's intellectual questioning and a youthful tendency toward hero worship.[7] He soon took Tucker as his special mentor. In his third year Woods wrote to his mother, "I look to Tucker for direction and the more I am with him the better I like him. He is a thoroughly business-like Christian. Not too much broadcloth, not too much piety. He takes such an active interest in all sorts of things that the fellows make a regular pope out of him."[8]

Woods was deeply affected by Tucker's presentation of social Christianity. In class he encountered a benign and heterodox "socialism," embracing economic ideologies from William Jevons and Henry George to Karl Marx. Tucker excoriated Andrew Carnegie's "Gospel of Wealth"; unfettered capitalism as well as "materialistic" socialism ignored the "ethical factor," the effect of the economic structure on character. Tucker told his students that distribution and not redistribution of wealth was the central economic issue, and that charity was no substitute for economic justice: powerful statements in the tumultuous atmosphere of the late 1880s.[9] Prepared by Amherst's Christian philosophers, Robert Woods found Tucker's teaching stimulating and lucid. Years later, one of his classmates recalled Woods's preoccupation with developing a social philosophy based on the religious motive, which would lead to "social" as well as "individual" salvation.[10]

As Woods honed his personal philosophy, he worried increasingly about his career choice. Surrounded by young men preparing for the ministry, he might well have been tempted to hear a "calling." He tried lay preaching and also worked as the Andover reporter to the *Christian Union*. By the end of his third year, with no clear vocation, Woods apparently gave in to a dark period of religious doubt and self-questioning.[11] As he struggled to connect his faith to a practical career, he could not discern the social role that would accommodate the lay ministry that most attracted him. In a meditation that year he wrote: "God has revealed himself in the nature of the human life and in the organic unity of mankind. . . . The object of the individual life . . . is to work out its possibilities. But each race unit has currents of its life out into its immediate environment, into all the race, and into all the universe. All a man's powers then are simply potentialities of relationship."[12] Tucker's proposal of a social settlement may have seemed to Woods literally a godsend.

During his six months in England Woods plunged into the heady

world of social and economic reform. His contacts with England's foremost activists, intellectuals, and churchmen suggest the openness of
speculation and debate in the elaborate infrastructure of middle-class
social concern built in the previous decade. He did encounter frictions
within this eclectic group of reformers. The early Fabian Graham Wallas
recalled years later that Woods was caught "between two pretty strong
fires": the Barnetts and their vigorous Toynbee coterie, and the early
Fabians, who deplored the meager achievements of the "scientific"
charity reformers.[13]

Part of Woods's success in penetrating British academic and reform
circles was due to his connection with Tucker, who already had a
modest reputation among the new economists and English Congrega-
tionalists.[14] As a visiting resident of Toynbee Hall, Woods felt very much
at the center of things. Besides serving as a salon for visiting academics
such as Alfred Marshall, who had just completed his *Principles of Economics,* Toynbee Hall had become a rendezvous for the New Unionists.
During the great dock strike of 1889, the settlement had passed muster
with these powerful labor figures by contributing men to organize
relief. The trio of leaders responsible for this successful action by un-
organized and unskilled laborers comprised Tom Mann, John Burns,
and Ben Tillett. They were persuasive propagandists for labor who
moved confidently among moderate as well as radical middle-class
reformers. Mann had been deeply influenced by Carlyle and Ruskin; he
built bridges from the workers' movement to the Social Democratic
Federation and the Fabian Society and to the churches, through several
Anglican Christian Socialists.[15]

Woods admired the New Unionists' idealism and moderation; he also
liked the Fabians' genteel, talkative, and opportunistic socialism. He
became particularly fond of William Clarke, the least contentious of the
early Fabians. A close student of American politics and culture and a
friend of William Dean Howells and the magazine editor Edwin D.
Mead, Clarke was temperamentally more comfortable with American
genteel reformers than with English socialists.[16] Clarke offered Woods
an entrée into the National Liberal Club and the chance to observe a
Fabian lecture tour in northern England. In Manchester Woods met
another congenial Fabian, Graham Wallas, who had fallen ill in a cheap
hotel. Woods stayed to nurse him and talk with him. He came to admire
the Fabians' reasonable gradualism, their heroic efforts to enlighten the
people through tracts and lectures, their preference for facts over
dogma, and their energetic endorsement of municipal socialism. None-

theless he maintained that Fabianism had "decided limitations from the humanistic and spiritual points of view," and he disapproved of Shaw's "unethical attitude."[17]

Woods's visit to England coincided with a resurgence of Christian Socialism. The Christian Socialist "revival" was a more diffuse movement than its predecessor inspired by Maurice and Kingsley. The ideologies and panaceas put forward in the 1880s offered an embarrassment of riches to newly radicalized clerics; a fairly amicable factionalism prevailed within the ill-defined movement. In contrast to the first Christian Socialist movement, High Churchmen dominated the leadership of the "revival" through the most powerful of several organizations, the Christian Social Union, founded in 1889 by Charles Gore and by T. H. Green's old student Henry Scott Holland. Oxford House, the second major English settlement, was headed by members of the CSU. Under their influence a number of young High Church graduates wedded radical politics to their religious commitment. Though Oxford House as an institution stayed aloof from the dock strike, several former and current residents gave their energies to the "new unionist" organizational work.[18]

"We are all Socialists now," intoned the parliamentary leader Sir William Harcourt in the 1880s.[19] Though the promiscuous adoption of the Socialist label must have struck "true" Socialists as a maddening form of co-optation, to the young American pilgrim it was an exhilarating promise of social progress. By 1890 politics and philanthropy, both old and new style, had become popular avocations among the increasingly heterogeneous British "middle classes"; a few individuals had even parlayed their concern into full-time vocations.[20]

One of the focal points of this new interest in the "social question" was the small but well-publicized settlement movement, the chief object of Woods's journey. By 1891 Toynbee Hall and Oxford House had been joined by a handful of other settlements to bring university men (and women) into touch with the poor. Their programs varied. Most of the work of Toynbee Hall, the "mother of settlements," was still educational, much of it through the university extension movement.[21] Toynbee Hall residents also continued to participate in politics and philanthropy outside the settlement. In contrast to Toynbee Hall, Oxford House was outspokenly denominational at its founding and remained strongly Anglican and active in the parish work in Bethnal Green. About 1890, several nonconformist denominations began their own settlements on the Oxford House model: the Wesleyan Methodists' Bermond-

sey Settlement near the South London docks and the Congregational-
ists' Mansfield House in Canning Town, headed by Percy Alden, who
would form particularly close ties with the early American settlement
leaders.[22]

Every settlement sponsored clubs, which came to symbolize the settlement idea and many of its tensions. While Toynbee Hall allied itself
with the ostensibly self-governing Club and Institute Union, Oxford
House offered a competing umbrella organization, the teetotal Federation of Working Men's Social Clubs, more directly controlled by settlement residents who hoped to mold the affiliates into vehicles for
social and civic education. Whether the settlement clubs were a potent
"civilizing and refining influence," as the settlement residents claimed,
is hard to determine; local women, at least, seemed to welcome the
clubs as an alternative to their husbands' patronage of public houses.[23]
The settlement boys' clubs were touted as beneficent influences on the
morals and conduct of their members. Most of the club leaders had the
good sense to lure in the street urchins with boxing and games.[24]

The English women's settlements, separate from the men's, did
largely the same work. The Women's University Settlement in South-
wark, founded in 1887, was jointly sponsored by the women's colleges
of Oxford and Cambridge and gradually drew workers from the London
colleges as well. In addition to its own clubs and classes, lectures and
picture exhibitions, this nonsectarian settlement participated in existing
charities and organizations, such as the COS, the Metropolitan Association for Befriending Young Servants, and the London Pupil Teachers'
Association. The settlement sponsored district nurses and, with Octavia
Hill's guidance, coordinated a training program for the COS and other
charity workers.[25] The other women's settlements, the Cheltenham College Settlement (1889) and Saint Margaret's House (1892), which was
affiliated with Oxford House, added church-related work to their other
activities. Many of the residents belonged to the Christian Social Union.
The women's settlements initially drew on the strong tradition of
middle-class women's social work in Victorian England, most recently
incarnated in Octavia Hill's housing and COS work; Margaret Sewell of
the Women's University Settlement called settlement work an "adaptation of accepted methods to special conditions of society."[26] But in
Britain as in America, women's settlements came to outnumber men's,
and the settlement movement became a vehicle for women looking for
a quasi-professional role in public life as well as a haven for some of the
single women who tacitly or overtly challenged the social stigma of the

spinster's life as at best second choice to marriage and rearing one's own children.[27]

In both England and America, one of the settlement movement's distinctive contributions to social thought was the promoting of social investigation as the foundation for rational public policy; this bias formed the underpinning of the welfare state in Britain and progressive social legislation in the United States. The groundbreaking work for both English and American social investigation was Charles Booth's *Life and Labour of the People of London* (1889–1903). Booth later testified that Samuel Barnett inspired this staggeringly ambitious project, and Toynbee Hall was happy to claim the connection.[28]

A successful businessman, Charles Booth had married into the highest circles of London intellectual life (his wife was Mary Macaulay). A lifelong fascination with working-class life led him in the early 1880s to London's East End and friendship with the Barnetts.[29] With growing skepticism Booth read the sensational reports of London poverty; he questioned the Social Democratic Federation's claim that a quarter of London's people lived in extreme poverty. In 1886, armed with the census reports of 1881 and an "almost fanatical faith" in the scientific method, Booth gathered a small team of assistants and began a painstaking street-by-street, house-by-house inquiry into the living standards of London households and the industries that supported them. As he worked, Booth occasionally imitated the earliest settlers by finding temporary homes in poor neighborhoods to seek the intimate meaning of his exhaustive statistics.[30]

Classifying the population by income and occupation, Booth developed the subsequently influential concept of the "poverty line."[31] His researchers drew detailed maps of East London districts and color-coded them according to eight "classes." They posted these in Toynbee Hall and Oxford House so that residents familiar with surrounding neighborhoods could check the findings. After eight weeks of intensive surveying of the destitute Tower Hamlets district, Booth had to conclude that the SDF's numbers were conservative; it was possible that fully 35 percent of the total population was living "at all times more or less in want."[32]

The first volume of Booth's *Life and Labour,* published in April 1889, created a sensation in England and the United States. Beyond statistics, the book offered densely detailed descriptions of the living conditions of the poor: the social disorders and physical diseases that plagued them, their makeshift household finances, and the wretched sanitary conditions of their streets and dwellings.[33] His survey galvanized the "practical sociologists" of the 1890s and early twentieth century: social workers, publicists, labor partisans, educators, Fabians, politicians, and settlement residents. Booth was jolted by his findings into advocating a state socialism that by "taking charge of the lives of the incapable would relieve us of a serious danger." Many agreed; indeed, he could claim much credit for the piecemeal but steady erection of Great Britain's "welfare state."[34] Even more important was the legacy of his methods to social science and social work; Beatrice Potter Webb of the Fabian Society took from her work with Booth a lifelong faith in the "application of the scientific method to social organization."[35] Toynbee Hall had to cope with a surge of applications to sponsor social "inquiries" in the late 1890s.[36]

The new science and the new religion marched together under the English settlement banner. As Booth released his first volume, Mary Arnold Ward—better known as Mrs. Humphry Ward—floated her scheme for a "New Reformation" settlement on the transatlantic wave of acclaim for her best-selling novel, *Robert Elsmere* (1888). Mary Arnold's grandfather was Thomas Arnold of Rugby; her uncle Matthew Arnold was Oxford Professor of Poetry during Mary's boarding-school years. Denied a formal university education, Mary made shift with family friends: Mark Pattison, Benjamin Jowett, and T. H. Green, who moved her from the evangelical influences of her girlhood into the orbit of Balliol's socially conscious liberalism. After marrying the classics tutor Thomas Humphry Ward, she built her own Oxford coterie as a popular young matron and a scholar of Spanish church history. In 1882 the Wards moved to London, where Mary Ward plunged deeper into the heated religious controversies of educated England.[37] Six years later she finished *Robert Elsmere,* her fictional call for a revitalized liberalism.

Her young hero Elsmere is a religious naïf who at Oxford falls under the spell of the Reverend Mr. Grey, whom Mrs. Ward frankly modeled on T. H. Green. Grey's "earnestness" and the "upward swell of a new religious revival" persuade Elsmere to take orders and accept a country living. His liberal faith crumbles under the insidious attacks of a local skeptic who denounces the "enthusiasm" Elsmere has imbibed from Kingsley, Maurice, and Ruskin. In a crisis of unbelief Elsmere turns back to Grey, who points him toward a new faith based on the human brotherhood exemplified by Jesus Christ. Turning his back on arid theological disputes, Elsmere offers a real-world testimony to his faith by founding a settlementlike institution, the New Brotherhood of Christ, in the slums of London. In the end he dies, a martyr to overwork.[38]

Robert Elsmere went into multiple printings in its first months in England and may have sold as many as 500,000 copies in the United States in its first year. Mrs. Ward brought to melodramatic life the theological disputes of the previous decades, and she captured the intoxicated idealism of the new credo of "personal service." William Gladstone and Walter Pater were among its English reviewers, while in the United States the popular impact of *Robert Elsmere* was compared to that of *Uncle Tom's Cabin*.[39] The *Andover Review* editors wrote a long appreciation. Rev. Lyman Abbott reassured readers of the *Chautauquan* that though doctrinally unsound, Mrs. Ward's novel was thought provoking and fundamentally moral: "The philosophy of Robert Elsmere was not Christian," Abbott concluded; "his life was."[40] Another American reader, Graham Taylor, agreed, blaming Elsmere's apostasy on his church's "rigidly narrowing range of thought and action."[41]

In 1890 Mrs. Ward brought her settlement to life as University Hall, which would combine scholarship in religious history and biblical criticism with the usual settlement activities. The new warden, Rev. P. H. Wicksteed, explained that the settlement would offer "direction and guidance to the practical manifestations of a new spirit of Christian Discipleship." Beatrice Potter was one of the original committee members.[42]

The English settlement movement was still in its infancy when Robert Woods reembarked for the United States. Despite his pleasure at the apparent convergence of so many reform initiatives in a moderate, humane, and essentially Christian "socialism," the extent of English social problems had staggered him. "I must admit," he told a friend, ". . . I find that we human beings are not nearly so far on as I thought we were."[43] But Woods chose optimism. As he wrote lectures on his English observations and laid plans for a Boston settlement, he reflected:

> If we do not have enthusiasm, faith, we are lost. Then when one has rescued one's self from the teeth of despair, and coming again into his faith finds that although he may not be far along, yet the world lies all full of opportunities and possibilities; that every genuine longing is a promise, one is ready to go back into the world again, feeling a new glow and inspiration. . . . I believe we must take every possible approach men have to the better life and induce them to take the next step. Take every possible means to show them the interest and attractiveness of righteousness.[44]

From the beginning of his work at Andover House, Woods would see himself as a kind of "lay exhorter," a role his Andover training and moralistic religious bent fitted him for.

Robert Woods was the most thorough of the early American observers of the English settlement movement, but another Amherst alumnus, Stanton Coit, had been there first. Returning from his doctoral studies at Berlin in 1885, he paused for three months at the young Toynbee Hall. Coit had left Amherst in 1881 after two postgraduate years as an English tutor, just before Woods arrived. Like Woods, he had been stirred and unsettled by the vital Christian atmosphere of Seelye's college. His religious questioning was seeded during his youth in Columbus, Ohio, by his mother's journey from Episcopalianism to Spiritualism and his own adolescent discovery of Emerson. He recalled being "transfixed" by Emerson's query, "How shall I live?" Later at Amherst, he was expounding on the need for a "cult" of ethics when a friend suggested that he should seek out Felix Adler, "the Radical," who was "*doing* the very thing of which *you* are *dreaming!*"[45] Adler sent his would-be disciple off to study philosophy at Columbia and then at Berlin. Coit's stopover at Toynbee Hall suggests the attraction of practical social experiments for the Ethical Culture converts. Back in New York, Coit went to work as an Ethical Culture lecturer, and he moved to the Lower East Side and founded in 1886 what he called a "Neighborhood Guild."

Coit's Neighborhood Guild was short-lived in its first incarnation. When he returned to England in 1887 to stump full time for Ethical Culture, he left the guild in the hands of his East Side neighbors and a few Ethical Culture associates, who failed to make it thrive on his formula. In 1891 the moribund Neighborhood Guild became the University Settlement under Coit's friend and co-worker Charles B. Stover.[46]

Coit's concept of a neighborhood guild owed much to Toynbee Hall, but he sharply criticized several facets of Barnett's settlement. He believed that true reform must build upon "the conscious organisation of the intellectual and moral life of the people," and he agreed that moral uplift and cultural enrichment were the primary aims of philanthropy and settlement work, but he took issue with the Toynbee Hall settlers' stubborn resistance to "method or system." A young men's club that offered its members no purpose except to smoke, box, and play cards could contribute only accidentally to social progress and character elevation.[47]

A firm believer in neighborhood organization, Coit felt that the pioneers of localism in social work, Thomas Chalmers and Octavia Hill, had both failed to exploit the "instinctive philanthropy" of the working classes.[48] "How grim a commentary upon the social life of the poor is it that they unite almost exclusively to procure funeral privileges and sick-money, and help when they are out of work! But how tender and unobtrusive such assistance, where neighbors are already knit together by a thousand high associations in play and song, in pursuit of the intellectual ends of life, in the enjoyment of art, literature, music, conversation, and nature!"[49] The neighborhood guild would integrate relief, education, and recreation, with the ultimate goal of developing the neighbors' consciousness of their common needs and interdependence.

Coit insisted that the strong leadership required to progress methodically toward set social goals must come ultimately from within the "working classes." Although "a few men and women of leisure" might assume command in the early stages of a guild, these outsiders should abdicate to indigenous leaders as they came forward. Ideally a few of the guild members might be paid for full-time investigation and social work.[50] Like Barnett, Coit emphasized the importance of personality in managing the guild, but he rejected the implication that "personality" was the preserve of the educated and cultured. "A personality of the type needed is perhaps more common among working people than among the more leisured classes. With the latter the conventionalities of society, rather than the opinions and tact of individuals, prescribe conduct."[51]

Thus Coit's subtle emendations of the settlement "patent" challenged some of its central and least examined assumptions. In his belief in a democratic wellspring of that precious substance, "personality," and his emphasis on developing local leadership, Coit anticipated the rhetoric and ideals, if not the reality, of the "Americanization" of the settlement movement. Though his New York Neighborhood Guild reverted to the settlement model, and though Coit himself spent most of the rest of his life in England as the virtual leader of the Ethical Culture movement, it is not surprising that American settlement leaders recognized him as the "father" of the American settlement movement.[52]

Robert Woods and Stanton Coit were exceptional among the young Americans traveling to England in these decades. Most of the others sought the artifacts of history and tradition, not the stirrings of new social movements. Vida Scudder, a young Smith College graduate, ar-

rived in Oxford in 1884, accompanied by her close friend Clara French
and chaperoned by their mothers, for a term or two of postgraduate
study. By coincidence she found herself at the storm center of the new
credo of religious social service, at a time when she was acutely vulnerable to its appeal.

Vida's parents had united two Boston families of social and intellectual standing. She never knew her father, who died as a Congregational
missionary in India when she was an infant. Her maternal uncle, Horace
Dutton, edited the *Atlantic Monthly*. Vida grew up in a "cheerful circle
of aunts, uncles, and cousins on both sides of the family."[53] As an only
child Vida spent much time by herself, lost in a precious fantasy world
of fairies and "colorful visions." Her reading was a Victorian mix of
Scott, Dickens, Emerson, Wordsworth, and the Bhagavad Gita (a tribute
to her father's Oriental interests), as well as popular children's books.[54]

Several long residences in Europe with her mother and an aunt
cultivated Vida's precocious responses to art and literature. During their
stay in France when Vida was about fifteen, she saw sights, attended
lectures, and enrolled in the same art school as another daughter of the
Boston intelligentsia, May Alcott. She read George Sand, Eugène Sue,
Victor Hugo, Alfred de Musset, and "naughty" books from the Paris
stalls. She also discovered a group of Catholic writers, including Félicité
de Lamennais, the comte de Montalembert, and Eugénie and Maurice
de Guérin, whom she later remembered as the most profound literary
influence on her young life. Both Vida and her mother had rebelled
against the family's puritanical Congregationalism the year before and
joined Phillips Brooks's Episcopalian Trinity Church. But Back Bay Episcopalianism was more satisfying to Mrs. Scudder, an avid reader of
Maurice, than to the mystically inclined Vida.[55] The passion of the
French Catholics intoxicated her, with the "strong deep sense of home-
coming which this experience alone can offer those to whom it belongs." These writers also initiated her into nineteenth-century social
thought. Even before Maurice and Kingsley, they would point out the
"revolutionary social implications" of Christianity that would become
"the master light of all my seeing."[56]

But before the certainty of maturity came a long, painful emotional
crisis that Scudder described in her autobiography as an omnipresent
and nightmarish feeling of "unreality," accompanied by the fear that she
was not a "real person" but was "hollow," a "phantom." Her failure to
grieve at her grandmother's death filled her with "horror" at her own
coldness and revealed "the shocking fact that I did not love anyone"—

not even her pliant and doting mother. In later life she blamed her emotional frigidity on her childhood immersion in "second-hand experience": "I had saturated myself with the records of life at its most dramatic and passionate. . . . I was a proud little thing; I did not like to grant that I had never known these great emotions. . . . But in point of harsh fact, nothing whatever had befallen me, nor was I ever to know human passion like Juliet, nor, I fear me, divine passion like St. Augustine."[57]

As early as 1890 Scudder began to formulate her indictment of an education too rich with the records of mature passions for a child, when as a young Wellesley instructor and a leader of the nascent College Settlement Association, she and her colleague Sophia Kirk wrote an imaginary dialogue titled "Influence and Independence" for the *Andover Review*. As "Julia," Scudder blamed the "curious unreality" of youth on this diet of predigested revelations: "The great book came to us too soon; we received it with a certain eagerness, but with minds too crude or weak for its deeper teaching; its finer truth was overlooked in excitement, or lost in dullness, and later it had become inert, useless to us. . . . We lead sham lives in our youth, and the sham knowledge deadens us for the reality."[58]

Vida attended private school until 1878, when her mother unexpectedly decided to send her to the new Girls' Latin School, where she studied the classics and mingled with girls from the South End. The next step for her and a few fortunate classmates was Smith College.[59] There Vida finally "waked up" to people, a "staggering and absorbing" experience. The "ecstasy" of her initiation into reality through these college friendships set the pattern of her future emotional life; ever afterward her intimate and domestic life was shared with women.[60]

Vida took advantage of Smith's fluid intellectual atmosphere. One of her English instructors invited Vida and a friend to draw up the course syllabus, into which they slipped Matthew Arnold, Browning, and even Swinburne. She studied philosophy with M. Stuart Phelps and economics and sociology with John Bates Clark, later of Columbia and one of the American theorists of marginal utility. Scudder and her classmates sat up past the ten o'clock curfew debating religion and the meaning of life. Their dilemmas were not all affectation; Scudder witnessed breakdowns among her peers, innocent cannon fodder for Dr. Edward H. Clarke and his misogynist colleagues. Vida herself spent her senior year confined to bed with a "double curvature of the spine." She managed to graduate with her class and set off for Oxford the next autumn.[61]

Study at Oxford was extraordinary for an American woman in the mid-1880s. Students at the Oxford women's colleges were not admitted to full university privileges until after 1900. Scudder attended lectures and secured tutorials by special arrangement.[62] Her year at Oxford was a crucial juncture in her life. She arrived just in time to hear Ruskin's last lectures as Slade Professor. She had long dreamed of traveling in Italy with *The Stones of Venice,* and she was eager to hear the "curious, wild, dangerous" ideas of Ruskin's later years.[63] Excitedly, if at a distance, Scudder shared the new social awareness of the undergraduates who had been influenced by Ruskin, Toynbee, and Green. She heard about the Barnetts' settlement experiment, only a year old. The luxury of the university lent a disquieting incongruity to her new thoughts. "Something within me stirred, responded, awoke. . . . The point of my desire was an intolerable stabbing pain," she wrote later, using an odd metaphor, "as Ruskin and the rich delights of the place, forced me to realize for the first time the plethora of privilege in which my lot had been cast."[64]

Despite a brief, incongruous fling with the Salvation Army, Scudder took from Oxford a new appreciation of High Church Anglicanism as a living ritual, a satisfying substitute for the Catholicism she had been drawn to in France.[65] It became clear that she might find a happier home in her own church than she had realized back in Boston. At the same time, along with many other American intellectuals, she was developing a "passionate sense . . . that the middle ages rather than the nineteenth century were my natural home."[66] Her imagination and mysticism came together in Oxford's rare atmosphere. She returned to Boston with two still unreconciled impulses: an urge toward the future, ignited by Oxonian "social radicalism," and a longing for the "spiritual traditions of the past" so seductively embodied in High Church Anglicanism. "That there was living connection between the two orders of truth, and that for me there was no certitude on either until they were fused, I did not as yet surmise."[67]

Nor was it clear what she would do next. After returning to Boston in 1885, Scudder floundered for two years. She joined women's clubs and wrote a paper to fulfill Smith's minimal master's degree requirements. Finally a family friend, George Herbert Palmer of Harvard, suggested that Scudder apply to teach English at Wellesley, then under the presidency of his fiancée, Alice Freeman. The same autumn that she began her long academic career, Scudder returned to Smith for a meeting of the Association of Collegiate Alumnae. With her classmates Helen Rand

and Jean Fine she discussed the settlement idea. Wouldn't such a project be popular in this country, especially among young women graduates? Over the next few years, as the idea grew with frustrating slowness, Scudder merged her religious and social ideas. She joined the Society of the Companions of the Holy Cross and connected herself with the Boston Christian Socialist W. D. P. Bliss and his Church of the Brotherhood of the Holy Carpenter. By 1890 she was moving rapidly toward socialism.[68]

Like Vida Scudder, two young Illinois women, Jane Addams and Ellen Gates Starr, first encountered the settlement idea during a trip to Europe in quest of culture, not social ideas. Addams and Starr had met as freshmen at Rockford Female Seminary in 1877–78. Though Ellen Starr had to leave school after a year to earn her living, she and Addams sealed their complex intimacy through long letters and hectic visits over the next ten years. Very different temperamentally, they shared a self-conscious interest in literature and ideas and a stern commitment to self-improvement.

Jane Addams was the youngest daughter of the richest man in tiny Cedarville, Illinois.[69] A millowner and banker, with investments in land and railroads, John Huy Addams had helped found the Illinois Republican party and sat in the state Senate from 1854 to 1870. Jane's mother, Sarah Weber Addams, died when Jane was two; until she was eight, when her father remarried, he and her older sisters were the center of Jane's world. Jane Addams adored her father; yet, as G. J. Barker-Benfield has suggested, her struggles against his control over her education and aspirations marked her adolescence and young womanhood. On one side was her real and very Victorian hero worship of him; on the other, her inchoate urge to follow her own will toward an education and possibly a career that fell outside the boundaries of his, and their culture's, conception of the proper role of a middle-class woman.[70]

Jane Addams's own account suggests that her father chose an understated and quasi-Socratic style of moral teaching for his youngest daughter that puzzled and challenged the serious little girl and riveted her to him. A Quaker by upbringing, he took his children to church and Sunday school but set no value on religious doctrine; he insisted only on personal moral integrity. His teaching on social distinctions was terse and concrete: Jane should wear an old cloak, not her new one, among her poorer Sunday school classmates.[71] Despite his belief that women and men had different tasks requiring different preparations, John Addams wanted Jane to be conversant with the classics of Western culture. By early adolescence she was conscientiously emulating him in this as in other things, by rising before dawn to labor through the tomes in the family library; the little cash bribes that he offered for every volume completed were probably unnecessary.[72]

Jane's stepmother, Anna Haldeman Addams, was a fashionable, dominating woman who tried to fill out Jane's training with novels, plays, parlor music, and the social graces. Their relationship, though cordial, was apparently often strained, doubtless because of the massive change in the psychic economy of the household caused by her father's remarriage, but also because Anna Haldeman, like John Addams, enforced a model of young womanhood with which Jane was at some level uncomfortable.[73] Jane did like one of her stepbrothers, George Haldeman, only slightly younger than she was. Apparently George, and certainly his mother, hoped that after he completed his education, he and Jane would marry. Despite her affection for him, Jane was not interested.[74]

Jane wanted to go to Smith College in Massachusetts. Her father dictated Rockford Female Seminary, closer to home, where her older sisters had gone and John Addams served as a trustee.[75] Despite her disappointment and probable disdain for an institution so unequal to its eastern competitor in prestige and academic quality, Jane Addams did well at Rockford. Though not yet a degree-granting institution, the tiny school was blessed with an eager student body and some stimulating instructors. Its formidable principal and founder, Anna Sill, clung to the seminary's Christian evangelical tradition as well as to her belief that women's proper social roles were domestic and religious. She was proud of the number of Rockford graduates who were missionaries' wives. She was also a pioneer of women's education in the Midwest, and by the late 1870s she had begun campaigning among the Rockford trustees for degree-granting status.[76] Rigid rules of conduct, housekeeping, religious observance, and daily routine were still enforced, and it is not surprising that Addams refers to Rockford as a "boarding school" in her memoirs. But some departments offered fully collegiate instruction, and the students had initiated a number of extracurricular activities.[77] A women's college was pushing its way through the constricted framework of a girls' Protestant seminary.

The obedient daughter blossomed in her own right at Rockford. The magnetic fascination of the mature Jane Addams was clear in embryo during her college years. Portrait photographs confirm what her contemporaries repeatedly suggested: her eyes, set in a small and slightly sharp face, were her most arresting physical feature. Imagination must recreate the voice and speech, low, attractive, and increasingly confident. These intangibles were complemented by her academic ability and her gift for leadership. "We never speculated as to why we always liked to go to her room," wrote one classmate in retrospect, "so that it was always crowded when the sacred 'engaged' sign was not hung out. We just knew there was always something 'doing' where she was, and that however mopey it might be elsewhere there was intellectual ozone in her vicinity." Another remembered that "whenever difficulties with Miss Sill came up for settlement, most of us 'let Jane do it' in presenting them." An astonishing anecdote survives from a "birthday fete" for President Mark Hopkins of Williams College, whose *Evidences of Christianity* was well known to the pious Rockford students. After the first toast, to Hopkins, a second was offered to Jane Addams, the "best evidence of Christianity."[78]

This story is revealing, though possibly apocryphal. On conventional scales of Christian observance and belief, Jane Addams must have taken at best a middling place among her fellow students. At Rockford she faced a constant, interesting, even seductive pressure to convert—more specifically, to accept Christ as her savior. She was happy to debate religious questions; she attended chapel without protest; she read the Testaments in Greek with a favorite instructor. But she resisted a final Christian profession. Though she later attributed her stubbornness to her father's latitudinarianism and "a sort of rationalism" that she shared with a few close friends, a better explanation is Christianity's lack of emotional appeal to her. As she meditated and argued these issues through college, it was Carlyle, not Christ, who gained an ever firmer grip on her imagination.

She discussed religion endlessly with her friend Ellen Starr. Ellen came from a less privileged background than Jane Addams. Her father, a small-town businessman, could find money for only one year of college tuition for his bright daughter. The greatest influence on her youth was her aunt Eliza Allen Starr, whose vivid personality and artistic talent won her a special place in Chicago society. She was an ardent Catholic convert, a fact perhaps less objectionable to her Chicago patrons because in her popular lectures on art she could relate religion and art in a Ruskinian manner. Eliza Starr took on her niece's education and social polishing. Her aunt helped Ellen leave her first teaching job in a public high school for a post at Miss Kirkland's School for Girls in Chicago.[79]

Though sorry to leave Rockford, Ellen liked teaching. In the bonds she formed with a few of her pupils she found some substitute for her interrupted college friendships. While Jane Addams was still at Rockford, Ellen relied on her for news of her friends and teachers.[80] Their correspondence suggests that while Jane Addams appreciated her friend's mind and relied on her as a sounding board, Ellen Starr had an intense personal attachment to Addams. Though she had a privileged place in Addams's affections, she shared her peers' slight awe toward Addams and a wistful sense that she must temper her affection for the sake of the friendship. Even as an adolescent, Jane Addams seems to have held people at arm's length. Occasionally her impersonality was almost cruel. In the summer of 1879 she wrote to Ellen,

> I am disappointed to think that you are not coming back to Rockford, that our social intercourse is probably over for all time, it is queer though, but a fact that I am glad when I know some people just so much and then stop . . . not that I am afraid to go any farther, but there is a sort of fascination to me, you remember them & retain the impression they leave, go steadily on your own way and meet some-one else, who will sort of finish out what they begun . . . two people honestly going ahead are better if they don't meet too much—don't need to "descend" you know—The condition which high friendship demands &c.[81]

These reflections on the idea that friendships, and thus people, might be virtually interchangeable suggest that Addams had some fear of or revulsion from intimacy. Ellen Starr was less complacent about their separation. In the early 1880s she wrote to Addams after one of their infrequent visits:

> I feel positively forlorn without the "disconcerted person" tonight. . . . I suppose, on the whole it is better that I cant see you very often. You are the one person . . . that I have seemed to possess, absent as present. I shall get to depending on you, bodily, in a little while, and that would be quite sure to make me trouble in the end. I can't help wishing, however, that we could sometime be in the same place long enough to do some work together. I believe we should work well.[82]

In 1889 her love for her friend moved Ellen to throw in her lot with the settlement experiment.

Ellen Starr's spiritual growth was strikingly similar to Vida Scudder's. She sought emotional and mystical components to personal faith. She hungered for certainty and constantly questioned the sincerity and depth of her religious sentiments. From the unsatisfying Unitarianism of her childhood, Starr finally converted to Episcopalianism after several years at Miss Kirkland's School, and close to her aunt, in Chicago. When Addams presciently suggested that her friend would ultimately move to Catholicism, Starr protested that one reason she liked the "'church of England'" was that "it doesn't consider union with it as an indication of anything accomplished, only of a desire for something."[83]

Addams was alternately challenged and irritated by her friend's theological concerns. She tried to explain her own evolving position: "Comprehending your deity and being in harmony with his plans is to be saved. If you realize God through Christ or not, that is not the point. . . . Christ don't help me in the least," she admitted; ". . . sometimes I can work myself into great admiration of his life and occasionally I can catch something of his philosophy, but he don't bring me any nearer the Deity."[84] In her third year at Rockford, Addams shrewdly distinguished between Ellen's need for religion and her own: "You long for a beautiful faith an experiance [sic] of this kind[.] I only feel that I need religion in a practical sense, that if I could fix myself with my relations to God & the universe, & so be in perfect harmony with nature & deity, I could use my faculties and energy so much better & could do almost anything. *Mine* is preeminantly [sic] selfish," she concluded perhaps disingenuously, "and *yours* is a reaching for higher things."[85] Jane Addams's bible had become Thomas Carlyle. She wrote to Ellen that she increasingly admired Miss Sarah Anderson—Ellen's favorite Rockford teacher—for her "sincere genuine character" and the simplicity of her reasoned faith, which reminded Addams of Carlyle's statement that "every God-created man is a hero if he only remains true to his creation." Miss Anderson told her rapt young friend that "I do not think we are put into the world to be religious, we have a certain work to do, and to do that is the main thing."[86]

Though Addams yielded to the ostentation of humility in calling her approach to religion "selfish," it was certainly bound up with her powerful preoccupation with her own destiny. In fact, the force of her desire for "work," as Carlyle called it, or more accurately a calling, was inversely proportional to her sense of just what it might be. During college she championed women's education as a preparation for "good works and honest toil" and argued for a more embracing vision of woman's historic role as a "breadgiver"—not merely submissive to man, but creatively employed in sustaining the race.[87] But she did not supply examples of the "toil" she proposed for women. She herself flirted seriously with the idea of becoming a doctor. Her stepbrother Harry Haldeman was a doctor; George Haldeman, just graduating from Beloit, aspired to a scientific career. Little wonder that she fixed upon this goal. But at a deeper level she was driven by a far less determinate ambition: to be a remarkable *person,* like those in one of her favorite verses of Matthew Arnold:

> Unaffrighted by the silence round them
> Undistracted by the sights they see
> These demand not that the things without them
> Yield them love, amusement, sympathy.[88]

She saw these lines as a portrait of a "self-poised, mighty life"; another reader might find them austere, even chilling. Her fascination with character and greatness, rather than a gift for intimate friendship, might also explain why in her third year she consciously chose "people for my observation, and conversation for my recreation." Rather than persevere in an attempt to believe in a divine Christ, she had decided to "yield myself to all nobility where ever I can find it, in hopes at length I may be lead [*sic*] to the Perfect or Ideal man, a very simple creed and the being satisfied with it may but show how shallow my religion is."[89]

Jane Addams was hardly shallow. It is difficult to guess how far she herself fathomed the depths of her motivations and inner conflicts over the next eight years. She graduated from Rockford in 1881, went home, and became ill. She had not given up her dream of going East, to Smith College or medical school, but her parents persuaded her to postpone any plans. During a vacation trip later in the summer, John Addams died suddenly of a ruptured appendix. To Ellen Starr, who hurried to Cedarville to be with her friend, Jane Addams wrote, "I will not write of myself or how purposeless and without ambition I am, only prepare yourself so you won't be too disappointed in me when you come. The greatest sorrow that can ever come to me has past and I hope it is only a question of time until I get my moral purposes straight."[90] In this letter to her closest friend, Addams's major emotional response to her father's death was chagrin at her moral lassitude. If her father's death was a test of her character, she felt she had failed it. She was now rudderless. Her ambivalent, passionately charged dependence on her father had denied her the "self-reliance" she paradoxically but under-

standably revered above almost any other quality. His death now bound
her more tightly to her family and his memory.

Repeatedly over the next eight years her grand plans were delayed or
abandoned owing to family problems and her intermittent ill health.
That first autumn she traveled to Philadelphia with her stepmother to
enroll at the Women's Medical College. After a term of study, Addams
landed with back problems at S. Weir Mitchell's celebrated Hospital of
Orthopaedic and Nervous Diseases.[91] In 1882 Harry Haldeman operated on her back; months of forced prostration followed. In 1883–84
Mrs. Addams shepherded Jane through a European grand tour. They
spent the next two winters in Baltimore, so that Mrs. Addams could be
near George, studying at Johns Hopkins, and introduce her stepdaugh-
ter to Baltimore society. This was not a great success. In Europe Jane
had sunk into a morbid state of psychic inertia and self-recrimination.
She had punctuated one newsy letter to Ellen Starr with the unhappy
reflection that "failure through ill-health is just as culpable and miserable as failure through any other cause. . . . I have been idle for two
years just because I had not enough vitality to be anything else, and the
consequence is that . . . I have constantly lost confidence in myself and
have gained nothing and improved nothing."[92] The two years in Baltimore were as "idle," by her definition, as the previous two. Depressed,
she admitted her emotional vulnerability and dependence. "For many
years it was my ambition to reach my father's moral requirements, &
now when I am needing something more I find myself approaching a
crisis, & look rather wistfully to my friends for help."[93]

Lacking focused ambition, Addams doggedly pursued an increasingly
arid self-cultivation. She read Carlyle's *Frederick the Great,* Ruskin's
Modern Painters (at Ellen's urging), and Browning (plus an essay titled
"The Idea of Personality as Embodied in Browning's Poetry"). She attended lectures at Johns Hopkins and took French lessons. She suggested to Ellen in 1886 that they prepare for their next visit by reading
something in common and developing "opinions and sentiments ready
to 'exchange.'"[94] Though she sometimes upbraided Ellen for indulging
similar temptations to idleness bred of precarious health, she also
praised her friend's industry: "don't you know, my dear, that you do as
much as I do, and more, in addition to all the time and vitality you give
to your girls and that I am filled with shame that with all my apparent
leisure I do nothing at all."[95] This was not quite true. Addams had heavy
family commitments. She helped her sister-in-law after her brother
Weber had a mental breakdown, and she spent much time intermit-

tently with her sister Mary and her nieces and nephews. Much of the burden of family business fell to her after her father's death. In Baltimore, between lectures and card parties, she tried charity work. She was moved by the children at a sewing school for the poor and the "colored women" at a nursing home, but there was no conversion experience.[96]

Throughout these years Ellen Starr bolstered and comforted her friend. While she poignantly took to heart Jane's "scoldings," she would not reciprocate, except to criticize Addams's spelling and punctuation ("You always were careless, Jeannie").[97] She even read Addams's Rockford essays to her students and reported back their naive praise. She must have been elated when Addams proposed in 1887 to dip into her paternal inheritance to make it possible for Ellen and their friend, Sarah Anderson, to travel with her to Europe. Ellen would finally see the great art she had been studying and teaching under the tutelage of Ruskin and her aunt Eliza, and she would spend uninterrupted months with her dearest friend.

By Addams's own account, it was in Madrid in the spring of 1888 that she first broached to Starr her idea of moving into a house in a poor neighborhood of Chicago. She suggests in *Twenty Years at Hull-House* that her horrified guilt at relishing a gory bullfight precipitated her resolution to break out of the "snare of preparation" and act to fulfill some of her grandiose dreams. Whether or not the bullfight provoked the epiphany she describes, the "scheme," as she and Ellen called it, quickly took imaginative shape.[98] When Starr returned to America, Addams and Sarah Anderson paused in England, where Addams attended a congress of foreign missions and looked around at some of the London reform efforts whose beginnings she had missed during her first trip in 1883–84. A chance encounter with Canon Fremantle in Canterbury won a letter of introduction to the Barnetts, and Addams observed Toynbee Hall with admiration. The settlement chimed with the notions of social service that had floated half-formed in her mind for several years. The conversion experience she had missed in Baltimore may have come to her here. "It is so free from 'professional doing good,' so unaffectedly sincere and so productive of good results in its classes and libraries so that it seems perfectly ideal."[99] By the next January she and Ellen Starr were living together in Chicago, dividing their time between hunting for the perfect house and explaining their "scheme" to everybody, from ministers to society matrons, who might be able to help.

The settlement idea was parented in both England and America by the new organismic "religion of humanity" and the potent notion that social science would explicate and resolve the problems of urban industrial society. The settlement movement made an easy transit from England to the United States, where it flourished in a milieu deeply influenced by the icons and concerns of Victorian Britain. The Social Christianity that commanded from the comfortable middle class a vigorous concern with poverty and social inequities drew inspiration and texts from English Christian Socialism. Willing workers, the most important element of the settlement idea, were being cultivated by American colleges and universities, hothouses of the ideology of Christian character and middle-class noblesse oblige.

In the late 1890s, the English settler Percy Alden wrote only partly tongue in cheek that the reason women seemed to dominate the American settlement movement was that "the men are so much engaged in commercial pursuits, and the aggregation of huge fortunes, that they have no time for altruistic effort or philanthropic endeavor."[100] There is a grain of truth in this caricature of American society. As in England, middle-class women had always been predominant in American philanthropy. Prosperous matrons and unemployed single women had time for the "good works" their culture extolled. Although the settlements strenuously distinguished themselves from traditional philanthropy, they appealed to a segment of the population still bound to slowly changing assumptions. For many of the new women undergraduates, college functioned as a glorified finishing school. The ideal of "liberal culture" as a good in itself, coming to a rhetorical climax in men's colleges, was handily transferred to women's education and subtly reinforced by propaganda for the instrumentality of the liberal arts in women's work as wives and mothers. Whereas men were expected to advance from liberal arts or technical education into a profession, most women lived with no such clear-cut expectation. Many energetic, capable women were tortured by the gap between the rhetoric stressing the broad serviceability of liberal education and the real vacuum where their vaunted mission to society should have been revealed.

The American settlement movement was *not* exclusively a women's movement. It is impossible to quantify meaningful differences between the personal motives actuating the men and the women entering the settlement houses. Among the handful scrutinized here, Graham Taylor, Robert Woods, and Stanton Coit found in settlement work a practical field for their essentially religious callings. Each felt constricted by available vocational choices and broke away from a conventional career path to participate in settlement work. Woods struggled the hardest to find a social role for the lay ministry to which he felt impelled, but even Taylor, a decade into a successful clerical career, rebelled against its constraints. But for Woods, Coit, and Taylor, social conviction preceded the personal search for vocation. The urge to reform a flawed society shaped their professional decisions.

The settlement movement bore a more complicated relationship to the lives of the women. Jane Addams floundered for eight years after college, held back by "the family claim" and her own obscure hesitations from pursuing the Carlylean destiny she had dared to dream of at Rockford. Vida Scudder discovered the "reality" she had craved in her college friendships, and she found satisfying work in college teaching, but a sense of the hollowness of socially inert education persisted and gained urgency from her unsettled spiritual life. Ellen Starr too had found at least a temporarily fulfilling vocation in teaching, but as with Scudder, deeper longings for spiritual fulfillment would fuse with her aesthetic thought to impel her toward social radicalism.

The settlement workers were from the beginning their own shrewdest critics. As they moved into reclaimed tenements and rambling mansions from their new neighborhoods' more prosperous days, they publicly scrutinized their own motives and goals. Like the English settlers, they disowned pious sentimentalism. They did hope to do good. But above all, in the American metaphor, they were "pioneers" on a "frontier"; they were embarking on an exciting, even audacious, adventure.

3
Moving In

The American settlement movement was deeply indebted to the English elaboration of the "personal service" ethic, yet the American setting was different. Democratic ideology, social fluidity, and a unique urban demography pressed against the received rhetoric of the settlement founders. Gradually the Americans developed a justification of their enterprise suited to their own climate. But even as it molded itself to a new environment, the American settlement movement carried permanent traces of its Victorian origins.

Like their English models, the American settlements were intended to benefit residents and "neighbors" alike, and ultimately the society beyond their neighborhoods. In "leavening" drab urban neighborhoods with young, well-educated residents, the settlements would, as Jane Addams put it, "add the social function to democracy."[1] To halt the atomization of American urban society, the settlers would bear witness to a community of social interests that belied artificial economic distinctions. Though most of the settlement workers tried to avoid the rhetoric of "moral uplift" made familiar by missionaries and charity workers and looked to the authority of social science to legitimate their enterprise, the settlement credo of the organic unity of society was framed and understood as a fundamentally ethical doctrine dictating ethically motivated action. To mitigate the altruistic cast of their work, they embraced the idea of reciprocity and claimed to receive as much as they gave in choosing to live among the poor.

In practice, the plasticity that had become a central tenet of settlement life contributed to the initial success of the American settlements. The residents' tentative overtures to their new neighbors reflected both settlement doctrine as they understood it and their appropriate diffidence as self-invited participants in neighborhood life.

Because the American settlers shied away from a fixed program of cultural or religious mission, they wrestled in the first decade with the contradictions between their intentions and their actions. Informal neighborliness was never jettisoned as a method or primary goal, but its nebulousness made it impossible to measure, as the settlers themselves admitted. Further, there was no fail-safe prescription for evoking friendship and trust in their new neighbors. When the settlers placed their faith in the beneficent influence of personality, they inadvertently created a critical vulnerability in their doctrine of the indefinite expandability of the settlement movement. Though there might be enough volunteers to staff hundreds of settlements, there was no guarantee that they would be naturally endowed with personal qualities that would win the loyalty of their neighbors. The leaders were acutely aware of this problem, to which there was no real solution. Nevertheless, the settlements flourished.

The settlements succeeded largely because their neighbors welcomed what the settlers almost apologetically offered: organized, regularly scheduled, and resident-led activities. Though the neighborhood adults often hung back from the settlement, aloof out of shyness, deference, or pride, the children and adolescents swarmed in and stretched the settlers' resources and imagination to their limits. Contrary to their initial hopes and expectations, the residents found that their clubs, classes, kindergartens, clinics, and summer camps formed a backbone of continuity that ensured settlement survival not just from year to year, but over decades. As the movement evolved, the structure and routine that carried the dreaded taint of institutionalism gave the settlements a raison d'être in the neighborhoods that simple sociability, often awkward and artificial, lacked. In turn, the settlements' persistence vested their spokesmen with credibility in causes that transcended the neighborhoods.

For most of the young settlement workers of the 1890s, moving into the industrial neighborhoods of the great American cities was a momentous step. From the partial shelter of their surrogate households, they realized ipso facto the settlement idea by confronting the lives and values of hitherto alien segments of society. The settlements offered their recruits, particularly the women, a sanctioned interlude of great personal autonomy, an active role in public life, and an often exhilarating extension of the kind of group life and personal fellowship that most of them had tasted during college. If it did not overwhelm, exhaust, or dismay the individual, the settlement experience was often extraordinarily stimulating and liberating. Like London's Toynbee Hall, a number of American settlements became magnets for the radicals and reformers who flourished in the Anglo-American fin de siècle and hungered for allies, platforms, and bases of operation. The settlements' critics often accused them of fostering a dilettantish bohemianism, a charge earnestly refuted but not always unfair.

The settlements adopted a cautious and placating posture toward the outside world, for several reasons. In the first place, they were surrounded by potential enemies with the power to undermine or vitiate their work. The settlements shouldered their way into the busy philanthropic field between the existing charities, many of whose methods they quietly deplored, and the churches, suspicious of these secular "missionaries" who eschewed religious teaching and practice precisely because of the risk of alienating communicants of other faiths. The settlement workers' righteous campaigns for clean streets, better tenement laws, and regular methods for inducting immigrants into citizenship roiled the dirty waters of city politics. The settlers pestered the police with reports of illegal gambling, prostitution, and saloon-law violations. They offered aid and comfort to union organizers in the stockyards and garment industries. They gave the floor to avowed socialists and anarchists. For all of these disturbing initiatives they offered careful explanations, because they could not risk confronting their competitors in politics and philanthropy, nor could they afford to offend their prosperous and often conservative "uptown" patrons.

The settlement workers' moderation was not merely opportunistic. They saw their role as mediators between competing social and economic interests, interpreters shuttling between the alien cultures of the recent immigrants and the entrenched and defensive "natives." The poor and exploited should have the right not to rise up, but to raise themselves up. Social solidarity must be achieved on both an organic and a pluralistic basis. In a period in which popular social analysis was characterized by dichotomous extremes—"rich and poor," "victims and parasites," "good and evil"—the settlement doctrine counseled tolerance, reconciliation, and a benign recognition of cultural and ideological multiplicity.

After Stanton Coit's Neighborhood Guild, the first American settlements were Hull-House in Chicago, the College Settlement on Rivington Street in New York, and Andover House in Boston. Each embodied a distinct model of organization, but they shared a fundamental belief in the settlement ideology as laid down by Canon Barnett. They opened their doors with the nervous hope of making themselves welcome and useful to their neighbors and an optimistic faith that their "work" would be shown to them.

The Rivington Street Settlement was the first venture of the College Settlements Association, not even named or organized as such until six months after the New York settlement opened. A rudimentary network among the women's colleges had been growing since Vida Scudder broached the settlement idea to Helen Rand and Jean Fine in 1887. Jane Addams and Ellen Starr, without any institutional affiliation, laid a similar groundwork of support by "working" Chicago philanthropists, churches, and socialites for eight months before moving into the old Hull mansion on lower Halsted Street in September 1889.

Addams and Starr promoted their "scheme" as an inverse philanthropy for restless and frustrated rich girls. They laid it out simply. They would take a house, "furnish it prettily," and live there "*naturellement*," inviting their neighbors and their uptown friends to visit them. They hoped other young women would come live with them. Though Ellen refused to take credit for their evolving idea, her experience at Miss Kirkland's School fed her understanding of what Addams would later call "the subjective necessity for social settlements." "I pity girls so!" exclaimed Starr, "especially rich girls who have nothing in the world to do. If ever the ordinary girl expresses any wish to do anything for her less fortunate sisters her mother throws cold water on it. . . . And then she shrivels up, & feels that she is of no use whatever, & that it was of course very foolish & presuming in her to think she could do anything."[2] Above all, as Ellen stressed to her cousin, there must be "no 'organization' and no 'institution' about it." The residents must not feel they were engaged in anything "queer or extraordinary: turning themselves into sisters or giving up the world or society or cutting themselves off from the things of the flesh or any such sentimental nonsense." Any "sacrifice" they made would be for their own benefit.[3]

Their promotional rhetoric did not always successfully avoid the condescension of traditional philanthropy. They wanted their little group to "learn to know the people & understand them and their ways of life: to give them what they have to give out of their culture and leisure and overindulgence, & to receive the culture that comes of self denial and poverty & failure." Several times they succumbed to the ready analogy of missionary work.[4] These lapses arose from the difficulty of envisioning such a novel and formless enterprise and the need to tailor their presentation to their audience. Though Addams and Starr had enough money to open Hull-House, thanks to Jane's inheritance, they strenuously sought the goodwill of philanthropic agencies and influential individuals, particularly important if they were to succeed in drawing the fellow workers they desired: society's cherished daughters.

They found an ample audience for their promotion. A wave of civic pride and boosterism, Victorian respect for the principle of self-help, and fears of a burgeoning uneducated populace had recently led Chicago's magnates to endow a number of civic and educational institutions, including the Young Men's Association, the Chicago Atheneum, the Art Institute, the Chicago Manual Training School, the Armour Institute of Technology, and the Industrial Art School. There were also several large church missions, among them Dwight L. Moody's Sunday school, the Armour Mission, and the Clybourne Street Mission. Finally, Chicago's society women had begun to gather in well-organized clubs commanding the machinery and funds for large charitable projects. The Philanthropic Committee of the Chicago Woman's Club was one of Addams's and Starr's first targets.[5]

The friends systematically penetrated these preserves, aided by Ellen's contacts through Miss Kirkland's School and through her aunt. They observed the missions and met several volunteers who also belonged to the Woman's Club. Addams spoke to the board of the Armour Mission, where she met the young architect Allen Pond, who assured her that she had "*voiced* something hundreds of young people in the city were trying to express." The young women persuaded patrons to arrange special receptions, such as Ellen Henrotin's tea for several dozen "young ladies." Jane boasted to her stepmother that they were becoming quite a "fashionable 'fad.' "[6]

They attributed their popularity to something "in the air," an "influence." Ellen privately credited Addams with being the "luminous medium" of something "outside herself."[7] After one saccharine newspaper article—part of the publicity the two women sought but tried to control—Addams joked that "I positively feel my callers peering into my face to detect 'spirituality.' "[8] Ellen Starr laughed too, but about this time she wrote that "a personality is the only thing that ever touches anybody."[9]

Though the friends promoted their "scheme" as unique, they knew that whatever was "in the air" had touched others as well. In early 1889 they received a circular letter from one of the Smith College group. In corresponding with her they discovered that though the easterners had collected enough money to rent a house, they were having trouble attracting volunteers. Ellen Starr rather smugly reported to her cousin:

"[Theirs] is to be confined to college women & is to be an organization which ours distinctly is not, & then I think [they are] less Christian than Jane is. Jane feels that it is not the Christian spirit to go among these people as if you were bringing them a great boon: that one gets as much as she gives." She felt that the Toynbee Hall men more truly exemplified the proper spirit, with no pretense to self-sacrifice or social superiority.[10]

There was less discrepancy between the two experiments than these reflections imply. Although some of the early rhetoric of the College Settlements Association did smack of the noblesse oblige of traditional charity ("helpful, personal contact" being the sole "method of friendship" by which "the higher is . . . to give an uplift to the lower"), the CSA also espoused reciprocity and stressed the settlement's educational value for college women.[11] In fact, the most significant contrast was in the settlements' organization. In vesting control in a membership representing the women's colleges and therefore not necessarily resident in the settlement city, the CSA consciously laid the groundwork for a "movement," expandable into other cities (eventually both Boston and Philadelphia had CSA settlements) and independent of the idiosyncrasies of personnel. Hull-House depended on the personal force of one woman for its survival and success. Though each of the CSA settlements found strong leaders for extended periods, changes in leadership did not signal the fundamental upheaval that occurred at Hull-House upon Addams's death in 1935.

Boston's Andover House, headed by Robert Woods, represented a third model for sponsoring and organizing a settlement. Although the leaders and most residents would come from the seminary, the preliminary appeal was mailed not only to younger seminary graduates, "familiar with its present methods of social study," but also to others in Boston's educational, religious, and philanthropic circles who might sympathize with the settlement's aims and join the association.

In the Andover House appeal, Tucker accused the Protestant church of being "niggardly of men." Social Christianity dictated the church's "new duty" of "loving one's neighbor"; the settlement was the best illustration of the "large use of Christian personality." The settlement could extend the church's "moral power," encouraging the "noble and generous desires" of poor as well as wealthy individuals. The settlement would be nondenominational, which Tucker and Woods saw as wholly compatible with its essentially religious and specifically Christian motivation.[12]

Several other early settlements were established under the auspices of organized religion. East Side House in New York, founded in 1890, was sponsored by the Church Club, an Episcopalian lay association. In 1894 Graham Taylor launched Chicago Commons through the Chicago Theological Seminary, and a group from the Union Theological Seminary established the Union Settlement in New York in 1895. However, equally typical of the settlement impulse was the experience of Charles Zueblin, who worked for the Methodist City Mission in Chicago after his return from Leipzig University in the late 1880s. Criticized for shunning evangelistic methods, Zueblin left the mission and turned to Northwestern University for support in founding a settlement.[13]

Many of the American settlement founders were motivated by religious faith. In the early years, they sometimes compared the settlement to the medieval Franciscan order. For a mystic like Vida Scudder this was a natural analogy, but Robert Woods used it too: "The better times cannot come except as we have in these days in our cities some influence like that of the Franciscans, who at the end of the Middle Ages went forth freely out into the world, among the people in the field, in the town, sharing in a measure their lives, and disseminating . . . the influences of Christianity and civilization, which, up to that time, had been sheltered in the monasteries."[14]

The settlers' use of this figure carried a critique as well as an affirmation of the relation of organized religion to modern urban problems. They agreed with Tucker that the Protestant church had failed to reach large segments of the population. They also felt that primarily religious social work was too narrow and could be counterproductive. They endorsed Barnett's distinction between settlements and missions: "A Settlement enables the rich to know the poor in a way not possible for a Mission, whose members go about with minds set on their object, and who are often held at a distance because of that object."[15]

There were many shades of opinion concerning religion in the settlement. In general, though, the settlement workers' aversion to denominational proselytism was tied to their consensus on the meaning of social Christianity: that it transcended doctrinal differences to embrace communicants of every faith. The values embedded in the Protestant culture most of them sprang from inevitably shaped the settlement idea, which can be seen as the final flowering of Victorian middle-class culture. On the other hand, the tolerant pluralism of social Christianity reflected the waning influence of evangelistic concerns in the religion of genteel and urbane Americans and laid the groundwork for the advocacy of cultural pluralism that became a hallmark of the American settlement movement.

Most of the settlements began as modified cooperative living arrangements. Often the sponsoring association or individuals paid the rent while the residents paid board and took at least the evening meal in common.[16] In a letter to Katharine Coman of the CSA in 1891, Jane Addams suggested that the "style of living" should be one "that the residents would naturally have if they lived anywhere else. I deprecate very much anything that makes the movement strained or unnatural."[17] Though residents were expected to keep their own rooms neat, the houses usually hired servants to do the cooking and heavier cleaning.[18] The settlers found it "natural" to plan their routines around the availability of servants, as most of them might have done in their own homes or at college. Still, some felt nagging doubts about whether hired service was self-indulgent or inappropriate in the settlements. If they sincerely sought to eradicate class divisions through action and example, how could they justify this anomalous distinction in their own households?

Jane Addams found this troubling issue posed most sharply by the personal credo of Leo Tolstoy, perhaps the most important influence on her thought in the late 1880s and early 1890s. In *What Then Must We Do?* (translated 1887), Tolstoy asserted that to live a truly Christian life one must actively share society's burden of physical labor. His own shocked discovery of the horrors of Moscow poverty in the winter of 1882 led him to reject the palliative of charity for a doctrine of absolute Christian purity of life. Jesus commanded, "Resist not evil"; to Tolstoy nonresistance implied not passivity, but a refusal to take a stance toward the world that set man's law above God's.[19] The announcement of this revelation, coupled with Tolstoy's retirement to his estate, Yasnaya Polyana, to live a simple life of hard labor stirred readers who had been struggling to define their obligations to poor and oppressed people. To them, Addams later recalled, he epitomized the individual who had "lift[ed] his life to the level of his conscience, to translate his theories into action."[20]

Little wonder that the spirit of Tolstoy haunted the settlement workers, engaged in an enterprise that was a tissue of compromises. In 1894 Jane Addams told her intimate friend Mary Rozet Smith that before she moved into Hull-House, she had had "an awful time" with the questions of conscience posed by Tolstoy, but now she found his position "untenable": "a man cannot be a Xtian by himself." Yet two years later Addams seized upon the opportunity to visit Yasnaya Polyana with Mary Smith and their cicerone, Aylmer Maude, disciple and translator of the great Russian. Their neurotically frank host rebuked the Americans for their fine clothes and chided Addams for being an "absentee landlord," deriving income from a farm she rarely visited, a fact that had already caused Addams much uneasiness. She found herself resolving during the journey home to spend two hours a day in the Hull-House bakery making bread—only to realize back at the settlement that this was a more "preposterous" compromise than any she had already made. To bake bread while visitors waited and mail lay unanswered would be pretentious and self-indulgent—a dubious route to "saving her soul."[21] Though Tolstoy's doctrine of nonresistance would be an important underpinning of her later peace work, she now rejected his dogmatic insistence that the essence of a Christian life was literal "bread labor." More troublesome than Tolstoy's antimodern impracticality was his disdain for human frailties and the paradoxical self-absorption that his thought invited.

The issue of the master-servant relationship in settlement life remained unsettled as long as the settlements' primary self-identification was as "homes" among other homes in their neighborhoods. In 1898 a committee of Chicago Commons residents drew up a ponderous "voluntary agreement" by which each resident would pledge to "avoid causing unnecessary labor or inconvenience" and to "assist as I have opportunity in the manual labor for the comfort and convenience of the household." Clearly reflecting sore points in daily routine, the agreement specified that residents were to keep their own rooms neat (though the servants apparently swept and cleaned them) and get down to breakfast on time. In addition, in this early "mixed" household, the men would tend the coal fires while the women served at table and washed the dishes. The committee hoped "to revolutionize the spirit and method of our domestic life, . . . [and] abolish . . . the social classification palpably existing between ourselves and our servants, and begin to create, within our household, a living example of Christian co-operation and brotherhood."[22]

The "Rules for Residents" periodically issued by similar house committees suggest that group life was no less trying and disordered in settlements than in any other mixed and extended household. (Being late to breakfast seems to have been endemic throughout the Anglo-American settlement world.) The fervent Chicago Commons document, with its ringing yet irresolute conclusions, reflected the continuing dilemma of what it meant to lead a "natural" life in a contrived social setting. Ellen Starr's mother professed herself "delighted" with the old Hull mansion but, as Jane Addams told her stepmother, "she did wish this beautiful old house was in a better neighborhood, without reflecting that if it were we would not be in it."[23] Robert Woods admitted that in living comfortably with "the usual necessities of civilized existence," the settlement workers were practicing a philosophy of "elevation by contact." The effort to avoid any hint of patronage would itself become unnatural and offensive.[24] Privately he maintained that "the relation between the settlements and their neighbors is an artificial one. I don't know that it can ever be otherwise."[25]

The settlers' initial reception depended less on their self-presentation than on the idiosyncrasies of the neighborhood. Their arrival piqued local curiosity and sometimes evoked offers of help. The janitor next door to 95 Rivington Street kindly showed Jane Robbins how to clean the stoop, and the neighbors were probably amused by the young women's first attempts to wash windows and shovel snow. At Denison House in Boston the residents unthinkingly went door to door to engage local women to do the cleaning; they felt they were making a "natural & friendly beginning." They were relieved that newspaper publicity did not seem to put off their neighbors: "I think they thought we had come to do some *other* people good & were glad of it," wrote Helen Cheever.[26] The women at Hull-House suffered petty vandalism and even personal attacks—a man spat in Addams's face as he passed her on the street one day—but they refused to call a policeman. They would let the neighbors determine whether they could stay.[27]

The new settlers planned to tailor their neighborhood involvement to local "needs," but it was hard to sit back and wait for something to happen and easy to fall back on familiar forms of social interaction and organization. By the end of their second month the Hull-House women, so adamant about "simple neighborliness," had inaugurated a boys' club. They discovered that poor neighborhood attendance at the first evening receptions was due less to the presence of the uptown "elite" than to their own ignorance of local mores. The German and Italian women were not used to going out in the evenings with their husbands. So Addams and Starr arranged receptions for the mothers and children; the uptowners could practice their German or Italian, play the piano, or cut out paper dolls. Gradually jeering and vandalism gave way to occasional visitors and requests for assistance. In mid-November Ellen reported proudly to her parents, "Two young men have called voluntarily, a woman has presented us with a bottle of catsup, & another has requested to leave her baby while she moved her household effects." Soon they were nursing the sick and even assisting at births.[28]

Addams and Starr discovered that the Hull-House neighborhood was not only an ethnic patchwork, with clusters of Irish, Italians, Germans, and East European Jews, but also a social amalgam. While most native-born Americans and older immigrant groups pushed outward, leaving their decaying houses to new immigrants and the ubiquitous "sweaters," the neighborhood's past persisted in "people of former education and opportunity" who had slipped from prosperity or never quite gained a foothold in the shifting economy. To them "the Settlement may be a genuine refuge."[29] This "element" rather than the immigrant colonies responded most warmly to the settlement's lectures, reading circles, and classes. Ellen Starr found an audience for an oral reading of George Eliot's *Romola*. A group of local public schoolteachers formed a Latin class.[30]

The Hull-House women had insisted that "the Settlement should not be primarily for the children"; they hoped to enrich the lives of the adults as well as the young people by working through natural social groupings, particularly families. But the children could not be turned aside. The kindergarten was soon joined by an array of children's groups. Reading, sewing, and other crafts provided a framework for the social interaction that was the main purpose of these clubs.[31]

Other settlements also found the neighborhood children clamorous and irresistible. The Rivington Street settlers had planned to concentrate on girls' activities but found they also had to accommodate the boys, who begged not to be left out.[32] The residents recruited the small children in their largely Jewish neighborhood by enticing them from the streets on Sundays with the promise of stories and singing. The little kitchen gardens tended by the "Good Seed Society" capitalized on the children's extravagant love of the flowers and greenery they rarely saw.

Settlement residents and other social workers repeatedly verified the cliché of the city dwellers' hunger for nature, most poignantly shown by the children.[33] The Rivington Street settlers told of the child found picking a heap of old rose leaves out of a barrel, one by one, and the child thrilled to be going to the "'real country, where you can catch flowers.'"[34] Other colorful accidents of nature in the city streets were greeted with almost atavistic awe and joy. Several years later a New York settlement resident described a scene on Rivington Street, where she heard a sudden "howling and yelling" one afternoon. Children ran in from the side streets and gathered in a crowd on the corner. "Some danced and waved their hands: all were wildly excited. Suddenly looking *up* into the sky, I saw a rainbow! The excitement lasted five or ten minutes."[35]

The significance of the child as a symbol of innocence in Victorian literature, and as the center of solicitous attention in the idealized Victorian middle-class family, had undoubtedly shaped the settlement workers' warm and sentimental responses to the neighborhood children. The children were the most plastic and trusting element of any population. Not only were they captivating and genuinely responsive, but they were the best candidates for the primary settlement purpose of shaping character through personal influence. The children also offered the most important entrée into the life of the neighborhood. The Rivington Street children spoke of the settlement residents as "teachers"; most likely their parents, initially puzzled by these friendly intruders into their lives, found this label apt and convenient. The settlement workers wanted to be accepted as friends and neighbors; ironically, their presence in the neighborhood was more lucid and "natural" when it could be understood as quasi-professional. But not all parents readily entrusted their children to the settlements. The most sensitive point of suspicion and conflict was religion.

After moving into 93 Tyler Street in Boston's South Bay in late 1892, the Denison House settlers called on the local Catholic priest. Like other Boston neighborhoods, the South Bay was changing with the influx of eastern European and Asian immigrants, but the immediate neighborhood was still largely Irish. Father Billings was an American convert from Methodism—"cordial, zealous, narrow & honest," the residents noted in their daily log. One of them, Helen Cheever, made it her special mission to win over Father Billings. She explained that, like him, the residents wished to instill morality and thrift in their neighbors through "friendly influence." Nonetheless, Father Billings raised obstacles to the settlers' proposals. He objected to their inviting young people in for "innocent pleasure"; he disapproved of anything that threatened the children's respect for the "sacredness of home." A lending library, unless confined to "Catholic" books, raised the specter of creeping Protestantism or even irreligion. The priest finally agreed to let the settlement work freely for a year, and "watch *results.*"

Within three months he paid an angry return visit. The women had broken their promise by having "clubs" in the house, and he had been forced to speak against them in church. Cheever protested that the few boys they had invited to the house had improved markedly in "meekness & gentleness"; the residents could not enter their neighbors' homes as freely as he could, so making friends with the children in the settlement was the best way for them to meet the adults. "Our ultimate object is to help the home," she pleaded, "only we must reach the same result by different means." Father Billings retorted that the settlers made "the fatal mistake of teaching the children disrespect to their parents" whenever they tried to influence them directly. Even if the parents were "bad people," he insisted, "I prefer bad home influence to outside influence."[36]

Ultimately the Denison House residents either shrugged off or placated Father Billings; by the end of their second year there were at least ten clubs meeting in the settlement. The vigilant priest had been fighting defensively, distrusting not just the settlement residents but also the "bigoted" judges, SPCC agents, and public schools, which taught children "more than they ought to know for their station." "Gentleness and suavity" didn't work on these people, he maintained. Father Billings and other neighborhood priests were themselves threatened by the gentle, suave methods of the largely Protestant, middle-class philanthropies and public agencies threatening the church's ascendancy over its communicants.[37]

The appropriation of the settlement label by church and missionary groups helped arouse popular suspicion of settlements. The Epworth League University Settlement in the North End of Boston epitomized the naked offensiveness of some religious settlements. "Let us retake the North End for Methodism!" cried the settlement's brochure in 1894. Characterizing the Italian and Jewish colonies as "plague spots" in the new city, the Epworth League aimed to win the souls of the immigrants while teaching them English and manual skills. They scorned the "nonsectarian" philanthropist who turned away from his own savior to "pose before His enemies as a pagan."[38]

Even the "regular" settlements did not consistently avoid religious work. Both Andover House and Graham Taylor's Chicago Commons maintained institutional links with nearby chapels. In his settlement's second year, Robert Woods inaugurated a Sunday evening "musical service" designed to appeal "to the simpler and deeper religious instincts of people, and . . . absolutely without the taint of proselytism."[39] Though most settlement residents espoused a tolerant, pluralistic attitude toward their neighbors' faiths, they blundered occasionally by staging children's Christmas parties in a Jewish neighborhood or planning recreation on holy days.[40] Given the Protestant tinge of social Christianity and traditional American Protestant chauvinism toward Jews and Catholics, the nonsectarian settlements may in practice have resembled the "religious" settlements more than they cared to believe.

As the settlement residents made their first overtures to their neighbors, they sought ways to accomplish the other part of their task: to get to know their neighborhoods as social and economic units in order to help make desirable reforms. Imbued with the optimistic teleology of much contemporary social science, the settlement workers believed that neighborly friendship was compatible with distinterested objectivity. Herman Hegner, an early resident of Chicago Commons, explained in the *American Journal of Sociology* in 1897 that the settlement "method" was "scientific" because it was "empirical, reciprocal, mediatory, and positive along the lines of social evolution." Studying the "real facts" of people's lives would lead to understanding that could speed up the process of social evolution.[41]

Robert Woods called the settlements "laboratories in social science." His foray into jargon leaves Hegner in the dust: "The range of inquiry under [social science] includes the investigation of normal statical conditions, of abnormal statical conditions, and of the observed effects of all processes which under reasonable hypothesis may work upon both sorts of statical conditions, to produce change in them along the lines of the normal dynamic development of society." His tone changes abruptly as he describes the resident's "stirring belief in the life-giving quality of culture."

> He holds every good thing a means of grace. He believes so deeply in what he has to bring that he is willing to do his work without seeing the results. He confers upon his neighbors, the working people, the signal honor and respect of trusting them with all those better things which refresh and strengthen his own life. He is, if he is truly educated, a believer in man, a democrat, a citizen of the world, and as such nothing human is foreign to him.

"Such is the scientist," he concludes, "in this new kind of laboratory." Comfortably juxtaposing clinical objectivity and value-laden subjectivity, Woods argued that social science could be true to its human subject only through intimate familiarity, as demonstrated by Charles Booth and Frédéric Le Play.[42]

Woods felt that the inductive method was most fruitfully used in the practice of "friendly visiting," the settlement's "distinctive" local effort. Ideally, each resident would take a particular interest in several groups of families. Boothlike, the resident would note the details of each family's environment, income and expenditures, daily habits and mode of living, characters, influence on each other and the neighborhood, and "all matters which affect their bodily health, labor, education, sobriety, honesty, nationality, and religion"—all *without* resorting to "the mechanical and inquisitive methods of the census-taker."[43] The settlement resident was *not* a "'visitor' in the professional sense of that term, going monotonously and regularly from house to house. He is simply a neighborly caller."[44]

This concept of "friendly visiting" derived from earlier forms of religious and charity work and had most recently been made the centerpiece of the charity organization movement, which by the 1880s had spread to the United States.[45] In criticizing the "professional visitor," Woods risked offending a powerful force in the philanthropic world. It was a rare lapse. Woods joined other early settlement workers in treating the charity organizers with wary and diplomatic amicability and even, at first, deference. The Denison House residents solicited the advice of their ward supervisor, who spoke of the needs and character of their neighborhood in categories that jibed with the attitudes and expectations of the new residents: "Personal influence the one way of helping effectively and the power of this, when truly exercised, marvellous," noted Emily Balch.[46]

Robert Woods first met the Boston charity workers as he sought the cooperation of other agencies with the new Andover House. Tucker gave him an introduction to Robert Treat Paine, Jr., longtime president of Boston's Associated Charities, founded in 1879 and subscribing to COS principles.[47] Annie Adams (Mrs. James T.) Fields called on Woods at Andover House. The vibrant and energetic wife of the publisher of the *Atlantic,* Mrs. Fields was a disciple of Octavia Hill and had helped found the Co-operative Society of Visitors among the Poor, a forerunner of the Associated Charities.[48] She enlisted Woods in her current projects and donated a map of Ward 17 and Booth's extant volumes to the Andover House library.[49]

Most of the settlement workers endorsed the premise of charity organization as it had migrated from England to America. They agreed that traditional relief practices were frequently inefficient, redundant, and wrongheaded. They too believed that cultivating character was critical to improving the condition of the poor. The Boston Associated Charities' slogan, "Not alms, but a friend," borrowed from London, captured the spirit of personal service and the faith in personal influence that motivated the settlement workers.[50] The "friendly visitors," attempting to combine personal friendship with the poor and dispassionate observation of their living situations, carried out the highest function of the "new" scientific charity, which like the settlement movement wedded Christian humanitarianism to respect for the authority of social science.

These philosophical congruences did not ensure harmony between the two movements. The settlement workers objected to the same malfunctions and perversions of the charity organization idea that the English critics had seized upon earlier. While Robert Treat Paine characterized the ideal charity as embodying not only "kindly sentiment" but also "manly vigor and resolute repression," the settlers could not square "repression" with the gifts of personality and culture they wanted to bring to and evoke in their neighbors.[51] Though Hull-House residents supported the founding of the Chicago Bureau of Charities in the depression winter of 1893–94, this cooperation did not inhibit later criticism. Jane Addams gently delivered a devastating indictment of organized charity in *Twenty Years at Hull-House* by recounting the story of her own naive attempt to apply its doctrines to the case of a frail shipping clerk who contracted pneumonia and died after taking her advice that he seek work on a nearby drainage canal before applying for more charity. Addams penitentially "kept track of" his two orphaned children for years afterward.[52]

Besides objecting to a fetishism of self-reliance, the settlement workers criticized the "friendly visiting" practiced by some of the less skilled and sensitive charity workers. These visitors condescended to their forced hosts; they meddled; they were impolite and disrespectful; they disregarded the religious and cultural customs of those they visited; they popped in perfunctorily or overstayed their welcome. Behind these criticisms lurked a disparaging comparison: "The settlement resident who is already on a good social footing has a distinct leverage over a friendly visitor from a charitable society," stated Mary Kingsbury Simkhovitch, a New York headworker.[53] This observation echoed Woods's earlier claim for the superiority of *resident* neighborhood work. No amount of goodwill and preparation could compensate for the intimate familiarity and local trust that belonged to a genuine inhabitant of the neighborhood.

It was finally this claim to a special relationship with the neighborhood that led the settlement workers to set themselves apart from the charity organizers. It took several years of daily grappling with local conditions for the settlers to formulate the most telling critique of organized charity: that the poor were caught in a mesh of environmental circumstances that "character building" alone could not cut through. In 1898 John Palmer Gavit, a plainspoken young resident of Chicago Commons, told the Baltimore COS leader Mary Richmond: "Charity at its best is an offensive thing to me, and I deprecate exceedingly the attempt to make a science of it. . . . I cannot feel that charity organization is better than another effort to patch up the damage done to fellow-men by the conditions under which we live."[54]

The strident call for social justice, not charity, soon to issue from the settlement movement sprang from the settlers' assertion that their work was not a traditional philanthropy but an attempt to heal society by restoring social intercourse between artificially sundered classes. Their claim of reciprocity in their neighborhood friendships, though often stilted and artificial in actuality, predisposed them to see their neighbors' lives as molded by circumstances beyond their individual control. Further, the settlement philosophy, emphasizing the multifaceted richness of human life and social interaction, had a built-in bias against the negative and one-dimensional concerns of organized charity.

However infrequently spoken, these criticisms of organized charity were implicit in the settlement impulse. No amount of diplomacy could forestall the charity workers' consequent suspicion and resentment of this brash and well-connected interloper. At a charities conference in 1895, a few veteran charity organizers deplored the settlers' enthusiastic gullibility. Mary Richmond complained about the "young women fresh from college . . . who have not taken any special study in social science whatever [and] are bowled over by the first labor leader, or anarchist, or socialist, or whatever he happens to be in that neighborhood. . . . It seems to me that charity organization, standing as it does for the development of character . . . has got a serious work before it in the years to come."

Richmond suggested that too many settlements had been established too quickly and threatened the hard-won influence of the older charity workers. Another speaker pointed out that Jane Addams herself had said settlement work was being "overdone"; in his gloss, settlement work had become a kind of "fad" too often undertaken "carelessly" and with "too much sentimentality."[55]

The settlement leaders bowed to some of these criticisms. Just as

Addams cautioned against too-rapid expansion, Robert Hunter admitted several years later that "gush and sentimentality" were "often . . . exhibited by the immature and untrained residents of the settlement," and that recruits classically reacted to their first exposure to poverty with "the desire to relieve every one's needs immediately, generously, and without question." Yet he indicted in turn the "Hamlet" syndrome among charity workers so drilled in the "philosophy of 'Don't, don't!'" that they became chronically unable to take positive action in the face of need.[56]

Mary Richmond eventually became a wary friend of the settlement workers, while she continued to advise them didactically against impulsive generosity and an overblown sense of their importance in the lives of the poor.[57] Her defensiveness in 1895 stemmed partly from her rueful recognition that the charity organizers, having successfully challenged the "old fogies" of philanthropy, had now themselves become old fogies, vulnerable to a younger insurgency.[58]

4
The Settlers Look Outward:
Housing, Health, and Labor

The settlement workers cooperated with organized charity and other private and public agencies to try to avoid institutionalism and duplication of efforts. The workers at Boston's Hale House explained in 1898 that they wanted to establish not "institutions which already exist in abundance," but rather "friendly relations with the people among whom we live, . . . that we may persuade them and their children to make the best use of privileges already offered them by the city and state."[1] But those governments had often failed to take measures to ensure health and safety, let alone provide the "privileges" of social and educational enrichment. The settlement workers leaped into the breach they perceived on all these fronts. During their first two decades they compiled a stunning record of cultural and civic initiatives.

Though the settlers intended to work with their neighbors for local improvement, it was easier to undertake experiments within the settlement houses. They built playgrounds in their own backyards; they engaged kindergarten teachers trained in the Froebel method; they began stamp savings and "penny provident" banks; they collected small libraries and supervised reading and study rooms; they sponsored vacation schools and summer camps.

As with most of the clubs and classes, these unilateral ventures reflected the settlement workers' values and priorities. The settlers assessed the "needs" of the neighborhood within the framework of their own social preconceptions. The voluntarism animating the settlements usually ensured that unpopular programs would die. When Hull-House began a public kitchen on the principles of Ellen Richards's "New England Kitchen," the neighbors were indifferent; one woman admitted that "she didn't like to eat what was nutritious, that she liked to eat 'what she'd ruther.'" The adjoining coffeehouse did not tempt away the patrons of the local saloons, as the residents had hoped, but found a clientele among the same groups that patronized the settlement's cultural offerings: local teachers, businessmen, clerks, and the Hull-House residents and their friends and visitors. "The experience of the coffee-house," wrote Addams, "taught us not to hold preconceived ideas of what the neighborhood ought to have, but . . . to modify and adapt our undertaking as we discovered those things which the neighborhood was ready to accept."[2]

More challenging were local experiments that required the cooper-ation of public authorities or the special trust of the neighbors. The settlements' contributions to public health were made against a frag-mented but discouraging opposition compounded of local ignorance, official obstruction or passivity, and the defensive suspicions of physi-cians. But they also found mentors and allies, some of whom had been crying in the wilderness for years.

Agitation for housing and appeals for public health reforms were intertwined. The importance of public and domestic sanitation to health had long been recognized, and the mistaken but ironically effective "miasmic" theory of disease transmission undergirded the efforts of nineteenth-century sanitary reformers to publicize the iron links be-tween environment and disease.[3] New York created the Metropolitan Board of Health in 1866, and in 1867 the first tenement house law established regulations as to room size, ventilation, and fire prevention; but it did not address the developers' crowding of building against building, worsened after 1880 by the ubiquitous "dumbbell" tenement, whose central airshaft functioned as "a culture tube on a gigantic scale."[4] In 1884 Felix Adler's addresses to the Ethical Culture Society sparked a new state commission on tenement conditions, and amend-ments to the Tenement House Law followed in 1887. In the 1890s the complementary skills and personalities of two other individuals con-nected with the settlement movement, Jacob Riis and Lawrence Veiller, finally put New York tenement reform on a solid basis.

A Danish immigrant who struggled to American respectability as a newspaper reporter and social gadfly, Riis galvanized the public in 1890 with a stark prose portrait of Lower East Side living conditions. *How the Other Half Lives* trafficked in the cultural stereotypes of the day, yet it transcended previous publicity with grimly appealing photographs and a strong environmentalist plea for reform through privately financed model tenements.[5] Despite a third commission in 1894, a new housing bill, and scattered private initiatives, there was still plenty of scope for the single-minded dedication of a young City College graduate, Lawrence Veiller, to the cause of housing for the poor. In 1898 he persuaded the New York COS to tackle housing reform and took the chairmanship of its new Tenement House Committee.[6] With Governor Roosevelt's support—Veiller's ally Riis was the former police commissioner's friend—Veiller lobbied the state legislature for a new state tenement commission and became its first secretary. In the next ten years, Veiller's indefatigable work established him as a national leader in housing reform. In 1910 he became director of his own creation, the National Housing Association.[7]

Riis became a friend and adviser of the early New York settlement workers, and in 1899 he and his wife Elisabeth took over a settlement that grew out of a chapter of the King's Daughters, on Henry Street on the Lower East Side.[8] Veiller was briefly connected with the University Settlement (the reincorporated Neighborhood Guild), and his dual allegiance to the settlement and the COS exemplifies the common interests and overlapping loyalties of the two movements, despite their frictions. Veiller's social convictions, shaped by his reading of Ruskin and Carlyle, gave him a kinship with the pioneer settlement leaders. His decision after leaving the settlement to become an expert, virtually a "professional," in one aspect of social reform was not unique among early settlement workers, but his conviction that decent housing was the key to social betterment reveals a mind-set that clashed with the "settlement spirit." Riis, with his compulsive involvement in myriad social causes, his concern to explore, document, and address the human impact of poverty, and the social conservatism reinforced by his memories of an idyllic Danish upbringing, better understood the settlement workers' primary commitment to building a human community by interacting with individuals. Increasingly, the settlement movement nurtured and supported enterprises such as Veiller's, while rejecting monocausal explanations of urban problems as the basis of its own philosophy.[9]

Initially the settlement workers did not plan to become involved in neighborhood health care. They moved into congested and noisome districts with admirable bravado in the face of risks to their own health.[10] One reason single people dominated the settlement movement was parents' fear of taking children into areas posing health hazards, which overrode the stoutest democratic ideals. Graham Taylor's Chicago Commons was one of the few settlements staffed by married couples with children.[11] In general, though, the residents exposed themselves not to mortal peril but to the daily unpleasantness of sometimes appalling local conditions. In a letter from Hull-House in 1892, after discussing their work to ease a local typhoid epidemic, Ellen Starr remarked plaintively that it was hard to love one's fellowman in the summer heat when he smelled bad—particularly, she added, the Russian Jew, "poor dog."[12]

The settlement workers' involvement with public health reform grew out of their inductive approach to social work and their focus on the neighborhood as the primary social unit. They quickly saw that their neighbors' health problems were multiple and interconnected, part of the fabric of community life. Local residents should be educated to understand the connections between poor sanitary conditions, recurring illnesses, and high mortality and to be vigilant against neighborhood nuisances. The settlement folk ignored the latent contradiction in the double thrust of their efforts. They joined campaigns for greater government control over sanitation and housing standards and public provision of elementary health care. Because some of their early opponents came from the medical profession and the political machine, the settlers formed an insurgency against the status quo that partly masked the implication of their programs: that they were building bureaucracies of experts and civil servants that were the antithesis of local self-determination.

The settlement movement's most important contribution to neighborhood health care was Lillian Wald's Henry Street Visiting Nurse Service, begun modestly from a top-floor tenement apartment on New York's Lower East Side in 1893. By her own account, Wald had never heard of a settlement house before that summer, when she moved temporarily into the College Settlement on Rivington Street with Mary Brewster, her friend and classmate from the New York Hospital nursing school.

Lillian Wald grew up in Rochester, New York, the pampered daughter of a middle-class German Jewish couple whose families had immigrated to America in 1848. Her father was a successful optical-goods dealer; her mother filled their home with beautiful things and fostered her children's fondness for books, art, and music. Lillian's religious training was at best relaxed; the family attended a Reformed temple that sometimes welcomed Christian ministers. She attended Miss Crittenden's nondenominational girls' school and was ready to sit for the Vassar entrance examination at sixteen, but the college officials felt she was too young. She returned to her girls' school for two more years.[13] At twenty-one, still living at home and working as a business correspondent, Wald was restless, if not unhappy. She wrote that year: "My life hitherto has been—I presume—a type of modern American young womanhood, days devoted to society, study and house keeping duties. . . . This does not satisfy me now, I feel the need of serious, definite work."[14]

Though these reflections reveal the kind of inchoate aspiration shared by Jane Addams, Vida Scudder, and other young women active in the early settlements, Wald does not seem to have been tortured by the same spiritual searching and personal doubts. Having forgone a liberal arts education, her sudden decision to attend nursing school suggests an impulsive penchant for practical activity. "I choose this profession," she explained in her application to the New York Hospital, "because I feel a natural aptitude for it and because it has for years appeared to me womanly, congenial work, work that I love and which I think I could do well."[15]

Whether she knew it or not, Wald's characterization of nursing as a "womanly," and by implication genteel, calling was well formulated to appeal to administrators in this early phase of professionalization in nurse training. She entered nursing school at a time of rapid growth in the number of trainees despite continuing divisions in the medical community over the role of nursing in health care. Several decades earlier, the Englishwoman Florence Nightingale had argued that the nurse should be trained and educated, oriented toward treating the person, not the disease, versed in preventive medicine and able to serve not just in the hospital but in the community. Faced with some obstructionism from both doctors and nonprofessional nursing staff, the first schools of nursing tried to build a corporate image of middle-class gentility and fostered the notion that nursing was a peculiarly appropriate calling for women.[16]

Wald found she enjoyed nursing, but she rebelled against her first taste of bureaucratic rigidity and cruelty at the Juvenile Asylum on 176th Street. Leaving the asylum, she enrolled at the Women's Medical College for further training. Soon an opportunity arose to teach a home nursing class among the immigrant Jews downtown on Henry Street.[17]

Since the first waves of the swelling migration of Eastern European Jews, the prosperous German and native-born American Jews had shown an anguished ambivalence toward their coreligionists; not wanting to be identified with the "downtown" Jews, they still felt the imperatives of religious custom and humanity. By the early 1890s they had established a range of programs whose chief aim, beyond relief, was rapid and thorough Americanization. Pious immigrants who resented the oppressive noblesse oblige of the uptown Jews responded by establishing their own synagogues, Hebrew schools, and *Lansmanshafts* or mutual aid societies. A vocal minority had brought a bent toward political and labor radicalism that would further trouble the waters of Jewish fellowship in New York.[18]

Thus by the early 1890s the Lower East Side sported a motley patchwork of charities and organizations. It is not surprising that when the vivacious and persuasive Wald proposed to move to the Lower East Side to extend nursing services to a desperately needy district, Mrs. Solomon Loeb and her son-in-law, Jacob Schiff, the head of Kuhn, Loeb and Company and a noted philanthropist, responded with openhanded generosity.[19] It was characteristic of the spirit if not the pattern of uptown Jewish philanthropy that neither the nursing service nor the settlement that grew up around it was specifically Jewish. In return for payment according to its means (which often meant no payment), any family might receive home care from a nurse who resided in the district.[20] Thus a nondenominational, humanitarian organization grew from the seed of an effort based on the Jewish imperative of mutual aid and benevolent stewardship, an outcome peculiarly congenial to successful American Jews who had sought assimilation while trying to remain faithful to their religious identity and heritage.[21]

The nursing service grew by steady though hard-won stages. Like previous home nursing associations, Wald and her co-workers met resistance from physicians accustomed to employing their own nurses or sending their patients to the hospital.[22] The Henry Street nurses, in contrast, preferred home care to hospitalization. Not only more economical, home care allowed the family to stay together even through an extended illness. When necessary, they referred patients to a physician or sent them to a hospital, often using their finest persuasive powers to overcome the local "hospital prejudice." Experience provided endless examples of the domestic and economic disruptiveness of illness in a poor community and bore out the efficacy of competent home care. Wald's early reports to her sponsors reflect her conviction that the nurses must address not just the family's physical ills but also its social and economic circumstances. The nurses placed children in school and sometimes foster care, helped men find work, and put their patients in touch with philanthropies to meet their special needs.[23]

Working for the first two years out of their tenement apartment on Jones Street, the nurses extended their caseload as far as they could. In 1895 Jacob Schiff provided the means to expand the nursing service and laid the groundwork for a full-fledged settlement by purchasing a house on Henry Street. In the Jones Street days, befriending the children had been easy and indeed inevitable. An early renovation of the Henry Street house transformed the backyard into one of the first playgrounds on the Lower East Side.[24] The expanded nursing staff was supplemented by workers who oversaw social and recreational activities.

Unlike most of her peers in the first generation of settlement leaders, Lillian Wald came to the movement with no deliberate apprenticeship to the social and religious ideas that undergirded the settlement movement. Yet she shared the energy, the restlessness, and most important, the personal magnetism of the other successful settlement leaders, and her upbringing had given her the cultural assumptions that shaped her response to urban social problems. Like the model settlement of early rhetoric, Henry Street was the elaboration of a remarkable personality.

The brutal depression winter of 1893–94 accelerated the nurses' education in East Side life. Wald later reflected that the "strain . . . left neither place nor time for self-analysis and consequent self-consciousness, so prone to hinder and to dwarf wholesome instincts, and so likely to have proved an impediment to the simple relationship which we established with our neighbors."[25] For all the early settlement workers, the depression was an ordeal by fire, testing the nature and depth of their commitment to their neighborhoods.

In most houses, social and cultural activities slowed while the residents sought relief and stopgap employment for their neighbors. Helena Dudley, the new headworker at Denison House, wrote: "For a settlement to devote itself to educational and social work exclusively at such a time would be as anomalous as for the Parisian of 1870 to devote himself to receptions and lectures during the siege, with the sick and dead lying in the street."[26] Jane Addams wrote to a friend abroad: "It takes something of an effort these hard times to keep up one's spirits, our neighbors are so forlorn and literally flock to the house for work."[27] The Rivington Street settlers concurred: "Only the most positive determination to keep our minds away from any suffering that we could not relieve made it possible for us to do our work."[28]

The settlers' preference for self-help over relief and their fears of demoralization among the unemployed made them eager volunteers in work-relief efforts. They multiplied their contacts with charities and city officials. At the CSA settlements in New York and Philadelphia the residents distributed tickets and brooms for street-sweeping jobs. At Rivington Street "we were able to . . . give a tone of friendliness to the whole work . . . even after there was a force of eight hundred men employed."[29] Denison House residents solicited funds from the ad hoc Citizens' Relief Committee to open a workroom for "the better class of sewing women who had never received charitable aid."[30]

Pressed to their emotional limits, the settlement workers fell back on their own doctrine for guidance in responding to the depression. To act as friends was their highest calling, and they were gratified by their neighbors' responses. "I have really been touched by the goodness of our neighbors to each other," Addams wrote, "and their sweet attitude toward us. The effect is a little like 'trouble in a family' which draws the members together."[31] The settlers gained confidence in their real usefulness during the depression winter. "We are neighbors among neighbors," asserted the Philadelphia women that year,

> and this implies much. When there is sickness or trouble there are calls to be paid. We stand between the various organizations of the city and the people for whom they are intended. . . . We look after the sanitary conditions of the neighborhood, report nuisances, try to have the streets properly cleaned; appeal to councils for more electric lights—and get them; we write letters innumerable to and for all sorts and conditions of men . . . we go and give talks to societies or schools who want to know more about settlements. Last, but by no means least, are our social engagements.[32]

The depression also plunged the settlements into what Jane Addams would call "a decade of economic discussion." Vida Scudder later suggested that the settlers were pulled outward: "We were swept into the strong currents of the world's unrest."[33] Their self-image as pioneers in applied social science forced the settlement workers to confront broader causes of economic crisis.

Even before the depression some of the settlements had sponsored lecture series that opened their doors to spokesmen of many political persuasions. Hull-House launched the "Working People's Social Science Club" during its first year.[34] Clarence Darrow inaugurated the weekly discussions with a talk on strikes. Over the next several years the meetings addressed taxation, Christian Socialism, Toynbee Hall, "the forgotten man," unemployment, American jurisprudence, municipal government, civil service reform, "the Negro problem," immigration restriction, the labor movement, economic theory, and socialism.[35] When the speaker sat down debate began, pitting socialists, anarchists, and Single-Taxers against each other. During the nineties the "free floor" flourished in several settlements, notably Chicago Commons. In post-Haymarket Chicago, this apparent encouragement of deviant opinion touched the settlements with the brush of radicalism, a taint never finally expunged despite the settlers' disclaimers and explanations. To Addams, Taylor, and other settlement workers who opened their doors to radicals, free speech was a "safety valve" and a right without which democracy was meaningless; to the rabid left-baiting Chicago press, the settlements endangered democracy by giving aid and comfort to its opponents. Graham Taylor came under fire for his weekly column in the Chicago *Daily News*. The paper's rivals exploited his connection with the Chicago Theological Seminary to link the teaching of sociology to the advocacy of socialism. Ironically, this connection was not wholly fanciful in the early years of academic sociology, but popular journalism made no distinction between the quasi-religious social organicism or the "gas-and-water" socialism endorsed by certain academics and the radical incendiarism with which they tried to associate the settlements.[36]

In the wake of the depression a number of settlements turned to labor organization, an equally risky activity. The American settlers followed the London dock workers' struggles and were tutored in labor's right to organize by John Graham Brooks, William J. Tucker, and Richard Ely. Witnessing the irrationality of industrial employment and the brutal sweating system in the tenement districts could give a "general belief" in labor organization the "driving force of a conviction," as Addams wrote in 1895.[37] But again, the settlement workers had to prove their good faith before labor quite trusted them. Union men tended to identify settlement houses with the churches and charities so frequently hostile to their interests.

The Hull-House women were fortunate in their first labor contacts. In 1890 or 1891, seeking interesting guests to meet some English visitors, Addams and Starr approached Mary Kenney, the organizer and president of the women's bookbinders union, then the only women's union in Chicago. She almost turned down their invitation to dinner. A feisty, independent working woman, Kenney had followed the bindery trade from Missouri to Iowa and then to Chicago, where poor working conditions turned her to unionism. Outspoken and fearless, she was accepted as a leader by fellow workers, male and female, and made connections beyond the shops through her campaign against unsanitary conditions in the factories. After she organized the bookbinders union,

Kenney was recruited by Samuel Gompers as an organizer for the American Federation of Labor. Disdaining philanthropists and wary of working-girls' clubs that spent more time planning outings than discussing working conditions, Kenney planned to ignore the Hull-House invitation until her mother, now living with her in Chicago, persuaded her to go.

"When I went into Hull-House," she wrote later, "I saw furnishings and large rooms different from anything I had ever seen before. . . . Miss Addams greeted me and introduced the guests from England and all the residents. My first impression was that they were all rich and not friends of the workers." Taking in her guest's truculent distrust, Addams questioned Kenney about her union and offered Hull-House as a meeting place. Over the next few weeks she won Kenney over by going door to door to advertise the meeting and pressed Kenney and her mother to become "guests" of Hull-House for a while.[38]

Kenney's acceptance marked the beginning of an important era for the young settlement. As an AFL organizer, Kenney lent credibility to Hull-House's gestures toward labor. Besides sponsoring the Bookbinders Union, Hull-House helped organize the women's shirtmakers union and the cloakmakers union, and over the next few years it hosted the cabdrivers union, representatives of the retail clerk workers, and strike committees of the garment workers and the clothing cutters.[39] In 1892 another labor leader and publicist, Alzina Parsons Stevens, moved into Hull-House. Abraham Bisno, a leading Chicago unionist, became an ally of the settlement, though he never quite understood the Hull-House women, who did not sing or dance or reveal any "sign of their sex life."[40]

The Hull-House residents mined a vein of support for labor among middle-class intellectuals and reformers. Henry Demarest Lloyd and his wife had given financial support to Hull-House since its beginning. Lloyd's intellectual sympathies could hardly have been more congenial to the early settlement leaders. Trained in the law, he went to work for the Chicago *Tribune* in 1872 and a year later married Jessie Bross, the only child of one of the *Tribune's* wealthy owners. The Great Railroad Strike of 1877 shook Lloyd and stirred his interest in finding what John L. Thomas has called a "civic religion."[41] He began to build a reputation as a crusading journalist fighting political and corporate corruption. Traveling in Europe after a nervous breakdown in 1885, he moved easily into the English network of reform movements and socialist agitation that would captivate the young American settlement founders.

He became especially fond of the Fabian William Clarke, whom Robert Woods liked so much. Lloyd returned to Chicago in time for the Haymarket trial. Outraged by the verdict, he joined William Salter of the Chicago Ethical Culture Society in the campaign for clemency for the "Anarchists." After their execution he plunged into labor advocacy and social reform.[42]

As godfather to the early Hull-House labor activities, Lloyd traveled frequently to South Chicago from his Winnetka home to address union meetings and coach strike committees. Scattered accounts of these early episodes offer a classic picture of one style of middle-class reform, the Hull-House living room crammed with anxious or stolid laborers, while their own leaders and journeymen agitators like Lloyd took turns exhorting them and uplifting musical selections were played in the pauses.[43] Awkward incidents were unavoidable. One evening a visiting cabdriver told Ellen Starr that he recognized the featured speaker, William Salter, as a customer who had recently abused him.[44]

Though the Neighborhood Guild in New York also participated in several union-organizing efforts in the late 1880s, Hull-House was the first predominantly women's settlement to take up the cause of labor. Female settlement workers were doubly handicapped in their overtures to labor by their status as "outsiders" with the working class and by their sex. Nevertheless, in the depression years Denison House and the Rivington Street Settlement followed the Hull-House lead. When Mary Kenney went to the AFL convention in Philadelphia in 1892, Addams asked her to stay with a new acquaintance, Helena Dudley, then heading the CSA's Philadelphia settlement. Kenney offered to take Dudley and a settlement visitor, Vida Scudder, to a convention session. Later she mischievously commented that her friends "were surprised to find that labor men could so ably discuss big public questions."[45]

The next year Dudley moved to Boston to head Denison House. One afternoon in November a neighborhood woman hurried in, distressed because a representative of the Knights of Labor had appeared at her garment shop to "force" the workers to organize a union. That evening Denison House sponsored a meeting to allow the union representatives, including John O'Sullivan of the United Garment Workers, to explain their aims to the "tailoresses." The women finally agreed to form a union and organize other women's shops, but only "if the ladies of the house would help them." Thus the settlement workers were drawn more deeply into Boston's labor world. At Central Labor Union meetings they were relieved to find that "the speakers, although limited in education and at times narrow in their views, often show a grasp of the subject and a wise conservatism which increases one's faith in democracy."[46] They agreed to sponsor a new organization, the Federal Labor Union, an alliance of workers and professionals whose chief aim was to instruct "people of all classes" about the "higher intellectual and moral ends" of the labor movement.[47]

Much of Denison House's labor work was shared with the Andover House residents, with whom they formed the Social Science Club in 1893 to explore labor organization from the medieval guilds onward.[48] When Mary Kenney married John O'Sullivan in 1894, her intimacy with Helena Dudley linked Denison House more tightly to the union movement as well as to the Hull-House residents. Through Kenney and Robert Woods, the Denison House residents met the English unionists John Burns, Ben Tillett, and Keir Hardie.[49]

This alliance of the young settlement movement with the fragile new union movement is somewhat surprising. The settlements depended on the goodwill and financial support of a wealthy minority whose biases and interests were threatened by labor organizers. The labor leaders in turn might well have feared co-optation by naive middle-class reformers with little comprehension of the workers' daily struggles or long-term interests.[50] But it was precisely this apparent conflict of interests that drew the settlement workers to the labor movement. They invoked their role as mediators to justify their labor activities. As Woods explained: "We believe that we shall be able by degrees to bring about a little of that illumination which is, after all, the great end of social science, and will enable men in different circumstances of life . . . to put themselves in each other's place."[51]

This philosophy translated into an emphasis on peaceful conciliation of labor disputes. The Hull-House residents took pride in their successful arbitration of an 1892 pieceworkers strike at the Star Knitting Works.[52] The Rivington Street settlers helped local tailors in an 1894 strike by forming committees to "wait on" the subcontractors and the Manufacturers Association to plead the strikers' cause.[53] The Federal Labor Union at Denison House, which helped organize eight hundred female garment workers in 1894, also intervened in labor conflicts in nearby Haverhill and Hyde Park, to advocate "conciliation and arbitration" as against the tried-and-true method of "starving out the workmen," which led only to "bitterness and suppressed hatred."[54] Confident that education and publicity were the first steps toward reform, they hoped to bring the estranged sides together in negotiations, circumventing violence and animosity.

Beyond their initial goal of intercepting conflict, the settlement workers conceived a greater aim, shaped by their social organicist ideals. They *did* hope to co-opt the labor movement. Pleased by what they had seen of the "most thoughtful of the wage earners," the "wisest trade unionists," they aspired to channel the nobler leanings of the workers into a "larger life."[55] In 1895, Jane Addams explained the "ethical" role of the settlement in the labor movement. In their zeal to win better wages and working conditions, the workers lost sight of the higher aims of brotherhood and democracy that the labor movement stood for at its best. The settlement could help the workers understand their true interests. Economic realities that forced workers to unite would push them toward a "social democracy" with an "educating and broadening aspect of no small value." Addams hoped they could be brought to "perceive the larger solidarity which includes labor and capital, and act upon the notion of universal kinship." The settlement's task was to hold the labor movement "to its best ideal," to steer it away from "class warfare" and toward the "all-embracing ideal" of brotherhood.[56] This philosophical stance jibed with that of Hull-House's early mentor on labor issues, Henry Demarest Lloyd, who more and more fancied his own role as that of "prophet-counselor" in the long, peaceful struggle to control the social destructiveness of unchecked big business.[57]

For a few settlement residents, commitment to the workers moved beyond mediation to partisanship. Through their involvement in labor struggles, both Vida Scudder and Ellen Starr came to embrace socialism. Both women were inducted into social thought by the writings of John Ruskin and the Christian Socialists. Ruskin and William Morris were the guideposts by which Ellen Starr charted her early artistic activities at Hull-House. Their doctrines concerning the organic relationship between art and the social order fed her increasing militancy. In an essay of 1895 she struggled to express the difference between the human "pain and struggle" that inspires and accompanies art and the suffering and degradation that stifles it. "Into the prison-houses of earth, its sweat-shops and underground lodging-houses, art cannot follow. . . . Art can never present humanity as overborne. It cannot let the hostile principle, pain, sorrow, sin, at the last conquer." Rejecting despair as a moral possibility or a subject for aesthetic expression, Starr found hope in a broader struggle that would both "feed the hungry" and release "the art-power of the whole nation and race by enabling them to work in gladness and not in woe."[58] Starr pursued both goals— social justice and the democratization of art—at Hull-House. She oversaw the settlement's early picture exhibitions, on the model of Toynbee Hall, and she built up studio art and crafts. After a bookbinding course with T. J. Cobden-Sanderson in London, she started a small studio with a few apprentices at Hull-House. But these efforts seemed increasingly paltry to her, and she threw herself enthusiastically into the union movement, until labor leaders began turning to Starr rather than Jane Addams for support.[59]

"I became a Socialist because I was a Christian," Starr declared in 1916. "The Christian religion teaches that all men are to be regarded as brothers, that no one should wish to profit by the loss or disadvantage of others; . . . 'Civilized' life is in grotesque contrast to all this."[60] Beyond her discipleship to Ruskin and Morris and her deep religious faith, Starr moved toward socialism for more personal reasons. Unlike Addams, Starr evoked from her associates a wide range of reactions. Mary Kenney O'Sullivan, tough enough to appreciate both Starr's sense of humor and her sometimes acidic frankness, came to love her "dearly."[61] Another resident less happily labeled Starr "the most aggressive truth-speaker in the house"; and a third, while testifying that Starr had "done much for the art sense of the neighborhood," admitted, "I don't like her particularly."[62] Alice Hamilton, who became a central figure in the settlement soon after her arrival as a shy, newly fledged doctor in 1898, was offended and intimidated by Starr's religiosity and her increasing temperamental volatility.[63]

Though it is difficult to piece together the intimate history of these extraordinary women, it is clear that by 1894 Addams's dependence on her Rockford friend had been weakened, first by the earliest fellow residents of the house, Julia Lathrop and Florence Kelley, and soon afterward by a wealthy young Chicago woman, Mary Rozet Smith, who quickly became Jane Addams's closest confidante and later may have been the only individual who knew a "private" Jane Addams.[64] It is possible that muddled and half-denied feelings of jealousy and superfluity intensified Starr's involvement in the labor activism that Addams, by contrast, approached gingerly and with growing ambivalence. Starr's temperamental warmth, her passion for justice, her need to be needed, and perhaps, finally, some impulse to annoy and distance herself from Jane Addams pushed her toward avowed socialism.[65]

As with Ellen Starr, the foundations of Vida Scudder's socialism were her fervent Christian faith and an increasing sense that the beauties of literature and art were hollow unless universally accessible. For her too, participation in labor struggles quickened ideological development. Scudder never moved into Denison House, choosing to stay at Welle-sley and keep house for her mother. Also, in a very real sense Scudder already inhabited a tight community of reform-minded women. Her fellow faculty members at Wellesley offered her professional and intel-lectual companionship, personal intimacy, and in many cases ideolog-ical sympathy and support.[66] But as a CSA founder she remained deeply interested in the settlement and was especially involved when her friend Helena Dudley was headworker. She came to admire the "spirit . . . of fiery adventure" of the local AFL leaders. Her contacts with Boston's genteel radicals—among them Robert Woods, John Graham Brooks, the Episcopal rector Charles Brent, and the Christian Socialist W. D. P. Bliss—multiplied in this period.[67] Her discovery of the *Fabian Essays* "clinched my socialism" and gave doctrinal form to the inchoate ideals she had absorbed from her long "saturation" in the writings of Kingsley, Maurice, and Ruskin. And like Starr, she believed that "unless I were a socialist, I could not honestly be a Christian."[68]

In her roman à clef of 1903, *A Listener in Babel,* Scudder traced the ideological and sentimental journey of Hilda Lathrop from a restless desire to escape stifling privilege and fulfill her "longing for untram-meled fellowship in supreme beauty," through six months in a settle-ment house, to her final espousal of socialism "not as a dogma of the end to be achieved, but as a description of the process to be fur-thered."[69] At the settlement Hilda listens to endless debates, Scudder's shameless device for presenting her views on charity organization, the labor movement, the failures of institutional religion, and "tainted money." But what finally moves Hilda to accept socialism, passionately yet provisionally, is the simple, almost oceanic feeling of human kinship with the men and women she meets at the settlement. At one evening concert she looks around at the tired adults and children. "A deep joy moved in her heart, —was it the joy of brotherhood, unchecked at last? She had always been rather averse to society, but here her old impa-tience died away, as she recognized in social intercourse at its simplest an eternal sacredness and beauty."[70] The novel is full of these moments of surrender, executed with the stylistic brush of the Victorians, yet poignant as autobiographical confessions. By her own testimony, Scud-der probably never achieved the personal, loving empathy with the settlement neighbors that her troubled heroine experienced. But glimpses of its possibility were surely the bedrock of her ideological growth, the catalyst for the fusion of religious and political passion that she called "socialism."

An avowal of socialism could mean many things in the 1890s. The "revolution by consent" of the Christian Socialists and the Fabians was consonant with the civil activism and appeals to middle-class conscience that characterized the settlements and other contemporary reform movements. As a woman and a member of Boston's patriciate, Scudder could command a hearing from her peers that a worker could not.[71] Ironically, Scudder was more "radical" than most of the labor leaders she consorted with. But the public rarely made those fine distinctions, and in some situations the settlements risked as much by advocating workers' grievances as they might have by espousing dogmatic radicalism. They were fortunate that against those middle-class citizens who felt with Mary Richmond that settlements were havens for "hot-heads" stood those who agreed with the great philanthropist Josephine Shaw Lowell, who made the astonishing statement that in any contest between labor and capital, "the laborers are the people . . . and their interests, therefore . . . are the important interests. . . . [W]e must be very sure," cautioned Lowell, "not to let the necessity for having money to carry on our work stand in the way of our telling the truth and saying what we ought to say and of feeling what we ought to feel."[72]

5
Leaders and Followers

During its second year the College Settlement on Rivington Street organized the Women's Home Improvement Club for local mothers who seldom got out of their houses. The club's success gratified the residents. The women willingly learned better housekeeping, nutritional, and child-care practices. They were grateful for cultural opportunities, like complimentary tickets to *Messiah*. They learned the value of mutual aid, particularly during the winter of 1893–94. They brought their husbands and children to the settlement for family social gatherings, unprecedented in the neighborhood. Finally, they began to realize their collective power to improve neighborhood sanitation and learned to report infractions and abuses to the city authorities.

The club governed itself from the beginning. About 1896 the majority took a momentous decision: the club would move out of the settlement and rent its own quarters to pursue social and educational work independently—to become, in effect, a settlement. The attempt failed. The College Settlement resident who recorded this story reported that the club members either neglected their families in favor of the work or failed to sustain their commitments to the clubs, play groups, and other activities. Within two years the club members petitioned to return to the College Settlement. They were received, one gathers, like prodigal daughters. The resident drew two morals: "That the mother of a working-man's family has neither strength nor time to give away; that the very conditions of tenement-house neighborhoods require trained, impersonal workers."[1]

One of the latent conflicts in the settlement enterprise was the potential contradiction between the premise that the educated middle class was by definition endowed with intangible "gifts" worthy of being shared with the less privileged and the goal of the settlement movement to foster self-help in poorer communities. Like the Rivington Street Home Improvement Club, Stanton Coit's Neighborhood Guild had foundered when outside leadership fell away. Aside from the limited time and experience that initially handicapped the leaders of these "indigenous" initiatives, the problem was the outsiders' natural reluctance to let go of their own creations, to allow neighborhood leaders to assert different priorities and sometimes different values.

In 1894 John Elliott, a young Ethical Culture teacher, founded the Hudson Guild on Stanton Coit's principles of self-government. At first just an assortment of young men's clubs meeting in rented space in New York's Chelsea district, the guild expanded steadily, was incorporated in 1897, and moved into its own four-story house on West 26th Street.

Growing up in genteel poverty in Princeton, Illinois, young John Elliott did not show any outstanding intellectual promise, but his parents, who had imbibed their Republican reformism during the Civil War era, were determined he should go to college. In his sophomore year he attended a campus lecture by Felix Adler and was converted to Ethical Culture. After he graduated in 1892, the society sent him to Germany to study philosophy and sociology. He earned his Ph.D. with a dissertation titled "Prisons as Reformatories" at the University of Halle and returned to New York, where he became Adler's assistant, speaking and teaching for the society and beginning his boys' clubs downtown.[2] Under the Ethical Culture aegis, Elliott met many of the early settlement leaders, including Dr. Jane Robbins of the College Settlement and Charles Stover and James Paulding, associated with the University Settlement. He tried volunteering with the COS but soon rejected its philosophy, and he did not choose to attach himself to the existing settlements. Instead he made Chelsea on the West Side the center of his activities. When the Hudson Guild was incorporated several years later, he stressed that it was to be a "neighborhood center," not a "settlement."[3]

This distinction rested on two principles: that the guild should be as financially independent as possible, and that the clubs and activities should be self-governing and initiated by the neighbors themselves. Though the guild never did become self-supporting, self-government, imposed by decree, seems to have been moderately successful. The guild was to be run democratically by a council that the members dubbed "Dr. Elliott's Sunday School Class." Composed of Elliott, other staff members, and delegates from the clubs and organizations, the council decided guild policy and discipline and handled the treasury of club dues. Elliott denied himself a vote but retained a veto, which could be overruled by a two-thirds vote of the council.

Elliott's occasional use of his veto provoked accusations of hypocrisy; a staff member once reportedly exclaimed, "I guess you can run things the way you want them better when you call it self-government."[4] But more important than the issue of Elliott's sincerity, which seems to have been profound, is the paradox illustrated by the Hudson Guild and endemic in the settlement movement. Elliott's personality ensured the guild's survival and even the degree of success its principles achieved. Elliott himself defined the "business of a social worker" as "that of coming to know other people so well that he can understand their fundamental interests and devise machinery for making their better social impulses effective."[5] If middle-class leadership was required to evoke appropriate forms of self-help from the working class, as settlement ideology suggested, much depended on the quality of that leadership. A second paradox emerges. The effectiveness of a scheme whose validity depended on its universal applicability was limited by the idiosyncrasies of its personnel.

The American settlements survived their trial period largely because of the imagination, magnetism, and doggedness of a remarkable cohort of leaders: Jane Addams, Vida Scudder, Robert Woods, Graham Taylor, John Elliott, Helena Dudley, and Lillian Wald. But the enterprise required followers: men and women willing to subordinate themselves to the ideas and direction of the headworkers. While many of the leaders fashioned lifelong careers in settlement work, most other early residents left the houses after several years, as expected, to marry or take up other work, or both.

By Allen Davis's reckoning, 90 percent of the early settlement workers were college graduates.[6] They would have heard of the settlement idea through campus missions, visiting speakers, sympathetic professors, or popular journals. It is fair to assume from what we know of the articulate veterans that most of the others were moved by a combination of religious or quasi-religious mission, restlessness or indecision about their goals, and a desire for adventure or self-testing. Many of these young recruits had little idea what to expect in their new homes and little or no analogous experience that might have familiarized them with their own capacities and quirks. They would look naturally to the settlement head as a counselor and guide, who might help them translate the perplexing and multiform local reality back into the language of ideals and aspirations that had inspired them in college. A new setting for youthful hero worship emerged.

The charismatic style of leadership shared by so many of the first generation of settlement heads was singularly appropriate to the mission and self-image of the settlement house. Not only the founders' religion of character, but also their enshrinement of home and neighborhood as the institutions on which social coherence might be built supported the emergence of leadership by personality. Settlement leaders concurred that the settlement should strive to emulate the functions and roles of a home, and they often compared their relationships to those of a family. This analogy was justified in several ways. As in a home, social interaction in the settlement clustered loosely around a daily routine of waking and sleeping, dining, and "chores" as well as the regular comings and goings of the residents. Within that framework of mundane routine, increasingly supplemented by planned group activities, social life was fluid, contingent, and random, often determined by the unpredictable needs and demands of outsiders: the neighbors or special visitors to the settlement. In this context the most effective leader could impart a feeling of security and continuity to the household; he or she would play a parental "anchoring" role and serve as a model for emulation and an authoritative source of encouragement and rebuke.

Jane Addams exemplifies the power of a personality to impart internal coherence to a settlement house. Both visitors and residents remarked on the void left by her temporary absences: "An empty, rather lonely house," was how Alice Hamilton described Hull-House one August, "very content as long as Miss Addams is there, but pretty forlorn when she goes off."[7] Addams understood and used her own magnetism. She cannily appealed not only to each individual's interests, but to his or her self-esteem. "She is the greatest of mortals," wrote one young woman resident who served briefly as Addams's secretary, "and far indeed from domineering over anybody."

> The residents are all her willing servitors, and she holds them all by reason of her very admirable qualities of mind & disposition. She is really a cosmic individual, and is able to get into relation with every sort of person by instinctively giving him what he wants and can assimilate. . . . She never drives anyone to work & indeed is most considerate in that regard. But it is impossible to live here and not feel to some extent the pressure of work to be done.[8]

Alice Hamilton, almost thirty when she moved into Hull-House in 1897, felt honored to nurse Addams through an illness. She was flustered when she had to share a room with Addams to make space for a visitor: "It gave me the queerest feeling to think of rooming with her"—as if she had been told to room with her housemother at boarding school.[9] Hamilton also felt the "pressure" of work constantly demanding attention. In her first year at Hull-House, she added a roster of evening duties to her daytime position at the Women's Medical College of Northwestern University: teaching hygiene and infant care to the Italians, increasingly "on call" to both the residents and the neighbors, and surrounded by the settlement's unrelenting visitors. "All winter long I kept feeling what a farce it all was and how Miss Addams was classing me with the people she is always talking about who have had scientific or literary training but who are utterly unable to put their knowledge into a form useful to simple people." On the verge of a breakdown, she was finally pulled away from the settlement by a fellow physician and given a rest. But held by her personal loyalty to Addams, she returned to the settlement.[10]

After a series of visits to Hull-House in 1894 while he settled in as professor at the new University of Chicago, John Dewey could understand the impression of chaos that overwhelmed Alice Hamilton several years later: "I sh'd think the irritation of hearing the doorbell ring, & never doing one thing without being interrupted to tend to half a dozen others would drive them crazy." He too fell under Addams's spell and admired Ellen Starr. But he noted of the other "'young lady' residents" that "many of them do not seem particularly intelligent except in quite particular ways; for general consciousness they fall back on loyalty to Miss A."[11]

This assessment was not quite fair either to Addams or to Hull-House. Addams commanded the respect and affection not just of naive college women but also of a group of strong, independent women who worked beside rather than for Addams and made Hull-House their base as they moved into state and national service. Julia Lathrop, one of the earliest residents, came home to Rockford, Illinois, after graduating from Vassar just as Jane Addams was beginning her final year at the seminary. Like John Addams, and like John Elliott's maternal grandfather Owen Lovejoy, Julia's father William Lathrop had been an active abolitionist; he was now a lawyer, Republican politician, and Rockford Seminary trustee. Her mother, Sarah Potter Lathrop, was a suffragist and a member of the seminary's first graduating class. Probably a little bored with her job as secretary in her father's office, Julia Lathrop responded warmly when Addams and Starr visited Rockford in 1889 to seek support for their "scheme." She came to live at Hull-House the next year and became interested in public welfare institutions. In 1893 the new governor of Illinois, John Peter Altgeld, appointed her to the Illinois

Board of Charities. She forged a career in advocacy of children, the mentally ill, and other dependents. In 1912 President Taft appointed her head of the newly created Children's Bureau under the Department of Labor and Commerce.[12]

Her coresidents described Lathrop as sensible, warm, witty, and quietly competent. Politically she stayed with the reform Republicanism of her youth. Her progressive stance on public responsibility for humane care of the dependent grew out of her early belief in the necessity of state stewardship as well as her compassion for the helpless.[13]

A very different character completed the inner circle that set the tone of Hull-House in the early years. At Christmastime 1891, Florence Kelley Wischnewetzky arrived on the Hull-House doorstep. Fleeing New York and a failed marriage, Mrs. Kelley (who took back her father's name) was thrown on her own resources to support her three young children. But she was very different from other young mothers who had turned to Hull-House for help. The daughter of Pennsylvania congressman William "Pig Iron" Kelley and Caroline Bonsall Kelley, a descendant of John Bartram, Florence Kelley graduated from Cornell University in 1882 with an undergraduate thesis on the history of the legal status of children. One of Cornell's first women students, she helped form the "Social Service Club" for the discussion of "all live questions social, moral and political." Refused admission to law school because of her sex, Kelley decided while traveling in Europe the next year to attend the University of Zurich. There she discovered Marxian socialism. With characteristic impetuosity and a convert's ardor, she plunged into political debate and began a decade-long correspondence with Friedrich Engels as she worked on a translation of his *Condition of the Working Class in England*. She married a fellow radical, Lazare Wischnewetzky, a Polish-Russian medical student. Though Kelley maintained contact with her mother, she broke off relations with her father and brother over politics.

In 1886 the Wischnewetzkys and their infant son moved to New York, where Lazare tried to establish a medical practice and Florence entered the American socialist movement. Disillusionment preceded her expulsion from the immigrant-dominated Socialist Labor party. She made other contacts among American radicals and reformers, including Richard T. Ely and, in 1890, the women at the Rivington Street settlement, to whom she offered a class in economics. Her marriage floundered and her husband grew abusive. In 1891 Florence took her children and moved to Illinois, where she sought out Jane Addams and Hull-House, which she knew through her work at Rivington Street.[14]

Hull-House found a place for Kelley, and the Lloyds made a home for her children in Winnetka. She was put in charge of the Hull-House Bureau of Labor, an evanescent placement service for working girls. The settlement paid her $50 a month plus board. She was overwhelmed by the "generous hospitality" of her new friends, particularly the Lloyds, who helped her win custody of the children in the divorce trial a year later.[15]

In her revulsion against her estranged husband she turned back to her family and asked their forgiveness for her "years of ingratitude"; but she did not turn her back on the political allegiances she had formed in Europe. An indefatigable investigator, she brought to Hull-House her tireless compulsion to expose the detailed workings of economic exploitation. In 1894 she praised Richard T. Ely's *Socialism and Social Reform* but took issue with his gradualism. She defended her own apparent hypocrisy: "I personally participate in the work of social reform because part of it developes [sic] along Socialist lines, and part is an absolutely necessary protest against the brutalizing of us all by capitalism. Not because our Hull-House work alone satisfies me."[16] Her investigation of the garment industry's sweating system for the Illinois Bureau of Labor Statistics led to an invitation from Carroll Wright, the federal commissioner of labor, to supervise the Chicago segment of a national investigation of slums. That work seeded Hull-House's major collective effort at investigative reporting, *Hull-House Maps and Papers* of 1895, and led to a broader inquiry into women and children in Illinois industry that resulted in the state's first workers' protective legislation in 1893. Governor Altgeld appointed Kelley to the new office of factory inspector after Lloyd turned down his initial offer. During these years Kelley also earned a law degree at Northwestern University so that she could prosecute factory abuses outside the constraints of politics. A change in administration left Kelley jobless in 1897. After floundering for a time she moved to New York at John Graham Brooks's invitation to head the National Consumers' League. She made the Henry Street Settlement her New York base between cross-country organizational tours.[17]

One young resident in the mid-1890s described the exotic Mrs. Kelley—"socialist, divorced wife of a Russian nobleman, and State factory Inspector"—as "one of the attractions of the house. . . . She is a bright, restless, strong-minded woman, very original, progressive, and executive, but not exactly pleasant for steady companionship, I should think. . . . Her incessant activity of mind might prove a trifle wearing."[18] Kelley had little time for the more genteel activities of the settlement, though she had a broad sense of humor and loved a late-night debate.[19] Her combination of irreverence and brisk professionalism was infectious; Alice Hamilton feared that Kelley influenced the residents to adopt a "pose"; "We are desperately afraid of thinking ourselves great reformers, or treating our work with an enthusiasm which would betray freshness and lack of real experience and we get into the habit which I think all large, clannish households do, of laughing at outsiders."[20]

Though there were always a few men residents and associates and a constant stream of male visitors, it is little wonder that Hull-House was always thought of as a "women's" settlement. Moreover, Addams's settlement was almost unique in transcending what could easily have been a stigma to be accepted by both women and men as a corporate participant in the national reform culture and a force in public life.

The other "women's" settlement to achieve the stature of Hull-House was the Henry Street Settlement. As at Hull-House, it was primarily the personality of the headworker, Lillian Wald, that won the settlement a place in city and national life. Like Addams, Wald commanded the affection and cooperation of both her peers and new settlers. Whereas Jane Addams was frequently called a "saint," Wald was affectionately known as "Lady," and often "Leading Lady," by patrons and residents of Henry Street.[21] The hint of theatricality was appropriate; she charmed visitors with her vitality and optimism and clearly enjoyed command in a way Addams did not outwardly reveal. Once when she pressed Alice Hamilton to stay in New York for a dinner party at the settlement, Hamilton commented privately: "Miss Wald has one little fault, she is pretty insistent and she loves to show off her circle."[22] Like Addams she had the gift of simultaneously flattering an individual with personal attention and making him or her feel uncomfortably inadequate. "It isn't what you do in your settlement that means such an inspiration," Frances Kellor gushed to Wald,

> its what you are in your wonderfully sweet way to the people—
> it seems to me sometimes that your voice has the sweetest
> sympathy in the world in it. . . . Whatever is good reverences &
> loves you and whatever isn't is very much grieved and shamed,
> cause it knows what you would think. Your life is too full you
> mean so much to so many that I can only see a little & I shall

never be big enough to *give* you anything so its going to be one-sided as I guess most of your friendships will have to be till *many* of us grow lots more.[23]

As Kellor's tone hints, Wald inspired a series of what her older colleagues called "crushes" among the younger residents, often the women. Mabel Hyde Kittredge, a Park Avenue society woman whose father was pastor of the Madison Avenue Reformed Church, found her way to Henry Street about 1900. She began with club work, then on Wald's urging took charge of a "model flat" to demonstrate housekeeping skills to local women.[24] Kittredge fell in love with Wald and became deeply dependent on her. For a while at least her affection seems to have been reciprocated. Wald reserved an evening each week for Kittredge, confided in her, and gave her presents. But even the Tuesday evenings were fractured by Wald's myriad commitments, and Kittredge was torn between shame at wanting more time and her urgent desire for Wald's undivided attention. "I would very much like to meet you on a desert island or a farm, 'where the people cease from coming and the weary are at rest'—will the day ever come? . . . I suppose that I didn't really need your friendship—as compared with some of the poor, starved, tired souls that you have given your helpful individuality to. . . . I am free and strong and alive and awfully happy—but some way as I think back over this year—I believe that I needed you—it may be as much as the others."[25] She resented the residents' view of her as just another of Wald's "crushes," in the same category as "the man who presented the swallow-covered jar" and "Miss Jacobus who makes me so nervous patting your hair." Once she admitted that competing with "endless" supplicants for Wald's attention "makes me lack that perfect sympathy with 'work for others' as exemplified by a settlement."

At the same time she realized that she had been attracted largely by Wald's "public" qualities. She was "proud" of Wald and the settlement and grateful for being awakened to her own potential to help others and the superficiality of her circumscribed life. "I am getting altogether too close to you—Lady Wald," she mused at one point early in their relationship; "or is it your life and all those doors that you have pushed open for me?" Another time she wrote, "Your approval of my work is very dear to me, and it is easy with such a push to go on and do still better."

Eventually several minor clashes between the two women over staffing the model flat, and perhaps Kittredge's cumulative frustration at being repeatedly shunted aside for more pressing matters, cooled the passion to a continuing friendship and working relationship. The model flat expanded under Kittredge's leadership into the Association of Practical Housekeeping, and during World War I Kittredge shared in Henry Street's work for peaceful arbitration as well as the city's food rationing effort.[26] Her career vividly illustrates the potential of a strong personality to recruit workers by catalyzing their casual or unfocused interest into participation through the power of affectionate emulation.

Not all the settlement leaders possessed these personal qualities. Robert Woods, a fervent believer in Tucker's dictum that the settlement represented above all a "lavish use of personality," was not charismatic. In 1899 Alice Hamilton observed Addams and Woods collaborating at a settlement conference. The "impersonal" Woods was the loser in her comparison: "Mr. Woods . . . has the highest ideals and very clear rational convictions, but he has no warmth, no human impulsiveness and personal interest in his attitude toward people"—though she preferred him to the "sentimental, rather mushy settlers" at the conference.[27] One of his residents, a leader of the women's branch of South End House (as Andover House was called after 1895), recalled that Woods revealed his "sense of play" only when he was "off guard," and that what she called the "smaller mind" tended to be "in some awe of him."[28]

Strong headworkers set the tone of their households as well as putting the stamp of their personalities and beliefs on the work of their settlements. Hamilton described Chicago Commons when Graham Taylor was away as "'Hamlet' with Hamlet left out."[29] Certainly Taylor shared with the Dane a tendency toward oratorical self-dramatization that emerges in his correspondence and public statements.[30] Though he lacked the personal magnetism of Addams or Wald, he seems to have radiated an avuncular warmth and infectious optimism that ensured the affection and respect of his residents.[31] This allowed him to assert a personal authority that evaded some other headworkers. The routine at Chicago Commons included an evening "vesper service," with prayers and hymns; Taylor felt strongly that such a ritual "affords unity of action and mutual fellowship," and the residents seem to have complied.[32]

In the first year at Andover House, Robert Woods confronted a less tractable resident group. He found the questions of how and how firmly to wield his authority as headworker perplexing and somewhat painful. He too wanted to institute daily prayers for the residents, but two of them rebelled. "I simply maintained the position I suggested to you," he reported to Tucker, "that daily prayer seemed to me essential to the idea of a moral & spiritual unity, and that it was not a thing that I could submit to a ballot. . . . I have promised to refer the whole matter to you. While it comes in the form of a protest to my action, yet I myself suggested this method, and have not assumed any sort of decisive authority. I have merely acted as representing the idea, and as thinking of our relation to the members of the Association and to future residents."

It was galling to realize that when he was away the morning prayers were omitted; even when he was there, the residents hurried away after breakfast and left him to preside over the housekeeper and the two Catholic maids, more pious or docile than the male residents.[33] Though Woods soon emerged as a strong leader in the national settlement movement and the guiding spirit of his own house, his personal reserve and superficial austerity made him more respected than loved.

As the movement grew, settlement workers began visiting other houses to confer about particular issues or just to find a friendly haven in a strange city. They found that each house possessed its own character, the intangible "atmosphere" imparted by the personality of the headworker and the idiosyncrasies of the resident group. A Hull-House resident who moved to New York in 1898 reported back to Chicago that "Miss Wald's was the only settlement which had the least bit of settlement atmosphere about it. The University Settlement and Rivington Street [were] bleak and businesslike."[34] Naturally, personal loyalties and the treacherous nature of first impressions color such comparisons. Several years later a Rivington Street resident cast similar aspersions on the Friendly Aid House of New York, which she judged "not at all homelike." On a tour of the other CSA settlements she found the Philadelphia settlement "charming" and the house itself "as enchanting as a Rhine castle." She reported that "the whole spirit is like 95 Rivington Street." But Denison House, though "lovely—most quiet and respectable," had "something of a mission and a school atmosphere: prayers after breakfast and no baths allowed after ten." Denison House did not seem hospitable to the neighbors: "I didn't see the boys and girls coming in and 'hanging around' as they do in Philadelphia and here, seeming to be at home and feeling they are welcomed anytime." On the other hand she appreciated the calm of Denison House, in contrast to the "high pressure" of New York, a feeling she attributed not only to the "atmosphere of the city," but also to the Rivington Street headworker, Elizabeth Williams: "Having such a capacity for work, [she] makes everyone else feel conscience-stricken if they are not rushing also."[35]

Most of the early settlement residents, just out of college, were several years younger than the founding group. Eager and impression-able, they responded to the same social and intellectual currents that first touched their leaders, but few were as deeply immersed in the seminal religious and social literature. When Florence Kelley began teaching economics to the Rivington Street residents in the winter of 1890–91, she was startled to discover their ignorance. "It speaks ill for the scholarly atmosphere of several of our leading girls' colleges," she wrote to Richard Ely, "that the 'settler's' [*sic*] are not only utterly blank concerning economics but have no habit of reading!" She "jeered and scoffed at them" until they agreed to subscribe to the daily newspaper, begin a settlement "library of economics," and set aside an hour a day for reading. "What must be the habit of mind among the *less* earnest college girls?"[36]

There are counterexamples: young people drawn to the settlement houses primarily by the proliferating literature of the "new philan-thropy," the Social Gospel, and after the mid-1890s the infant American settlement movement itself. As a young doctor and researcher in the mid-1890s, Alice Hamilton first heard of the settlements from her cousin Agnes, who had stayed at home in Fort Wayne, Indiana, and become a leader in local religious and philanthropic organizations as her cousins Edith and Alice went off to college and professional school. A devout Presbyterian, since adolescence Agnes had steeped herself in the Christian Socialists, Maurice and Kingsley, who inspired her to de-vote her time to "personal service" to the less fortunate of Fort Wayne. From the English writers she went on to the social criticism of the Americans Richard T. Ely, George Hodges, and Francis G. Peabody. Intrigued by what she read of the new settlement movement, she helped extend invitations to Florence Kelley and Graham Taylor to speak in Fort Wayne. It was Agnes who suggested that her cousin Alice might try to live in one of the Chicago settlements when she took up her position at the Northwestern Women's Medical College. After she moved into Hull-House, Alice discovered that she had been accepted as a resident largely because Kelley had met and liked Agnes and her other Fort Wayne cousins—which made Alice feel like a "miserable hypo-crite" and wish that Agnes were there "to do the things they will expect me to do."[37] Agnes visited Alice during her first year at Hull-House in 1898. Several years later she left Fort Wayne herself to live in the Light-house Settlement run by the Presbyterians in Philadelphia.[38]

Even for serious readers, the hectic pace of the settlements and the attractions of "real life" left little time for quiet study. "I haven't studied much this winter," admitted Florence Cross, a Rivington Street settler, "because the flesh and blood people around me made books seem vain and profitless." She had graduated from Wells College in 1897 and gone to work for three years at the George Junior Republic, a farm school for city youth in Ithaca, New York. Lively, cheerful, and popular with children, Cross exemplified the settlement worker who respected the theory but above all relished the experience of settlement life. "O won't I show you things!" she teased her parents as they planned to visit her in the exotic Lower East Side. "I'll take you into back alleys and rear tenements that will make you want to fly back to Rochester. We can go to the Chinese theater and hear them bang and yell till you're deaf, to the Italian marionette, where you'll wonder how many daggers under each ragged coat, or the Bowery vaudeville where one can drink beer with a very short-skirted lady by just winking at her to 'come on.'" Her headworker urged her to pursue a master's degree in sociology at Columbia. Cross agreed, partly to please Miss Williams, whom she admired, and also because it was clear that an advanced degree would enhance her record if she decided to continue with social work. This motive for further study would become increasingly common among the settlement workers. Unconsciously echoing the plaint of the settlement founders in an altered context, she sighed, "This continual preparation for something bigger and greater beyond tries one's patience."[39]

Working beside those settlers who balked at studying social theory were the few who, like Vida Scudder and Ellen Gates Starr, were propelled by their settlement experience toward more doctrinaire ideological positions. Robert Hunter, the son of a wealthy carriage manufacturer in Terre Haute, Indiana, graduated from Indiana University in 1896 with a concentration in social science and economics. He went to work for Chicago's Bureau of Charities and became organizing secretary in 1899. He lived in several Chicago settlements before moving into Hull-House the same year. Hunter quickly made important connections in the fluid world of social reform. On a trip to England in the summer of 1899 he visited the economist John Hobson, Keir Hardie, and Gertrude Toynbee, who was apparently charmed by the young American and gave him a portrait and an autograph of her brother Arnold.[40] In 1901 Hunter published a study of Chicago's tenement houses, and shortly afterward he was invited to become headworker of the University Settlement in New York. His new wife's brother, James G. Phelps Stokes, was also connected with the University Settlement and gave

Hunter an added entrée into elite city circles, where Hunter energetically promoted settlements, municipal reform, and child labor laws. In 1904 he resigned his headworker position to write *Poverty,* an angry exposé of the national dimensions of poverty, with a particularly bleak assessment of the exploitation of child labor in mines and factories. Though he distinguished poverty from pauperism, Hunter demonstrated their close connection by analyzing the conditions the poor had to struggle against to escape degrading dependence. He ended with a call for national industrial regulation and social legislation. In 1905 Hunter followed Stokes into the Socialist party.[41]

Like his fellow settlement recruits, Hunter embraced a meliorist version of socialism that envisioned a benign state regulating the economy and society to ensure social justice, generally equated with the central ideal of the settlement movement: the right of each individual to unimpeded social development.[42] Most of the settlement converts to socialism did not so much reject as lose patience with the settlement as a vehicle for social change, though a few manifested a separatism that cast their more moderate leaders into the uncomfortable role of temporizing Puritan fathers. "Poor Mr. [W. H.] Noyes has been having a dreadful time of it," reported Alice Hamilton to her cousin Agnes. This "big, impulsive, rather ill-balanced man" had moved from Hull-House to head his own settlement sponsored by Chicago's Ethical Culture Society. "He has gone through another crisis in his convictions and he now believes that only undiluted Socialism will do, that Settlements are a hindrance to progress and he must give up his place."[43] (Moreover, Noyes had compounded his marital difficulties by falling in love with the kindergarten teacher.)

Robert Woods struggled with several similar cases in the first year of Andover House. He reported in exasperation to Tucker that "Bevington . . . is out of sympathy with neighborhood work. He seems to have gone into it out of sentiment, and now when he finds sentiment does not melt away difficulties, he becomes thoroughly convinced that the way to improve [the neighborhood] is by improving the world in general through reforms and agitations. He expresses himself as thinking the club work to be petty and even wrong, when we might be joining the 'great movements of the time.' . . . It seems sad that we can't get men who will face the issue."[44]

Woods was one of the most fervent and literal proponents of the "neighborhood" principle of settlement work, which when carried to extremes was gently ridiculed by Jane Addams as "geographical salvation"—the idea that the locality was the only fountainhead of genuine social change.[45] Other settlement leaders agreed wholeheartedly with Woods that the settlement should be a method rather than an institution and should further a process as well as striving for concrete results. In this sense, ideologically inspired programs for social reform were inconsistent with the settlement enterprise, though the settlements made a point, in true liberal fashion, of welcoming residents and visitors of all political persuasions. But the intended spirit of the settlements was appropriately captured by the woman who elevated "flesh and blood people" over books. Another resident, queried about the influence of settlement life on her social ideas, responded, "I don't know that my attitude changed, but my point of view certainly did, or perhaps it would be more true to say that now I have several points of view."[46] Other residents more cogently testified to the success of the settlements in challenging their preconceived notions about poverty and the economic system by presenting them with the homely and complicated lives of the individual poor.[47] No matter what label they adopted, or what degree of ideological confusion they admitted, just by being in the congested neighborhoods of American cities the settlement workers realized half of the original settlement intention: unmediated personal contact with the poor.

The other half of the settlement mission—to exert personal influence on the individuals in their neighborhoods, in order to enrich their lives and improve local conditions—was challenged by the immensity and complexity of the problems they uncovered. "One by one," Canon Barnett had said. Yet even those settlers who rejected doctrinaire solutions were sometimes frustrated by the small impact of their deliberately piecemeal approach to social improvement. The settlement workers had set themselves the task of maintaining the tense and delicate equilibrium between the subjective, ethically charged, and personal method of their endeavor and its logical and urgent tendency toward systematic expansion. Moreover, it became clear that the effective growth of the settlement movement could not take the one-dimensional form of a proliferation of houses to reach every neighborhood of every city—Woods's dream, caricatured by Addams as "geographical salvation." The settlement principle of "personal dedication" in the spirit of social Christianity pulled the movement in one direction, while the settlement workers' deference to the authority and objectives of social science as the engine of effective change dictated a different structure and set of priorities. By the late 1890s, the successes of the early settlements had generated a dynamic that pushed the movement from its grounding in Victorian social ideas to a dominant position in modern social work.

6
Immigrants and Culture

The First Generation

The American settlement workers honored Canon Barnett's dictum, "one by one." Emphasizing personal influence and character building, their ultimate goal was to affirm each person's unique potential. But while their philosophy tacitly posed the individual as the irreducible unit of social life, the settlement workers also saw individuals as integrally connected with larger entities. Each person would fulfill certain roles and expectations within the family, and beyond the family was the neighborhood. The settlers' commitment to localism stemmed historically from the settlement's roots in the English parish system and bore a practical relation to the settlement philosophy of personal service. It also represented the settlers' reaction to their perception of fragmented, depersonalizing life in the industrial city. "To a man lost in the city wilderness," wrote Dr. Jane Robbins, "friendliness is priceless."[1] In this respect the settlement movement formed part of a conservative response to modernization. The urban neighborhood should echo the best aspects of village or town, offering its residents a sense of rootedness and intimacy as a bulwark against impersonal exploitation by the modern economy.

In its American incarnation the neighborhood principle became a vehicle for a new rationale for cultural pluralism (the term was not coined until several decades later by William James's student Horace Kallen).[2] The homogeneity and social stasis of multigenerational continuity central to nineteenth-century European visions of traditional village life were illusory in the American city neighborhood. The multi-colored maps painstakingly drawn by the settlement workers after Booth's example eloquently illustrated the multiethnic and unstable complexion of their districts. A link between economic and geographic mobility made many poor neighborhoods into social strainers, with ethnic groups arriving en masse, then separating into ranks according to degree of economic success. Often the groups' natural leaders moved out as they moved up. Individual success tugged against group well-being; the settlers found their two main goals ranged at opposite poles.

In the face of irresistible change, the settlement workers strove to accommodate traditional values to the social demands of urban indus-trialism. They substituted social interaction for social history as the principal stimulant to local bonding. They applied the premise that shared experience led to social unity to the problem of neighborhoods splintered by cultural differences and mutual suspicions. The most acute settlement workers plundered new theories in sociology, educa-tion, and psychology to modernize and secularize the Christian Socialist vision of an organic, interdependent society.

The earliest settlers discovered the special demands of dealing with first- and second-generation immigrants as challenges superadded to their preconceptions of settlement life.[3] The settlement ideal of adap-tation to local needs plunged the houses into the issues and problems arising from unrestricted immigration and the policy of laissez-faire toward the bewildered "greenhorns." In a period of rising nativism, perhaps the settlements' major contribution to national dialogue on immigration was their insistence on viewing the immigrant as the *victim* as much as the *cause* of America's social and economic troubles.[4]

The settlers' personal attitudes toward the immigrants fell across a wide spectrum. Many of the settlement workers shared the chauvinism, if not the fears, of their fellow citizens toward the "new immigrants" from southern and eastern Europe. The language of the settlement investigators sometimes slipped from generalization to stereotype as they recorded the "racial" characteristics of their neighborhoods. In a chapter called "The Invading Host" in *Americans in Process,* a South End House study of 1903, the Jews were noted for their "instinct for sharp practice in trade," while the Italians were characterized as "an excitable race."[5] As a group, though, the settlers were probably less overtly condescending in their discourse about the immigrants than most other native-born Americans. As with the issue of religion, usually tightly bound up with the immigrants' ethnic origins, the settlement workers' first imperative was to avoid alienating their new neighbors by aggressive or insensitive actions.

The issue of ethnicity was even more complicated than that of reli-gion. Whereas most immigrants clung to their customary faith, with adjustments to American institutional contours, their attitudes toward their ethnic and linguistic heritage were often more ambivalent and therefore made them more vulnerable.[6] Younger immigrants particularly learned to dread the "greenhorn" label and felt their own languages, dress, and customs as stigmas in an intolerant environment. From outside, the immigrant "colonies" of the tenement districts seemed stubbornly insular; at closer range, as the early settlement workers perceived, they were all in various stages of painful and disordered transition.

Like other social service agencies, the settlements offered classes in English, civics, and the hagiographic rudiments of American history. But they also gradually refined their programs in ways that reflected both their received values and their own ambivalence toward the goals of "Americanization." The settlement workers were among the first to appreciate the Old World cultural survivals in the immigrant colonies. While many native-born Americans scoffed and some earlier immigrants distanced themselves from later arrivals, American settlement workers brought a different perspective to the neighborhood festivals and parades. Jane Addams once exclaimed: "Nothing is more beautiful than the gay celebrations in the Italian quarter in Chicago on Garibaldi's birthday. Nothing is brighter than the march of the mutual benefit societies along the streets."[7] The settlers discovered that settlement social evenings came to life with pictures, songs, and dances from the immigrants' native lands. National and religious festivals added color to a drab neighborhood and brought its residents together.

Besides nurturing community sentiments, the festivals and celebrations appealed to the settlement workers' own aesthetic sense. A spontaneous gathering of Italians in Boston evoked this warm description from two settlement women: "The court in which a large number live is transformed as if by magic, and the Bella Napoli, with all its gayety, its lights and shadows, suddenly stands out upon the scene of the North End of Boston. Everything is there, —the song, the tambourine, the accordion, and lastly the dance and the glass of Chianti."[8]

Many of these young Americans found in these exotic celebrations the brighter side of the urban "reality" they sought. Here were genuine manifestations of the European folkways they had read about in college, nostalgic survivals of "simpler," preindustrial cultures.[9] Lillian Wald expressed the sense of regret that underlay the settlement workers' evolving rationale for cultural pluralism: "Great is our loss when a shallow Americanism is accepted by the newly arrived immigrant, and their national traditions and heroes are ruthlessly pushed aside."[10]

In 1904 Vida Scudder joined forces with an "Italian gentleman,"

Francesco Malgeri, to initiate a new kind of social work with the growing Italian community in Boston. Scudder's European travels, her passion for literature, and her Anglo-Catholicism, particularly her recent
discovery of Saint Catherine of Siena, formed the background for her
fascination with the Italian immigrants.[11] She responded warmly to
Signor Malgeri's concern that educated Italians were lumped indiscrim-
inately with their countrymen and given no opportunity to use their
talents in this country. "Our desire was less to work for the poorer
elements than to express our gratitude for the gifts brought us by the
better, and to avoid what Mrs. Florence Kelley called 'the sordid waste
of genius' among them."[12] Scudder was distressed by these Italians'
disaffection with American life, their cynicism toward politics and resentment of the cheapening of Italian family life and social ideals. She
hoped to find a positive channel for their "initiative" and "enthusiasm
for an abstract idea" and to break down the cultural barriers that isolated them from American society. "They are well worth knowing," she
informed her compatriots. "The poets and thinkers of the Latins, from
Mazzini and Carducci to Georges Sorel, are on the tips of their tongues;
their minds are atingle with the European issues, political and religious,
concerning which we read in the magazines."[13] Scudder had discovered a diamond in a dustbin.

The centerpiece of her collaboration with Malgeri was the "Circolo
Italo-Americano," which aimed to give these elite Italians the chance "to
meet Americans of the better class on a social footing."[14] For the Americans, Denison House offered classes in Italian language and history.
Evening meetings of the Circolo featured Italian songs, "recitations,"
and political talks, while at Sunday afternoon lecture-concerts the Italians could hear speakers on American issues and ideals.[15]

Through associating with the Italian-Americans closest to her own
background, Scudder could feel "America in the making"; she envisioned "what the emergent people might become, when the glory and
honor of many diverse nations should have entered through its gates
and created its citizenship."[16] Unconscious snobbism coupled with a
romanticized sense of historical kinship broadened her path to this
cosmopolitan ideal. Other settlement leaders had also grown up viewing Garibaldi and particularly Mazzini as republican heroes from the
same mold as Abraham Lincoln.[17] Their reverence for the Italians' heritage stretched back through the Renaissance and Dante to the glories
of Rome. Other national groups likewise appealed to their selectively
cultivated historical imaginations. Jane Addams understood why an

audience of Greeks remained politely indifferent to her tales of the
Pilgrims: "I was uneasily conscious of the somewhat feeble attempt to
boast of Anglo-Saxon achievement in hardihood and privation, to men
whose powers of admiration were absorbed in their Greek background
of philosophy and beauty."[18]

Thus the settlement workers viewed the immigrants through a double lens. From one angle, the immigrants could be respected and appealed to as the legatees of ancient and rich cultural traditions; with
only a slight shift in perspective they stood uprooted and perplexed in
the modern American city as poignant survivors of earlier, simpler, and
more integrated societies. Their role as "culture bearers" exalted their
humanity as well as evoking some undemocratic reactions; Jane Addams
agreed with Scudder that the settlement should "bring [the immigrants]
in contact with a better type of Americans"—a sentiment that reflected
the settlers' biases.[19] At the same time, the need to assimilate these
displaced persons dominated the settlers' efforts on their behalf. Robert
Woods summarized the settlement aspiration: "To honor what is genuine in the spirit of nationality among each of the complex elements of
our working population, while exalting those American loyalties which
can unite them into a common citizenship."[20]

This ideal was practically impossible to achieve not only because of
the centrifugal pressures of American society, but also because it required the temporal juxtaposition of clashing modes of life. Addams's
own wording of this aim—"to preserve and keep whatever of value
their past life contained"—betrayed the counterhistorical thrust of the
settlement effort. Her settlement's major institutional contribution to
the celebration of immigrant "gifts" to American life was all too aptly
called the Hull-House Labor Museum.[21]

The "museum" evolved to integrate traditional arts and crafts into the
urban neighborhood, largely as a way of healing generational rifts. The
Hull-House residents had discovered that some of their neighbors were
expert in the arts and crafts of their native countries. Not only were
these skills atrophying from neglect in the new environment, but the
craftsmen's own children often showed indifference and even scorn
toward their accomplishments, part of a broader syndrome of generational conflict that struck settlement workers everywhere as the immigrants' primary social problem.

Another impetus for the new "museum" was the residents' feeling
that their existing arts programs had done little to fertilize the cultural
life of their neighborhood, despite the popularity of the Art Gallery,

endowed in 1891, and the traditional art studios.[22] The residents had founded the Chicago Arts and Crafts Society in 1897 to foster Ruskin's image of manual labor as "dignified and beautiful," but even as they launched this ambitious program they doubted that modern industrial labor could be magically transformed into "something expressive of the mind and interest of the workers."[23] Though Ellen Gates Starr clung to her faith in the social function of good craftsmanship, she chafed at the fact that "the people who most deserve to have choice books" could hardly afford her bindery's laboriously produced volumes.[24] No matter what the inner rewards to the pupil-craftsman, a disjunction persisted between the working lives of the Hull-House neighbors and the aesthetic experiences the settlement offered.[25] But while the Labor Museum similarly embodied the ideals of Ruskin and Morris, it would add a new dimension partly suggested by John Dewey's evolving educational theories. The museum aspired to enrich community life by using handicrafts to exemplify the possibility of experiential and historical continuity between the Old World and the New.

The first decade of her Hull-House experience had prodded Jane Addams to seek ever more effective expression of the settlement's holistic premises. Urban American conditions had outstripped the Victorian terms of the earliest settlement pronouncements. In 1897 she published a seminal article called, simply, "A Function of the Social Settlement." Dense and elusive, this brilliant paper attempted to apply new theories of knowledge and education to the settlement experience. Again Addams criticized the dissociation of books from life, formal education from modern problems. But now she invoked the scorn of her friend John Dewey for inert knowledge, accumulated and verified but never applied to "securing a method of action"; and she cited William James's evolving pragmatism, which suggested that "beliefs" were really "rules of action" and the "test of truth" was "the conduct it dictates or inspires."[26] Using these ideas, she offered a new definition of the settlement as "an attempt to express the meaning of life in terms of life itself, in forms of activity." Implicitly criticizing the rhetoric of some of her settlement colleagues, notably Robert Woods, she argued that the true settlement spirit was not analytical, but synthetic: that the settlement was not a " 'sociological laboratory' " for gathering facts, but a place where acquired knowledge might be tested and, if valid, employed.

Addams's emphasis on the concepts of experience, vitality, and organicism suggest that she was struggling toward a new idea of the settlement as a *process,* a stage for social interaction that presented a unique opportunity to link Dewey's educational theory and James's pragmatism to transform traditional ideas of social service into a broader vision of social life. "Just as we do not know a fact until we can play with it, so we do not possess knowledge until we have an impulse to bring it into use; . . . [to] throw into the stream of common human experience one bit of important or historic knowledge . . . which before belonged to a few."[27]

Her new rationale for the settlements' insistence on social reciprocity in an organic society broke the barriers between public and private by suggesting a new way to understand the interdependence of collective welfare and individual well-being. *Life itself* could aspire to art's traditional function in "freeing the individual from a sense of separation and isolation in his emotional experience."[28] This fusion of separate and even antagonistic entities—the individual and the group, private and public, self-gratification and altruism—could be carried into the temporal realm as well. That was the essence of Addams's concept of the Labor Museum. The museum's centerpiece was a living exhibit of seven traditional modes of spinning and weaving, arranged in a "historic sequence" that concluded with contemporary factory processes. The exhibit illustrated the unity of endeavor over time and cultural boundaries.[29] It embodied a mode of education that recognized the connectedness of past and present, economy and society. Addams suggested that the child offered knowledge in this form "will never see a piece of cloth without a certain recognition of the historic continuity of effort . . . ; but better still perhaps such a child, having learned something of the lives of textile workers for thousands of years . . . , will be interested perforce in the textile workers of the present moment and will know how superficial an education must be which is not based upon and adapted to the industrial life of its age."[30]

Inseparable from the universal function of "industrial education" was the particular and personal role the Labor Museum could play in family and community life in the Hull-House neighborhood. One of Addams's favorite stories concerned an Italian girl who attended a cooking class at Hull-House while her mother demonstrated spinning at the Labor Museum. Ashamed to be seen at the settlement with her traditionally dressed mother, Angelina would enter by a separate door. Then one evening the girl found her mother in the spinning room surrounded by an admiring group of visiting educators and heard her lauded as "the best stick-spindle spinner in America." Afterward she had a new appreciation for her mother's previously embarrassing accomplish-ments.[31] Angelina's mother, too, might well have found that her work at the Labor Museum had restored a sense of pride and self-worth eroded by life in an American city. The museum and the workshops put the immigrant craftsman in the teacher's role—"a pleasant change," Addams wrote, "from the tutelage in which all Americans, including their own children, are so apt to hold them."[32] With uptowners as well as local residents drawn to the museum's exhibits and classes, the settlement could extend and deepen its role as a center of cultural exchange.

The Hull-House Museum was unique, but there were a few settle-ment analogues that combined a respect for the intrinsic value of art and crafts with the attempt to add color and unity to community life and evoke from immigrant colonies the natural "gifts" they could offer American society. The Italian program at Denison House incorporated a "revival" of native Italian arts and crafts.[33] A few years earlier, the Henry Street residents had begun to sponsor an annual spring festival in their Lower East Side neighborhood. One of the residents, Rita Wallach, explained that these local festivals were a form of experiential education that allowed young people to "reliv[e] those experiences which in former times occupied man's leisure—when he still was un-spoiled by the commercial spirit, and his spontaneous joy in the beauty of life caused him to express himself artistically in poetry, painting, song or dance."[34] Wallach demonstrated the same complex amalgam of con-descension and admiration that characterized Addams's and Scudder's perceptions of the immigrants' cultural backgrounds. Neighborhood festivals would let the immigrants "voice [their] artistic yearnings," she argued, implying that they were not only the heirs but the survivors of "primitive," prescientific European societies. She also suggested that reviving these cast-off traditions would not only strengthen intergener-ational relations among the immigrants, but enrich American culture: "May we not as a nation, young in art . . . receive from the older civilizations a new impetus and a leavening force to that commercialism which too often deprives mankind of its heritage of beauty?"[35]

The settlements did enliven the popular artistic life of their cities and helped arouse interest in ethnic contributions to American life. But they were less successful in achieving their complementary goal: to recreate community life in the immigrant neighborhoods by instilling pride in the immigrants' heritage. The combination of therapy and tutelage that marked these large schemes for enriching community life was fragile not only because it rested on questionable historical and anthropological premises, but also because it demanded an ultimately untenable equilibrium between cultural autonomy and social assimilation. Nowhere is this strain more evident than in the settlements' relationship with the young people of their neighborhoods.

The Second Generation

The settlement workers struggled to restore the family's integrity and traditional authority structure by rekindling filial respect in the second generation, but this effort proved insidiously self-defeating. In effect, the settlement tried to mitigate the divisive impact of American society on the immigrant family by offering itself as a mediator between parent and child. Father Billings revealed this fundamental insight in his hostility to the Denison House residents. The settlement workers' decision to represent the interests of the poor and foreign-born led logically to their benign usurpation of local authority in both the private and quasi-public realms. Though they espoused conservative family values and local self-determination, the means they adopted undermined these ends. Their endorsement of cultural pluralism stopped at the point at which the immigrants' mores inhibited the second generation's ability to succeed in American society. Through their clubs, classes, recreation programs, and summer camps, the settlements offered local youth the skills and values necessary to social adaptation that they could not acquire at home. With the most benign intentions, the settlement workers taught filial loyalty while acting in certain critical areas in loco parentis.

In one matter the settlement workers interposed themselves between parent and child without apology. "Early residents were shocked," Woods and Kennedy later wrote, "to discover the number of parents who regarded offspring as potential sources of revenue."[36] In factories, sweatshops, retail stores, and the street trades, young children routinely labored long hours to bring home pennies. As the settlement residents began to investigate child labor, they were less distressed by callous employers than by complicitous parents. In many cases, as Florence Kelley and Alzina Stevens discovered in Chicago in 1894, children did serve as the sole possible support of a family. But in other cases parents demanded the children's wages for such purposes as early payment of a mortgage.[37] Whether through greed, ignorance, short-sightedness, or genuine need, some parents conspired with employers to evade the poorly enforced labor laws.

The settlement workers called for better laws and rigorous enforcement. The Hull-House residents led a successful fight in Illinois for
effective child labor laws.[38] In New York, settlement residents advised a
legislature-appointed committee on child labor in 1895. In 1902 Robert
Hunter chaired the settlement-dominated New York Child Labor Committee, which also included Florence Kelley, as head of the National
Consumers' League, and Lillian Wald. Two years later the New York
groups spawned the National Child Labor Committee. In Jersey City,
Cornelia Bradford of Whittier House headed a lobbying drive for protective legislation for youth. Boston settlement workers joined a fight
for child labor protection that focused on the street trades.[39]

Horrified by the abuse of children inadequately shielded by their
families, the settlers extended their mediating and protective role by
petitioning the state to exercise a benevolent paternalism through legislation and regulation. Lillian Wald expressed this position bluntly in a
letter to Jacob Schiff in 1914: "I want the best that there is in the whole
world for the poor, and the less discriminating they are, the less sophisticated, the more it is up to the State to guard them."[40] In the
absence of responsible private authorities, government should forcibly
guarantee the American promise of justice and opportunity. The settlers
believed that these concepts included what Florence Kelley called "the
right to childhood": provision of the minimal conditions conducive to
the child's healthy development.[41] Further, they argued, public policy to
protect children was dictated not only by humanitarianism but by the
national interest. Robert Hunter asserted in 1904 that "[child labor] is a
waste of the nation's most valuable asset, —manhood."[42] In *Some Ethical Gains through Legislation* (1905), Florence Kelley agreed: "The
noblest duty of the Republic is that of self-preservation by so cherishing
all its children that they, in turn, may become enlightened self-
governing citizens." Even fish, she pointed out, had their own national
commission. Were children not worthy of the same solicitude?[43]

The settlement workers' harshest indictment of urban life was its
effect on children. Robert Hunter drew a romantic picture of preindustrial community life, in which children played, studied, and shared the
healthful labor of a rural economy under the watchful eyes of their
parents: "The home was the centre of the moral, educational, industrial,
and social life."[44] Industrialization had "destroyed" the home by allot-
ting its functions to other agencies while neglecting to replace its social
and recreational role in the child's life. Because city life could not

thwart children's instinct for play, their games were jarringly superimposed on the harsh surfaces and hostile routines of the city:

> The teeming tenements open their doors, and out into the dark passageways and courts, through foul alleys and over broken sidewalks, flow ever renewed streams of playing children. Under the feet of passing horses, under the wheels of passing street cars, jostled about by the pedestrians, driven on by the policeman, they annoy every one. They crowd about the music or drunken brawls in the saloons, they "shoot craps" in the alleys, they seek always and everywhere activity, movement, life.[45]

Hunter's use of the "stream" metaphor in this powerful passage was deliberate and multilayered. The settlement workers accepted the psychological premises of child-centered education that they themselves had forwarded through the settlements' Froebel kindergartens. The most effective education would nurture the child's innate instinct for play, the seed of healthy development. By comparing the play of urban children to a stream running through the city landscape, Hunter played on the contrast between nature and the "unnatural," country and city life, preindustrial and industrial society. Like Kelley, he compared children to other forms of nature to point up the irony of society's apathy toward them: "Our gardens are given a place apart; flowers and plants are tended and drawn out by wise hands, which supply unobtrusive and safe guidance; but the childhood of our city is without its place, without its tending, and without its guidance."[46]

The settlement writers chose their natural conceits with care. Far from prescribing a benign neglect that would allow children to grow "wild," they invoked protected species and cultivated gardens to suggest, following the ethos of Lester Frank Ward, that public policy could be used to select and mold the socially desirable tendencies of "natural" human development. Hunter echoed his own metaphor and clarified his philosophical stance by quoting Goethe's statement that "character is developed in the stream of life." Society should monitor the course and purity of that "stream," so that in each child the "roots of character and of the soul of man" were bathed in good, not evil, influences.[47] The children's innocent plasticity was, ironically, the source of their corruption. Seeking games, they imitated all facets of street life, even the evil and dangerous; looking for adventure, they slipped into petty crime.[48]

Ten years later Philip Davis, a Boston settlement worker, struck the same notes in pleading with his city to take the children "off the streets." Davis too argued that the unprotected street child was "in a peculiar sense, public property of which the community is trustee." For Davis, "community" meant two things: the smaller, "accidental" community of the neighborhood, and the broader polis, formally responsible for safeguarding the human resource of its children. Because American urban conditions had destroyed the protective abilities of the traditional community, urban children were now properly considered "wards of the State."[49]

The settlers were pouring old wine into new bottles—employing new educational and psychological concepts to frame the litany of evils associated with city life in terms of their influence on children. They also transposed the fundamentally religious justification of communal watchfulness over the individual soul into secular terms. Collective self-interest dictated society's duty to protect and shape its youth in order to ensure the future wealth and well-being of the nation.

Adolescence had long been recognized as a distinct developmental stage that sharpened vulnerability to certain stimuli and temptations. By the mid-nineteenth century, a middle-class consensus held that during this period of rapid sexual maturation the child—particularly the girl—should be shielded from corrupting knowledge and sexual temptation. As Joseph Kett points out, the evolution of this view coincided with and partly stemmed from accelerated urbanization; not surprisingly, the desirable prolongation of innocence was often associated with "simple" country living, while the city became a "hotbed" of vicious influences on the suggestible adolescent.[50]

Raised in the mid-Victorian climate, the settlement workers initially shared these assumptions about youth. Their first contribution to the busy dialogue on adolescence after 1900 was to insist that the solicitude reserved for middle-class youth should be extended to poor and working-class young people. Ultimately the settlers adopted an ambivalent and conflict-laden approach to these adolescents. On the one hand, their sympathy for the problems of working-class urban adolescents universalized the society's romanticizing of youth; just as all children shared the "right to childhood," all adolescents confronted the dilemmas of coming-of-age. On the other hand, the policies settlement leaders put forward to integrate these young people into the industrial order tended to fix them in the social stratum they had been born into.

Once again Jane Addams spoke most compellingly for a new perspective on urban adolescents. In *The Spirit of Youth and the City Streets* (1909), she posed the crisis of juvenile delinquency as a failure in cultural interpretation of the needs of youth. Again placing her subject in a large historical and evolutionary context, she proposed a universal human impulse to look to youth for self-renewal, to "depend upon" the young for "gaiety and enthusiasm."[51] Offering a variation on the ubiquitous stream metaphor, she asserted that industrial society represented men's first failure to provide "channels through which this wine of life might flow, and be preserved for their delight." Like other settlement writers on urban youth, she presented society's obligation to nurture and protect its young as a positive appeal for cultural continuity and social health. She came close to acknowledging what was also true for the commentators on younger children: while professing to seek greater responsibility for the welfare of the young, these writers were in fact laying on the children the heavy burden of a collective longing for innocence.

Addams wrote frankly of the "sex susceptibility" that joined the play impulse in older children as a "force" blindly propelling their actions.[52] Properly channeled, this "force" fueled the imagination that produced art and drama and laid the "foundations of domesticity." Whereas earlier writers had emphasized the physical as well as moral degeneracy that accompanied the unhealthy "depletion" of energy in sexual activity, Addams saw nascent sexuality as intricately linked to the play instinct and the "love of pleasure," and she warned against "damming up" this "sweet fountain."[53] Though she too deplored the consumption of "vast stores of vital energy" by an unmediated sexual drive, she called for the "diffusion" rather than suppression of sexual impulses. The solution was not the artificial infantilization of adolescents, but the cultivation of their imaginations so as to "substitute the love of beauty for mere desire, to place the mind above the senses."[54]

Addams indicted the modern city for its contradictory responses to young people's restless search for pleasure. She faulted both repression and commercialization. The private dance halls were generally linked to saloons, yet they provided one of the only settings where young men and women might meet. Likewise, the cheap theaters and new moving picture shows, which offered many urban young people "the only possible road to the realms of mystery and romance," presented vapid and morally offensive dramas and spectacles, only worsened by an occasional veneer of false piety. Yet young people hungered for the theater's promise that "life was noble and harmonious," despite the "cruelties and trivialities" of their daily lives in the factories, shops, and streets.[55]

Like many others, Addams found these manifestations of popular culture personally distasteful, and she indulged in the alarmist warning that repeated exposure to dance halls and vaudeville theaters incited children to vice, crime, and even mental illness.[56] As with the settlement workers' attempts to resuscitate immigrant crafts and "folkways," both cultural elitism and antiurban, even antimodern, attitudes colored their programs and pronouncements, and Addams shared these attitudes. But several distinctly *modern* strains of analysis and prescription over-shadow the hints of nostalgia and cultural parochialism in the *Spirit of Youth*.

Though Addams deplored the "vulgar" drama prevalent in the city theatres, she also argued that these shows and songs were popular because they reflected the audience's own experience: "Recitals of city adventure contain the nucleus of coming poesy and romance, as the songs and recitals of the early minstrels sprang directly from the life of the people."[57] The emergence of a new "folk art" in this context was regrettable because the commercial structure of urban entertainment precluded active audience involvement in its development. In these circumstances Addams judged that middle-class intervention and guid-ance were not only justified, but urgent.[58]

She extended to popular culture the reasoning that got the settle-ments involved in labor organization, industrial regulation, and politics. Powerless to defend themselves, the people needed articulate advo-cates to protect them from exploitation—at least until they were ready to act in their own behalf. Regarding democracy as an evolving ideal, the settlers were never populists. As a character in Vida Scudder's *Lis-tener in Babel* put it, "I protest against being called undemocratic be-cause I know the difference between refinement and vulgarity."[59] To Addams it seemed impossible for the people's tastes and instincts to develop autonomously in the contemporary city, so it became crucial to bring enlightened and morally sound influences to bear upon them. But she also recognized the need for aesthetic forms that addressed the realities of people's urban industrial experience. "We cannot expect young people themselves to cling to conventions which are totally un-suited to modern city conditions, nor yet to be equal to the task of forming new conventions through which this more agglomerate social life may express itself."[60]

Another novel element of *The Spirit of Youth* was Addams's prescription of performing arts as a substitute for commercial entertainment. Drawing again on psychological and educational theory that stressed activity and experience as the catalysts of true education, she suggested that participation in drama and music offered young people a conduit for the "self-expression" important at that age. The amateur actor, technician, or scene painter became an active purveyor of beauty. Addams also commended drama, music, and pageantry as social activities, drawing people together to cooperate in a project and, in a larger sense, fusing individuals to the continuing life of society: "What is the function of art but to preserve in permanent and beautiful form those emotions and solaces which cheer life and make it kindlier, more heroic and easier to comprehend; which lift the mind of the worker from the harshness and loneliness of his task, and, by connecting him with what has gone before frees him from a sense of isolation and hardship?"[61]

Her advocacy of the performing arts reflected a settlement trend growing since 1900. Taking culture to the people had been a touchstone of settlement identity since the movement's inception. Taking a leaf from Canon Barnett's book, the Neighborhood Guild, Hull-House, and Woods's South End House had sponsored annual art exhibitions and campaigned to open city museums on Sundays.[62] Settlement art classes had been inspired by the arts-and-crafts movement and the settlements' interest in promoting the immigrants' cultural gifts to America. Social singing and small concerts often formed the focal point of Victorian-flavored evening gatherings in the settlements. Pushing beyond social and informal music, Hull-House and the Rivington Street Settlement started music schools in the early 1890s. Emilie Wagner, the head of the Rivington Street Music School, offered an anecdote that illustrates the settlers' faith in the moral influence of good music. One "ragged little girl" had come to the settlement asking for violin lessons. Her rapid progress effected a revolution in the life of her family: "At the time this child commenced her musical work her family lived in dark, sordid rooms and had fallen into a careless, ambitionless state. The little girl's playing soon awakened in them a desire for better things. Her father's memory was stirred with the thought of what he had once been in his youth at home, his self-respect and ambition were revived, and now he is a prosperous wage-earner."[63] Once again, art was the agent of spiritual redemption and the catalyst for a merging of Old World past and American present.

The settlements moved slowly into full-scale amateur drama, held back partly by Victorian doubts about the theater's propriety.[64] But as college graduates, most of the residents had likely seen or participated in the forms of theater familiar on nineteenth-century campuses: classical plays, declamation, pageants, and pantomime. Many residents had used forms of dramatic activity in their club work. Younger children naturally enjoyed fantasy and mimesis, and there could be no objection to older children's dramatic readings of Shakespeare and Victorian poetry. The settlements' sponsorship of festivals and pageantry, and the growing popularity of "little theater" after 1900, paved the way for more formal amateur drama in the houses. The Hull-House Dramatic Association came together about 1897 and spawned the Hull-House Players. About ten years later, Henry Street attracted two young volunteers, Alice and Irene Lewisohn, who used their talent and wealth to build up the settlement's activities in drama and dance. In 1914 they established the Neighborhood Playhouse, which became the most impressive and renowned artistic contribution of the American settlement movement.[65] To be sure, few other houses approached the proficiency, or publicity, achieved by these two groups; in fact the Neighborhood Playhouse used professional lead actors, designers, and directors. But by 1910 many of the settlements listed "dramatics" among their regular activities.[66]

The growth of the performing arts in settlement programs reflects the settlement workers' leadership in tackling the problems of urban youth through new concepts of education. At the same time, the arts programs grew naturally out of the settlements' previous philosophy and practice. The evolving role of art in the settlements illustrated the application of Victorian values to perceived modern social needs that shaped and characterized the social thought of the Progressive Era. From the beginning, the English and American settlements had stood on the radical platform that art belonged to all the people. The Ruskinian tradition asserted that art had moral significance, a stance that provided a yardstick for measuring the value of a work of art and lodged art firmly in a social framework.[67] The settlement workers offered the riches of culture to the poor as their unclaimed birthright. At the same time, they believed that under the gentle tutelage of art, the poor might find the moral energy to begin to improve their own lives—like the family of the little music-school pupil.

The locus of change in the settlement arts programs after 1900 was not philosophy, but emphasis and process. The introduction of drama and dance—folk and formal as well as social—and the expansion of music education were conceived as integral to the "education for life" that the settlement workers advocated.[68] These programs emphasized the value of experience and interaction in healthy individual development as well as trying to act as substitutes for the "arts" of the city street. But they also rested firmly in the philosophical tradition of art in the settlement as a vehicle of moral education, promoting the growth of individual character through social interaction, and as an effort to make culture truly democratic not by conceding dominion over taste and form to the vulgar majority, but by extending to everyone access to the "best which has been thought and known in the world."

As the settlement workers put their ideals of art into practice, they stumbled once again into a contradiction that became an open debate by the 1920s. In offering their urban neighbors "the best that there is in the whole world," in Wald's unconscious paraphrase of Arnold, they eventually had to confront the consequences of toppling one kind of "aristocracy" in favor of another. Arts programs designed for social purposes would not necessarily serve the needs of the minority of truly gifted pupils they attracted, and vice versa. In the case of music this dilemma was especially sharp. By 1910 there was a handful of special "music school settlements" concentrated in Boston and New York. Though not professional schools, they catered to the talented amateur ready for the discipline of good training. They professed the same social and educational goals as the regular settlements, striving to cultivate character and enrich neighborhood life through the medium of musical appreciation and performance.[69] But they also intended to serve as magnets for the gifted who would otherwise receive no training; to "save and develop the talent of working-class children," in the words of Boston's South End Music School.[70] These twin aims, the social and the artistic, were not necessarily compatible. Not surprisingly, settlements in areas where music schools were strong, notably New York, gradually attenuated their own musical activities. Even where "social music" was maintained, it was clearly seen as a "second," or inferior, level of art.[71] The performing arts were refractory to "democratization"; they stubbornly imposed their own hierarchy. In sponsoring these music schools, the settlers went beyond their gift of vicarious middle-class status through cultivated taste to offer their neighbors that fundamental bourgeois ideal: the "career open to talent."

This bifurcation of the settlements' arts programs symbolized one of the most compelling issues of self-definition that the settlers faced. If they actively encouraged social mobility, they would drive deeper the wedges between parents and children and abet the fragmentation of community endemic to the American city. Yet honoring the status quo by fostering family and neighborhood cohesiveness could constrict the horizons of the young people whose lives they touched. In the end, the settlers followed the only practical course; they compromised.

Robert Woods habitually mourned the "waste of ability and genius" common in American industrial society, and he helped popularize Felix Adler's evocative description of settlements as "talent-saving stations."[72] Yet about 1900 he began to argue that ideally the settlement did not address the needs of the "submerged grades" of the habitually dependent or the "aristocracy of labor" that was moving up and out, but rather the vast in-between: the "working class proper." He held that these independent, capable, yet unambitious people were essentially "collectivists" and that the settlement's true mission lay in fostering "every helpful form of association," from neighborhood improvement groups to labor unions, that would strengthen their tendencies toward cooperation and mutual tolerance.[73]

Woods's anatomization of a naturally stratified subpopulation seems a far cry from the heady early vision of a class-free society, and his characterization of the "working class proper" as peculiarly fit for exercises in solidarity represents a constricted application of the rallying ideal of universal brotherhood. The image of the settlement as a "talent-saving station," a rescue mission for misplaced and overlooked human resources, suggests the form of accommodation with prevailing social dynamics that the settlements chose. For the handful with exceptional gifts, the settlement workers would create the conditions to actualize the American promise of "equal opportunity." To the vast unremarkable majority, they would offer the skills and amenities that would allow an intelligent adjustment to the realistic boundaries of their lives.

Nowhere was this tacit acquiescence in a truncated scale of opportunity for working-class youth more apparent than in the settlers' approach to school reform. John Dewey's influence on the settlers' educational thought is once again palpable here. At the time of his greatest intimacy with Jane Addams and the other Hull-House residents, after his arrival in Chicago in 1894, Dewey reflected in a private letter, "The school is the one form of social life which is abstracted and under control—which is directly experimental."[74] The settlers' belief in public provision of cultural and social amenities predisposed them to concur in Dewey's assessment of the school as a positive instrument of social engineering. They joined critics of the archaic narrowness of formal education, its separation of brain and hand, and its irrelevance to the lives of urban children. They called for the transfer to public schools of settlement-initiated activities in recreation, the arts, manual training, and evening education for adults. In Boston and New York particularly, they helped to achieve in the decade after 1900 a dramatic expansion in the programs and concerns of the schools. "Not a child shall be lost seems to be the motto," wrote two Boston settlers enthusiastically.[75]

Jane Addams's views on educational reform epitomized many of the settlers' highest ideals. Addams hoped that the Hull-House Labor Museum would serve as a model for reconceptualizing public education. She saw Dewey's theories of task-oriented education as the foundation of a universally relevant "industrial education." All children, especially those destined for manual labor, should understand the history and processes of industrial production so that their mental world was not restricted to their own fragment of the manufacturing process.[76] With Kelley and Woods, she called for the extension of compulsory education through the "two wasted years"—the ages of fourteen to sixteen— so that instead of flitting from job to job in a futile search for novelty and interest in dead-end occupations, young people might receive realistic preparation for fulfilling economic lives.[77] "Education alone," she asserted in *The Spirit of Youth,* "has the power of organizing a child's activities with some reference to the life he will later lead."[78]

After 1900, the settlement leaders found allies in the quest for school reform among partisans of the "manual training" movement, who had subtly but significantly different goals and motives. Their combined lobbying contributed to curricular changes that represented at best an unimaginative version of the "industrial education" Addams had envisioned. In the 1870s the earliest spokesman for manual training, Calvin Woodward, had used terms congenial to the settlement leaders two decades later; universal manual training, integrated with traditional studies, would "elevate, . . . dignify, . . . liberalize, all the essential elements of society."[79] Woodward's ideas gained support through the 1880s, chiefly from businessmen who were primarily concerned to challenge the unions' power over the work force in a period of high immigration and increased demand for unskilled and semiskilled labor.[80] Manual training, centered in the public schools, promised to become the handmaiden, so to speak, of English and civics lessons in the efficient adjustment of first- or second-generation immigrant children to their new environment and their future in the American economy.[81]

In November 1906 several manual training advocates formed a new organization, the National Society for the Promotion of Industrial Education. Seeking a coalition of disparate interests behind an unobjectionable platform, the organizers invited several social workers, including Robert Woods and Jane Addams, to participate in the first convention.[82] Speakers used rhetoric that portrayed their various goals as congruent. As the final speaker, Jane Addams reminded the enthusiastic assembly that "science is only part of life"—that it was time to divert their attention from the speed of the machine to the welfare of the worker. Addams would not give up her own conception of industrial education: that workers with a sense of the place of their own labor in the structure and history of the industry would do better work more happily. "It is now up to us," she pleaded, "to see what we may do toward the application of the art of life to industrial education."[83]

As they echoed Addams, the most astute of the settlement workers at least partly understood the social implications of vocational education. One of the good consciences of the settlement movement, John Dewey, came to oppose vocational training on two related grounds: as a damaging limitation on the child's educational development, and "an instrument in accomplishing the feudal dogma of social predestination."[84] Robert Woods, increasingly the settlement spokesman for a realistic acceptance of class differences, disagreed, criticizing the "weirdly Utopian" notion that vocational education violated "American principles of social equality" by fixing a child's career too early and preempting upward mobility. A well-planned system of industrial education would actually extend opportunities by promoting children "from school to school" until their natural talents were fully tapped. Like Kelley and Hunter, Woods reasoned that the child's interests and the national good were interdependent. To him, "true social equality" involved matching each child's inherent abilities with an appropriate occupation, thus "making available the whole of that prime essential wealth of the nation which lies in the nascent capacities of the new generation."[85]

The settlements' increasing intervention in the lives of the young people they dealt with had found a justification. Envisioning the future of vocational education, Woods spoke without apology of settlement leaders and social workers as "taking to some extent the place of the responsible parent to boys and girls of the less resourceful classes."[86] In 1910 the administrators of Boston's North Bennet Street Industrial School stated starkly that "the ideal of personal culture has been largely modified or replaced by that of efficiency. . . . the mere fact that a child possesses a capacity is no reason that the school should aim to develop it. On the contrary, many capacities, since they bear no relation to social life as at present constituted, may well be let alone." Though few settlement workers would have concurred in the suggestion that "personal culture" was outmoded either as an individual desideratum or as a social good, they increasingly endorsed the proposition that "a science of education rests on the basis of social and economic progress and demands."[87] The settlement folk had elaborated their philosophy on the faith that in the ideal society, private and public interests were identical. Their method of approaching this goal—friendly interaction with the residents of poor urban neighborhoods—embodied their belief that social progress should be cooperative and consensual. Yet their choice of texts—the writings of sociologists, economists, historians, and philosophers—betrayed their corresponding conviction that the determination of what constituted the social good might best be made by experts: individuals specially prepared to undertake informed speculation on the course of public life.

For almost two decades the settlements had survived the contradictions inherent in their founding philosophy, but by 1910 latent strains had emerged. The settlement folk did not want to abandon their advocacy of democratic self-determination, but they could not accept the distressing results of political and social laissez-faire. They moved toward an ever firmer belief in the necessity of benign intervention in the public and even private lives of their neighbors and, by extension, the collective membership of what Woods called the "less resourceful classes."

7
Settlement Work and Social Work

From the beginning of their movement the settlement leaders had shared ideas and experiences through correspondence and face to face. The first *Bibliography of Settlements,* listing both American and English settlement houses, was compiled by the College Settlements Association in 1893 and regularly updated throughout the first decade.[1] Also in 1893 the settlers held their first major conference in Chicago in conjunction with the World's Fair. They met in that forum to underline their concern with national and international social issues as well as to publicize the distinctive aspects of the settlement philosophy—part of their early effort, as Woods put it, to "keep the Settlements from being merely part of the drudging machinery of charity."[2]

The settlement workers held national conferences sporadically over the next fifteen years to discuss common concerns and revivify the "settlement spirit" through mutual inspiration.[3] As in their own neighborhoods, the settlers' eagerness to project a novel corporate image did not prevent them from reaching out to kindred organizations. Settlement workers began attending meetings of the National Conference of Charities and Corrections in the early 1890s. At the NCCC's national convention in 1896, a special session explored "Social Settlements and the Labor Question." The speakers, including Julia Lathrop, James Reynolds of the University Settlement, and Charles S. Loch of London's COS, construed the topic broadly enough to allow for a wide-ranging exposition and defense of settlement work in its first American phase.[4] There were several more discussions of the settlement movement in following years; more commonly, settlement leaders delivered papers on extramural topics such as public education, child labor, and organized charity.[5] In 1909 the members of the NCCC tacitly acknowledged the significance of the settlements in the field of social work by electing Jane Addams their president.[6]

The settlement workers' visibility in philanthropy and social welfare was partly due to their collective genius at self-promotion, as well as their individual talents and tenacity. More important to their acceptance, though, was the changed philosophical climate in which they worked after 1900. Between 1900 and 1910, the most forceful and articulate leaders in social work came to accept the idea that poor environment, not defective character, generated poverty, and therefore that a vital part of their own mission was to uncover and strike at the social, economic, and physical causes of poverty.[7] Nowhere was this shift in emphasis more dramatic than in the New York Charity Organization Society.

In the late 1890s the New York COS acquired a handful of talented young workers who were able to lead the society in new directions precisely because they did not mount a direct assault on the prevailing philosophy of charity organization but worked from within to expand the boundaries of philanthropy. Like Josephine Shaw Lowell, the revered COS founder who turned to active labor support in the 1890s, these younger leaders did not initially believe that charity organization was incompatible with social action that addressed environmental causes of poverty.[8] With the crucial support of Robert W. De Forest, president of the society, these activists happily used the staid COS as a platform for their ventures. While Lawrence Veiller enlisted the cooperation of settlement workers and other social workers with his Tenement House Committee, the young general secretary, Edward T. Devine, obtained the COS's support for a campaign against tuberculosis that tapped the energy and expertise of the Henry Street nurses and other New York settlement workers.[9]

In 1897, a year after being hired as secretary, Devine was asked to edit a new journal for the society. Named *Charities,* it was to stand beside the older *Charities Review* as a more lively and accessible bulletin of news and opinion in the philanthropic world. Devine's personality largely ensured the success of the journal in its various incarnations over the next decades. Raised on an Iowa farm, Devine attended Cornell College in Iowa and then worked as a teacher and principal in the public schools. His life was changed by a chance encounter with a visiting teacher from a nearby school district, Simon Patten. Patten had received his doctorate in economics at Yale, but family pressures and a mysterious impairment of vision deflected him from a university career. While he worked with Richard Ely and others to found the American Economic Association in 1885, Patten supported himself by teaching school.[10] When he met Devine, Patten had just been appointed professor of political economy at the University of Pennsylvania.

Devine was fired by his talk with Patten about economics; a year later he borrowed some money and followed Patten to Pennsylvania, then went to Germany for graduate study. Back in Philadelphia, he supported his studies by working for the American Society for the Extension of University Teaching. At an economics conference in 1896 he met Franklin H. Giddings, a Columbia sociologist and a member of the central council of the New York COS. Giddings subsequently recommended the young Pennsylvania Ph.D. for the position of secretary to the COS.[11]

During its first six or seven years, *Charities* attracted a steady readership of social workers. In 1901 the *Charities Review* merged with *Charities;* two years later Paul U. Kellogg, a twenty-three-year-old newspaperman from Michigan, joined the staff as assistant editor, followed by his brother Arthur. The Kellogg brothers, particularly Paul, seem to have brought a philosophical boldness and cogency to *Charities* that reinforced Devine's efforts to create an innovative national publication.[12]

In 1905 a new publication committee presided over a merger with Graham Taylor's the *Commons.* Since 1896 the Chicago journal had served as the national organ of the settlement movement, featuring articles on large topics by big-name contributors such as Henry C. Adams, Charles H. Cooley, Richard Ely, John Dewey, Washington Gladden, Jane Addams, and Henry Demarest Lloyd.[13] The merging journals also absorbed Lee K. Frankel's *Jewish Charity.* Remarkably, their symbiotic philosophical relationship succeeded from the start, despite the reservations of the Boston philanthropist Joseph Lee, who argued to Paul Kellogg against taking on the *Commons,* "because that stands for Trade Unions and Settlements (don't it?) and because I do not think that they 'are the people.' I think their idea of democracy is the European idea that it consists in putting the under dog on top; whereas of the 2 dogs, if one is to be on top, I imagine the one who is used to it will be the best."[14] Lee had misread the settlements' political philosophy and missed the new course *Charities* had begun to chart under Devine and the Kelloggs; the historical antagonism between the two movements was rapidly fading.

In 1905 Devine was appointed to the Schiff Professorship of Social Economy at Columbia, newly endowed by Henry Street's patron Jacob Schiff. In his inaugural lecture, Devine argued in an earlier tradition that academic social scientists had a duty to create in their students an "enthusiasm for social service," with an emphasis on promoting human efficiency by battling the conditions that perpetuated ill health and ignorance.[15] His election to the presidency of the National Conference of Charities and Corrections the next year suggests that the majority of the members endorsed Devine's new emphasis on social reform as a main concern of welfare work. In his presidential address, he stridently asserted that the new priority in philanthropic work must be a full-scale attack on the causes of dependence and debility, "which are beyond the control of the individuals . . . whom they too often destroy."[16] Devine did not condemn the economic system; instead he took moral high ground by indicting greedy malefactors for the ills of child labor, prostitution, gambling, inadequate wages, and poor housing. Legislation and regulation offered the best means to check the guilty rich. He accused his colleagues in organized charity of having focused on "personal weaknesses and accidents" to the neglect of "the environmental causes of distress."[17]

Charities and the Commons continued the investigative journalism that *Charities* had begun before the merger.[18] The most remarkable of these investigations was the Pittsburgh Survey of 1907–09, funded by the new Russell Sage Foundation.[19] The establishment of the Sage Foundation "for the improvement of living and working conditions" had elicited rapturous enthusiasm from social workers, educators, and reformers. Robert W. De Forest and other consultants had helped Sage's widow, Margaret Olivia Slocum Sage, to earmark the $10 million endowment for projects that would contribute to long-term social amelioration, with emphasis on research and education. The foundation's agreement to fund the Pittsburgh Survey suggested that the trustees concurred with what Devine called the "new view" of philanthropy.[20]

"We want to make the town real—to itself," wrote Paul Kellogg. The survey directors aimed to occupy some stretch of analytical ground between the census and yellow journalism.[21] Theirs would be the most thorough investigation of a single city since Booth's *Life and Labour,* but in their attempt to be both exhaustive and evocative, to tabulate statistics and describe the texture of life in the steel city, the researchers could look to recent precedents from the settlement workers' investigations to Lincoln Steffens's and Ida Tarbell's muckraking exposés of urban politics and Standard Oil.[22] The Pittsburgh Survey, first published in three special issues of *Charities and the Commons* and subsequently in six volumes, represented the Progressive Era's lushest flowering of the belief that knowledge and publicity were the first steps to reform.[23]

The large team of researchers and advisers included a number of settlement workers. Robert Woods, a Pittsburgh native, and Florence Kelley joined the advisory committee. William H. Matthews opened Pittsburgh's Kingsley House to the visiting researchers.[24] Crystal

Eastman, who investigated industrial accidents for the survey, met Mary Simkhovitch and Paul Kellogg while she was studying law at Columbia, and she lived in Greenwich House for a while before taking on her work in Pittsburgh.[25]

In April 1909, in symbolic acknowledgment of the significance of the Pittsburgh Survey, *Charities and the Commons* was renamed the *Survey.* As the editors tactfully explained, "The old name, to many of us as familiar and welcome as the face of a friend, proved a stumbling-block to new readers."[26] In 1912 the *Survey* cut its remaining ties to the New York COS and reincorporated independently. Devine and the Kellogg brothers retained editorial control, and Robert W. De Forest accepted the presidency of the new Survey Associates.[27]

Coincident with the Pittsburgh Survey, Edward Devine mounted a campaign to introduce his readers to a new social theory. In 1905 he had helped appoint his mentor, Simon Patten, to the new Kennedy Lectureship at the New York School of Social Work. In 1907 Patten published those lectures as *The New Basis of Civilization.* From 1907 through 1909, *Charities and the Commons* carried excerpts from Patten's book and responsive editorials, reviews, and letters.[28]

For almost twenty years, Patten had been exploring the implications of his belief that industrialization had created a potential "age of abundance." Old social assumptions predicated on chronic scarcity must be jettisoned. Working from a utilitarian ethic promoting "the greatest good of the greatest number," Patten argued that an age of material abundance would allow a redistribution of wealth sufficient to eradicate poverty by lifting the poor to a higher plane of existence. His ideas carried tremendous implications for the philosophy and practice of philanthropy. Since environmental ills were the main barrier to social progress, the "service altruism" that characterized nineteenth-century social welfare thought—and had sprung initially from a *rejection* of utilitarianism—should be transformed into an "income altruism" that would address the problems of poverty through the "distribution and rapid circulation of the social surplus."[29]

The nub of Patten's argument for environmental remedies for poverty, and his attack on "service altruism," was his theory of character formation. He sketched a democratic physics of character distribution: "The weak latently possess the powers that the strong display; and the sudden transformation of the weak into the strong, which we see daily, reveals the inherent qualities of human nature."[30] In an age of abundance, character was formed not through sacrifice and hardship, which

sapped vital energies, but through "regeneration" fostered by opportunities that brought out latent powers. Character change could result
simply from the individual's positive interaction with the economy;
because neatness and cleanliness ensure his success in a free labor
market, the young man gradually incorporates these traits into his character. "As time passes, the habits formed for purely selfish, economic
needs become new motives in the improving type of man."[31]

Patten's belief in the beneficent social effects of abundance extended
to his views of recreation. He claimed controversially that popular
amusements, even of the more "vulgar" kind, could offer a twofold
enrichment of working people's lives. The worker who found pleasure
and relaxation in theaters or amusement parks would be more inclined
to punctuality and steadiness in order to earn the money for his
recreation.[32] Further, like Jane Addams, Patten believed in the educational value of vicarious experience, and he argued that popular theater
appealed to the experience and imagination of its audience more effectively than the uplifting programs of genteel philanthropists: "The
renewed imagining of hate, love, terror, curiosity, danger, daring, and
fury—all the elemental stuff—concentrates the thoughts and momen-
tarily rouses mental forces to a keener effectiveness than any scheme of
night schools has yet discovered."[33] In time, Patten suggested, these
"primitive" amusements would yield to higher pleasures, but not by
coercion or repression. "Vice must first be fought by welfare, not by
restraint. . . . Men must enjoy, and emphasis should be laid again upon
amusement so extended and thorough that primitive people may be
incorporated by its manifold activities into the industrial world."[34]

Patten's concept of "social control," a term he borrowed from his
fellow economist E. A. Ross, reflected the strange combination of natural
evolution and purposeful policy he advocated. "Social control" to Patten
was the sifting out of social from unsocial character traits that produced
the consensual beliefs and values most conducive to social survival.[35] In
a period of scarcity or widespread threats to life, a "restrictive" social
control would prevail: "ideals and institutions lapse into barren formu-
lae, traditional rule, and defiant superstitions."[36] In contrast, a "surplus"
in material goods and thus in social and moral energy created the
potential for a new kind of social control, based on values generated by
the moral and intellectual power freed by economic security. The "attractive" social control possible in an age of abundance would substitute
positive social rewards for the "crude traditions and punishments of our
ancestors."[37] This was not an automatic process. "Income will change

conditions, but opinions yield only to the public service of devoted and self-sacrificing men." Patten had discarded "service altruism" in philanthropy, but he reinstated it as a motive for individuals to dedicate their intellect to the welfare of the whole society.[38]

Patten's ideas fed into the struggle to redefine the concerns of social work. He had been interested in these issues at least since the early 1890s, when he had encouraged his students, among them Devine, to pursue careers in philanthropy.[39] In the final chapter of *The New Basis of Civilization,* he offered "A Programme of Social Work." Reiterating his environmentalist beliefs, Patten challenged social workers to examine their personal motives. Those more concerned with the creation of "new and higher virtues" than with the "elevation" of humanity should give up social work per se and devote their intellect to cultural progress. Social workers should give up individual character molding and concentrate on environmental reform in order to clear the way for the "regeneration" that must begin with widespread access to material plenitude.[40]

Patten's ideas challenged the philosophy of the settlement movement as well as more traditional forms of philanthropy. A debate began in *Charities and the Commons* that ranged Patten against such able advocates of the status quo as Mary Richmond and the Boston charity organizer Zilpha Smith. Patten argued that the "good neighbor" model of charity work relied on a flawed analogy; true "neighborliness" was possible only between members of the same social, religious, or national group, where it fostered an ever-widening group solidarity. The "good citizen," bound to his society chiefly by economic ties, was a superior conceptual model for the philanthropist. The "good citizen" would serve his own interests by promoting efficiency of production and distribution in order to raise the living standards of all other citizens. Patten loosed a volley at charity organizers: "Mere goodness must be replaced by efficiency and the trained paid agent must replace the voluntary visitor who satisfies her curiosity at the expense of those she meets, and in the end loses her faith in humanity or turns socialist."[41]

Most of the settlement leaders had long supported the position that improved conditions were necessary to eradicate poverty. Patten praised what he perceived as the healthy evolution of the settlement philosophy. From pushing brooms through "reeking" gutters, hoping to inspire local housewives to do likewise, the settlement residents had graduated to seeking structural change: garbage collection and street paving underwritten by the city.[42] Patten also praised the development that had most worried the settlement founders: the settlement's evolution from a simple home among homes to an institution sponsoring formal social activities. This jibed with his conviction that only members of the same ethnic or religious group could genuinely share "neighborly" interests. But his suggestion that settlement workers let go of their earlier self-image as simply neighbors among neighbors came at a time of self-conscious vulnerability among settlement leaders. To be sure, many settlement workers had carved themselves areas of expertise along the lines Patten charted: housing, public health, labor policy, and municipal government. But what was to be the self-definition of those who devoted most of their energies to settlement work?

The settlement workers' continuing efforts to define their role in the world of social service dovetailed with the elevation of social work to a profession at the turn of the century, largely through the establishment of formal training for social workers.[43] By 1900, philanthropists and social workers, including settlement leaders, agreed that social workers should be trained, but predictably they differed over the nature of that training. Mary Richmond of the COS, one of the most strenuous proponents of a "training school for applied philanthropy," was wary of affiliating such a school with a university, for fear that the student would neglect "practical" in favor of "theoretical" education.[44] In contrast, most of the settlement workers remained true to their own tradition of close relations with the universities. They still believed in a vital relation between knowledge and life—more specifically, between social science and social life. Further, they continued to draw their workers from the colleges and universities, and they depended on the recruiting efforts of sympathetic professors, chaplains, and alumni organizations.[45] Robert Woods promoted social work to college graduates by portraying it as a kind of "unofficial statesmanship," patriotic service long familiar in England but hitherto scorned in America. The settlements offered professionals of all types the opportunity to apply their expertise to the broader welfare.[46]

A few settlements, including South End House, had regularly awarded fellowships to students interested in studying particular aspects of neighborhood life. The fellowships helped realize Woods's ideal of the settlements as "laboratories of social science" and served as recruitment tools.[47] But the settlements, like the charity organization societies, needed competent workers for their internal programs. They were able to benefit from close cooperation with the new schools of social work established at the turn of the century.

The New York Charity Organization Society began sponsoring a summer school in philanthropy in 1898. Half the enrollment of the first three sessions of the summer school was drawn from the universities; the admission requirements included a college degree or at least one year's experience in "philanthropic work."[48] The course covered the traditional concerns of organized charity: the treatment of needy families in their homes, the care of destitute, neglected, and delinquent children, medical charities, and the institutional care of adults, as well as neighborhood improvement, which included settlement work. Lectures by visiting specialists were supplemented by visits to local institutions. In 1903 the school's new two-year course included a recommended three-month residence in one of the settlements. This helped establish a stable reciprocal relationship, with the settlements contributing a small but steady percentage of students in the first few years.[49]

The Boston School for Social Workers was founded in 1904 under the direction of the longtime charity organizers Jeffrey R. Brackett and Zilpha D. Smith. Unlike its New York predecessor, the Boston school immediately sought university affiliation; Harvard and Simmons College agreed to a joint sponsorship. While the Boston school likewise taught the techniques of casework, the curriculum also focused on "improvement of general conditions of living" and brought in such speakers as Florence Kelley and Mary McDowell, headworker of the University Settlement in Chicago. Robert Woods served on the board, and the course sent many of its students into the Boston settlements for experience.[50]

The Chicago Institute of Social Science and Arts, directed by Graham Taylor, opened in 1903 under the auspices of the University of Chicago's Extension Division. For its first three years the institute followed the New York school in offering lectures by social service experts and visits to representative institutions.[51] It became clear after President William Rainey Harper's death in 1906 that he had been supporting the school from his private funds, and the Chicago Commons trustees agreed to rescue it from its uncertain fate with the university. In 1908 the rechristened Chicago School of Civics and Philanthropy received a grant from the Russell Sage Foundation to create a department of investigation and research.[52] The department, first headed by Julia Lathrop, was soon taken over by Sophonisba P. Breckinridge, a lawyer, Ph.D. in political science, and specialist in household administration at the University of Chicago. As her assistant Breckinridge chose Edith Abbott, another Chicago Ph.D. and a disciple of Sidney and Beatrice Webb. From 1908 to

1920 Edith Abbott and her sister Grace, a social activist and immigration expert, lived at Hull-House. While Taylor presided over the Chicago school, Breckinridge and Abbott built up its reputation. Increasingly frustrated by Taylor's leadership, the two women decided that training in social welfare administration and research had to become fully professional in scope and rigor. In 1920 they persuaded the University of Chicago to annex the Chicago school as a new Graduate School of Social Service Administration.[53]

The settlement leaders allied themselves with the new social work schools largely because investigation and cooperation were watchwords of the original settlement approach. The settlement workers' ambivalence toward organized charity had never halted communication between the two movements. As their neighbors' advocates, the settlers had learned how important it was to know about local medical, mental health, and penal institutions. Any settlement resident could benefit from understanding the methods of charities and welfare institutions taught by the social work schools. As these agencies began to accept the ideas underlying the "new philanthropy," particularly the importance of reckoning with the individual's environment, settlement workers would have found their practices increasingly congenial.

The settlements' burgeoning programs provided another motive for cooperating with the social work schools. Departments of recreation, arts, group work, and immigrant aid needed workers with training and experience. By 1900 the settlements were being further absorbed into the complex world of social work by the fluid movement of workers from one kind of social service to another. The "Employment Exchange" published by *Charities* and its successors sketches the stories of these new migrant professionals: "Young woman, graduate of an eastern college, wishes to enter settlement work at nominal salary while she is earning her experience. Has had some work as investigator for a charity organization society." "Settlement worker and teacher of manual and domestic art and music, wishes position as headworker in a settlement. Ten years' experience in New York City." "Canadian woman of experience in hospital and settlement positions, is free to take position as housekeeper and club-worker in a settlement." "Woman who has had considerable experience in settlement work would like employment as almoner, or as pastor's assistant." "Young man who has had experience both as probation officer and as head-worker in a settlement, wishes position which will enable him to study the social problems of a small city."[54] Headworkers' files began to fill with letters of inquiry from a heterogeneous array of candidates for specific jobs within the settlement.[55] Some of the applicants were clearly impressed by what they had heard about the grittier aspects of settlement life. One prospective resident of New York's University Settlement wrote to the headworker that he was "studying up a little about tenements, plumbing, etc., so as not to be entirely ignorant when I enter."[56] There was a particularly heavy traffic in summer workers, often students at the social work schools eager to get room, board, and experience while attending courses. Both parties benefited from these arrangements; while the regular workers took their vacations or staffed the settlements' summer camps, summer recreation programs at the settlements could continue.

Not all settlement leaders were comfortable with this marriage of convenience to professional social work. Constant reassessment of its own methods and goals characterized the settlement movement, and the period of the settlements' greatest growth, from 1900 to the First World War, was studded with thoughtful evaluations of the settlements' proper stance toward the revolution in social work.

In 1903 Vida Scudder warned Boston settlement workers against losing "the finer and rarer quality which characterized the first phases of the movement."[57] Nine years later Scudder told fellow directors of Denison House that Helena Dudley's departure marked the end of the "family aspect" of the settlement, which had become "a large institution demanding expert workers in all its departments, and more adequate salaries."[58] Not without regret, Scudder had capitulated to Simon Patten's vision of the settlement as institution.

Other settlement leaders were less resigned to inevitable change. Graham Taylor maintained that the best settlements still elevated the "personal" over the "institutional" and rewarded initiative and "personal spontaneity."[59] Gaylord White, headworker of the Union Settlement of New York, believed that the settlement still offered an alternative to the church and special agencies as a center of intimate knowledge of a neighborhood. "When the minister calls unexpectedly, the chances are that the mother of the family will hastily throw her apron over the can of beer that stands on the table; when the settlement resident calls the chances are that he will be cordially invited to share the contents of the can." While many settlements had capitulated to the "necessary evil" of growth, White also saw "a tendency to revert to the simplicity of the early days of the movement," a trend that foreshadowed "permanency for the method."[60]

Mary Simkhovitch, the head successively of the Friendly Aid House and Greenwich House in New York City and one of the rising settlement spokesmen after 1900, developed an evolutionary theory of the settlement as institution. The earliest settlers could not properly act before "soaking in . . . impressions" in their neighborhoods. Next came "interpretation": communicating what they had found to the broader public. Finally they could act to help their neighbors. To change settlement organization and methods in response to perceived local needs was *mandated* by settlement ideology. The growing clubs and classes called for "expert supervision and good management," money, and facilities. These developments were appropriate as long as the settlement continued to act from genuine knowledge of the needs and desires of its neighborhood.[61] Simkhovitch anticipated the gradual deinstitutionalization of the settlement as public agencies took over certain of its activities. The settlement would continue to be a "nursery" for social experiments and new groups that needed a "home." "This nurture of budding neighborhood life coming to group consciousness will perhaps be the last sign of institutional life in the settlements."[62]

By invoking the traditional role of the settlements as experiment stations, Simkhovitch suggested that their current hypertrophy was only part of a long, natural, and inevitable cycle. Following Addams's lead, she adopted the term "pragmatism" to describe the settlement philosophy: "The settlement is by its very nature suspicious of theory and on guard against any ready-to-wear views of life." Simkhovitch advocated reverting to the "old-fashioned" idea of the settlement as "a family, whose task is the task of all families, to help bring about in the community . . . a larger conception of neighborliness." She invoked Charles H. Cooley's recent work on the social primacy of "neighborhood" in *Social Organization* to argue for the lasting relevance of the original settlement philosophy. Her association of family life with a pragmatic philosophy of social interaction was one way to establish continuity in the history of the settlements. By appealing to pragmatism she could justify change while tying past values to evolving realities.[63]

Insisting on the settlements' continuing role in the urban neighborhoods allowed the settlers to "domesticate" recent social work theories by using them to evaluate the settlement's performance in terms of its own tradition. In social work as in industrial production, "efficiency" had become the great but ill-defined desideratum.[64] Although the word has a cold ring in connection with human welfare work, an essentially humanitarian logic led the nascent social work profession to adopt the efficiency ideal. To be sure, a form of efficiency was embedded in the now-discredited ethos of the early charity organization movement: to prevent the duplication of material aid by zealously tracking each family's applications for charity. But subsequent philanthropists and reformers had reconceived the concept of "waste" to connote the waste of human resources—health, talents, character—by an impersonally malevolent economic system. "Efficiency" in social work would conserve human resources by attacking their enemies. Mary Richmond argued that in her concept of "social diagnosis," "efficiency" did not mean rigidity but rather referred to accountability in social work.[65] The settlement workers could hardly quarrel with such an ideal. As Gaylord White conceded, "In this age of 'efficiency tests,' . . . the settlement cannot hope to escape . . . the necessity of rendering an account."[66] Mary Simkhovitch offered guidelines for settlement efficiency: knowledge of the district and of "all sorts" of people, cooperation with other agencies and local groups, and "executive capacity," demonstrated by a neat annual balance sheet and a cordial greeting to callers.[67]

Such "standards" of efficiency for settlement work, even though derived from the self-defined role of the settlements, carried important implications for the future of the settlement worker. Simkhovitch acknowledged that "most of all we need the trained, devoted, highly-equipped persons on whom the success of . . . the settlement ultimately rests." The richest source of workers was still the universities, and the "most ardent spirits" must be deflected from their attraction to the "more radical movements" into the settlements, through better publicity.[68] But the settlements' coming-of-age entailed new and subtly different expectations of these recruits. To be truly useful, untrained residents should arrive willing to make a commitment to acquire experience and then stay to use it. The changing needs of the settlements conspired with their gradual absorption into the social work network to make settlement residence increasingly a career rather than a short-term plunge into vital experience for young people headed toward other careers or marriage.

Jane Addams continued to plead for a holistic and inclusive vision of social work. While students of economics and sociology were clearly needed in the reconstruction of urban industrial life, so was the humanist: "To any young person who wishes to go into the social [field] . . . , I would say bring with you all that you can that softens life, all the poesy, all the sympathetic interpretation. You will need it all; and every scrap of history and language that you know, all of that which has made your own life rich, will be fairly torn off your back as you pass through those crowded city quarters."[69] Thus Addams reaffirmed the Victorian faith in culture as a social solvent, in the changed context of early twentieth-century social thought and social service. By her lights the settlement would flourish as long as it remained a center of shared experience, as long as "life itself" was its currency of exchange and reason for existence. Settlement workers must measure themselves by the same standard. Because the settlement was a process rather than a set of goals, settlement residents should bring not just a skill but their whole personality: education, beliefs, experience.

As with Addams's pronouncements on other settlement-related issues—industrial education, immigrants, urban youth—few settlers would have disagreed with her stance on the necessary attributes of the settlement worker. Settlement leaders acknowledged that the traits they valued most in their workers were the intangible qualities of personality that made them effective in dealing with the neighbors. But they also almost uniformly stressed the desirability of special training. "The main things in regard to a successful social worker as I see them are matters of temper[a]ment, character, etc. and training is really a secondary matter," wrote John Elliott to Lillian Wald in 1911; but after general education he recommended further training in kindergarten teaching, nursing, recreation, art, or domestic science, and he wanted all his workers to have organizational skills.[70] Another settlement leader stated that what she looked for in a children's worker were "personal qualifications, such as love of children, sympathy, insight and a sense of humor," but she also advocated a college education ("on account of the breadth of outlook and independence of thought"), kindergarten training, and a "knowledge of and real interest in social problems" gained from experience or from a school of social work.[71] A third headworker looked for honesty of purpose, self-control, and high ideals, as well as specific training and a college degree of the "highest standard."[72]

These discussions of the best preparation for settlement work took place in the context not only of the rapid professionalization of social work but also of the elaboration of intersettlement organization. The Chicago settlements were the first to unite in a common organization, in 1894. Boston settlement workers formed the South End Social Union, with Woods as its driving force, in 1899 and the Boston Social Union in 1908. The New York Association of Neighborhood Workers organized in 1900.[73] These city federations seem to have been sparked by the desire to present a united front on public issues and legislative initiatives. Woods carefully insisted in 1906 that the settlement's primary affiliation was still with its own neighborhood: "It is hardly conceivable that any settlement or group of settlements should be established to head toward some large scheme for the city as a whole before patiently going through the stage during which a full knowledge of local conditions is gained and the social initiative of local people to some extent elicited."[74] From the beginning the federations served more parochial settlement purposes. The South End Social Union borrowed a COS tactic in setting up a registration system to ensure that no individual claimed membership in more than one house; this system eventually helped migrants to new neighborhoods transfer their membership to the closest settlement. Settlements also compared notes on club work, programs in hygiene and sanitation, and local visiting. It became convenient and economical to "share" experts in some fields like the arts and recreation. Finally, intersettlement activities such as athletic meets and dances were organized.[75]

In 1911 the settlers took the next step. At the National Conference of Charities and Corrections convention in 1910, during Jane Addams's presidency, a call went out to settlement workers to convene in Saint Louis in May. The meeting appointed a committee of ten to lay plans for the first meeting of a National Federation of Settlements, held in Boston in 1911. The new NFS proposed to reinforce federated settlement action in individual cities, enhance cooperation with other forms of social work, and develop a uniform policy toward common settlement problems. The first committee, chaired by John Elliott, was charged to consider "the means of reaching colleges and universities and interesting young men and women in the settlements."[76]

The premise of the settlement movement had been that people of education had a special gift to offer the poor. "Culture" was the gift, and the individual's personality and character formed the conduit through which the "sweetness and light" of culture would flow. There was a strong if largely unspoken assumption that education itself imparted the elements of character—an assumption central to Victorian social thought and carried on in the rhetoric of American liberal arts education at the end of the nineteenth century. This assumption was not vitiated by adding training in specific skills to the repertoire of the settlement candidate. Settlement leaders continued to prefer residents

who had received a broad liberal education as a foundation for expertise in social work. The two were not seen as mutually exclusive. As
Edward Devine said in defense of professional training:

> If I wanted to quench enthusiasm, and lessen the desire to be
> of real use in the world, I can hardly imagine a more asinine
> way of going about it, than by putting earnest and competent
> young people for a year in a good training school in which
> their steel is to be tempered, in which developing powers are
> to be disciplined, in which their perception of the work to be
> done is to be clarified, in which they are to catch added inspi-
> ration from associates and instructors, in which, in a word, they
> are to find themselves and get a truer measure of their partic-
> ular powers and of the task that needs them.[77]

The settlements' alliance with the new social work profession represented one way to fill their self-appointed role as centers of social
knowledge and interpretation. The curricula of the social work
schools, particularly those in Boston and Chicago, reflected the new
trends in social thought, epitomized by the work of Simon Patten, that
indicted environmental factors beyond the individual's control for perpetuating poverty. While casework, group leadership, and institutional
management formed the backbone of training, students could also gain
experience in social research and analysis, often under the guidance of
settlement veterans.

One may argue that the professionalization of settlement work substituted a bureaucratic expertise for the Victorian noblesse oblige that
fundamentally motivated the early settlers—that, in effect, the social
equality embodied in natural and friendly relations for which the settlement founders strove continued to elude them. In crucial ways the
settlement leaders shared the faith of the Progressive Era in what they
saw as benign and constructive social control and manipulation by
"expert" functionaries. The partial professionalization of settlement
work was of a piece with the settlers' gradual assumption of authority in
the public and private lives of their neighbors. But the evolving settlement ideology continued to value the extension of genuine "democracy" to those on the margins of economic life and political power.
Further, the changing nature of settlement work merged with the spe-
cialization of function that characterized the maturation of American
economic life and spilled over into the social order. Settlement workers
could offer their neighbors the "gift" of expertise, which they them-

selves had acquired not strictly by accident of birth but in that market-place of skills, the new American university. The aura of professionalism in the settlements, faint as it might have been, suggested a new quid pro quo more fluid and democratic than the founding ethos that had asserted the class-bound nature of the social order even as it strained against it.

8
Politics, War, and the Meaning of Progressivism

Although settlement leaders reached a consensus based on ambivalence toward the major institutional issues they faced after 1900, fissures in their esprit de corps began to open over appropriate responses to events outside the houses. Like other Americans, the settlement leaders might have claimed the common label "progressive," but the pressures of politics and war revealed significant differences over what "progressivism" implied. The settlement philosophy was not sufficiently encompassing or monolithic to prevent rifts over major social issues, but its elasticity, combined with longtime mutual respect, affection, and interest in the movement's survival, allowed the leaders to close ranks once again to face the dilemmas of the 1920s.

The separate trajectories of Robert Woods and Jane Addams would reach the extreme poles of the settlement leaders' range of belief regarding the policies dictated by their dedication to the settlement movement as a vehicle of civic and social reform. Addams was a pacifist who rejected *conflict* of any type as a means to reform or even to subsequent reconciliation of differences. In the prewar period she reluctantly bent her principles to endorse a Progressive party platform that accepted militarism as a means to international ends. During the war her ability to compromise found its limit, and she chose to continue to speak out for peace at the risk of her popularity. Robert Woods, the advocate of an increased acceptance of the "natural" divisions in American society, followed *his* progressive bent toward policies that would isolate groups posing the threat of contagion to mainstream American society. He heralded wartime mobilization as a model for peacetime social control and organization.

The Making of Urban Progressives

The settlement workers' efforts to define, extend, and uplift the culture of urban neighborhoods paralleled their attempts to influence politics. The American political arena was peculiarly suited to uncovering the ironies and contradictions in the settlements' quest for popular self-determination through the midwifery of elite example and leadership. From the ward-level urban battles of the 1890s to the quixotic Progressive campaign of 1912, the settlers reached ever farther beyond their neighborhoods to find the leverage they needed to improve their neighbors' lives.

The settlement workers' self-education in publicity and single-issue pressure tactics—political tools of the literate and articulate—palpably increased their political influence and led them away from their ideal of face-to-face democracy. They grudgingly absorbed the lesson that, at least in politics, the power of personality to effect change through moral suasion was limited. Like the taste of the urban working class for vaudeville and dance halls, their neighbors' stubborn loyalty to the ubiquitous ward boss perplexed and frustrated the settlement workers, who increasingly turned to techniques that worked rather than give up their visions of change.

In the 1890s a few settlements ventured into city politics, encouraged by the English settlement workers' successes in municipal administration. The American settlers had three related aims in entering city politics: to secure officials sympathetic to their reform proposals, to cleanse the system of unethical practices, and to encourage a broader and more enlightened participation among their neighbors. Their first campaigns were a frustrating education in the tenacity of self-interested political power abetted by the voters' complicity in their own victimization.

The Hull-House residents were among the first to wage open warfare against an obnoxious local politician. By 1896, after several reform initiatives had been quashed by their alderman, the powerful and corrupt "Johnny" Powers, Hull-House decided to oppose Powers himself.[1] After an initial failure, Hull-House ran its candidate again in 1898, and a truly annoyed Powers pulled out all the stops. Backed by the streetcar magnate Charles Yerkes, Powers passed out bribes and favors, and his henchmen harassed the reformers. Obscene letters taunted Addams with trying to do a man's work, and Powers swore that Hull-House would "be driven from the ward and its leaders . . . forced to shut up shop."[2] Powers won and continued in office for another decade while Hull-House, far from "closing up shop," achieved international prominence. Absorbing the lessons of their defeats, the settlement workers bypassed Powers by forming alliances with reformers citywide to pressure the mayor's office, lobby at higher levels, and plant settlement-trained administrators in state and national office.

In a speech during the campaign of 1898, subsequently revised for the *International Journal of Ethics,* Addams grappled with the relationship between the traditional ward boss and his constituents.[3] She argued that the voters' startling indifference to corruption must be understood through the social dynamics and ethical boundaries of poor and largely immigrant urban neighborhoods. To these "primitive" people, with their "unsophisticated" moral code, the ward boss was a good man, worthy of respect and emulation. "Abstract virtues are too difficult for their untrained minds to apprehend, and many of them are still simple enough to believe that power and wealth come only to good people." The ward boss found them jobs, gave them Christmas turkeys, arranged the release of delinquent children from custody. His standing account at the funeral parlor underlined his beneficence and gave him a central place in the community's "archaic" rituals of death and mourning.[4] He himself exemplified a lower stage of "moral evolution" in which any act of seeming unselfishness must actually redound to his own benefit.[5] Because the most potent source of moral education was "example and precept," the "personality which seized the popular imagination" could mold the social ethics of immigrants anxious to conform to American social standards. A longtime incumbent like Powers could "lower the standards" of a community by warping local perceptions of citizenship and law and preempting more enlightened forms of tutelage and example.[6]

Addams's innovative interpretation of municipal politics rested upon the settlement ideology of personal influence. Other settlement reformers had previously deplored the social impact of political corruption, but Addams added another analytical dimension by examining contemporary urban politics in a historicist and relativist context, a perspective that characterized her later writings as she applied currents of late nineteenth-century social thought to pressing social problems.[7] She appealed to her readers' sympathies by portraying the logic and humanity of the motives of alien groups in adapting accustomed ways to new and difficult circumstances. "Ethical Survivals in Municipal Corruption" was in one sense uncharacteristic of her writing because it implied a qualitative gulf between the "primitive" social ethics of an immigrant community and the sophisticated, abstract ethical concepts of her audience. The article objectified the urban neighborhood in a quasi-anthropological fashion. But her concept of evolutionary ethics did invoke the analogy of individual moral education, and she pointed out parallels between the community's emulation of its ward boss and the significance of hagiography to the religious communicant. Also latent in her analysis was a provocative reading of Victorian hero worship as an embodiment of pragmatic, instrumentalist, and perhaps "primitive" ethics.[8]

In *Democracy and Social Ethics* (1902), Addams criticized good-government movements. Prosperous citizens tended to separate politics from their "moral or social life"; they forgot that the proper end of politics was improved social conditions and overlooked the "educative value" of the political process.[9] Though the readiest solution to voter irresponsibility was to distance government from the electorate, Addams strongly opposed this "hidden agenda" of Progressive urban reform. Removing politics from the people would debilitate democracy and shrink the vital scope of the individual citizen's social life. Instead, the reformer should emulate the ward boss in standing clearly "by and for and with the people" to seek a "like sense of identification" as a lever of moral influence.[10]

Many settlement houses endorsed Addams's preference for genuine civic education over prophylactic isolation by sponsoring lecture series and classes, adult clubs, and "civic" or voters' organizations.[11] Some settlements, most of them led and staffed by men, emulated Hull-House in openly entering local politics. The settlements' influence in city politics depended not only on the residents' aptitude for political rough-and-tumble, but also on the idiosyncrasies of the locale and the shifting fortunes of parallel reform efforts. In Chicago, despite the Hull-House debacle of 1898, reform forces were well entrenched by the turn of the century.[12] Energized by Raymond Robins, an itinerant laborer turned reformer, Chicago Commons did better than Hull-House in rallying local sentiment for good-government candidates, partly because two-party voting still prevailed in the Seventeenth Ward.[13] Graham Taylor and other settlement workers participated in the Municipal Voters' League, formed in 1896 by a group of businessmen, professionals, publicists, and reformers, largely to encourage campaigns like those of Hull-House and Chicago Commons against corrupt aldermen. By 1903 the league had broken Yerkes's power.[14] The Chicago settlement workers had found allies sympathetic to their own preference for (at least nominally) voter-controlled reform.

New York settlement workers had been active in politics since the early days of Stanton Coit's Neighborhood Guild, whose *Journal* boasted in 1889 that local ward bosses were beginning to recognize that "all college men have not had the action educated out of them."[15] But fifteen years later the New York settlers and their reform allies could claim only sporadic success in putting their own men in city government. Chicago's ward-based approach to reform faltered in New York, where Tammany Hall was well entrenched and unified.[16] The settlements did establish civic organizations, the largest being the Citizens' Union first headed by James B. Reynolds of the University Settlement in the 1890s. In 1897 Reynolds wrote to Jane Addams only half-jokingly that, like her, he had been in "the slimy ooze of politics," rallying support for an anti-Tammany mayoral candidate. When the reform candidate Seth Low, president of Columbia, won in 1901, he appointed Reynolds his secretary.[17]

Norton Goddard, cofounder of the Friendly Aid House, also took a stab at electoral politics. A staunch Republican, Goddard founded a Civic Club at the settlement, located in a "rough" neighborhood on the East Side. The club backed antimachine candidates and campaigned against neighborhood evils, but it never established a strong local base.[18] The Fellow Citizenship Association of East Side House took a more diffuse and indirect approach to political action. The resident manager, Clarence Gordon, claimed that East Side House stood "for POLITICS not *party*" and encouraged each voter to follow his conscience rather than "cast his ballot . . . because of friendship for or indebtedness to the East Side House corporation." Gordon contended that members of the association had been largely responsible for Seth Low's narrow district plurality against the "candidate for vicious government."[19]

In 1897, 1901, and 1903 many New York settlement workers campaigned for Seth Low, and each time their stake in his victory increased. During Low's incumbency of 1902–4, settlement workers and their allies had promoted reforms in education, public health, and housing.[20] They wailed at Low's defeat in 1903, but when the smoke cleared the results were not as devastating as some had feared.[21] Though some reform appointees had been dismissed in favor of loyal Democrats, others survived, prompting Lincoln Steffens to suggest that Tammany had learned to be discreet, if not honest.[22] In 1909 the settlers' candidate was defeated by a "reform" Tammany mayor, William Gaynor, who appointed as parks commissioner Charles Stover, one of their own, and as chief commissioner of accounts Raymond Fosdick, a former Henry Street resident.[23]

Boston politics presented still another landscape to settlement workers eager to promote social reform and enlightened citizenship. In 1896 a coalition of Yankee and Irish Democrats elected Josiah Quincy III, of impeccable New England lineage, as mayor.[24] Quincy believed that municipal government was responsible for the public's well-being, and he hoped to tap the "public-spirited and successful class of people" who usually did not serve in elective office. One of his first acts was to appoint Robert Woods to an unpaid commission that recommended a system of public baths; several gymnasiums and playgrounds followed.[25]

Though the settlers appreciated Quincy's cordiality and reform-mindedness, they hesitated to hail the millennium. Under the mayor was a board of aldermen with a fair sprinkling of machine retainers. In 1897 William Clark of Lincoln House, in the "toughest" South End ward, founded a political club that adopted a platform of honest government and modest municipal improvements, then made the bad mistake of personally standing for alderman. A speech at the Twentieth Century Club played into his rivals' hands; they used his candid comments about his district to turn the voters against him. Clark had to give up his campaign and try to repair his settlement's damaged local standing. Robert Woods wrote privately, "I think [Clark] must keep on telling 'the truth in love' about our districts, but I have doubts as to the expediency of local political action."[26]

The settlement workers were loath to renounce city politics just as they had begun to realize some of their cherished reforms. The Lincoln House fiasco led to strategic regrouping. In 1900 Woods joined Addams in arguing that reform directed to the methods rather than the aims of city politics was "futile," because it failed to stir the masses of urban voters, who were largely moved by "class, race, and religion." Instead, the settlements should develop promising local leaders and "[bring] to the local consciousness individual needs which are common needs, public needs": they should promote measures, not men, and slowly build an enlightened and "independent" body of voters throughout the city.[27]

With the ascendancy of a cruder and more colorful generation of Irish politicians, the settlers watched Boston politics degenerate. In "Traffic in Citizenship" (1903), Woods analyzed machine politics in several adjacent wards; without naming names, he depicted the politicians John Fitzgerald and Martin Lomasney in such unflattering detail that they threatened to sue for libel.[28] Also in 1903 the power of the new politicians pushed the reformers to launch the Good Government Association, the independent movement they had previously avoided. Woods and other settlers cooperated with the "Goo-Goos" over the next decade to try to oust Fitzgerald's gang and install honest progressives. Except for their victory in promoting at-large city council elections, the reformers made little headway.[29]

Thus the settlement workers developed a troubled ambivalence toward local politics. As the settlement historian Albert J. Kennedy recalled, by the turn of the century the settlements had given up backing reform candidates in favor of advising incumbents, testifying at hearings on municipal affairs, and working for better services and facilities.[30] Many settlements, particularly those founded after 1900, never played an active role in city campaigns. Although the settlement workers had not failed abjectly, they had discovered that the settlement could compromise its local standing by avowing partisan loyalties. The clash of values sometimes grew sharp and damaging in the heat of campaign. Ideally, the settlement agenda should be adopted and democratically effected by its beneficiaries. Woods declared in 1908: "The two great watchwords in settlement are possibilism and permeation, —taking the practical next step as shown by the outstanding conditions, and creating a leavening influence in the midst of the various groupings of the people themselves which will make that next upward step a natural and inevitable one to them also."[31]

The settlement workers were undoubtedly sincere in advocating community self-determination. After 1900 their reform fervor led them into inconsistency as they increasingly chose state and national government as the appropriate arenas for activism. They did this partly because they had to reach beyond municipal law and administration to "get at" most issues regarding industry and labor. Further, they were goaded as much by success as by failure; their own and their allies' achievements as lobbyists, commissioners, and administrators at all levels of government encouraged them to play to their apparent strengths in enacting a reform agenda.[32] They found like-minded co-workers beyond the provincial confines of their own cities, particularly as their professional organizations forged tighter links among them.

The personality of Theodore Roosevelt pulled a number of the settlement workers further into national politics. When Roosevelt was police commissioner of New York City from 1895 to 1897, his friendship with Jacob Riis brought him to the University Settlement and Henry Street, where he captivated the residents with his relish for the variety and excitement of the Lower East Side and his outspokenness for "fair play" in enforcing Sunday saloon closing and free speech even for obnoxious ideologues.[33] In his brief term as governor he heeded the suggestion of the New York COS that he appoint a State Tenement House Commission. Roosevelt showed an affinity for government by commission that appealed to reformist social workers frustrated by legislative politics.[34]

Elevated to the presidency by McKinley's assassination, Roosevelt confirmed the social workers' faith in his intention to effect social justice by fiat. The New York settlement workers milked their old connections with him to push their pet causes.[35] Roosevelt was particularly cooperative on child labor. The National Child Labor Committee formed by New York social workers in 1904 was publicly incorporated by Congress in 1907. The president sponsored a White House Conference on Dependent Children that led ultimately to the creation of the Children's Bureau, signed into law by President Taft.[36] Though Roosevelt moved cautiously in backing legislation, the settlement workers continued to be excited by his hortatory moral leadership. The suggestion that Jane Addams be with the president on his inaugural platform in 1905 seemed thoroughly appropriate; as Riis wrote to Wald, Roosevelt "stands for all the settlement means to our cities. . . . The settlement naturally 'belongs' where the President stands."[37] In *Charities and the Commons* in December 1906, Edward Devine suggested that "the most potent social force in America at present is the personality of the president." He praised Roosevelt's recent message to Congress promoting corporate regulation, labor reform, and conservation as "an expression of noble enthusiasm, and of practical statesmanship wholly directed towards higher standards of life and conduct, industrial democracy and social control."[38]

During the Taft administration Julia Lathrop took over the new Children's Bureau, while a group of social workers that included several settlement leaders campaigned for an industrial relations commission, finally created by the Hughes-Borah bill signed by Taft in August 1912.[39] But Taft's moderate commitment to fairness in the marketplace frustrated social workers looking to the federal government to cut the Gordian knot of interest-group competition and influence at the municipal and state levels. In 1911 a committee of the National Conference of Charities and Corrections wrote a platform of "Social Standards for Industry." In 1912 their hopes intersected with Theodore Roosevelt's boundless personal ambition to launch the short-lived Progressive party.

As Roosevelt marched angrily out of the 1912 Republican convention, the social workers left, discouraged by the bosses' indifference to their industrial platform. A small committee, including Paul Kellogg, journeyed to Oyster Bay to sound out Roosevelt. He liked their platform. In August the social workers turned out for the Progressive convention in Chicago and helped write every one of their planks into the platform. Industrial measures included regulation of hours and conditions of labor, particularly for women, abolition of child labor, housing improvement, and most controversially, federal unemployment, accident, and old-age insurance. Political planks that the social workers happily endorsed included direct primaries, the initiative and referendum, and not least, women's suffrage.[40] Though the Chicago convention may have resembled a genteel revival, it was hardly the quasi-comical collection of political naifs that some historians have sketched.[41] The Progressive platform was not unrealistic by 1912. Further, if Roosevelt the politician was sometimes uncomfortable with the single-minded reformers, they in turn made what to some were distasteful concessions to the realities of coalition politics.

Jane Addams confronted particularly sharp dilemmas in supporting the Progressive party. During his presidency Roosevelt had written to her: "Will you let me say a word of very sincere thanks to you for the eminent sanity, good-humor and judgment you always display in pushing matters you have at heart? I have such awful times with reformers of the hysterical and sensational stamp, and yet I so thoroughly believe in reform, that I fairly revel in dealing with anyone like you."[42] Beyond the flattery, this note reveals important truths about both Roosevelt and Addams. Even when they differed ideologically, they both leaned toward possibilism and accommodation as the wisest approach to social change. The politician and the settlement worker, both dealing with heterogeneous constituencies, found compromise a necessary means to their own ends. Even deeper lay a shared vein of personal conservatism; both Roosevelt and Addams feared social upheaval and sharp breaks in historical continuity. They were partisans of social concert and order, and each worked toward a peaceful realignment of the balance of power in American society—the achievement of social justice based on consensus. This essential similarity allowed these two powerful individuals to submerge their differences to work together toward a shared vision of harmonious national life.

Yet there were important differences between these remarkable contemporaries. Roosevelt the cowboy, policeman, and Rough Rider relished a good hard fight with a clearly defined enemy; in 1912 he "stood at Armageddon and battled for the Lord." Conflict was a test of character and will; victory vindicated one's beliefs. Addams's deepest attitudes toward conflict could not have been more alien to Roosevelt's. Tolstoyan "nonresistance" suffused her thought on social relations and social change. In the mid-1890s she stopped John Dewey in his tracks by persuading him that "antagonism," far from being a necessary phase of social readjustment or historical evolution, was an artificial and essentially evil impediment to social growth.[43] She sought not to vanquish her opponents but to persuade them of the rightness of her position; her vast literary output was in content and style a testimony to her faith in the power of the word to reorient the reader's stance toward the world.

From her speech seconding Roosevelt's nomination at Chicago through the grueling months of the campaign, Addams committed all her energies to the Progressive cause, but perhaps not all her heart. Characteristically, she had consulted some of the Hull-House trustees about the propriety of her partisan stance before attending the convention, and she devoted much of the next four months to defending her decision against critics of either her "radicalism" or her willingness to stomach certain Progressive planks.[44] It was difficult to accept Roosevelt's bow to southern prejudice in refusing to seat the black southern delegates to the convention and equivocating on Negro suffrage, which she had outspokenly defended.[45] Addams was more troubled, however, by the platform's call to build two battleships a year and fortify the Panama Canal. By supporting such a document, did she not violate her impassioned commitment to peace?

"I confess that I found it very difficult to swallow those two battleships," she admitted in *McClure's Magazine* in November.[46] Though at one level rather strained, her explanation for this inconsistency represented a profound continuity with her evolving thought on the connection between human welfare and the enfranchisement of women. For Addams as for a number of other Progressive women, including Lillian Wald, the seal of the party's good faith was its endorsement of women's suffrage.[47]

Addams's argument for women's entrance into political life resembled that of many suffragists who contended that their "natural" interests gave them a stake in the political process; that the domestic and nurturing roles of women should embrace aspects of community life such as health, education, and social morality that drew on their special knowledge and instincts. Addams hoped the large female contingent at the Progressive convention indicated that "public spirited women are ready to give up the short modern role of being good to people and to go back to the long historic role of ministration to big human needs."[48] Since the 1890s Addams had supported women's participation in civic affairs and urged Chicago women to use their municipal vote.[49] Her advocacy of women's public roles reflected her belief that private life was inseparable from public life—that the individual could not limit her social obligations to a biologically defined sphere without truncating her own social growth and impoverishing community life.[50]

Though Addams started from an exceptionalist premise, she went beyond many other feminists of this stripe to urge that industrial society cultivate values growing out of the female instincts to nurture and protect. In *Newer Ideals of Peace* (1907), Addams tried to demonstrate the connection between the womanly concerns for food and safety and a benign cosmopolitanism that would outlaw war as inimical not only to life itself but also to the values necessary to the social prosperity of industrial society. The "newer ideals" would not require a surrender of virility or vitality. An abstract love of humanity based on the a priori principles of eighteenth-century humanism must be replaced by social bonds based at once on warm-blooded compassion and on a tough empirical approach to social problems. With William James she sought a "moral substitute for war" that would demand the same exhilarating dedication of moral courage and mental acuity to the solution of a different set of problems.[51] Building upon the pragmatic emphasis on shaping ethics through action and process that had characterized her writing for a decade, she achieved a brilliant rhetorical fusion of traditional "male" and "female" values and styles of confronting life.[52]

Addams leaned on her record as a peace advocate to defend her seeming apostasy in 1912. She contended that her previous appeal for peace had been couched in the imperative of a "new internationalism" that deplored bloody and wasteful peacetime destruction through disease, malnutrition, and industrial accidents. Judged by that standard, the Progressive party's stance for democracy and social welfare might counterbalance its deplorable acceptance of war as a recourse in international disputes. Weakly she argued that the casualties of major nineteenth-century wars compared favorably with the casualties of American industry.[53]

Not all settlement workers supported the Progressive party in 1912, but many of their leaders participated in the campaign and then stayed on after the defeat for a fruitless attempt to establish the 1912 coalition as a permanent force in American politics. They labored through the Progressive Service, a network of reform lobbyists created after the election, to transform the platform into a machine for legislative and electoral advances. Harold Ickes organized the Illinois contingent, which included Addams, Grace and Edith Abbott, Raymond Robins, Mary McDowell, the head of the University of Chicago Settlement, Graham Romeyn Taylor, the settlement leader's son, and Louise de Koven Bowen, a Hull-House trustee. Robert Woods supported the Progressive cause in Boston, as did Katharine Coman, a Wellesley friend and associate of Vida Scudder and a patron of Denison House. Wald and Henry Moskowitz of Henry Street and Mary Simkhovitch of Greenwich House joined the Progressives in New York.[54] The Progressive campaign and its aftermath offered a new kind of political education and sealed their commitment to national politics as an extension of their work in the neighborhoods and municipalities. Coming just a year after the incorporation of the National Federation of Settlements, the organization of the Progressive movement as part of mainstream national politics reinforced the settlers' growing faith in concerted political action on the national level.

Like their spiritual leader Jane Addams, most of the settlement workers had rejected adversary politics on the model of the radical parties and labor groups in favor of persuasion and "permeation" to achieve intergroup harmony. Nonetheless, the settlement workers' program gradually opened a gulf between their methods and goals. Ironically, their ambivalence toward imposing their politics on their neighbors propelled the settlers into spheres beyond their neighbors' power to penetrate. While Addams and others pointed out the pitfalls of the Progressive ideal of government by commission, the settlement workers found that such bodies could effectively parlay their expertise into social change. Their increasing influence as advocates of social and industrial reforms accentuated their role as stewards or protectors of the nation's disadvantaged. As spokesmen for the interests of immigrants, workers, and the poor, the settlers called themselves "mediators" and "interpreters," and they styled the settlement house a "listening post." But their communication with a growing body of allies in social work took increasingly official, quasi-professional forms. Political success joined professionalization to propel the settlement movement toward an institutionalization that the original settlers had eschewed.

The Settlement Workers and the Great War:
Progressivism's Two Roads

The settlement workers shared their contemporaries' shock at the coming of the European war. Unlike most Americans, they were forced to confront the war's social effects from the beginning, as the guns of August frayed the ties that bound many of the immigrants to their European families and communities. When American entrance into the war posed the ultimate loyalty test to the "hyphenates" and fixed upon them the suspicions of a new and virulent strain of American patriotism, the settlements felt a new urgency in their old role of standing protectively between their neighbors and the ill-informed hostility of American public opinion.

The war forced the settlement leaders to reckon with the conflicting implications of their progressive faith. They spoke with one voice for an active neutrality in the early stages of the war; internationalism had become part of the American settlement credo and demanded that the settlers extend their mediating roles to the European conflict. By 1916 the preparedness debate was making inroads into settlement unity, and American entrance into the war split the settlement workers into factions, with Robert Woods and Mary Simkhovitch carrying the banner for a militaristic progressivism that would exploit national mobilization to advance social reform, while Jane Addams and a few other diehards clung stubbornly to a pacifistic progressivism that rejected wartime totalitarianism as a means to the end of a purified, just America.

Virtually all the major settlement leaders agreed that Americans' welfare was intimately related to the world's fortunes; their own neighborhoods vividly demonstrated this abstract proposition. Continuing ties to British social workers kept the settlers abreast of social legislation and labor politics in England and gave them a network of connections that eased travel in England and Europe. Though these long-term ties to European colleagues and communities provided the framework for the settlers' deeply felt internationalism, it was given a dramatic dynamic by their increasing involvement in Russian affairs after 1905.

The testimony of Jews and political exiles in the Russian immigrant colonies familiarized the settlement workers with the terrible saga of Russian suffering and failed revolt. Jane Addams had lectured around the country on Tolstoy's ideals and Russia's social problems after her pilgrimage to Yasnaya Polyana in 1896. Several years later, Hull-House became indirectly involved with the transplantation to Manitoba of the Doukhobors, a pacifist, agrarian Russian sect. Aylmer Maude organized this venture, and Tolstoy himself financed it. The settlement became a way station for friends of the exiles, and in 1904 Maude offered the leftover funds—two hundred dollars—to Hull-House.[55] In New York, the Henry Street Settlement and the University Settlement were swept up in the agitation of local Russian communities by new waves of exiles and pogrom victims after 1900. The settlements were in close touch with the exiles' revolutionary committees, who must have recognized in the settlement workers not only compassionate friends, but also influential liberal allies.

In the first flush of enthusiastic outrage the settlers usually did not discriminate ideologically among the Russian agitators; the learned and aristocratic anarchist Peter Kropotkin received a warm and reverent welcome along with the socialist novelist Maxim Gorky and the liberal constitutionalists Nicholas Tchaikovsky and Alexis Aladyin.[56] The Russian who became the settlers' beloved symbol of the revolutionary cause was Madame Catherine Breshkovsky, or "Babushka," the "Little Grandmother of the Revolution," who first visited the United States in 1904 after a twenty-two-year exile in Siberia. She charmed settlement workers and other liberals in New York, Chicago, and Boston and formed lasting friendships with Jane Addams, Lillian Wald, Helena Dudley, and Alice Stone Blackwell, editor of the *Woman's Journal.* Her warmth and courage personalized the Russian struggle for the Americans; her reimprisonment by the czarist government in 1910 outraged them.[57] Breshkovsky's first American visit inspired the formation of the Friends of Russian Freedom, to aid the Russian revolutionaries by donating funds to support outlawed printing presses, maintain the families of political martyrs, and combat famine. The Friends boasted a stellar committee that united the social work, academic, religious, and financial communities.[58]

The Americans had other eyewitnesses in three reformer-journalists— George Kennan, Ernest Poole, and William English Walling—who began traveling to Russia and sending back reports. Poole and Walling were both residents of the University Settlement in New York.[59] In his indictment of the czar, Walling focused on the self-sacrificing heroism of the students who risked exile and imprisonment to forward the revolution: "It is not a snobbish movement of the rich toward the poor. . . . They have not gone to college to learn how to make a personal success or how to become scholars and gentlemen and live apart from the mass. Like all Russians they are democrats by instinct, too subtle and too refined to imagine life as a brutal battle of all against all."[60] Walling's passionate account implicitly compared Russian and American youth. Social service in the United States offered little scope for heroics; further, those who entered the settlements were taught not to view their work as a form of "self-sacrifice." However heartily they accepted this image of the democratic social worker, some may have quietly longed for a more dramatic dedication to human welfare. The respect, even reverence, American liberals accorded to the Russian revolutionaries may be partly explained by a kind of vicarious heroism. Ten years later the Harvard graduate John Reed would exemplify the young American drawn irresistibly into the greatest adventure of the era.[61] It is not surprising that the Americans took pride in inspiring the first Russian settlement experiment in Moscow in 1905.[62]

After the outbreak of war in August 1914, the settlement leaders girded for action on two fronts. While they prepared to meet local problems engendered by war, they sought appropriate corporate responses to the international calamity. The war touched their neighborhoods almost immediately as immigrant men departed to serve their native countries and families were left in grief and disarray.[63] As the settlement leaders reoriented their staffs to cope with their neighbors' wartime crises, they reached out to each other and like-minded groups and individuals to help mold public responses to the war and promote peace.

In September 1914, Lillian Wald and Jane Addams cosponsored a round-table conference at the Henry Street Settlement, to bring together "in humbleness and quiet, some of us who deal with the social fabric." The group published a statement in the *Survey* in March 1915. Signers included Addams, Wald, Edward T. Devine, Paul Kellogg, Florence Kelley, Graham Taylor, John Haynes Holmes, Judge Julian C. Mack, Congressman William Kent, and Rabbi Stephen S. Wise.[64] Mary McDowell, headworker of the University of Chicago Settlement and president of the NFS in 1914–15, mandated a meeting of settlement workers in Washington in January 1915 to "forward a constructive peace program."[65] To promote the idea that "it is patriotic to live for one's country, not to die and kill," she suggested that local settlement federations help develop social substitutes for military training.[66] The Boston Social Union had already gathered in October 1914 to hear Joseph Lee on "substitutes for war." Since war was both a "natural instinct" and a "high ideal," argued Lee, the social workers' task was to replace one ideal with another—to substitute art, drama, and play for the attractions of war.[67] In this prescription he followed William James and Jane Addams in suggesting that the common denominator of these activities was the human impulse toward action.

The notion of a facile "substitution" of one collective impulse for another presupposed a malleable popular urge toward collective idealism that was the optimistic face of late nineteenth-century fears about the manipulability of masses of people. The outcome pointed up the flaw in this formulation of the dynamics of social emotion. It proved difficult to arouse people about the need for a substitute for war when the nation was not in fact at war. Though the European war affected the American economy, political discourse, and the life of immigrant neighborhoods, as yet it made no demands upon the nation as a whole. The Boston Social Union took a stab at concrete recommendations such as cooperating with the Women's Peace party to lobby for physical education in the public schools, "with a view to improving physical, mental, and moral qualities."[68] Other proposals were vaguer. The Committee for Substitutes for War suggested, among other things, that the press be persuaded to publish articles "urging the democratic worth of the people in times of peace . . . in order to create public opinion."[69] The social workers presciently feared the corrosive effects of unleashed "martial" passions on intergroup relations and the cosmopolitan tolerance they had tried to foster. Though the anticipatory attempt to erect barriers of sentiment and principle against this amorphous threat proved futile, the effort itself was significant. The roots of the government's intensive campaign to mold public opinion during the war lay not only in the precedent set by the nascent advertising industry, but also in the more diffuse progressive faith in the possibility of educating people to a collective sense of morality and idealism that could then be mobilized for specific objects.

A few settlement leaders worked to intervene directly in the war. While Lillian Wald became president of the Union against Militarism, Jane Addams joined a remarkable group of women who convened in Washington in January 1915 as the Women's Peace Party. Their platform called for a convention of neutral nations to try to formulate an "early peace." Addams was elected chairman, and Sophonisba Breckinridge served as treasurer.[70] Addams later recalled that because pacifism was still widely accepted in early 1915, "the members of the new organization scarcely realized that they were placing themselves on the side of an unpopular cause."[71] In Chicago the Women's Peace party mustered an "emergency federation of peace forces" at a convention in March, and in Boston the party won the BSU's cooperation in forwarding measures against militarism and the war.[72] In March the Women's Peace party sent a delegation to the International Congress of Women at The Hague, over which Jane Addams was asked to preside.[73] The Hague convention selected a committee to carry the group's resolutions, featuring a Conference of Neutrals to end the war, to the governments. The women found all doors open; the men in power listened politely to their proposals but remained unmoved.[74]

By late 1915, Addams and other vocal pacifists began to feel the sting of public disapproval. For Addams the turning point was her abortive involvement in Henry Ford's quixotic plan to bring peace to Europe by privately arranging the conference of neutrals that others had failed to bring about. To maximize publicity, he hired a ship to take the American participants across the Atlantic. The press had a field day with Ford's Peace Ship, but before the idea became an object of ridicule, Addams had agreed to sail with the group. (Graham Taylor turned down his invitation on the grounds of his "loyalty to the peace cause"!)[75] Addams became increaisngly alarmed at Ford's vulgar publicity. Just before the Peace Ship sailed, she took to her bed with a convenient though apparently genuine illness that ultimately earned her the double obloquy of allying herself with Ford's project and "jumping ship" when threatened with embarrassment.[76]

By early 1916 debates over American preparedness had ruptured the social workers' consensus on the war. The *Survey* reflected these new divisions as staff members and readers battled in print over appropriate attitudes to the war.[77] In a speech at Boston University in June 1916, Mary Simkhovitch outlined a preparedness philosophy that became increasingly popular among social workers. Skirting international ramifications, she tried to redefine "preparedness" to embrace social as well as military goals. "Preparedness" was really the older Progressive concept of "efficiency," only with a "gayer, more lively sound." Both terms meant the "raising of a national consciousness and national standards." The United States could "no longer tolerate the dangers of illiteracy and preventable disease," which undermined any attempt at world leadership. Simkhovitch stressed the federal government's responsibility to erect and enforce standards of health and education.[78]

America's entrance into the war resolved some tensions in the social work community and created others. For the pacifists Wilson's commitment to war was the ultimate calamity, extinguishing their fading hopes for a mediated settlement and tapping all the passions and prejudices they had dreaded. For Jane Addams, personal anguish mingled with philosophical distress. She recalled of herself and other pacifists: "We never ceased to miss the unquestioning comradeship experienced by our fellow citizens during the war, nor to feel curiously outside the enchantment given to any human emotion when it is shared by millions of others . . . one secretly yearned to participate in 'the folly of all mankind.' "[79] To separate herself from the spiritual life of her society for principle's sake flew in the face of the pragmatism Addams had embraced in the cause of a larger and richer social life.[80] The Progressive campaign of 1912 had strained her power to subordinate a revulsion of principle to a vision of that larger life; the Great War demarcated the limits of compromise.

Other settlement leaders made the pragmatic adjustment to war that Addams found so difficult. Like Mary Simkhovitch, they could envision war as a vehicle of their own long-cherished aims. They joined other liberals, whose chief spokesmen were Walter Lippmann and the other editors of the *New Republic,* in welcoming the necessity of massive government intervention in the economy as an opportunity to draw up a blueprint of the ideal peacetime regime. They also hoped to direct the social and spiritual energies released by war to building a just and cohesive society.[81]

As president of the NFS, Mary K. Simkhovitch rallied the settlements in April 1917 to act in concert during the emergency. The first task was to clean up the settlements' public image. As Woods commented, "The great force of the social workers, as a group, should be to show that all are ready to do the full duties of citizenship under all emergencies."[82] In a letter to the New York *Evening Post,* Simkhovitch tried to remove the albatross of Jane Addams's well-publicized views from the movement's neck. Calling Addams the "foremost woman in America, and, as I think, in the world," Simkhovitch accepted the "painful" necessity of repudiating the views of the settlement pacifists. She contended that the majority of settlement workers now believed that America could not "stand apart" in this great struggle for a "democratic world." She pleaded for the rights and well-being of immigrants and labor in the war crisis. "It is not in the districts where the settlements are situated that disloyalty is shown," she asserted.[83]

Several weeks later, Simkhovitch polled the member houses of the National Federation of Settlements on a six-point settlement war program. In telegraphed assents, the respondents endorsed wartime prohibition "to increase the food supply," adequate compensation to the soldiers and their families, taxation on nonessential consumer items, and the maintenance of labor standards already legislated. Following the lead of the Canadian settlements, which had been functioning in wartime conditions for several years, the American houses hoped to maintain their regular programs while taking up special home front tasks. Stepping up athletics and other youth activities seemed urgent in view of increased juvenile rowdiness and delinquency in some settlement neighborhoods.[84]

The settlements rightly anticipated a wartime drain on their resources. Some male residents were drafted, while others departed to do war work outside the settlements. Some women also left to serve with the Women's Land Army, the Red Cross, or as in the case of some Henry Street nurses, the Committee on Home Nursing. Many remaining residents diverted their time to the local draft boards, the Food Administration, and Liberty Bond drives.[85] Some settlements actively recruited part-time volunteers from the colleges; South End House relied heavily on men from Harvard College and the Medical School, who were exempt from the draft. In most houses women filled the men's places, even in the club work with boys, which had been traditionally assigned to men.[86]

Besides taking charge of local draft registration, Red Cross work, bond drives, and conservation campaigns, many settlements tackled what they perceived as the twin problems of recreation in nearby military camps and protective work with young girls. The War Camp Community Service was specially commended to social workers by Secretary of War Newton D. Baker, who told readers of the *Survey* that "wholesome recreation" would create an "invisible armor" of moral strength to protect American soldiers from the temptations that assailed them away from home.[87] Joseph Lee served as president of the Service. Robert Woods and the BSU took pride in their contribution to recreation and social programs for the men stationed near Boston; they contended that settlement experience was the best training for these ad hoc wartime programs.[88] The Boston settlers also cooperated with military authorities in attacking city vice. Woods had long been a vocal temperance advocate and had served a term on the Boston Licensing Board; he was an enthusiastic partisan of national prohibition, not just for its conservation value but in the interest of controlling public morals.[89]

For Woods, the wartime campaigns for prohibition and social purity were emblematic of the opportunities that militarization had brought to social workers. In late 1917 he rejoiced that "every branch of social work has been called into War Service"; the government's use of social workers' ideas and expertise proved their "soundness."[90] This circular reasoning typified the zeal with which Woods threw himself into the war effort. As president in 1918 of the National Conference of Social Work (the renamed NCCC), Woods promoted his vision of the "regimentation of the free"—the organization of American society on the model of wartime mobilization to work for health, welfare, and economic justice and prosperity, with social workers as a "national army of the constructive humanities." In his enthusiasm for social control in both private and public spheres and his unconditional faith in benign totalitarianism, Woods epitomized one extreme permutation of the progressive mentality. "In no previous . . . generation," he asserted, "would it have been possible that every nook and corner of our cities, would have been under the close, responsible, friendly surveillance of men and women representing much that is best in our national life—that in this way the dangers to a nation at war coming from nests of dissipation, of contagious disease, of crime, of disloyalty, of espionage, of actual resistance to the government, could be everywhere effectively minimized."[91] Woods's indiscriminate lumping of political, social, and physiological evils under the implicit controlling metaphor of contagion and infection was one logical elaboration of the concept of "social organism." The social worker became in his vision an epidemiologist working to check the spread of dangerous "diseases."[92]

The most pressing and delicate wartime issue the settlements faced was the relation of their foreign-born neighbors to the war effort. Never before had the United States' unique demography been so starkly underlined as in this world clash of nationalist passions. Collectively, the settlements remained true to their tradition as "listening posts" and "interpreters." The settlement workers renewed their two-pronged, sometimes contradictory campaign for a reasonable and humane approach to "Americanization." On the one hand, they reasserted their commitment to cultural pluralism. Mary Simkhovitch insisted, "To Americanize I do not mean New Englandize or Old Colonialize. . . . We desire indeed to keep the ideals of our forefathers as to liberty, economic opportunity and religious freedom, but there are also . . . [i]deals of culture and association, and . . . [w]e ought to welcome and conserve variety in our newcomers."[93] Mary McDowell borrowed Randolph

Bourne's concept of "transnationalism" to advocate "a new kind of nation of many peoples 'whom God hath made of one blood.' "[94] On the other hand, the settlement workers had always supported the kind of "Americanization" that included instruction in English language, civics, and American history and had sometimes overlooked their own contribution to generational and acculturation tensions among immigrants. But when the war came, the settlement spokesmen hewed to their own tradition of viewing "Americanization" as the accommodation and adjustment of the immigrants' customs, languages, religions, and political assumptions to their new American environment.

The Immigration Act of 1917 had imposed a literacy test designed to exclude the southern and eastern European groups most feared by American nativists. After the United States entered the war, new legislation was proposed to coerce "100% Americanism" by eradicating all signs of immigrants' lingering loyalties to their native countries.[95] In 1918 the National Federation of Settlements opposed any requirement that foreign-born people "learn English with a view to enforcing the suppression of their native speech." Pointing to the settlements' long-time practice of offering voluntary classes in English and citizenship, the NFS insisted that coerced acculturation would only breed "misunderstanding and bitterness" in the immigrants, who would be reminded of the silencing of linguistic minorities by Old World autocracies.[96]

The settlement workers accepted a special responsibility to mitigate the harsh reaction of public opinion against the immigrants. After war was declared, Simkhovitch sent a letter to NFS houses exhorting them to serve as calming influences in their own communities: "Now is the very time to love our neighbors as ourselves."[97] In every public statement the settlement workers underlined their neighbors' patriotism. As Simkhovitch said, "Newly arrived foreigners are great jingoes. They are more American than Americans."[98] Another headworker boasted of "our boys" in the army that "it is gratifying to see their pride in their physical fitness and their eagerness to fit their uniforms in other ways as well," and she praised "the mothers who have so unselfishly given their sons to the country."[99] Mary McDowell told the story of a Lithuanian man who turned his life's savings of one thousand dollars into Liberty Bonds, explaining " 'I give it all for this country where my daughter she has learned more from the American schools than the biggest man knows in my village at home.' "[100]

The settlement leaders also stressed the continuing hardships of the immigrants' lives in America that made their patriotism even more remarkable. Pleading for a more humane approach to Americanization—including outlawing the term itself as "savoring too much of denationalization"—Charles Cooper pointed out the exploitation that foreigners still suffered in the labor market and the court system.[101] Mary McDowell concurred: "The unskilled worker wants a home of his own and tries desperately to meet the monthly payments. In the struggle, his wife often has to go to work, either at night or in the day time and the children are neglected. Can we wonder why they do not flock to our evening schools to learn English after long days of monotonous ugly work?"[102]

As the settlers tried to focus on long-range social goals, they also reminded the public and their patrons—in letters, leaflets, and annual reports—of their own special role in serving their neighborhoods. Clubs, recreation, and vigilance against local nuisances were all part of "Americanization" as the settlements understood it. "A settlement is a family in which men and women, possessed of some of the advantages that America can give, live in the midst of a foreign people. The settlement program includes much more than naturalization papers and English classes. Its purpose is the safeguard of American standards of living."[103]

The armistice threw the settlements into the chaos and minutiae of demobilization, reconstruction, and a devastating influenza epidemic.[104] They also began proudly to assess their role in the war and look forward to resuming their work strengthened by the apparent endorsement that wartime social and economic policies had given their progressive vision of social democracy. Once again Robert Woods voiced the settlement workers' most sanguine predictions: "Even amid the embarrassments which the war brings to it, social work is destined to have a far wider dissemination of its essential aims; it is to be much more broadly and powerfully organized; it is to receive much larger and more general support from the community as a whole and from the public administration. It holds some of the chief resources through which the world must be restored." Yet he ended on an incongruously cautious note: "But we shall need to pray for it in the days of its prosperity."[105]

9
The Settlements' Search for Normalcy

As they tried to resume normal activities while helping their neighbors cope with the war's aftershocks, the settlements found themselves embroiled in a battle not of their choosing: a campaign to defend their own loyalty. Though the settlement workers were unprepared for postwar accusations of radicalism and subversion, it is not surprising that they should have been caught up in the great Red Scare that distilled the diffuse anxieties of a nation abruptly released from wartime discipline. To the settlements' long record of aiding and defending labor and the immigrant—the targets of postwar suspicions—was added the recent vocal pacifism of some of their most prominent leaders and their sympathy with the Russian Revolution.

The settlement founders had faced such charges before. The Chicago settlements in particular had planted themselves in a volatile situation, with a business community largely hostile to labor organization and a middle-class population with vivid memories of the Haymarket bombing. The Chicago Commons "free floor," the Hull-House women's sympathy to labor unionists and Russian exiles, and Mary McDowell's work at the University of Chicago Settlement to organize the meatpackers under the American Federation of Labor had all earned the opprobrium of conservatives and many industrialists.[1] In 1901 Jane Addams and Graham Taylor courted public misunderstanding when they defended the right to counsel of Abraham Isaacs, the editor of an anarchist publication, arrested by the Chicago police for allegedly inspiring and collaborating with McKinley's assassin.[2] Addams raised an even greater storm by protesting police behavior in the "Averbuch affair" of 1908. A young Russian Jew who appeared on the doorstep of the Chicago police chief's home had been shot to death by the chief's son in anticipatory self-defense. The assumption that the man had been an anarchist bent on violence touched off a police raid on the Russian Jewish colony. Addams and other settlement leaders intervened to demand a fair inquiry and secure a reliable autopsy on the body of the suspected assassin. While they won no points with avowed anarchists hoping to milk the tragedy for propaganda, the settlers were equally condemned by the public, who interpreted their aid and comfort to Averbuch's family and countrymen as sympathy with anarchism. In an article for *Charities and the Commons* in May 1908, Addams defended the settlements' stance for constitutional procedure while disavowing any tolerance of anarchism. What the Russians learned from the Averbuch affair, she wrote, was that the American promise of democracy and civil liberties was hollow: that the methods of the American police were not much different from those of the czarist government they had fled. The settlements had been the Russians' only recourse for aid in securing justice.[3] The letters of support and admiration Addams received after the appearance of her article—which she typically circulated among associates and patrons— suggest that the settlements' critics, at least those of any influence, were safely outnumbered by people who understood the settlers' approach to the dilemma of radicalism in the immigrant communities.[4]

In 1914 a comparable show of liberal support was evoked by a series of incidents at the University Settlement of New York. The headworker, Robbins Gilman, had occasionally made the settlement available as a cold-weather shelter for the unemployed. When he was told that some of the men he was aiding were members of the Industrial Workers of the World, he declared that he refused to discriminate against the needy on the basis of their political affiliations. On another occasion he made a speech that condemned police brutality against the IWW and praised the union's members as "intellectually keen . . . red blooded men in sharp contrast to the Bowery type of the hopeless 'down and out.' "[5] Gilman's remarks received prominent press coverage. When shortly afterward he resigned from the headworkership, seemingly under pressure from his board, letters of indignation and support poured in, many from other headworkers and social workers who shuddered at the apparent precedent. In the end one of the board members begged Gilman to publish a denial that his resignation had anything to do with the IWW incidents.[6]

Nonetheless, evidence suggests that even the most politically tolerant settlements developed some skittishness toward certain radicals. Though Emma Goldman was first received warmly as a friend of Peter Kropotkin and Catherine Breshkovsky, both Addams and Wald received with increasing caution her repeated requests for support in her court battles. As the most notorious anarchist in America, Goldman threatened the settlements with guilt by association.[7] Though the settlers defended free speech and civil rights and had a compassionate sense of the alienating effects of the immigrant experience that might foster radicalism, most of them were not radicals, and they all deplored political violence.[8]

The settlements had weathered earlier accusations of radicalism because of the broadly progressive and sympathetic social context in which they worked. Though the spasms of repression and violence directed against aliens and radicals before 1914 cannot be considered aberrant in American political life, they coexisted with a general acceptance of the legitimacy of the settlements' progressive and humanitarian goals. The settlements had, after all, emerged from several intellectual and religious currents in the mainstream of Victorian culture. After the war, the settlement workers gradually reckoned with the fact that they were operating in a more constricted milieu. It was easy to refute specific accusations of radical and un-American sympathies, but no amount of explanation and exculpation seemed to accomplish the reintegration of settlement ideology with larger American political and social ideals.[9]

Denison House in Boston was an early target of postwar reaction. Though the outspoken socialist Helena Dudley had resigned as headworker in 1912 so as not to impair the settlement's effectiveness, the next headworker, Geraldine Gordon, had been a pacifist before the war. In 1919 several of the house's supporters suddenly refused to help raise funds because of the settlement's "very radical and anti-capitalistic position." Further, a rumor reached the settlement that a federal investigation of the house had been planned for the summer of 1919 but then called off. Both the board of directors and the residents split over the proper relation between the private views of the settlement workers and the public position of the house on "important issues of the times."[10] Concord was not restored. In February 1920 the board asked Gordon to "go away for a rest"; in March her resignation was accepted.[11]

The most concentrated public attack on the settlements' goals came from the Lusk Committee of the New York State legislature, which convened from 1919 to 1921 to investigate radical and seditious activities in New York. In 1921 the committee's report indicted the New York settlements for practicing a pernicious kind of "Americanization" that placed "radical and revolutionary ideas on a parity with the ideals of American Government." The settlements allowed radicals to speak from their platforms and harbored "parlor Socialists and philosophers" who corrupted susceptible young people.[12] The members of the United Neighborhood Houses fought back aggressively in the press. Their counsel, Harold Riegelman, defended the settlements' record and challenged the committee to produce a single example of a resident's encouraging "disloyalty, sedition, or anarchy."[13] Mary Simkhovitch and Lillian Wald also offered testimonials to the settlements' public service and patriotism from prominent citizens and politicians.[14] Some settlers did favor conciliation; Helen Jessup of the Riis Settlement wrote to the president of the UNH that the New York settlements should participate more vigorously in the "English to Foreigners" drive in order to refute recent criticism.[15]

Because the Lusk attack was public and quasi-official, the New York settlers could present a public defense through the press. Other offensives against the settlements were sporadic and individual. Some settlement patrons withdrew their financial support. Graham Taylor reported in 1921 that the "reaction and unrest" of the postwar period had affected a few large subscriptions to Chicago Commons—though he did not specify whether the donations were withheld on political grounds or simply dried up in the general economic dislocation.[16] Like Denison House, a few settlements were penalized for their headworkers' private views. Lillian Wald recalled later that for her own pacifist activities "I was disciplined by the torture-chamber method of having the money withdrawn which enabled the nurses to care for the families of the soldiers no less than the other sick."[17] The settlement worker who suffered the most sustained and varied campaign of abuse was, not surprisingly, the one who had come to symbolize the settlement spirit to the American people in the prewar period—Jane Addams.

Addams had not renounced her pacifism after war was declared, but she had willingly allowed Hull-House to be turned into a center of home front activities.[18] She herself worked as a public speaker for the Food Administration under Herbert Hoover, which allowed her to return to an issue that had intrigued her since college: the special relation of women to the physical sustenance of humankind.[19] Despite growing hostility to her pacifism in the year before America's entry into the war, Addams was apparently well received as a speaker for the humanitarian cause of feeding the hungry.[20] After the armistice, however, she gave her critics new ammunition by journeying to Europe to convene with the newly renamed Women's International League for Peace and Freedom, which was laboring to influence the peace terms, particularly regarding famine relief. After witnessing the misery of the starving Germans firsthand, Addams made a plea to Americans for donations to the Friends Service Committee for German relief.[21]

The only issue more likely to arouse Americans' suspicions was the other one she took up in 1919 and 1920: defense of the aliens, some of them old friends of hers, who had been rounded up without warrant in the Justice Department raids.[22] The public attacks on Addams began in earnest in 1920. Speaking at the Rockford, Illinois, Kiwanis Club, one Charles Ferguson charged that there had been far too much "Hull House" taught at Rockford College. R. A. Gunn, a member of the American Protective League, fired a volley of charges at Addams and her associates, the "Hot House Hull-House variety of Parlor Bolshevists." In line with her habit of responding concretely to personal attacks, she published careful refutations of Gunn's and Ferguson's charges.[23] The Chicago *Tribune* baited Addams, and she received abusive mail.[24]

Addams's most persistent assailants in the 1920s were members of right-wing and military groups, who developed a cottage industry of uncovering supposed networks of Bolshevism and subversion in the United States. The infamous "spider web" chart, which flourished from 1923 to 1927, linked a list of individuals with a list of organizations by a dark tangle of lines to demonstrate the insidious and ubiquitous nature of communist influence in American life. Besides such obvious candidates as Eugene Debs, William Z. Foster, William D. Haywood, Morris Hillquit, and Norman Thomas, the chart included Addams, Roger Baldwin of the young American Civil Liberties Union, Florence Kelley, Vida Scudder, Mary McDowell, and Julia Lathrop. The peace organizations listed included the WILPF, and the "Red Radical—Communist—Subversive" category began with the ACLU. The Labor Department, the Children's Bureau, and Congress were all honored as harboring tainted individuals.[25] Other organizations that spotlighted Jane Addams as a threat to American democracy were the American Legion and the Daughters of the American Revolution, to which Addams had been elected in 1900.[26] By 1927 Addams was a featured villain in DAR pamphlets against subversion. Of her membership she remarked, "I thought it was for life, but apparently it was only for good behavior."[27]

As postwar passions faded, some ventured forth in Addams's defense.[28] In January 1927, following a brouhaha over the American Legion's attack on Addams, a group of her Chicago colleagues and NFS members staged a civic dinner for Addams. Laudatory telegrams poured in, including a message from President Calvin Coolidge praising

Addams for her "service of humanity."[29] She was doubtless pleased to be feted; her general bearing of humility did not preclude lifelong pleasure in honors and awards. But her writings of the 1920s and 1930s hint at bitterness over her ostracism, particularly by her fellow settlement workers and the social work community. She suggested that the settlements had betrayed their mission and broken faith with the "simple people" in failing to serve as an "interpreter" during the Red Scare.[30] In *The Second Twenty Years at Hull-House* (1930), she indicted the social workers of the 1920s for "playing it safe," sacrificing their concern for social justice in their "panic" over corporate survival. She had joked grimly before the NCSW in 1924 that if improved dental care were suddenly identified with a particular social theory, the social workers "would be frightened and feel that they must drop it."[31]

There is little question that the prewar acceptance of social reform as an integral aspect of social work gave way in the 1920s to a conception of social work as a constellation of skills and services designed to bring troubled individuals into functional harmony with society. This trend has generally been analyzed as a shift from a concentration on the environmental determinants of poverty to a renewed, though altered, concentration on individuals' responsibility for their own social situation. Instead of removing the social and economic barriers to human fulfillment, the social worker would attempt to change people's behavior and outlook to help them "adjust" to their society, an orientation that certainly entailed, if it was not dictated by, a decreased emphasis on the removable ills of the social order.

The diminution of reform ideals among social workers after the war may be partly attributed to caution in a politically repressive atmosphere. But in many threads of social work in the 1920s, progressive ideals lived on, and there was no sharp turn toward a readily identifiable "conservatism." Further, many of the trends in social work that fructified in the 1920s, particularly the triumph of "casework" and increased acceptance of the relevance of psychology and psychiatry to social work, began before the war and had as much to do with the dynamics of an emerging profession as with the political climate.

Settlement work in the 1920s offers an equally complicated picture of continuity interwoven with change only partly attributable to an altered political context. Virtually all the settlement workers, no matter what their political beliefs, read the signs of the times with foreboding. Charles Cooper, the new headworker of Kingsley House in Pittsburgh, found in 1921 that "Pittsburgh has reacted to extremely conservative

views, especially along industrial and social lines." Cooper advised discretion; he claimed to work successfully with an "extremely conservative Board" by "biding my time." To Paul Kellogg he protested that the
Survey's aggressive stance on social and political issues did more harm
than good.[32] On the other hand, the settlement leaders who had lobbied for social reforms before the war continued several crucial campaigns in the 1920s, notably those for a national child labor law and for
decent housing.[33] The attempt to pass a constitutional amendment outlawing child labor gave reactionaries an outlet for their purple rhetoric.
Alice Hamilton reported from the Illinois legislature in 1925: "The hall
was packed with Catholics sent by the Cardinal and with ladies of the
Civic Federation. In the afternoon they let loose and every outburst
against Bolshevism, Mrs. Kelley, Moscow, Grace Abbott, nationalization
of children and all the other Tommy-rot was applauded . . . A Harvard
professor's wife . . . said that Hull-House was a branch of the Soviet
government . . . while Miss Addams was the most dangerous woman in
America. Of course the amendment is lost."[34]

While the settlers honored their progressive tradition by working for
child labor laws and reformed housing, they remained true to another
facet of progressivism by recommending prophylactic measures against
the infectious immorality of the times. In this aspect of their work they
remained in step with widely held American attitudes in the postwar
decade.

Throughout the 1890s and up to the Great War, the settlement workers had been among the foot soldiers of the moral purity campaigns that
characterized urban progressivism. Their offensives against prostitution
and the neighborhood saloon were fueled by their concern with the
environment of family and community relations; most settlement workers did not manifest the single-mindedness of some crusaders against
vice, for whom sexual and passional immorality functioned as intensely
focused symbols of their anxieties about the changing social order.[35]
The settlement workers may have seen sexuality and drunkenness primarily as threats to order and self-control, but they treated these issues
in pragmatic rather than symbolic or hyperbolic terms. Their arguments
for temperance and "social hygiene" focused on the welfare of the
family and the impact of saloons and brothels on juvenile delinquency,
violent crime, and public disorder.

The settlement workers cautiously welcomed the Eighteenth Amendment. A number of their studies beginning in the 1890s had denounced
the saloon's key position in the web of urban crime and vice, and some

houses had attempted to gain police cooperation in acting against obnoxious local establishments, but the characteristic settlement recommendation had been to find a "substitute" for the saloon's more positive social functions before absolutely closing it down.[36] As a group, the
settlers supported wartime prohibition as a conservation measure and
an aid in maintaining local moral standards during the emergency, but
their disappointing experience with even moderate municipal statutes
regulating the saloons made some of them skeptical toward absolute
prohibition in peacetime. The most enthusiastic settlement partisan of
national prohibition was Robert Woods, who had been closely involved
with liquor regulation in Boston.[37]

Woods first dealt with the liquor issue in 1907 when the governor
appointed him chairman of the trustees of the Foxboro State Hospital
for Dypsomaniacs. In 1910 Woods persuaded the Boston Social Union,
basically his creature, to back him in a fight for the "bar and bottle bill,"
whose passage ended the double licensing of saloons for retail sales.[38]
Three years later his allies secured Woods's appointment to the Licensing Board, where he further annoyed liquor interests by tightening
administration of the liquor laws and reducing the number of licenses
granted. He was not reappointed.[39]

Woods always stressed that he approached the problem of drink from
the standpoint of a neighborhood worker. Though a teetotaler himself,
until 1916 he walked a moderate's tightrope by supporting temperance
through regulation rather than elimination of drinking. At least as early
as 1907, though, he was moving toward a view of alcohol that logically
culminated in prohibitionism. He had become convinced that alcohol
and "degeneracy" were tightly connected and that the best treatment of
"degenerates," a "constant leaven of evil" in the neighborhood, was
"disposal" through institutional segregation and treatment.[40] His experience with the Foxboro Hospital reinforced his belief in segregation
and gave him a new, dispassionate language in which to discuss alco-
holism; he could describe it as a medical problem rather than a moral
horror. At a session on "Drunkenness" at the 1911 convention of the
National Conference of Charities and Corrections, he argued that an
effective campaign against tuberculosis would include treatment and
aftercare for alcoholics.[41] By 1916, after his discouraging term on the
Licensing Board, Woods decided that local regulation or prohibition
was ineffective in reducing alcohol consumption, and he came out for
national prohibition.[42]

Woods's advocacy of prohibition jibed with his evolving progressive philosophy. Segregating the alcoholic degenerate would serve the same dual purpose as segregating the mentally unfit, providing the afflicted with humane care while ridding the community of a noxious influence.[43] Like other settlement workers and reformers, Woods had always stressed the relation between the saloon and prostitution. In 1919 the American Social Hygiene Association published an article by Woods that dramatically broadened this identification of alcohol with unhealthy sexuality. Prohibition, he wrote, would allow the raising of "an entire generation whose pre-natal life has not been damaged by alcohol." Venereal disease would be checked and the divorce rate would drop as individuals were "release[d] from the handicap placed by alcohol on the higher brain centers." Finally, national prohibition would tacitly establish the "ethical principle . . . that certain phases of conduct which have often been thought of as private and personal are . . . matters of inviolable public concern." Woods traced a straight line from the social organicist ethic of the late nineteenth century to the beneficent "neo-Puritanism" represented by Prohibition, which would control the "age-old evils of misdirected appetite and passion through the resources of science and democracy."[44] The prohibition laws reasserted the community's right to impose standards on the individual's private behavior, the seventeenth-century prerogative that had been eroded in a contractual society.[45]

Most settlement workers came to view Prohibition as a mixed blessing for their neighborhoods. Settlement workers in Boston and Chicago testified to improvements in family conditions and neighborhood order.[46] But as enforcement problems multiplied with the increase in bootlegging and speakeasies, the settlers began to fear the erosion of moral standards, especially among young people.[47] In some neighborhoods the settlers tried to cooperate with police to enforce the law.[48] Though they recognized their golden opportunity to develop the "social substitute for the saloon," the form was still problematical; one New York settlement worker suggested that a successful substitute "must not be too purposeful nor entirely purposeless."[49]

In 1926 the National Federation of Settlements, with Paul Kellogg's cooperation, undertook a study of the effects of Prohibition on neighborhood life. Kellogg and Bruno Lasker recruited Martha Bensley Bruère of New York to head the study, partly because they felt that Wald and Addams, with their "streak of feminism," would have "more confidence in a woman."[50] In a vivid impressionistic report, Bruere skillfully pieced together a complex and contradictory picture of the impact of Prohibition and the question of its "success" or failure. Social workers, including most settlement leaders, seem to have favored continuing Prohibition despite their clear-eyed assessment of its costs and failures. Jane Addams, Raymond Robins, and Lillian Wald were among the realists who endorsed an extension of the "experiment."[51] Though neither Addams nor Wald seems to have shared Woods's fervent faith in Prohibition as the foundation stone of a new scientific democracy, both invoked possible future benefits as well as present improvements in local life to justify their support. As chairman of the NFS's Prohibition Committee, Wald cautioned the public in late 1932 that a retreat from Prohibition would invite the "tragic renewal of conditions destructive of home life and of respect and dignity."[52]

Many social workers noted that Prohibition seemed to have curtailed prostitution as a well-organized commercial trade.[53] Though they had waffled initially on Prohibition, the settlement workers had never hesitated to take a strong stand against prostitution. Again, they brought their perspective as observers and advocates of working-class communities to the question of eliminating the "ancient evil." They railed against the "double standard" that implicitly sanctioned segregating rather than eliminating prostitution by endorsing the need of the "normal man" for sexual release.[54] Graham Taylor served on the Chicago Vice Commission appointed in 1910, which came out unanimously against the segregation of vice (i.e., prostitution) as unworkable, demoralizing, and ethically wrong.[55] Later testifying before the newly established Chicago Vice Committee, Taylor stressed his shock at the large proportion of "defective" women among the prostitutes they had interviewed. He advocated segregating the defective—the "insane," the "weak minded," and the "apoplectic"—and sterilizing defective men.[56]

Not only was Taylor worried about the subnormal woman victimized by procurers, one of his first brushes with prostitution in his neighborhood was a mother's plea for help in finding her missing daughter. An informant led the settlers to an apartment where the girl was being held against her will, a victim of the "white slave trade."[57] Though there has been retrospective debate over the extent of this trade in young girls, there is some reason to believe that reformers' fixation on the problem was not merely a culturally nurtured hysteria or a sensationalist device to call attention to the larger problem of prostitution and moral purity—though both opportunism and hysteria fed this offensive against the white slave trade.[58] Focusing on white slavery also permitted a shift in perspective from the prostitute as Eve to the prostitute as victim.

Two years after *The Spirit of Youth and the City Streets,* Jane Addams entered the national discussion of prostitution and the white slave trade with *A New Conscience and an Ancient Evil,* first serialized in *McClure's* in 1911. Drawing on her experience and the records of the Juvenile Protective Association, established by her friend and Hull-House associate Louise de Koven Bowen, Addams examined prostitution as only one aspect, though a tragic one, of the larger problem of urban adolescence. Her case histories were pathetic tales of the exploitation of innocence by the malevolent forces of industrial society. Girls and young women driven by the need to survive, by love for helpless family members, by an innocent desire for pleasure in a grinding daily industrial routine "fell" into prostitution and, ruined, lost any hope of a happy, normal life. Addams indicted the usual villains—procurers and "white slavers," and the police department in collusion with them—but she also exposed the physical, economic, and psychological roots of moral weakness. Sounding the same notes she had struck in *The Spirit of Youth,* she described the inhuman regimen of the factory and department store and the isolation of domestic labor and invoked the frequent psychological result: the "desolating feeling of belonging nowhere. All youth resents the sense of the enormity of the universe in relation to the insignificance of the individual life, and youth, with that intense self-consciousness which makes each young person the very centre of all emotional experience, broods over this as no older person can possibly do." To escape such loneliness and despair, the girl often turned to any pleasure or company available.

Besides the usual negative and repressive solutions to the problem of prostitution, Addams again recommended the public provision of healthy recreation for young people and regulation of their working conditions. Further, angered by the prevalent assumption that the toleration of vice allowed "virtuous" women to walk the streets safely, she called for moral education and "social control": the cultivation of male self-control and society's insistence on a "single standard" of sexual morality. Characteristically, she also looked forward to women's enfranchisement as a major step toward a civic conscience intolerant of the callous exploitation of poor women.[59]

Walter Lippman judged *A New Conscience* "an hysterical book," "sentimental and naive," and some historians have agreed.[60] Certainly Addams artfully used her genuine distress and compassion to arouse her readers, but the book is not hysterical. Perhaps there is a kind of naïveté in Addams's stubborn hope that the darker compulsions and attractions of sexuality could be educated or legislated out of existence. But the kinds of exploitation she described did constitute a significant element of commercial prostitution. Addams offered a complex analysis of the causes of prostitution, and her solutions were continuous with her progressive and compassionate concern with the coming-of-age of working-class youth in an urban industrial society.[61]

The settlement workers had always viewed their work with youth as prophylactic as well as educational. Because of their exposure to the dilemmas of immigrant family life, the settlers were sharply aware of the city's seductive attractions for young people. Just before the war, the settlement workers began to express a heightened solicitude for the moral safety of adolescents, a preoccupation manifested in special NFS studies on the adolescent girl and the adolescent boy and carried into the war years as the settlements joined the moral purity campaign. In particular, the popular culture of the immediate prewar years had aroused a special vigilance that persisted into the 1920s.[62]

Early motion pictures seemed if anything worse than the vaudeville melodramas. The settlement workers were among the middle-class reformers who, as Lary May has argued, saw the movies as undermining family values by attractively portraying youthful sexuality and rebellion. In Boston settlement workers actively lobbied for state censorship to supplement what they felt was the ineffective work of the National Board of Review—apparently with little success.[63] In a number of cities, the settlements responded to their inability to control the commercial movie houses by sponsoring their own showings of morally acceptable films: a decision that typified their mission to provide palatable alternatives to urban popular culture and also recognized the inexorable growth of the cinema's popularity beyond the urban working class. The movies were here to stay.[64]

The settlements approached the "dance problem" in the same manner. By 1913 a new menace to the morals of youth had joined the sale of liquor in the public dance halls: the "new dances" inspired by ragtime, more athletic and sexually suggestive than the sedate waltz or fox-trot.[65] The settlement workers joined forces with other moral purity campaigners and the civil authorities in some cities to deplore this debasement of a civilized social activity.[66] Some settlements offered dance classes that taught only those dances that were not "inherently unrefined"; settlements in all cities held more dances, and the new steps were sternly prohibited.[67] One of the tasks of the War Camp Community Service, in which many settlements participated, was monitoring the public dance halls—a thankless and probably futile task.[68] The Roaring Twenties brought new headaches for the settlement workers. One house, perhaps feeling impotent to stem the tide entirely, specifically ruled out the "high kicks" of the Charleston.[69] Intersettlement organizations in Boston and New York published detailed guidelines for proper social dancing. The United Neighborhood Houses of New York suggested that "refined persons should refuse to dance on a floor where couples touch cheeks, take 'neck holds,' make exaggerated movements or shake the upper parts of their bodies."[70] As with the movies, the reformers' campaigns to control the dance halls were partially successful. The halls themselves found it profitable to tap an increasing middle-class market by sprucing up their appearance and standards of decorum. The appeal of the new dances knew no class distinctions; they too flourished.[71]

The persistence of Victorian social and moral values went deeper in the settlement movement than these shudders at the new sexual "freedom" manifested by the cinema's indecencies and the suggestiveness of the Charleston. The settlements' work with youth continued to be decisively shaped by the aims first enunciated in the 1890s. The traditional settlement emphasis on character building, the heritage of the Victorian milieu in which the settlements first flourished, saw its apotheosis in the youth work of the 1920s. Lea Demarest Taylor, the headworker at Chicago Commons after her father retired in 1922, reminded her staff in 1924 that "the building of character . . . should really be the ultimate aim of all club or class work."[72] Young people's clubs, especially those for boys, throve in the postwar settlements. In tandem with their heightened concern with the "street life" of the young people, dating from the prewar years, the settlers devoted unprecedented energy to defining the goals and methods of club work.[73]

Athletics became the centerpiece of the boys' activities. Sports and games in real gymnasiums attracted the boys to the houses like no other feature and were seen as ideally suited to bring out desirable character traits. This conjunction of games and character building is not surprising in the era that saw the coincidental rise of college athletics and the climax of the rhetoric of Christian manhood in the colleges. In 1920 the head of the Chicago Commons physical department outlined his aims: "to promote . . . the highest physical, mental, and moral efficiency of the boys as essential in the development of the highest type of manhood."[74] A few years earlier, the physical director at Henry Street had put the case even more vigorously: "The gymnasium today is a manhood factory and manhood is more than a bunch of muscle and more than a skilled machine. Manhood is a strong human body, the vehicle of a sound mind and the home of a big, clean soul. Character is the thing we seek to cultivate."[75] A riflery instructor agreed: "Personally, I am shooting at the same target with Jesus Christ, and sooner or later I endeavor to get each boy on the range that he, also, may shoot with me."[76]

The boys' clubs pursued the same goals through a broader range of activities. "The raising of the standard of discipline and honor, and increase in house spirit and respect and self-government" were the aims of the boys' department of the University of Chicago Settlement.[77] Club activities that might cultivate these qualities were varied; besides athletics, the boys might enjoy woodworking, money-raising projects for the house or club, and with some groups, debate or discussion. Many of the club leaders tried to teach parliamentary procedure and encouraged self-government within the group.[78] One leader testified that "When they suggest, 'we just talk,' I think the very best opportunity to find out, what is troubling a boy, or what he is interested in, is at hand."[79]

Girls had traditionally received less social attention than boys, as Mary McDowell pointed out. "Even when boys are very naughty they are dramatic and hold attention. The faults and follies of girls . . . may be even more serious than the waywardness of boys but the public is quicker in running to the call to save the boys than they are to save the girls."[80] By 1912 the settlements had begun to redress the imbalance; the first major project of the National Federation of Settlements was a study of the adolescent girl, conducted by Robert Woods and his young protégé, Albert J. Kennedy, and published as *Young Working Girls.* In the same vein though less poetically than Addams in *The Spirit of Youth,* the authors described the special pressures on working-class adolescent girls, the dangers of urban pleasures, and the contributions the settlements and other agencies could make toward mitigating these problems.[81]

Woods's and Kennedy's suggestions of good girls' club programs reflect the settlement theorists' characteristic mixture of progressive educational ideals and conservative social assumptions. Not surprisingly, the result was uncannily similar to the prescriptions for women's higher education at the turn of the century. As with the boys, prime emphasis was laid on building character through constructive activity. Girls should be encouraged to develop their individual talents and personalities; they should learn group loyalty and self-government; and they should have outlets for their physical and creative energies in gymnastics, dancing, drama, and singing.[82] In addition, an ideal program of club and class work should address the special concerns of the girl as a future "housewife and mother." "Housework should be made a fine art and linked with all that is best in life." In sum, the young girl's settlement experience should be fashioned to bring out her latent attraction to the "refinements of life" and thus prepare her for her role in the family and society.[83]

Most settlement workers seem to have shared this vision of the ideal club program for girls. The Chicago Commons residents tellingly described their task as aiding girls to make an "adjustment to life."[84] While the club leaders worked to cultivate in girls the qualities they found more prevalent among the boys—group spirit and "clubbability," interest in organized activities, and individual initiative—they also reinforced sharp role distinctions. At a girls' leaders' meeting of the United Neighborhood Houses in 1924, several participants recommended a special athletic program for girls that would stress "group work and the development of general physique instead of training individuals for record-breaking." One woman pleaded the settlement workers' "moral responsibility" to "frown upon" strictly competitive behavior like "going in for speed at track meets," and she reminded her colleagues that girls should not be allowed to jump on the hard gym floors, "on account of the jar."[85]

With both boys and girls, the settlement workers continued to act in loco parentis while protesting their primary interest in reinforcing the original family unit. "The settlement approach to the neighborhood is through the family," asserted Chicago Commons in 1927. Program directors urged club leaders to get to know the parents.[86] At the same time, the settlements' continued existence was predicated on the insufficiency of the local family and community to carry out normal social functions and rituals, including the induction of young people into a healthy adulthood. Lillian Wald annually held a "coming out party" for the older girls' clubs. In her invitation letter she explained to the young women: "This means in the minds of mothers and chaperones of society that a new dignity has come upon you, that you are more responsible and that more can be expected of you."[87] In matters that impinged on the family's traditional role in monitoring children's sexual coming-of-age, the settlers trod with extreme caution. They had to balance their desire to intervene in the social process that led to prostitution and other sociosexual ills against their justified fears of arousing the ire of

local families and the wider settlement audience. Further, the settlement workers shared their society's general skittishness toward sex.
Though some advocated explicit instruction in sex, most were far more
comfortable with education by suggestion and example, such as in
sponsoring "wholesome" dances and informal social events where boys
and girls could meet in a homelike setting.[88]

In their work with young people, the settlers continued to stress
good leadership in language almost identical to that of the 1890s. In
1913 Rita Wallach Morgenthau explained the Henry Street philosophy of
club leadership:

> We say the most precious thing in life is human personality, the
> right of the child to self-expression, to social expression, and
> the right to play under favorable conditions. . . . The club
> leader's function is to pour into the child's life all the cultural
> material at her command, so as to produce the desired devel-
> opment of the child. . . . [S]imultaneously the club leader is
> extending her horizon, developing her own personality, her
> own talents, and thus while giving expression to these talents
> she is sharing a vital experience with her group.[89]

Almost twenty years later Karl Hesley, the director of clubs at Henry
Street, affirmed the continuing vitality of the old concepts when he
borrowed the tried-and-true formula of circular assertions for a letter of
reference: "I consider his influence in character-building most effective
through example of his own character more than by anything he
teaches. For an organization that stresses character development as
carefully as we do, this statement should bear considerable weight."[90]

The settlement workers universally agreed that the best leaders led
through the force of their own personalities as well as sympathy with
the needs and standards of the young people they worked with. In 1922
a settlement propagandist told the story of a New York street gang that
had metamorphosed into a promising club because of the tactful leadership and example of a former Princeton football star. "It took simply
contact with something a little better than street corner standards to win
their devotion."[91] Another man had no success with one apathetic
group of boys until their cherished pool table was vandalized and he
suggested that they repair it themselves. This inspired in the boys a new
interest in woodworking and planted the seeds of a whole crop of
worthy character traits: cooperation, organization, initiative, loyalty to
the house, and respect for community property.[92]

The settlement movement had always been dominated numerically by women, and the war had further skewed the balance by stripping the houses of their male residents. In the twenties, many men who might have been drawn to settlement boys' work could find employment in organizations such as the YMCA and the new Boy Scouts movement.[93] The settlers generally agreed that boys' clubs ought to be led by men just as girls' clubs naturally required a woman's guidance. Though the reasons for same-sex leadership were rarely spelled out, there were basically two: the desire for a manly role model for boys and the need to keep a tight, and tacitly physical, rein over the unruly youngsters. One boys' worker slipped into a more inclusive chauvinism when he strongly urged that the settlement directors hire a man to run their summer camp: "It should be far more easy to secure a man than a woman with a sense of camp necessities and operation, for indeed common sense and intelligence are greater requisites than any other."[94]

Despite personnel shortages, the larger settlements continued to pay at least lip service to the importance of training their club and activity leaders. At the larger settlements the department heads were generally salaried residents, but the club leaders were increasingly part-time volunteers, so it became even more urgent to ground them in settlement principles and supervise their early work.[95] Some saw the settlements' increasing reliance on volunteers as a way to rekindle the original spark and allow the settlements to serve once again as a meeting ground for diverse sectors of the society. In the early 1920s Arthur C. Holden, a Princeton graduate and settlement booster, argued that the professional worker was a "necessary evil." He harked back to the founding concept of the settlement as simply the residence of educated men and women in poor neighborhoods. "What is needed most of all is a greater number of intelligent visitors . . . who will find in the settlement community the inspiration and the means to a broader social understanding, and who will be moved through the vision of social justice to apply conscious effort toward the improvement of human relationships."[96]

A few houses, notably Henry Street, tried to recruit some leaders from the clubs themselves. In 1921 Charles Cooper of Kingsley House pointed out the propaganda value of that policy: "It answers one of the criticisms of the settlement movement; that we have not developed leadership in the neighborhoods themselves; possibly the featuring of such work may bring back the settlement into prominence again."[97] The settlements heartily welcomed the "local boy made good": the man or woman who had come up through the clubs, gone on to college, and now wanted to donate some time to the settlement.[98] Besides providing positive models, local young people could sometimes keep order and mediate disputes more effectively than "outsiders."[99] Few settlements depended heavily on local leadership, however. Given their belief that young people profited most from leaders of character polished by education and cultural refinement, it is not surprising that settlement leaders' democratic passions stopped short of an indiscriminate mixing of outside and indigenous leaders.

Settlement leaders who advocated using volunteers as a way to return to the roots of the settlement impulse bucked a strong current in social work of the 1920s: the addition of psychiatry to the tools of the social worker's trade. The mental hygiene movement had been launched before the war by Adolf Meyer and Clifford Beers. Meyer, a Swiss-born psychiatrist, brought the philosophy of psychiatric practice into line with progressive social work by insisting that mental health was the product of the dynamic interaction of individuals with their social environment. Rather than isolating the mentally ill in institutions or returning them to an unaltered social situation, Meyer stressed the development of a treatment program within the institution that took into account the social factors bearing upon the individual, followed by therapeutic aftercare involving family and community in the patient's readjustment. Extending treatment from the institution into the community created a professional function that would soon be filled by the psychiatric social worker.[100]

The mental hygiene philosophy was peculiarly compelling to some settlement workers because of its insistence on the importance of family and social environment as media for the formation of "personality." An equally potent attraction may have been the mental hygiene advocates' legitimation of the interventionism already practiced by the settlement workers, particularly since much of the energy invested in psychologizing social work was channeled into work with children. An important offshoot of the mental hygiene movement was the "child guidance" concept of the 1920s.[101] As midwife of the Chicago Juvenile Court and the Juvenile Protection League, Hull-House was intimately involved with the creation of the first Juvenile Psychopathic Institute. Julia Lathrop attended the founding meeting of the National Committee for Mental Hygiene in New York in 1909. She helped found the Chicago branch of the Mental Hygiene Society and recruited Dr. William Healy to head the new Juvenile Psychopathic Institute, spearheaded and largely funded by the philanthropist Ethel Sturges Dummer. Healy's work turned on the conviction that an individual's delinquency was the product of "multiple" idiosyncratic causes. The institute added a new dimension to the work of the Juvenile Court and the Juvenile Protection League as advocates of children in trouble.[102]

In 1917 Healy left the now-difficult Chicago situation to move to Boston as head of the new Judge Baker Foundation, dedicated to extending child guidance services beyond the court system.[103] Forming an early connection with the Boston Social Union, in 1924 Healy found occasion to praise the settlements' contributions to his work with delinquents. The Bostonians modestly attributed their success to the small size of Boston settlements and their districts, which allowed residents to get to know individual children and their families.[104] They could also have acknowledged the persuasive leadership of Robert Woods, who had long advocated the prophylactic segregation of the "feeble-minded" and in 1913 commended to fellow settlement workers the "new and deeply suggestive lines of psychological inquiry and experiment" that pointed to the formative importance of childhood emotional experience.[105] In the 1920s South End House sponsored one of the first "habit clinics" to extend child guidance into the preschool years, the period that disparate schools of psychological thought had come to agree was critical in forming the personality.[106]

In other cities, too, the settlement workers acknowledged the relevance of the mental health movement to their work in the 1920s. Psychiatric terminology and commendations of the importance of psychology in effective work with young people slipped more frequently into the settlers' discourse. (One speaker cautioned a group of girls' workers that "one of the ten commandments for social workers is 'Thou shalt not develop an inferiority complex in anyone.' ")[107] Workers trained in the schools of social work certainly were exposed to the facile Freudian terminology that swept all before it in social work in the 1920s, and probably also to the antagonistic philosophy of the behaviorists. Many social work professionals held as a new article of faith that a knowledge of psychology was indispensable to effective casework.[108] The application of psychology to group work per se was still on the horizon, but some settlement spokesmen pleaded for an end to the "trial and error method" of club work in a favor of a more systematic and scientifically based technique. As one woman protested, "At a time when other professions and the business world are coming to rely more and more upon the expert application of psychological principles to solve their particular problems, the settlement seems still to rely chiefly upon the emotional faculty [for] light and guidance."[109]

With the possible exception of work with young children, though, the new emphasis on psychology in social work seems to have had a largely superficial impact on the settlement movement, for several reasons. Despite their growing preference for trained workers for all activities, the settlement heads worked with limited funds and continued to rely on volunteers guided by a skeletal staff of salaried, quasi-professional workers. The settlements' own training programs, where they existed at all, could hardly provide an extensive grounding in clinical psychology. More important, the settlements continued to be clearinghouses rather than vital centers of those professional services that most heavily absorbed the developing philosophy and techniques of psychological social work: social casework, mental health work, and individual child guidance.

Though the settlements were not heavily affected by the incorporation of psychology into social work, this trend jibed with the settlement spirit of the 1920s as well as with key elements of the settlement tradition.[110] The settlements had centered their educational and social work on character building and had stressed "personality" (a term generally accompanied by the vaguest descriptions, if any) as the prime requisite of the settlement worker. In the 1920s these concepts lived on in the settlements' club work and their attempts to counter the moral threats of modern urban life with wholesome substitutes in recreation, group activities, and the arts. Practical financial constraints forced large portions of the settlements' programs to remain in "amateur" hands, thus resolving de facto any philosophical conflict over the degree of professionalizing the settlements could absorb without a major shift in ideology and purpose.

The settlements had never seen their character-building work and their efforts to improve working and living conditions as fundamentally contradictory. There was no reason the inner reform of the individual and the outer reform of the environment could not reinforce each other. In the reactionary aftermath of the war, many settlements toned down their advocacy of reform or at least put more energy into justifying their intimacy with the immigrant communities, their notorious defense of free speech, and their apparent "softness" toward alien radicals and organized labor. Did this partial retreat from controversial causes signal their acceptance of a new philosophy of social work based on adjusting people to the status quo?

Yes and no. By the 1920s, the settlements were no longer havens for those who sought fundamental social change. Yet such radicals had always constituted a small minority of settlement residents. The settlements may have relinquished their status as beacons of progressive innovation in social welfare after the Great War, but we must also recall that they had never willingly adopted a posture of dissent from a broader consensus on what constituted social justice among people of goodwill. They styled themselves educators, interpreters, and even leaders, but never rebels. Settlement leaders of the second generation were sharply conscious of the proud heritage they carried forward into the 1920s and beyond. Dialogue about the larger aims of the settlement movement never ceased. As the first generation aged, the question of the movement's direction took on a new urgency.

10
Whither the Settlements?

By the mid-1920s much of the national administration of the settlement movement had devolved onto two of the younger leaders, Charles Cooper and Albert Kennedy. On the outsized scale of longevity established by the founding generation, these two were striplings: Cooper, headworker of Kingsley House in Pittsburgh, was fifty-one in 1925, and Kennedy, long associated with South End House and from 1928 headworker at the University Settlement in New York, was forty-six. Kennedy had been assistant secretary of the National Federation of Settlements from 1911 to 1922, then took over as secretary from Robert Woods in 1923. Cooper became president of the NFS in 1925 after Woods's sudden death and remained president until 1930. Together these two men presided over one of the most intensely introspective periods of the settlements' corporate history. It was appropriate that they found themselves, unexpectedly, the spokesmen for two distinct views of what the settlements stood for and what future direction they ought to chart.

Cooper's postwar jitters about the outspoken radicalism of a few social workers must be understood against the backdrop of Pittsburgh's raw and often repressive conservatism. Cooper had attempted, futilely, to mediate in the great steel strike of 1919. After he took over at Kingsley House he tried strenuously to engage Pittsburgh's business and professional communities in friendly dialogue about social issues in the "Hungry Club," a monthly meeting featuring speakers and discussion.[1] While Cooper deplored a confrontational style that would alienate potential sympathizers and financial backers, he also insisted that the settlement continued to play a special role in social reform, dictated by its original mission as an interpreter between social and economic groups. He was frustrated by postwar suggestions that the settlement idea was played out; as he wrote to Woods in 1921: "What . . . I believe hurts the settlement movement here the most is the feeling that the settlement has served its purpose. It seems to be coming from both the radical and conservative groups . . . as if there was some sort of a propaganda against the settlement movement."[2]

Cooper saw the most insidious threat to the settlements' continued vitality in the swelling Community Chest movement. The idea of coordinating all philanthropic resources in the community, to ensure a fair and efficient distribution of funds among social welfare services, predated the war but received its greatest boost from the experience of the "war chests," which often forcibly extracted donations from workers and businesses to be applied to semipublic war-related services.[3] Cooper had in fact been one of the original advocates of this method of financing social services in Pittsburgh; but when the Chamber of Commerce began investigating the feasibility of a Pittsburgh Chest in 1921, Cooper smelled a rat. "So far," he wrote Paul Kellogg, "they have not called the agencies into consultation or participation."[4] With alarm Cooper watched the hurried formation of the Chest plan, which froze out experienced social workers and centered control in the Chamber of Commerce. He pleaded with Kellogg to use the *Survey* to "open up" the issue—"of course, without reference to me or any of us by name." Cooper feared that the discreet battle he would have to wage against the Chamber of Commerce was really a fight to the death; as he told Kellogg, the Chests had become "very dangerous to social progress and to social workers. I don't want you to think I am crazy on this subject, but I believe it is the biggest question in social welfare work of America today . . . [I]t is 'Come in and be controlled or stay out and be crucified.' "[5]

Pittsburgh's move to the Chest was forestalled by Cooper and some more outspoken allies, but until his untimely death in 1930 Cooper monitored the national progress of the Chest movement and its effects on the vitality and diversity of settlement work.[6] In 1928 he wrote to Kennedy, "The urge of the Chest movement is to conformity and standardization, and the Settlement movement stands in the way of this. We must have some general free agencies in social work, and I think the lot has fallen to the Settlement movement, but it will mean trouble with the Chest group."[7] A retrospective assessment suggests that Cooper's fears were well grounded. In her study of the settlements in the Great Depression, Judith Ann Trolander finds that in those cities where the Chest operated—virtually every major city except Chicago and New York—the settlements were not in the forefront of social reform movements of the 1930s. She also points out the tight and often unilateral control of settlement policies, personnel, and daily settlement programs that Chest boards were able to assert.[8]

Cooper was the most vociferous settlement opponent of the Chest movement, though characteristically he limited his frankest comments to his private correspondence and kept his name out of public criticisms of the movement. Other settlers agreed that the Chest was not the best method of settlement finance; the pressing problem was to locate reliable alternatives.[9] Settlement funding had been especially precarious since the war. While some larger settlements had suffered temporarily because of their prominence as targets of reactionary political attacks, many smaller settlements lived hand to mouth in the time-honored way of young establishments.[10] Though the NFS addressed the issue of settlement finance throughout the decade, the national organization could do little except offer advice on methods of fund-raising. Cooper put together a report titled "Settlement Finance" in 1924 and followed it in 1929 with a short study of settlement endowments.[11] Endowments were understandably popular in the 1920s. Some of the larger and older settlements secured substantial endowments after the first troubled postwar years.[12] Fund-raising continued to be a perennial—or more accurately, annual—headache for headworkers and their boards, however. Anniversaries often served as vehicles for fund drives. South End House, for example, mounted a drive in 1923 to celebrate its twenty-fifth anniversary (presumably under that name, since Andover House had been founded in 1893). Starting with a goal of $125,000, the drive was extended to 1930—Boston's tercentenary—and the final goal increased to $300,000.[13]

Other houses relied on annual contributions from loyal subscribers, occasionally supplemented by special drives. The Henry Street Settlement had unusually large needs, maintaining the nursing program as well as the arts and regular settlement activities. Though Jacob Schiff frowned on endowments—"Each generation must do its own altruistic and philanthropic work"—he approved a deficit fund, and he and Wald rode herd on the other members of the board to participate in solicitations.[14] Henry Street was one of the first settlements to hire public relations experts to publicize its activities and coordinate fund drives. In 1918 the settlement engaged the public relations pioneer Ivy Lee to manage publicity—but Lee "did not make good" and was dismissed.[15]

Besides Wald's popularity among liberal New Yorkers and the settlement's careful cultivation of wealthy patrons, the Henry Street Settlement may have been unusually successful in raising money precisely because of its special, expensive programs. It was relatively easy to illustrate the financial needs of visiting nurses, a neighborhood playhouse, summer camps, and a recreation program. It was more challenging to arouse enthusiasm for the more nebulous mission of the settlements: their traditional functions as good neighbors, "listening posts," purveyors of true Americanism to immigrants. It was hard to "sell" the settlements as beacons of progressive reform, not just because of the conservative political climate of the 1920s, but also because the fruits of reform were often intangible. In 1921 nothing came of Robert Woods's idea that the Carnegie trustees should grant a large sum to each of eight or ten leading settlements to sustain them through the hard times.[16] In 1926 the Carnegie Corporation awarded $25,000 to the NFS to create a "Settlement and Community School Music Council."[17]

The settlements' financial problems in the 1920s were linked to the philosophical debate over the direction of the settlement movement. In formulating their fund-raising goals—and sometimes contemplating the stark question of survival—the settlers were forced to reckon with their ultimate aims and whether these should change to fit an altered social context. In a letter of 1925, as the NFS office regrouped following Woods's death, Cooper told Kennedy that he saw "two tendencies" in the contemporary settlement movement. The first was the one Kennedy seemed to advocate: the settlement as "an experimental, educational institution with a special emphasis on arts and craft." The second, for which Cooper himself carried the torch, was the old concept of the settlement "as a liberalizing influence in all phases of life." Especially now, he felt, with attacks on liberalism in politics, industry and religion, the settlement should renew its old pledge to "finding . . . underlying unities back of the conflicts in thought and life today" and address large questions such as "Peace, Industrial Adjustment, Government, International Relations, Free Speech, Fundamentalism."[18] He suggested bluntly that the push toward compartmentalism and concern with technique that accompanied an emphasis on the arts and special education was "all fine and good, but secondary." Cooper was mounting the same revolt against "standardization" that fueled his campaign against the Community Chest. He had renewed the protest of the young settlement movement against routine and institutionalism, and against the complacency inherent in forgoing risky innovation in favor of buttressing tried-and-true activities.[19]

Cooper's belief that Albert Kennedy personified the settlements' inward-turning tendency was in some ways unfair. Among his contemporaries Kennedy had perhaps the broadest experience of settlement life and concerns. Having taken a degree in divinity at Rochester and served as a minister in Minnesota for several years, Kennedy came to settlement work with a fellowship at South End House to study economic change and sociology. He was "director of investigations" at South End House from 1908 to 1914, served as assistant secretary of the NFS, and collaborated with Woods on the *Handbook of Settlements* and the eloquent and compendious *Settlement Horizon* of 1922. He worked in regular settlement activities, including boys' work, and helped to develop wartime community programs used by settlements nationwide.[20] Only as secretary of the NFS did he turn his attention to settlement arts programs, by advocating special departments to organize arts work and disseminate information on administration and technique.

Kennedy was dismayed at being pigeonholed as a "conservative with a special interest in the arts and crafts," but he defended the legitimacy of his concern with high standards of achievement in settlement activities. Though it might be true that the settlers were becoming too "concrete," he parried, "My feeling is that we used to be too nebulous." He questioned whether the settlements should shoulder primary responsibility for discussing large social issues when there were organizations with the expertise and resources to handle complex questions such as peace, capital punishment, economic issues, and religion. The settlements should foster *local* discussion and monitor the impact of these issues on their neighborhoods. Finally, Kennedy argued, Cooper had delineated an unnecessary "dualism" of settlement interests. Some members of the NFS would be alienated by a commitment to the priority of large, abstract questions. Each settlement should concentrate on what its residents did best; the task of the NFS was to coordinate and harmonize "the widest possible diversity of fine interests."[21]

The Kennedy-Cooper debate touched off a new round of stocktaking when Kennedy circulated Cooper's letter among settlement leaders around the country. Though most of the headworkers who responded agreed with Kennedy that there was room for both "technique" and inspiration in the settlement movement, they expressed a longing for the old days of progressive leadership and a conviction that the settlement had a continuing role as an "interpreter," as Lillian Wald wrote. Harriet Vittum of the Northwestern Settlement in Chicago asserted that the settlements must "understand that they are experiment stations and they are willing to help people who are just beginning to think, to think aloud, and that they will not be afraid." S. Max Nelson invoked the old settlement metaphor when he wrote, "I like to think of the settlement as a log-fort on the frontier. For certainly we are [on] as difficult a frontier as ever existed." Lou-Eva Longan, Mary McDowell's understudy at the University of Chicago Settlement, mourned the settlement's "liberalizing influence" as a "phase of the past." "I am in sympathy with the trend toward closer organization, with the effort toward what modern industrialism terms 'efficiency,' but I see and I *feel* its dangers. . . . I feel we are apt to go astray and lose our souls." Though young workers brought "highly specialized, technical training," they lacked "any particular feeling concerning the brotherhood of man or understanding of the principles which some of us hold very dear."[22]

In 1926 the NFS asked headworkers to comment on "Settlement Goals for the Next Third of a Century." The range of responses must have heartened Kennedy, with his catholic approach to settlement philosophy. The headworkers cited greater emphasis on small-group and individual work, more rigorous training for residents, ever-stronger programs in the arts, and a more effective "education" of settlement and community fund boards. Most headworkers also espoused political and spiritual aims. Cornelia Bradford of New Jersey's Whittier House offered an ambitious platform of progressive political goals culminating in world peace. Another headworker called for the settlements to stress those "spiritual, religious and moral truths which make for a higher type of character." Charles Cooper stated flatly that "the Goal of the Settlement house is a new world."[23]

By 1928 the current of settlement opinion seemed to be flowing so strongly in Cooper's direction that Kennedy offered his resignation as secretary of the NFS.[24] Cooper begged Kennedy to reconsider. "The Settlement movement must be broad enough and deep enough to include great-souled people like yourself who want to bring the cultural advantages to all people, and . . . also to include those Settlement people who see the misunderstandings and conflicts in life today and who believe with their whole heart that the Settlement has a mission in this field."[25] In a remarkable meeting in 1928, the executive committee rejected Kennedy's resignation and took a vote of confidence in his accomplishments. The committee itself took responsibility for any imbalance of emphasis that had fettered the settlements' work in tackling national economic and social issues. Committee members agreed on the importance of NFS leadership, especially for settlements led by younger workers. John Elliott, Lea Taylor, George Bellamy of Hiram House in Cleveland, and Paul Kellogg, a longtime member of the committee, proposed that the NFS undertake a study of unemployment as the first initiative in a rededication to broader social issues. The project would be modeled on the Prohibition study in concentrating on the human impact of unemployment, already a major problem in settlement neighborhoods.[26]

Albert Kennedy stayed on as NFS secretary until 1934, when he was succeeded by Lillie Peck, the protégée of Boston's veteran settlement worker, Ellen Coolidge of South End House.[27] The unemployment study was delegated to Helen Hall, headworker at the University Settlement in Philadelphia, who coordinated the gathering of case studies. Two books resulted: Hall's *Case Studies of Unemployment,* used by Congress in reckoning with unemployment after the depression hit in 1929, and *Some Folks Won't Work,* an account akin to Bruère's Prohibition report in tone and content, written by the free-lancer Clinch Calkins.[28]

In 1928 the NFS took another step to reassert the vitality of the settlement movement by founding a journal devoted exclusively to settlement concerns. From its name, *Neighborhood,* to its projected content—articles on settlement philosophy, special programs, international settlements, and the history of the American movement—the journal stood as a declaration of the settlement movement's continuity with its own traditions and its innovative influence in American life. Kennedy served as editor, and the advisory board integrated older and younger leaders. As a special feature, the journal would include photographs of the founders "fit for framing."[29] *Neighborhood* flourished for four years until the general economic disaster dried up its funding.

The American settlement leaders took particular pride in helping to found the International Federation of Settlements in 1922. Their connection with the English settlements had become more of a sentimental and inspirational relationship than a functional alliance.[30] Samuel Barnett's death in 1913 gave the Americans a sad occasion to recall their roots in the Christian Socialist ferment of late Victorian England and their spiritual debt to the English churchman. Henrietta Barnett conveniently orchestrated the American settlers' mourning by forwarding the numerous British letters of condolence, clippings, and obituaries.[31] The American settlers made other personal contacts with their English counterparts in the period before the war. Touring English settlement workers, politicians, and labor leaders had made a point of visiting the leading American settlements. The Fabians were particularly faithful; the Webbs, Graham Wallas, and H. G. Wells all stopped at Hull-House on their way through Chicago.[32] Indeed, Jane Addams was the chief point of contact between the American settlers and English reformers. After one visit John Burns reportedly said, "The greatest man in America is a woman."[33] W. T. Stead struck a different note when he called Addams "the sweetheart of humanity."[34] In 1913 Maude Royden, an English suffragist, begged Addams for a propaganda contribution: "Your name carries the very greatest weight over here . . . thousands of people would read [your words] who would never look at any other Suffrage writing."[35]

The outbreak of war rekindled hope that a traditional ideological sympathy could be stepped up to a working alliance. When some of the American women paused in England on their way to the Hague conference in 1915, the English settlers lionized Addams while various groups exploited her popularity for the peace cause. She made several public speeches and met representatives of the Fellowship of Reconciliation.[36] Beatrice Webb invited her to attend a Fabian-sponsored peace conference.[37] Henrietta Barnett eagerly played hostess to her beloved American friend and fellow peace partisan. "I cannot help thinking you should talk to some big folk," she wrote to Addams. "Would you like to see the Queen? She is quite a good sort."[38]

After the war came renewed efforts to create a transatlantic settlement community. The American settlers tried unsuccessfully to persuade the Rockefeller Foundation to underwrite the British settlements until they could struggle back to financial health after the war.[39] The formidably energetic Henrietta Barnett pulled the Americans into several other projects in the next decade. As the doyenne of the English settlement movement and the self-appointed apostle of friendship between the English-speaking peoples, Mrs. Barnett ultimately became something of a burden to the Americans, who appreciated her strenuous gestures of goodwill but, preoccupied with postwar issues, had difficulty matching her enthusaiasm for various Anglo-American projects. In 1919 her two-volume biography of Canon Barnett was published and, thanks to a private gift, was distributed to all the American member houses of the NFS.[40] In 1920 Mrs. Barnett planned a lecture tour in the United States and Canada, including an invited appearance at the NFS, a project that gave both pleasure and trouble to the American settlers who scrambled to book lectures for Barnett after the Pond agency of Chicago gave up in despair. There was apparently little public enthusiasm for her intended topic of housing reform.[41]

In 1924 Mrs. Barnett floated the idea of an Anglo-American "Barnett Fellowship," to be held alternately by an Englishman and an American, to promote cross-cultural understanding through research and observation in settlements and other social agencies. The NFS agreed to raise half of the $25,000 endowment and appointed Jane Addams to head the American fellowship committee. It took three years of heavy-handed solicitation among the American settlements and not always amicable negotiation with the British committee, headed by Mrs. Barnett and the Toynbee Hall warden, J. J. Mallon, to launch the fellowship. Cornelia Bradford spoke for many American headworkers when she wrote to Kennedy, "It is a struggle for a New Jersey settlement just to live and all are suffering most acutely at present from lack of funds to carry along their work." Finally in February 1927 Addams could report to Kennedy that the promised sum had been hand delivered to Mrs. Barnett in London. The first American fellow was dispatched to England the next year.[42] Close on the heels of the fellowship plan, Mrs. Barnett renewed her campaign for another Anglo-American project: the rescue from developers of a piece of London land called "Bunker Hill," to be preserved as a monument to Anglo-American cooperation in the Great War. But the settlements had been milked dry for the Barnett Fellowship, and the Americans politely begged off.[43]

The American settlers' postwar solicitude for the English settlements and their interest in European relief and reconstruction underlay their collective commitment to an international organization of settlements. There had been a handful of Continental settlements before the war, including a Parisian settlement founded in 1897.[44] The French settlements tended to follow the English rather than the American model, as outgrowths of Catholic or Protestant denominational social work.[45] During the war several of the settlements turned to relief and medical work, and several more were founded for that purpose. After the war one of the leading French settlements, La Résidence Sociale, turned to the American settlers for help in the relief work that had fallen to the French settlements. In 1920 Ellen Coolidge of South End House traveled to France to help organize the French settlement movement.[46]

Fifty-four years old in 1920, Coolidge came from an old Boston family with a special kind of cosmopolitan background; her uncle had been ambassador to France, and she had made her first journey abroad to visit him. As a longtime resident of South End House, she had been exposed to Robert Woods's missionary approach to settlement work. While Woods persuaded the British settlements to federate in 1921 in anticipation of a drive toward international cooperation, Coolidge worked on the French. In 1922 the Fédération des Centres Sociaux was formed, and Coolidge was elected its president. She promptly turned the office over to a Frenchwoman.[47]

With Coolidge, Woods, and Addams representing the American NFS, plans were made for the first International Conference of Settlements at Toynbee Hall in 1922. Representatives from over one hundred settlements in twenty nations attended. Predictably, the meeting was more inspirational than palpably constructive. The spiritual high point came after several days of suppressed tension, when the senior settlement representatives of France and Germany sealed their agreement to cooperate with an embrace in the Toynbee quadrangle.[48] The conferees vacillated between aspiring to a kind of League of Nations status in social issues and carefully acknowledging the limited scope of their settlements' expertise.[49] Ensuing conferences, held in 1926, 1929, 1932, and 1936 (the last conference before the war), tried to relate the settlements' concrete interests to wider social issues. The conferees considered settlement contributions to the progress of social relations, social service in relation to the community, the bearing of the "present crisis" on settlement work (in 1932), and the settlements and "mass suggestion" (in 1936).[50]

The apparent ambiguity of the International Federation's self-conceived role mirrored the energetic debate among American settlers as to the settlement's social function and the proper scope of its external concerns. In America, in Europe, and in Asia, where a handful of settlements had been established by missionaries and Western-educated nationals, settlement workers naturally saw themselves as representatives of a cosmopolitanism enunciated by the founding settlement philosophy and embodied in their humanitarian concerns. The founding of the Internation Federation in one sense sealed this commitment to a broad view of their mission in the world. Yet, the complexities of international relations, the multiplication of academically certified experts in health, welfare, education, and social and political science, and the proliferation of private and public agencies dedicated to specific aspects of social welfare and social relations effectively truncated the settlements' field of action and sent them searching for the unique contribution they might make to their own societies and to international comity.

The pressure the settlement leaders felt to renew their sense of purpose came not only from the need to reorient themselves in a new world but also from the increasing urgency of indoctrinating younger leaders to carry on where the older ones would soon leave off. A molding and testing process began in the mid-1920s. In 1928 Cooper appointed a program committee for the NFS convention made up exclusively of younger headworkers, as a "challenge" to them from the older generation.[51] The neophytes did not always come up to snuff, as John Elliott confided to Lillian Wald after an NFS conference: "Between ourselves, I did not feel that the youngsters were many of them enormously promising although some of them were, and may be we have put too much of an inferiority complex on them."[52] The Old Guard's esprit de corps and undiminished watchfulness over their corporate creation created a loose but effective machinery for monitoring the statements and policies of the novices. In 1932 the new male headworker at the Riis Settlement made the egregious error of comparing women headworkers unfavorably with men in a newspaper interview. Jane Addams picked up the item in Chicago and sent the clipping uptown to Lea Taylor, then president of the NFS, with the comment, "I think that the Federation of Settlements might consider disciplining this young man. It's a voice of forty years ago." Taylor mailed the clipping to Albert Kennedy at the University Settlement in New York. Equally disgusted, Kennedy promised to speak to the young man. A public apology for making "a terrible ass of himself" would not be out of order for the hapless sinner, Kennedy suggested. "It certainly is a bad start for the headworker of an old and respected settlement."[53]

Headworkers like Kennedy and Lea Taylor, whose experience spanned the settlement "generations," felt a special responsibility for ensuring that the torch was passed. There is no evidence that Taylor felt uncomfortable with the peculiarly literal filiopietism of her position. After graduating from Vassar she returned to Chicago Commons and worked her way up through the ranks, becoming head resident in 1922.[54] She felt a deep obligation to perpetuate the traditions of the Commons and the settlement movement in general; she stubbornly continued vespers despite the increasing indifference of the residents, and in the late 1920s she instituted a special monthly residents' meeting for "training" in the "history, aims and endeavors of the settlement movement."[55]

In a symposium of young headworkers in *Neighborhood* in 1930, one man turned the tables on the Old Guard by charging that the tacit aims of the settlements had not kept pace with the changing needs of the neighborhoods. Between the Scylla of "a general and vague vocabulary of the aims of the work" and the Charybdis of young workers who could speak only in terms of "the new sociology, the new psychology, the new education etc." lay an "appalling ignorance of purpose" in both staff and volunteer workers. The result, he asserted in a familiar vein, was overconcentration on specific programs and an insufficient sense of the ultimate direction of the settlements.[56]

Consensus on appropriate training for settlement workers continued to elude the leaders. By the late 1920s, the tightly run Henry Street Settlement was advising applicants that some training was almost mandatory, but it lapsed into vagueness when pressed for a specific program. Lillian Wald informed one social service placement officer that Henry Street workers were encouraged to take courses in one of the New York schools of social work: "The profession of social work requires at the present time definite training."[57] About the same time, one of Wald's assistants wrote to a young applicant that it would be very difficult to indicate what "specific training" was necessary in such a broad field as settlement work, aside from "a knowledge of the fundamental problems of society. There is no type of training or education which cannot be called into use."[58] Headworkers generally agreed that workers in well-defined fields like kindergarten and nutrition must seek the training available in universities and schools of social work. The settlements had pioneered in these fields, and it would have been unseemly to allow standards of work to slip back into amateurism.[59] A few independent programs in less professionally demarcated areas, such as Neva Boyd's training course in recreation operating out of Hull-House, won wide respect from settlement leaders.[60]

Beyond education in the tools of one's trade, some settlement leaders continued to pay lip service to the relevance of academic social science to settlement work. A New Haven headworker asserted that a settlement worker "really must have some training in sociology, economics, psychology, a smattering of industry, health and civics in addition to his or her special interest or accomplishment."[61] Another spokesman turned this prescription on its head by arguing that settlement work itself was "an appreciation course in economics and sociology." To the part-time volunteer, "wage scales, death rates, population densities" became the " 'stuff lives are made of' and to the getting of knowledge has been added understanding."[62]

This glowing tribute to experience as an education for settlement workers suggests that in many ways the settlement movement had come full circle in its quest for a new rationale. A set of tensions had been built into settlement doctrine at the movement's inception that offered either an invitation to failure or the key to success, according to the degree of vigilance the settlers could maintain over their own enterprise. In honoring the dictates of adaptability to their environment and the elevation of process over results, the settlements had cultivated an elasticity that had allowed them to expand in the directions of their greatest successes. Those very successes had threatened another facet of settlement identity: its anti-institutionalism and commitment to spontaneity. The elaboration of arts and recreation programs and the gradual absorption of an ethic of expertise implicated the settlements in the movement toward professionalism in social work, a trend they had actively abetted at a number of points. Welfare professionalism was in one sense the antithesis of the settlements' philosophical foundation in the idea of universal brotherhood and spiritual equality embodied in social Christianity. Yet it was also the logical culmination of the settlement pioneers' faith in social knowledge as the key to reform.

The challenges of social and political change in the 1920s reinvigorated and complicated the settlement workers' self-assessment. They found themselves making what seemed to some an artificial choice between their "internal" and "external" activities: between continuing their traditional commitment to social reform in the wider society and, in effect, cultivating their own gardens. It was not so much that these alternatives were inherently contradictory as that one seemed to bleed energy from the other; either the settlement workers concentrated on the "larger questions" of national life or they burrowed into the minutiae of successful local programs. Further, each choice posed a problem to the settlement's role in society. As Kennedy argued to Cooper, many social issues were better handled by special interest groups with the resources and expertise for agitation and policy molding. The settlement workers had become amateurs in some of the very fields they had opened up: public health, labor organization, immigration policy. In some of their internal programs in recreation and child care, the settlers had to face the consequences of their own success. Many municipalities *had* shouldered the burden of providing facilities for recreation, and the establishment of special child guidance clinics as well as the rapid development of the public school curriculum had made some settlement programs redundant or obsolete.

Of course, American cities had hardly become the utopias of early settlement dreams. There had been significant improvements, as the aging Robert Hunter reflected in 1936: "Our campaigns against tuberculosis, sweat shop labor, the shark type of pawnbroker, child labor, unsanitary conditions, the dreadful 'lung block,' have all been moderately successful, and these things are now generally recognized as inexcusable evils in a country as rich as ours."[63]

On the debit side, housing for the poor remained wretched, unions were still not tolerated in many industries, "vice" continued to flourish, and when the Great Depression hit full force in 1929, the unemployed found themselves as nearly resourceless as they had been in the dreadful winter of 1893–94. These were problems to which the settlement workers had devoted intense energy. The settlement leaders also showed what today we would see as "blind spots" in their identification and condemnation of major social problems. In its first forty years the settlement movement did not ameliorate, or even directly address, white society's systematic discrimination against black Americans. Though several of the white founders of the NAACP had settlement connections, institutionally the settlements failed to make any significant contribution to white Americans' consciousness of racism or to furthering black people's rights and opportunities.[64]

Further, as Cooper repeatedly emphasized, the atmosphere of liberalism that had allowed the settlements and other reform groups to make inroads into urban problems at the turn of the century had almost completely dissipated by the 1920s, leaving a clear field for intolerance, repression, and a popular attitude of political complacency and ignorance of social problems. Given this catalog of public ills and unfinished business, surely there was still room in national life for the settlement idea, if only the proper mode of reconsecration could be found.

In 1936, a year after Jane Addams's death, Albert Kennedy reflected:

> Ever since that memorable day in 1926 when I opened a note from Jane Addams containing her contribution to the Symposium on "Goals" and read the luminous sentence, "The only goal of the settlement is to bring the inspiration and resources of the higher life to a larger number of people" I have felt in intellectual equilibrium as to what settlement work is all about. . . . Our goal is the fullest and most rounded life for everybody in the degree that each can take up into his experience the wealth of the universe.[65]

The settlement idea, claimed Kennedy, was above all a *method,* a technique for bringing the "higher life" to all. Only the failure of that method could vitiate the settlement. But what did the method consist of? In trying to answer that question, Kennedy pinpointed the central vulnerability of the settlement movement. "We have preferred to trust in the hunches of a certain number of admittedly superior and unusual minds, such as Jane Addams and Robert Woods. The settlement movement, more than any other technique I can think of, has been one of action by superior personalities. There is no assurance that we can replace them. The technique or method of the settlement is, in overwhelming degree, the mental and emotional habits of these leaders." By Kennedy's lights, the settlement movement's greatest strength was in the end its greatest weakness; its founding idea carried the seeds of its own decay.

The women and men who launched the settlement movement in the United States and nurtured it through its remarkable first four decades *were* extraordinary individuals; in a real sense, history is biography for the American settlements from 1890 to 1930. Liberally educated at a time of rapid change in American higher education, they absorbed the rhetoric of Christian social organicism that characterized the new social sciences and the Anglo-American cult of character that suffused fin de siècle justifications of a liberal arts education in the age of the university. The settlement workers moved out to the frontier—as they would say—of the new social scientific approach to social problems that stressed empirical investigation of living and working conditions and carried in its wake an emphasis on the environmental causes of poverty. At the same time, their "method"—living naturally as neighbors to those they hoped to help, establishing face-to-face relations based on mutual trust and respect—was profoundly subjective and drew its potency from its resonance with the deepest cultural assumptions of potential settlement residents. An individual's character constituted both spiritual and worldly capital; it was the most precious thing one could offer to and cultivate in another person.

As the settlements expanded the realities of settlement work changed, but the initial conception of the settlement worker died hard. In one important sense the introduction of salaried workers vitiated the original concept of the settlement as a living arrangement, a deceptively simple and fundamentally radical assault on the class divisions the founders perceived in the American industrial cities. In another sense, though, the partial professionalization of settlement work, as of all social work, suggests a different affirmation of democracy; a free market in acquired skills might gradually replace the noblesse oblige inescapably present in the settlement venture. A more subtle but equally profound continuity in social work values may be found, I think, in the ascendancy of the "case" model in twentieth-century social work, harking back not only to the then-innovative plan of the Victorian charity organizers but to the idea that motivated them: that face-to-face contact between helper and helped, based on the efficacy of personal influence in promoting behavioral and attitudinal change, is the "one best system" in social welfare.

During their heyday from 1890 to the Great War, the American settlement workers made tremendous contributions to campaigns for improved living and working conditions, protective legislation for children, public health, public education, and political reform. They joined other reformers in inveighing against the "twin evils" of urban life, prostitution and the saloon, and they resisted the popular culture of their time by seeking to replace vaudeville and the dance halls with forms of recreation and entertainment they viewed as more wholesome and uplifting. Of course these activities constituted a multifaceted attempt at "social control": the imposition of middle-class culture and values on the lower classes. I hope I have demonstrated, though, that most of the settlement leaders truly believed in "social democracy" as they conceived it, and some made imaginative and influential contributions to new conceptions of cultural pluralism that recognized, with greater or lesser success, "immigrant gifts" to American society.

Though the settlement folk honored conventional morality, for themselves and their neighbors, they also posed sharp though sometimes unintended challenges to the status quo. This paradox is nowhere clearer than in the ramifications of the preponderance of women in the settlements. Historians have rightly focused on the significance of the settlement movement in offering hundreds of middle-class women a working sphere beyond their own households. Women were drawn to the movement largely because the settlement idea tapped qualities and roles that their culture had enthroned as feminine virtues: domesticity, nurturance, a special solicitude for the homely details of daily life, and moral guardianship over family and community. At the same time women held positions of genuine equality with men in leading the movement and became influential spokesmen on public issues that had previously been the domain of men. The movement's wealth of strong female leadership affected its ideological evolution and practical influence at several levels. The most immediate impact was on the men and women in the settlement "rank and file" who witnessed and experienced female leadership, often for the first time, and on the male leaders, reckoning from the beginning with women who individually were often more popular and charismatic than they themselves were.

Further, it may be argued that the settlement workers had an important influence on middle-class Americans' attitudes toward the cities, and that the strong presence of women in the movement profoundly affected the settlers' collective message concerning urban life. The settlement workers stressed the gratifications and fundamental normality, as well as the trials, of life in the industrial cities. They reduced the city to human scale by treating that complex agglomeration of peoples and forces—both abstract and concrete—as an extended household. The settlement itself was, in the first instance, simply another household, but one whose life intentionally embraced and spilled over into the lives of the surrounding households. The socialization of most of the women settlers had made them peculiarly fitted for and comfortable with this approach to social reform. Envisioning and effecting change from the neighborhoods outward, publicizing the incidents of their daily lives, the settlers called attention to the random, idiosyncratic, natural rhythms of urban life rather than the relentless, unforgiving, and somewhat sinister industrial rhythms and routines that had come to epitomize the *threat* of the city for so many Americans. The settlement workers injected color and detail into the monochromatic image of the urban landscape.

The settlement movement was at once sui generis and promiscuously tangled up with almost every strand of American reform culture of the late nineteenth and twentieth centuries. Above all, the movement was the vehicle for an idea, or perhaps more accurately, an affirmation or article of faith. The settlement idea embodied and perpetuated the spirit of social Christianity that transformed the Victorian worship of character and personality into the assertion of the value of every human life and its vital connection to every other human life. In the settlement medium, the Christian philanthropic model of personal service was to be transformed into an ideal of spiritual democracy. The settlements institutionalized the religion of humanity that was one of the most potent products of Victorian middle-class culture and served as one of the most powerful conduits of Victorian social thought into the twentieth century. For good or ill, that portion of the complex and multifaceted settlement legacy has yet to be dissipated.

Manuscript Sources

Includes Abbreviations of Frequently Cited Collections.

Chicago Historical Society, Chicago, Illinois.
    Chicago Commons. Records. (CCR)
    McDowell, Mary. Papers.
    Sikes, Madeleine Wallin. Papers.
    Taylor, Lea Demarest. Papers. (LDTP)
University of Chicago, Chicago, Illinois. Special Collections.
    Abbott, Grace and Edith. Papers and Addenda.
    Presidents' Papers, 1889–1925.
Columbia University, New York, New York. Rare Book and Manuscript Library.
    Kelley Family. Papers.
    Wald, Lillian D. Papers. (LDW-CU)
Harvard University, Cambridge, Massachusetts. Houghton Library. Woods, Robert A. Papers. (RWP)
University of Illinois at Chicago, Chicago, Illinois. The University Library.
    Addams, Jane. Memorial Collection. (JAMC)
University of Minnesota, Minneapolis, Minnesota. Social Welfare History Archives.
    Alliance of Cambridge Settlement Houses (Cambridge, Massachusetts). Records.
    Hamilton-Madison House (New York City). Records.
    Kellogg, Paul Underwood. Papers.
    Kennedy, Albert J. Papers. (AJKP)
    National Federation of Settlements and Neighborhood Centers. Records. (NFSR)
    Survey Associates. Records. (SAR)
    United Neighborhood Houses of New York City. Records. (UNHR)
    United South End Settlements (Boston). Records. (USES)
Minnesota Historical Society, Saint Paul, Minnesota. Division of Archives and Manuscripts.
    Gilman, Catheryne Cook. Papers.
    Gilman, Robbins, and Family. Papers.
Newberry Library, Chicago, Illinois.
    Taylor, Graham. Papers. (GTP)
New York Public Library, New York, New York.
    Jacob A. Riis Neighborhood Settlement. Records. (JARR)
    Kelley, Nicholas. Papers.

Thomas, Norman. Papers.
Wald, Lillian D. Papers. (LDW-NYPL)
Radcliffe College, Cambridge, Massachusetts. Schlesinger Library.
Brooks, John Graham. Papers.
Denison House. Papers. (DHP)
Hamilton, Alice. Papers.
Hamilton Family. Papers. Microfilm. (HFP)
North Bennet Street Industrial School (Boston, Massachusetts). Papers.
O'Sullivan, Mary Kenney. Manuscript Autobiography.
Simkhovitch, Mary Kingsbury. Papers.
White, Eva Whiting. Papers.
Smith College, Northampton, Mass. Sophia Smith Collection.
Addams, Jane. Papers.
Kitchelt, Florence Ledyard (Cross). Papers.
Starr, Ellen Gates. Papers. (EGSP)
Southern Illinois University, Carbondale, Illinois. Center for Dewey Studies.
Dewey Family. Letters. Microfilm.
State Historical Society of Wisconsin, Madison, Wisconsin. Division of Archives
and Manuscripts.
Lloyd, Henry Demarest. Papers. Microfilm (1971).
University Settlement Society of New York City. Papers. Microfilm
(1972). (USSP)
Swarthmore College, Swarthmore, Pennsylvania. Swarthmore College Peace
Collection.
Addams, Jane. Correspondence. Microfilm. (JA-SCPC)

Notes

Preface

1. Recent and forthcoming works on the American settlement movement and its immediate context include contributions from Clarke Chambers, Ruth Crocker, Howard Karger, Daniel Levine, Kathryn Kish Sklar, Barbara Sicherman, and Judith Trolander. The English settlement movement is also receiving considered attention from such scholars as Asa Briggs and Anne McCartney, Seth Koven, and Standish Meacham. (All these works are acknowledged at appropriate points in the Notes.)

2. Clarke A. Chambers, "Toward a Redefinition of Welfare History," *Journal of American History* 73(September 1986): 407–33.

3. The most strenuous advocate of this view is Howard Jacob Karger, *The Sentinels of Order: A Study of Social Control and the Minneapolis Settlement House Movement, 1915–1950* (Lanham, Md.: University Press of America, 1987), esp. vii–xiv. See also, e.g., Raymond Mohl and Neil Batten, "Paternalism and Pluralism: Immigrants and Social Welfare in Gary, Indiana, 1906–1940," *American Studies* 15(Spring 1974): 5–26.

Prologue

1. Walter Besant, "On University Settlements," in *University and Social Settlements,* ed. Will Reason (London: Methuen, 1898), 4.

2. Among the most important studies of the "social question" in nineteenth-century England is Gertrude Himmelfarb, *The Idea of Poverty: England in the Early Industrial Age* (New York: Knopf, 1984). Himmelfarb makes it clear that while debates raged over the best solutions to poverty, consensus prevailed that poverty *was* a major social problem and that it was fundamentally a *moral* problem. See esp. 12–13. Still important is Gareth Stedman Jones, *Outcast London: A Study in the Relationship between Classes in Victorian Society* (New York: Pantheon, 1984 [1971]). Particularly important here is part 3, "Middle-Class London and the Problem of the Casual Poor," esp. 241–54, on pauperism and "indiscriminate alms-giving."

3. Thomas Carlyle, *Past and Present* (London: Chapman and Hall, 1870), 352.

4. Thomas Carlyle, *Chartism* (London: J. Fraser, 1840), 55–56.

5. Thomas Carlyle, *On Heroes and Hero Worship* (London: Chapman, 1840), 358.

6. John Ruskin, *Modern Painters,* in *The Works of John Ruskin,* 39 vols., ed. E. T. Cook and Alexander Wedderburn (London: Allen, 1904), 5:69.

7. John Ruskin, *Unto This Last* (New York: John Wiley, 1872), 125.

8. Alec R. Vidler, *F. D. Maurice and Company* (London: S.C.M. Press, 1966), esp. 43–48, 76–80, 161–80, 205–20. See also Frederick Maurice, ed., *The Life of*

Frederick Denison Maurice, Chiefly Told in His Own Letters, 4th ed., 2 vols. (London: Macmillan, 1885), 1:130–38, 158–59, 173–84.

9. On the inception, ideas, and personnel of the Christian Socialist movement, see E. H. Seligman, "Owen and the Christian Socialists," *Political Science Quarterly* 1(June 1886): 206–49; Philip N. Backstrom, *Christian Socialism and Cooperation in Victorian England* (London: Croom Helm, 1974), esp. 29–47; Torben Christensen, *Origin and History of Christian Socialism, 1848–1854* (Aarhus: Universitets Forlaget, 1962).

10. The chief sources for Hill's life and work are E. Moberly Bell, *Octavia Hill* (London: Constable, 1942), and C. Edmund Maurice, ed., *Life of Octavia Hill as Told in Her Letters* (London: Macmillan, 1914). On Ruskin's association with Maurice, see John Dixon Hunt, *The Wider Sea: A Life of John Ruskin* (New York: Viking, 1982), esp. 211–12, 244–45. Resonances between Ruskin's and Maurice's ideas may be found in their concepts of "sacrifice" and "obedience." For both, sacrifice was the nexus of social unity, the rejection of selfish private ends for ennobling social ends; likewise, both saw "obedience" as the individual's capitulation to a higher law, social or religious, in the cause of social order. C. Edmund Maurice, *The Doctrine of Sacrifice Deduced from the Scriptures: A Series of Sermons,* new ed. (London: Macmillan, 1879); John Ruskin, *The Seven Lamps of Architecture* (New York: Wiley and Halstead, 1857), esp. 14–16, 18–20, 170; Edward Alexander, *Matthew Arnold, John Ruskin, and the Modern Temper* (Columbus: Ohio University Press, 1973), 33–37.

11. Octavia Hill, *Homes of the London Poor* (London, 1883; reprinted London: Frank Cass, 1970), 66: a collection of essays written between 1866 and 1875 to justify and explain her work.

12. David Owen, *English Philanthropy, 1660–1960* (Cambridge: Belknap Press of Harvard University Press, 1964), 135–36, 216–19; Himmelfarb, *Idea of Poverty,* 147–76; Daniel Levine, *Poverty and Society: The Growth of the American Welfare State in International Comparison* (New Brunswick, N.J.: Rutgers University Press, 1988), 24–28; Helen Bosanquet, *Social Work in London, 1869 to 1912: A History of the Charity Organisation Society* (London: J. Murray, 1914), 5 ff.; Charles Loch Mowat, *The Charity Organisation Society, 1869–1913: Its Ideas and Work* (London: Methuen, 1961), 3–7.

13. Quoted in Bosanquet, *Social Work in London,* 53–54.

14. Bosanquet, *Social Work in London,* 63–67; Mowat, *Charity Organisation Society,* 34–37; *Spectator* 55(16 December 1882): 1616–18; Beatrice Webb, *My Apprenticeship* (New York: Longmans, Green, 1926), 197–200. Two subsequent commentators have suggested that the COS's detractors worked from a skewed perception of the society's philosophy of "self-help." Rather than endorsing the "atomic individualism" of *laissez-faire,* the COS held an essentially idealist conception of independence that stemmed from the belief that moral independence—good character—was the foundation of meaningful citizenship or participation in collective life. Andrew Vincent and Raymond Plant, *Philosophy, Politics and Citizenship: The Life and Thought of the British Idealists* (London: Basil Blackwell, 1985), 99–105.

15. Fremantle expounded his mature theology in the Bampton lectures of 1883; the published version was entitled *The World as the Subject of Redemption.*

When offered to English readers in 1885, this collection of Fremantle's Bampton lectures of 1883 "fell almost flat." Picked up by several prominent Christian activists in the United States—Richard T. Ely and Graham Taylor among them—it slowly gained popularity. Its second edition, sponsored by Ely in 1895, found an audience in England as well as America. See W. H. Fremantle, *The World as the Subject of Redemption* (New York: Longmans, Green, 1895), ix–xvi, xxii, 98–99, i*–iii*; Graham Taylor, *Pioneering on Social Frontiers* (Chicago: University of Chicago Press, 1930), 388. Also see G. Kitson Clark, *Churchmen and the Condition of England, 1832–1885* (London: Methuen, 1973), 276–78.

16. On Barnett's life and thought, the most compendious source is Henrietta O. Barnett, *Canon Barnett: His Life, Work, and Friends,* 2 vols. (Boston: Houghton Mifflin, 1919). The classic history of Barnett's settlement is J. A. R. Pimlott, *Toynbee Hall: Fifty Years of Social Progress, 1884–1934* (London: J. M. Dent, 1935); Asa Briggs and Anne Mccartney, *Toynbee Hall: The First Hundred Years* (London: Routledge Chapman and Hall, 1984); and the most recent and ambitious in connecting the settlement to cultural change and political reform, Standish Meacham, *Toynbee Hall and Social Reform* (New Haven: Yale University Press, 1987). Seth David Koven challenges some of Meacham's pessimistic conclusions regarding the influence of the settlements on British political life and the districts they purported to serve. See "Culture and Poverty: The London Settlement House Movement 1870 to 1914" (Ph.D. diss., Harvard University, 1987).

17. Barnett, *Canon Barnett,* esp. 1:78, 85, 144–45. On the separate paths taken by the COS and the settlement founders from their common cultural roots, see Samuel Melcher, "The Influence of Nineteenth-Century British Social Work," *Social Service Review* 38(June 1964): 181–84.

18. The Barnetts collected their essays of the late 1870s and 1880s, written largely for genteel periodicals, in Samuel A. Barnett and Henrietta Rowland Barnett, *Practicable Socialism: Essays in Social Reform* (London: Longmans, Green, 1888). See "Relief Funds and the Poor" (1886), in *Practicable Socialism,* 30; "University Settlements" (1883), in *Practicable Socialism,* 97.

The early 1880s saw a number of exposés of British urban poverty, the most notorious being *The Bitter Cry of Outcast London,* allegedly written by Andrew Mearns and issued by the London Congregational Union (1883); the slim pamphlet was promoted by W. T. Stead in the *Pall Mall Gazette;* see Frederic Whyte, *The Life of W. T. Stead,* 2 vols. (London: J. Cape; New York: Houghton Mifflin, [1925]), 1:103–5. Simultaneously a host of radical organizations sprang up, led largely by middle-class reformers, including H. M. Hyndman's Social Democratic Federation (1881), the Fabian Society (1884), and the Socialist League (1885). On the political furor of the eighties, see Peter d'Arcy Jones, *The Christian Socialist Revival, 1877–1914* (Princeton: Princeton University Press, 1968); Stanley Pierson, *Marxism and the Origins of British Socialism: The Struggle for a New Consciousness* (Ithaca: Cornell University Press, 1973); Martin Pugh, *The Making of Modern British Politics, 1867–1939* (New York: St. Martin's Press, 1982).

19. For fuller accounts of this genealogy, see Meacham, *Toynbee Hall and Social Reform,* 1–23; Koven, "Culture and Poverty," chaps. 1, 2.

20. Edward Denison, *Letters and Other Writings,* ed. Sir Baldwyn Leighton (London: R. Bentley, 1872), 29. For Denison's life, see the preface, by Sir Baldwyn, iii–xi. Denison's elevation to martyr status was largely accomplished by J. R. Green, an Anglican churchman and later "new" historian, in "Edward Denison—In Memoriam," *Macmillan's Magazine* 24(September 1871): 376–83; reprinted as "A Brother to the Poor," in *Stray Studies from England and Italy* (New York: Harper, 1876), 9–29.

21. Alfred Milner tried to do for Toynbee what J. R. Green had done for Denison in *Arnold Toynbee: A Reminiscence* (London: E. Arnold, 1895); quotation on 24. See also Gertrude Toynbee, *Reminiscences and Letters of Joseph and Arnold Toynbee* (London: H. J. Glaisher, [1910?]).

22. On Green and his place in Benjamin Jowett's Balliol, see Melvin Richter, *The Politics of Conscience: T. H. Green and His Age* (Cambridge: Harvard University Press, 1964), esp. 52–72; W. R. Ward, *Victorian Oxford* (London: Frank Cass, 1965), 210–65; Geoffrey Faber, *Jowett: A Portrait with Background* (Cambridge: Harvard University Press, 1957), esp. 355–59. See also "Memoir" by R. L. Nettleship in *Works of Thomas Hill Green,* 3 vols. (London, 1891; reprinted New York: AMS Press, 1973), 3:xi–clxi; Ramon M. Lemos, Introduction to T. H. Green, *Prolegomena to Ethics,* ed. A. C. Bradley (New York: Apollo Editions, 1969), v–xxvi.

23. Quoted in Pimlott, *Toynbee Hall,* 42–43.

24. Barnett, *Canon Barnett,* esp. 1:304–9; Webb, *My Apprenticeship,* 202–3; Henry W. Nevinson, *Changes and Chances* (New York: Harcourt, Brace, 1923), 87–91. Seth Koven's history of the early London settlement movement makes it clear that Toynbee Hall and Oxford House were established within months of each other. I choose to concentrate on the genesis of Toynbee Hall in my account because though most of the subsequent English settlements followed Oxford House's denominational settlement model, the American visitors to London almost invariably visited and took lessons from Toynbee Hall. See Koven, "Culture and Poverty," esp. chap. 2.

25. Barnett's vision of the social settlement is best laid out in "University Settlements," in *Practicable Socialism,* 96–112. See also Meacham, *Toynbee Hall and Social Reform,* esp. 44–50; Pimlott, *Toynbee Hall,* 33–39; Briggs and Macartney, *Toynbee Hall,* esp. 8–9, 22–24; Koven, "Culture and Poverty," chap. 2.

26. One review and analysis of historians' definition and use of "social control" as a model of class interaction is F. M. L. Thompson, "Social Control in Victorian Britain," *Economic History Review,* 2d ser., 34(May 1981): 189–208.

27. Robert A. Woods and Albert J. Kennedy, *The Settlement Horizon: A National Estimate* (New York: Russell Sage Foundation, 1922), 30.

28. Quoted in James Adderley, *In Slums and Society: Reminiscences of Old Friends* (London: T. F. Unwin, 1916), 48.

Chapter One

1. See Arthur Mann, "British Social Thought and American Reformers of the Progressive Era," *Mississippi Valley Historical Review* 42(March 1956): 672–92.

2. Aaron Ignatius Abell, *The Urban Impact on American Protestantism, 1865–1900* (Hamden, Conn.: Archon, 1962), 27–56.

3. Sydney E. Ahlstrom, *A Religious History of the American People* (New Haven: Yale University Press, 1972), 763–804; Henry F. May, *Protestant Churches and Industrial America* (New York: Harper Torchbooks, 1967), 80–87. On the theological diversity of the Social Gospel, see, e.g., David Lyon, "The Idea of a Christian Sociology: Some Historical Precedents and Current Concerns," *Sociological Analysis* 44(Fall 1983): 234–37.

4. Ahlstrom, *Religious History,* 610–13, 781; William R. Hutchison, *The Modernist Impulse in American Protestantism* (Cambridge: Harvard University Press, 1976), 43–48; A. S. Chesebrough, "The Theological Opinions of Horace Bushnell as Related to His Character and Christian Experience," *Andover Review* 6(August 1886): 113–30.

5. William Jewett Tucker, *My Generation: An Autobiographical Interpretation* (Boston: Houghton Mifflin, 1919), 59–62; Hutchison, *Modernist Impulse,* 80–83.

6. Tucker, *My Generation,* 54, 77.

7. Theodore T. Munger, *On the Threshold,* rev. and enl. ed. (Boston: Houghton Mifflin, 1891), 229–46.

8. The early centers of liberalism were urban pulpits in the East and some of the northeastern seminaries, notably Harvard (Unitarian), Andover (Congregational), Union (Presbyterian), and the Episcopal Theological Seminary in Cambridge, with an important outpost established in the mid-1890s at the University of Chicago's Divinity School, initially Baptist but in practice multidenominational. See Ahlstrom, *Religious History,* 775–76.

9. For Ward's impact on the Social Gospel, see William G. McLoughlin, *Revivals, Awakenings, and Reform* (Chicago: University of Chicago Press, 1978), 162–66; James Dombrowski, *The Early Days of Christian Socialism in America* (New York: Columbia University Press, 1936), 10–12.

10. William J. Tucker, "Some Present Questions in Evangelism," *Andover Review* 1(March 1884): 233–44; also see Tucker, "Social Problems in the Pulpit," *Andover Review* 3(April 1885): 297–302.

11. John Graham Brooks, "Social Questions in the Light of the Social Organism," *Lend a Hand* 1(January 1886): 9–13.

12. Thomas L. Haskell, *The Emergence of Professional Social Science: The American Social Science Association and the Nineteenth-Century Crisis of Authority* (Urbana: University of Illinois Press, 1977), 200, 203; James E. Mooney, *John Graham Brooks, Prophet of Social Justice: A Career Story* (Worcester, Mass.: privately printed, 1968).

13. Henry C. Potter, "A Phase of Social Science," *Century,* n.s., 7(November 1884): 113–16.

14. Francis Greenwood Peabody, "The Philosophy of the Social Question," *Andover Review* 8(December 1887): 561–73.

15. The results of a survey of social science instruction in American colleges conducted by the American Social Science Association were printed in *Journal of Social Science* 21(September 1886): xxxiv–xlix. The same issue offered a sample social science curriculum; see 13–20. As Haskell notes, the curriculum

was organized not according to the emerging social science disciplines, but rather along the lines dictated by the ASSA's departmental divisions of education, health, trade and finance, social economy, and jurisprudence.

16. The second monograph, in 1908, was on social settlements: William I. Cole, *Motives and Results of the Social Settlements Movement,* Publications of the Department of Social Ethics in Harvard University 2 (Cambridge: Harvard University, 1908); Ahlstrom, *Religious History,* 795; F. B. Sanborn, "The Social Sciences: Their Growth and Future," *Journal of Social Science* 21(September 1886): 7–8.

17. William Jewett Tucker, "The Outline of an Elective Course of Study," *Andover Review* 11(January 1889): 85–89; 11(March 1889): 310–14; 11(April 1889): 424–27; 15(February 1891): 220–23; 16(August 1891): 188–92; Tucker, *My Generation,* 161, 172–78.

18. Louise C. Wade, *Graham Taylor: Pioneer for Social Justice* (Chicago: University of Chicago Press, 1964), 23–36; Graham Taylor, *Pioneering on Social Frontiers* (Chicago: University of Chicago Press, 1930), 362–72.

19. Wade, *Graham Taylor,* 38; Taylor, *Pioneering,* 378. The new president of Hartford Theological Seminary was Chester D. Hartranft, who had been Taylor's crewmate and religious mentor during Taylor's undergraduate and seminary years at Rutgers.

20. Wade, *Graham Taylor,* 40–44; Taylor, *Pioneering,* 379–93.

21. Taylor, *Pioneering,* 390.

22. See chapter 7; also Steven J. Diner; *A City and Its Universities: Public Policy in Chicago, 1892–1919* (Chapel Hill: University of North Carolina Press, 1980), 6–51.

23. Haskell, *Emergence of Professional Social Science,* 100. Haskell analyzes the rise and decline of the ASSA in the context of the "crisis of authority" among the American gentility in the post–Civil War era. For him the ASSA is less important as a manifestation of reforming zeal than as a stage in the establishment of sources of intellectual authority in an industrial society. See also L. L. Bernard and Jessie Bernard, *Origins of American Sociology: The Social Science Movement in the United States* (New York: Thomas Y. Crowell, 1943), 527–44. Other literature on the organization and philosophy of the ASSA includes several retrospective articles in its journal: F. B. Sanborn, "The Work of Social Science, Past and Present," *Journal of Social Science* 8(May 1886): 23–29; Sanborn, "Social Sciences," 1–12.

24. Richard T. Ely, *Ground under Our Feet: An Autobiography* (New York: Macmillan, 1938), 43–45, 145–47.

25. There are various accounts of the founding of the American Economic Association. See Ely, *Ground under Our Feet,* 121–44. A reinterpretation is offered by Patten's biographer, Daniel M. Fox, in *The Discovery of Abundance: Simon N. Patten and the Transformation of Social Theory* (Ithaca: Cornell University Press, 1967), 37–39. On professionalization versus reform in the new organization, see A. W. Coats, "The First Two Decades of the American Economic Association," *American Economic Review* 50(September 1960): 555–74, and Haskell, *Professionalization of Social Science,* 178–89.

26. Ely, *Ground under Our Feet,* 65–77; Richard T. Ely, "Socialism," *Andover*

Review 5(February 1886): 146–63; Ely, *Social Aspects of Christianity* (New York: Thomas Y. Crowell, 1889), 100–110, 123–32. Dorothy Ross traces Ely's retreat from advocating "socialism" after being threatened with dismissal from Wisconsin in "Socialism and American Liberalism: Academic Social Thought in the 1880s," *Perspectives in American History* 11(1977–78): 45–52. Also see James T. Kloppenberg's positioning of Ely among other American and European thinkers striving to carry social thought from socialism to social democracy: *Uncertain Victory: Social Democracy and Progressivism in European and American Thought, 1870–1920* (New York: Oxford University Press, 1986), esp. 199–246.

27. Ely, *Ground under Our Feet*, 78–79; Richard T. Ely, "Philanthropy," *Chautauquan* 9(October 1888): 16–18; Benjamin G. Rader, "Richard T. Ely: Lay Spokesman for the Social Gospel," *Journal of American History* 53(June 1966): 61–74.

28. Ely, "Philanthropy," 16–18; see my Prologue, note 15.

29. Dombrowski, *Christian Socialism in America*, 17–29.

30. Clyde C. Griffen, "Rich Laymen and Early Social Christianity," *Church History* 36(March 1967): 45–65; William R. Hutchison, "Cultural Strain and Protestant Liberalism," *American Historical Review* 76(April 1971): 390–93; Robert T. Handy, "The Protestant Quest for a Christian America," *Church History* 22(1953): 10–17; Henry F. May, *Protestant Churches and Industrial America* (New York: Harper Torchbooks, 1967), vii–xv.

31. See James Turner, *Without God, without Creed* (Baltimore: Johns Hopkins University Press, 1985), esp. chap. 8.

32. Howard B. Radest, *Toward Common Ground: The Story of the Ethical Societies in the United States* (New York: Ungar, 1969), 14–29.

33. Leo Jacobs, *Three Types of Practical Ethical Movements of the Past Half Century* (New York: Macmillan, 1922), 110.

34. Reproduced in Gustave Spiller, *The Ethical Movement in Great Britain: A Documentary History* (London: printed for the author at the Farleigh Press, 1934), 5.

35. Spiller, *Ethical Movement in Great Britain,* 4–18.

36. The numbers of students in liberal arts colleges alone numbered 16,600 in 1860 and 82,000 in 1900. Colin B. Burke, *American Collegiate Populations: A Test of the Traditional View* (New York: New York University Press, 1982), 215. Burke argues that rhetoric outstripped reality in the significance of innovative technical and scientific programs in colleges and universities. The most popular of the newer professional programs were law, medicine, and education, and more traditional liberal arts offerings drew a majority of students through 1900. See chap. 5, "The Colleges in Perspective," esp. 212–24. See also Laurence R. Veysey, *The Emergence of the American University* (Chicago: University of Chicago Press, 1965), 1–12, chaps. 2, 3; Frederick Rudolph, *The American College and University: A History* (New York: Knopf, 1962), 264–86, 329–54; Jurgen Herbst, *The German Historical School in American Scholarship: A Study in the Transfer of Culture* (Ithaca: Cornell University Press, 1965), 23–51.

It is interesting to compare Burke's figures with those of a contemporary observer, Arthur M. Comey, in "Growth of the Colleges of the United States," *Educational Review* 3(February 1892): 120–31. To arrive at a comparison of "traditional" college enrollments before and after the Civil War, Comey eliminated both women and "preparatory" (precollegiate) students from the figures he gathered from colleges and universities across the nation. His figures suggest that between 1850 and 1890, while the nation's population increased by a factor of 1.6, the number of male collegiate students multiplied by 3.5, from 8,837 in 158 institutions in 1850 to 31,516 in 282 institutions in 1890. In fact the greatest decadal increase came between 1890 and 1900; Burke's figures say that liberal arts, normal school, and medical school enrollments doubled, while law school enrollments tripled. Technical schools showed a far smaller rate of increase: from 10,000 students in 1890 to 12,000 in 1900. Burke, *American Collegiate Populations,* 216.

37. Rudolph, *American College and University,* 290–95. Brown University under Francis Wayland had adopted an even more flexible system than Harvard's in 1851, for essentially the same reason: the irrelevance of the classical curriculum to the changing society and economy. But Wayland's new regime was short-lived; in 1856 Brown recruited an acceptably conservative president and returned to the old curriculum. See Rudolph, *American College and University,* 237–40.

38. Quotation from a debate between Eliot and the more conservative President James McCosh of Princeton: "The American University," *Critic* 6(28 February 1885): 103.

39. Burton J. Bledstein, *The Culture of Professionalism: The Middle Class and the Development of Higher Education in America* (New York: W. W. Norton, 1976), 248–59; Rudolph, *American College and University,* 136–55. Rudolph argues that the "extracurriculum" grew from the antebellum seeds of debating and literary societies, established by students reacting against the stifling evangelistic cast of early American collegiate education. See also Edith L. Sheffield, "Student Life in the University of Michigan," *Cosmopolitan* 7(June 1889): 107–19; Daniel Coit Gilman, "The Future of American Colleges and Universities," *Atlantic Monthly* 78(August 1896): 177.

40. College officials also knew that sentimental alumni were generous alumni.

41. W. H. Johnson, " 'Does College Training Pay?' " *Lippincott* 44(November 1889): 722–27.

42. Daniel Coit Gilman, "Is It Worth While to Uphold Any Longer the Idea of Liberal Education?" *Educational Review* 3(February 1892): 105–19; see also Gilman, "The Group System of College Studies at the Johns Hopkins University," *Andover Review* 5(June 1886): 565–76.

43. See Matthew Arnold, *Culture and Anarchy,* ed. with an intro. by J. Dover Wilson (Cambridge: Cambridge University Press, 1960 [1932]), 43–71; Veysey, *Emergence of the American University,* chap. 4.

44. See Oscar Handlin and Mary F. Handlin on turn-of-the-century colleges as "custodians of culture," in *The American College and American Culture: Socialization as a Function of Higher Education* (New York: McGraw-Hill, 1970), 50–55.

45. G. H. Palmer, "The New Education," *Andover Review* 4(November 1885): 393–407; see also one response from a Yale man, George T. Ladd, "Education,

New and Old," *Andover Review* 5(January 1886): 1–18. On character and the development of the "whole man," see George E. Peterson, *The New England College in the Age of the University* (Amherst, Mass.: Amherst College Press, 1964), 30–51; on the settlement movement as an outgrowth of the evolution of the ideals of liberal arts education, see 172–94.

46. Nathaniel Butler, "The College in Relation to the University," *Citizen* 2(December 1896): 328–32; quotation on 330.

47. John E. Bradley, "The Higher Life of the College," *Education* 17(December 1896): 193–203.

48. Charles F. Thwing, "The Relation of the College and University to the Community," *Education* 11(March 1891): 417–22; Thwing, *Within College Walls* (New York: Baker and Taylor, 1893), 45–47.

49. Thwing, *Within College Walls,* 39, 52.

50. Thwing, *Within College Walls,* 31–33, 39–40.

51. For M. Carey Thomas's response to Clarke, see "Present Tendencies in Women's College and University Education," *Educational Review* 35(January 1908): 69. On Clarke, and on physical education for women, see Anna McClure Sholl, "Women's Colleges," *Bachelor of Arts* 1(November 1895): 767–71. May Wright Sewall also refers to Clarke in "The Education of Women in the Western States," in *Women's Work in America,* ed. Annie Nathan Meyer (New York: H. Holt, 1891), 77–78.

Rosalind Rosenberg analyzes the debate over the cultural fear that American women, and by extension, American society, would be harmed by their higher education: *Beyond Separate Spheres: Intellectual Roots of Modern Feminism* (New Haven: Yale University Press, 1982), 5–27. This concern for women's health was partly a covert expression of anxiety about the "unsexing" of women by education. It is true that many middle-class women complained of ill health in the mid-nineteenth century. Both their illnesses and the attitude of the medical profession toward women's complaints seem to have been intricately connected to social assumptions about the proper roles of women; it was often said that the best cure for female debility was dedication to domestic duties. By this standard, higher education would clearly threaten a woman's physical well-being. See Ann Douglas Wood, " 'The Fashionable Diseases': Women's Complaints and Their Treatment in Nineteenth-Century America," *Journal of Interdisciplinary History* 4(Summer 1973): 25–52. See too Barbara Miller Solomon, *In the Company of Educated Women: A History of Women and Higher Education in America* (New Haven: Yale University Press, 1985), 56–57; Thomas Woody, *A History of Women's Education in the United States,* 2 vols. (New York: Science Press, 1929), 2:98–130; Charles F. Thwing, *The College Woman* (New York: Baker and Taylor, 1894), 76–114. Thwing includes a compilation of responses from members of the Association of Collegiate Alumnae on the chief hazards of college to women's health. See also Kate Holladay Claghorn, *College Training for Women* (New York: Thomas Y. Crowell, 1897), 72–88: Claghorn advises parents what to look for in physical accommodations and dietary arrangements in colleges.

52. Solomon, *Educated Women,* 63; Roberta Wein, "Women's Colleges and Domesticity, 1875–1918," *History of Education Quarterly* 14(Spring 1974): 31–

47. The 1887–88 figures of the United States commissioner of education are given in the translator's introduction to Helene Lange, *Higher Education of Women in Europe,* trans. L. R. Klemm (New York: D. Appleton, 1897), xxvii–xxix. The 1900 estimate is offered by Burke, *American Collegiate Populations,* 218.

53. May S. Cheney, "Will Nature Eliminate the College Woman?" *Publications of the Association of Collegiate Alumnae: Magazine Number,* ser. 3, no. 10(January 1905): 4.

54. Cheney, "Will Nature Eliminate the College Woman?" 1–9; Claghorn, *College Training for Women,* 3; Thomas, "Present Tendencies," 65; Millicent Washburn Shinn, "The Marriage Rate of College Women," *Century,* n.s., 28(October 1895): 946–48; Frances M. Abbott, "A Generation of College Women," *Forum* 20(November 1895): 377–78. Also see Woody, *Women's Education,* 2:204–10; Solomon, *Educated Women,* 116–22.

55. Thirty-seven percent of all Vassar graduates in 1895 were or had been teachers, as were 49 percent of Bryn Mawr graduates, or 86 percent of those who had worked outside the home. See Abbott, "Generation of College Women," 379; Kate Holladay Claghorn, "The Problem of Occupation for College Women," *Educational Review* 15(March 1898): 217; Woody, *Women's Education,* 2:322–26.

56. For example, tabulated statement on occupations of Vassar alumnae in Abbott, "Generation of College Women," 383; Solomon, *Educated Women,* 122–39.

57. Woody, *Women's Education,* 2:216–23; Horace Davis, "Collegiate Education of Women," *Overland Monthly,* 2d ser., 16(October 1890): 337–39; George P. Schmidt, *The Liberal Arts College: A Chapter in American Cultural History* (New Brunswick, N.J.: Rutgers University Press, 1957), 141–42; Solomon, *Educated Women,* 80–83, Thomas, "Present Tendencies," 72–74.

58. Mary Roberts Smith, "Shall the College Curriculum Be Modified for Women?" *Publications of the Association of Collegiate Alumnae: Magazine Number,* ser. 3, no. 1(December 1898): 2.

59. See, e.g., Mary A. Livermore, *What Shall We Do with Our Daughters? Superfluous Women and Other Lectures* (Boston: Lee and Shepard, 1883), 48; Edward T. Devine, "The Economic Place of Woman," *Publications of the Association of Collegiate Alumnae: Magazine Number,* ser. 3, no. 10(January 1905): 13–23; Ellen H. Richards, "Some Further Considerations on College Curricula," *Publications of the Association of Collegiate Alumnae: Magazine Number,* ser. 3, no. 1(December 1898): 23.

60. Smith, "Shall the College Curriculum Be Modified for Women?" 7–8.

61. For example, Kate Morris Cone, "Some Further Considerations on College Curricula, IV," *Publications of the Association of Collegiate Alumnae: Magazine Number,* ser. 3, no. 1(December 1898): 33; Smith, "Shall the College Curriculum Be Modified for Women?" 10.

62. Solomon, *Educated Women,* 85–87.

63. Claghorn, *College Training for Women,* 238–41.

64. Thwing, *College Woman,* 164–65. Thwing recommends college settlements and the COS as outlets for the philanthropic skills of women graduates.

65. Samuel Warren Dike, "Sociology in the Higher Education of Women,"

Atlantic Monthly 70(November 1892): 668–76. William L. O'Neill fairly calls Dike a "moral conservative with liberal social views." Dike was one of those who raised the alarm about the rising divorce rate in the late nineteenth century, yet he also opposed draconian measures to limit divorce. He corresponded with Richard Ely and Charles F. Thwing, among others, and was an early member of the American Economic Association. See O'Neill, *Divorce in the Progressive Era* (New Haven: Yale University Press, 1967), esp. 48–56. See too Bernard and Bernard, *Origins of American Sociology,* 614, 655; Tucker, *My Generation,* 54.

66. He also advocated limiting college women's required class hours, not only to encourage "masterful handling" rather than "sheer acquisition" of knowledge, but also for reasons of health. Dike, "Sociology," 676.

67. For other expressions of this doctrine of womanly "exceptionalism," see Josephine Lazarus, "Higher Education: A Word to Women," *Century* 41(December 1890): 315–16; Devine, "Economic Place of Woman," 13–23.

68. Rosenberg, *Beyond Separate Spheres,* 43–53.

Chapter Two

1. Jane Addams, *Twenty Years at Hull-House* (New York: Macmillan, 1910), 3–5, 37–39.

2. The only source for Woods's early life is Eleanor H. Woods, *Robert A. Woods: Champion of Democracy* (Boston: Houghton Mifflin, 1929), a laudatory biography by his widow. Where possible, I have quoted from LS in the Robert Woods Papers in Houghton Library, Harvard University, rather than from the elided versions provided by Eleanor Woods. See also William Jewett Tucker, *My Generation: An Autobiographical Interpretation* (Boston: Houghton Mifflin, 1919), 180–82.

3. Woods, *Robert Woods,* 1–7.

4. Woods, *Robert Woods,* 8–17.

5. Quoted in Woods, *Robert Woods,* 18.

6. Tucker, *My Generation,* 185–221.

7. Quoted in Woods, *Robert Woods,* 20.

8. Quoted in Woods, *Robert Woods,* 24.

9. Tucker, *My Generation,* 178–80; also Tucker, " 'The Gospel of Wealth,' " *Andover Review* 15(June 1891): 631–45.

10. William I. Cole, "Robert A. Woods, 1865–1925: An Address before the Andover Alumni Association, April 14, 1925" (found in the Records of the United South End Settlements, Social Welfare History Archives, University of Minnesota). Woods later wrote of Amherst: "It was one of the very first centres in the country at which the old philosophy of individualism was eliminated and the new teaching of the organic unity of mankind developed in its moving power." Quoted in Woods, *Robert Woods,* 14.

11. Woods, *Robert Woods,* 22–25.

12. Quoted in Woods, *Robert Woods,* 32.

13. Quoted in Woods, *Robert Woods,* 38. Woods unwittingly took sides in a sharp encounter brewing among the charity voluntarists when he admired the

work of "General" William Booth of the Salvation Army: see Robert A. Woods to William J. Tucker, 10 September 1890, Robert A. Woods Papers, Houghton Library, Harvard University (hereafter cited as RWP); Robert A. Woods, *English Social Movements* (London: Swan Sonnenschein, 1892), 170–82; C. S. Loch, Bernard Bosanquet, and Philip Dwyer, *Criticisms on "General" Booth's Social Scheme from Three Different Points of View* (London: Swan Sonnenschein, 1891).

14. Woods to Tucker, 10 September 1890, RWP; Owen Chadwick, *The Victorian Church: Part II, 1860–1901* (London: A. and C. Black, 1970), 100–104.

15. Asa Briggs and Anne Macartney, *Toynbee Hall: The First Hundred Years* (London: Routledge Chapman and Hall, 1984), 46–49; J. A. R. Pimlott, *Toynbee Hall: Fifty Years of Social Progress, 1884–1934* (London: J. M. Dent, 1935), 84–87; Woods, *English Social Movements,* 18–24; Tom Mann, *Memoirs,* Fitzroy edition (London: McGibbon and Kee, 1967), 60–67, 79–80, 85–97. On Toynbee Hall's stance toward the dock strike, see Seth David Koven, "Culture and Poverty: The London Settlement House Movement, 1870–1914" (Ph.D. diss., Harvard University, 1987), chap. 3.

16. Herbert Burrows and John A. Hobsen, eds., *William Clarke: A Collection of His Writings* (London: Swan Sonnenschein, 1908), xi–xxix; Peter Weiler, "William Clarke: The Making and Unmaking of a Fabian Socialist," *Journal of British Studies* 14(November 1974): 77–108; William Clarke, "Industrial," in *Fabian Essays in Socialism,* ed. George Bernard Shaw, 6th ed., with a new intro. by Asa Briggs (London: Allen and Unwin, 1962), 94–134; William Clarke, *Walt Whitman* (London, 1892), 27.

17. Woods to Tucker, 10 September 1890, RWP; Woods, *Robert Woods,* 38–39, 49–61, 69–70.

18. Peter d'Arcy Jones, *The Christian Socialist Revival, 1877–1914* (Princeton: Princeton University Press, 1968), 85–94, 164–98; Koven, "Culture and Poverty," chap. 3; Woods, *English Social Movements,* 62–66; Stephen Paget, ed., *Henry Scott Holland: Memoir and Letters* (London: J. Murray, 1921), 168–74. For a contemporary view see Paul Monroe, "English and American Christian Socialism: An Estimate," *American Journal of Sociology* 1(July 1895): 51–63.

19. Quoted in James Adderley, *In Slums and Society: Reminiscences of Old Friends* (London: T. F. Unwin, 1916), 193.

20. See Woods's analysis in *English Social Movements,* 61–62.

21. Briggs and Macartney, *Toynbee Hall,* 28–33.

22. Woods, *English Social Movements,* 112–14; Will Reason, ed., *University and Social Settlements* (London: Methuen, 1898), 179–80.

23. A. F. Winnington Ingram, "Working Men's Clubs," in *the Universities and the Social Problem,* ed. John Knapp (London: Rivington, Percival, 1895), 45–49; T. S. Peppin, "The Clubs of the Club and Institute Union," in Knapp, *Universities,* 199–214; Gerald Fiennes, "The Federation of Working Men's Social Clubs," in Knapp, *Universities,* 217–35; Woods, *English Social Movements,* 104–7; Koven, "Culture and Poverty," chap. 4.

24. Reason, "Settlements and Recreation," 76–78; Hugh Legge, "The Repton Club," in Knapp, *Universities,* 131–47.

25. *Eighth Annual Report,* Women's University Settlement for Work in the

Poorer Districts of London, June 1895 (London, 1895), 16. Earlier *Annual Reports* detail the activities and personnel of the settlement. Also see Woods, *English Social Movements,* 108–10; Margaret A. Sewell and E. G. Powell, "Women's Settlements in England," in Reason, *University and Social Settlements,* 89–90.

26. Sewell and Powell, "Women's Settlements," 95.

27. Koven, "Culture and Poverty," chap. 6; Martha Vicinus, *Independent Women: Work and Community for Single Women, 1850–1920* (Chicago: University of Chicago Press, 1985), 211–31.

28. Briggs and Macartney, *Toynbee Hall,* 17–19, 36–37; T. S. Simey and M. B. Simey, *Charles Booth: Social Scientist* (London: Oxford University Press, 1960), 63–70; Beatrice Webb, *My Apprenticeship* (London: Longmans, Green, 1926), 209–15.

29. Belinda Norman-Butler, *Victorian Aspirations: The Life and Labour of Charles and Mary Booth* (London: Allen and Unwin, 1972): on the "intellectual aristocracy" of London, see 98; Henrietta O. Barnett, *Canon Barnett: His Life, Work, and Friends,* 2 vols. (Boston: Houghton Mifflin, 1919), 2:52–54.

30. Simey and Simey, *Charles Booth,* 98–106; Webb, *My Apprenticeship,* 207–8.

31. Simey and Simey, *Charles Booth,* 78–89; Webb, *My Apprenticeship,* 216–26.

32. Simey and Simey, *Charles Booth,* 89–90.

33. Interestingly, his work fell almost soundlessly into British academic sociology, at that time far more theoretically oriented than Booth, who was committed to inductive methods and unwilling to enter a dialogue with the academic sociologists. Simey and Simey, *Charles Booth,* 241–56; Harry Elmer Barnes, "The Fate of Sociology in England," *Papers and Proceedings. Twenty-first Annual Meeting, American Sociological Society* 21(December 1926): 35–46.

34. Quotation in Simey and Simey, *Charles Booth,* 108; Webb, *My Apprenticeship,* 239–48. On Booth's study and its subsequent publicity, see Daniel Levine, *Poverty and Society: The Growth of the American Welfare State in International Comparison* (New Brunswick, N.J.: Rutgers University Press, 1988), 115–18.

35. His wife's cousin, Potter came to Booth's work disillusioned by her experience of the subjective philanthropy of Octavia Hill. Her subsequent decision to leave Booth's work to investigate the cooperative movement in northern England began an estrangement that was completed by her marriage to Sidney Webb in 1891. Norman-Butler, *Victorian Aspirations,* 100–101, 108–15; Simey and Simey, *Charles Booth,* 111–13; Webb, *My Apprenticeship,* 327–45.

36. Barnett, *Canon Barnett,* 2:53–59.

37. Mrs. Humphry Ward, *A Writer's Recollections,* 2 vols. (New York: Harper, 1918), esp. 1:15–30, 133–84, 233–34, 2:64–73. In 1881 Mrs. Ward wrote a pamphlet called *Unbelief and Sin,* which rebutted the antiliberals' charge that religious doubt was tantamount to sin. The pamphlet was immediately suppressed on a technicality: the printer's name had inadvertently been omitted. Ward, *Recollections,* 1:216–26.

38. Mrs. Humphry Ward, *Robert Elsmere,* 2 vols. (London: Macmillan, 1888).

39. Ward, *Recollections,* 2:75–92.

40. [Editors,] " 'Robert Elsmere,' " *Andover Review* 10(September 1888): 297–306; Lyman Abbott, "Robert Elsmere: An Open Letter," *Chautauquan* 9(February 1889): 291–93.

41. Graham Taylor, *Pioneering on Social Frontiers* (Chicago: University of Chicago Press, 1930), 386.

42. Mrs. Humphry Ward, *University Hall Opening Address* (London, 1891), esp. "Appendix: Paper Issued by Committee of University Hall," 41–44. The settlement relocated in 1897 to a building in Bloomsbury donated by the philanthropist Passmore Edwards, whose name was adopted in gratitude. Later innovations included the first play center and the first vacation school in London settlements, as well as work with handicapped children. Ward, *Recollections,* 2:146–51; Reason, *University and Social Settlements,* 181–82; Woods, *English Social Movements,* 115–16.

43. Robert Woods to Rev. Wragge, 22 June 1891, RWP.

44. Woods to Wragge, 22 June 1891, RWP.

45. Stanton Coit, [personal memoir,] in *The Fiftieth Anniversary of the Ethical Movement* (New York: D. Appleton, 1926), 193–204. A fuller variant of this statement is reprinted in Gustave Spiller, ed., *The Ethical Movement in Great Britain* (London: printed for the author at the Farleigh Press, 1934), 177–79. See also J. Hutton Hynd, *The Creative Task of Rational Religion: A Memorial Tribute to Dr. Stanton Coit* (Saint Louis: Ethical Society of Saint Louis, 1944), 3–4; *Dictionary of American Biography,* suppl. 3, 175–76.

46. Caroline Williamson Montgomery, comp., *Bibliography of College, Social, University and Church Settlements,* 5th ed., rev. and enl. (Chicago: Blakely Press, 1905), 86–87.

47. Stanton Coit, *Neighborhood Guilds: An Instrument of Social Reform* (London: Swan Sonnenschein, 1891), 4, 85–88. Coit acknowledged his kinship with the Broad Church philosophy; see Susan Budd, *Varieties of Unbelief: Atheists and Agnostics in English Society, 1850–1960* (London: Heinemann Educational Books, 1977), 224–31.

48. Coit, *Neighborhood Guilds,* 17–25.

49. Coit, *Neighborhood Guilds,* 27.

50. Coit, *Neighborhood Guilds,* 71–77.

51. Coit, *Neighborhood Guilds,* 117–20.

52. Albert J. Kennedy wrote in 1944, "Dr. Coit put his own, and a thoroughly American impress, on the patent. This was, that the imaginative and emotional interest of the people of local neighborhoods might be the kindling to light political and social fires of reform." Kennedy, memo to George E. O'Dell, editor, the *Standard* [Ethical Culture Society, New York], 20 February 1944, Records of the National Federation of Settlements, Social Welfare History Archives.

53. Vida Dutton Scudder, *On Journey* (New York: E. P. Dutton, 1937), 1–30; Theresa Corcoran, "Vida Scudder," *Notable American Women: The Modern Period,* 636–38.

54. Scudder, *On Journey,* 34–35.

55. Scudder, *On Journey,* 38.

56. Scudder, *On Journey,* 41–43.

57. Scudder, *On Journey,* 50–51.

58. V. D. S. and S. K., "Influence and Independence," *Andover Review* 16(July 1891): 173.

59. Scudder, *On Journey,* 33–35, 57–60.

60. Scudder, *On Journey,* 65.

61. Scudder, *On Journey,* 68–73; L. Clark Seelye, *The Early History of Smith College* (Boston: Houghton Mifflin, 1923), 53–64.

62. Scudder, *On Journey,* 77; Annie M. A. H. Rogers, *Degrees by Degrees: The Story of the Admission of Oxford Women Students to Membership of the University* (London: Oxford University Press, 1938), 112–24.

63. Scudder, *On Journey,* 77–78, 82–83.

64. Scudder, *On Journey,* 83–84.

65. Scudder, *On Journey,* 36–37, 43, 85.

66. Scudder, *On Journey,* 78; T. Jackson Lears, *No Place of Grace: Antimodernism and the Transformation of American Culture, 1880–1920* (New York: Pantheon Books, 1981), 209–15.

67. Scudder, *On Journey,* 91–92.

68. Scudder, *On Journey,* 90–96, 109, 119.

69. There are a number of secondary accounts of Jane Addams's girlhood and education, of and the psychological "crisis" of her postcollege years. The most informative, though not analytical, is the biography by her nephew, James Weber Linn, *Jane Addams: A Biography* (New York: D. Appleton-Century, 1935). Allen F. Davis gives a shrewd account of her early life in *American Heroine: The Life and Legend of Jane Addams* (New York: Oxford University Press, 1973). In *The New Radicalism in America, 1889–1963: The Intellectual as a Social Type* (New York: Knopf, 1966), Christopher Lasch focuses on the objective roots in her youth of her later argument for "the subjective necessity for social settlements"—that her society condemned her to inactivity while bestowing on her useless gifts of culture and economic privilege.

70. G. J. Barker-Benfield, " 'Mother Emancipator': The Meaning of Jane Addams' Sickness and Cure," *Journal of Family History* 4(Winter 1979): 396–99. Allen Davis pinpoints this "hero worship" as the compelling intimate foundation of her youthful intellectual life in *American Heroine,* 3; on John Huy Addams, see Linn, *Jane Addams,* 1–22; Daniel Levine, *Jane Addams and the Liberal Tradition* (Madison: University of Wisconsin Press, 1971), 3–11.

71. Addams, *Twenty Years at Hull-House,* 13–14.

72. Addams, *Twenty Years at Hull-House,* 12–13, 47.

73. Linn, *Jane Addams,* 29–31; Lasch, *New Radicalism,* 20–22. Daniel Levine stresses, rightly, I think, the centrality in Addams's young life of her antagonism toward her stepmother—made ironically clear by her virtual omission of Anna Haldeman from *Twenty Years at Hull-House.* Levine, *Jane Addams,* esp. 11–12.

74. Linn, *Jane Addams,* 31–36; Davis, *American Heroine,* 29.

75. See Barker-Benfield on this conflict: " 'Mother Emancipator,' " 397–98.

76. Jill Ker Conway, "Anna Peck Sill," *Notable American Women,* 3:290–91.

77. Linn, *Jane Addams,* 40–64.

78. Linn, *Jane Addams*, 48–52.

79. Allen F. Davis, "Eliza Allen Starr," *Notable American Women*, 3:350–51; Ellen Gates Starr to Eliza Allen Starr, [1889?], Ellen Gates Starr Papers, Sophia Smith Collection, Smith College (hereafter cited as EGSP).

80. Ellen Gates Starr to Jane Addams, 11 August 1878, EGSP.

81. Addams to Starr, 11 August 1879, EGSP.

82. Starr to Addams, [n.d.,] EGSP.

83. Starr to Addams, 3 December 1885, EGSP. Starr converted to Catholicism in 1920.

84. Addams to Starr, 11 August 1879, EGSP.

85. Addams to Starr, 29 January 1880, EGSP.

86. Addams to Starr, 22 November 1879, EGSP.

87. Davis, *American Heroine*, 19–20; Addams, *Twenty Years at Hull-House*, 48.

88. Quoted in Jane Addams to Ellen Gates Starr, 13 February 1881, EGSP.

89. Addams to Starr, 15 May 1880, EGSP.

90. Linn, *Jane Addams*, 65–66; Addams to Starr, 3 September 1881, EGSP.

91. Barker-Benfield, " 'Mother Emancipator,' " 403–5; Davis, *American Heroine*, 27. On Mitchell, see Ann Douglas Wood, " 'The Fashionable Diseases': Women's Complaints and Their Treatment in Nineteenth-Century America," *Journal of Interdisciplinary History* 4(Summer 1973): 31–32.

92. Addams to Starr, 8 June 1884, EGSP.

93. Addams to Starr, 6 December 1885, EGSP.

94. Addams to Starr, 7 February 1886, EGSP.

95. Addams to Starr, 7 February 1886, EGSP.

96. Linn, *Jane Addams*, 66–69; Davis, *American Heroine*, 31, 41–42.

97. Starr to Addams, 3 December 1885, EGSP.

98. Addams, *Twenty Years at Hull-House*, 85–87.

99. Jane Addams to Alice Haldeman, 14 June 1888, Jane Addams Memorial Collection, University of Illinois at Chicago (hereafter cited as JAMC); Ellen Gates Starr to Caleb Allen and Susan Childs Starr, 19 February 1888, EGSP.

100. Percy Alden, "American Settlements," in Reason, *University and Social Settlements*, 138.

Chapter Three

1. Jane Addams, "The Subjective Necessity for Social Settlements," in *Philanthropy and Social Progress; Seven Essays*, by Jane Addams, Robert Woods, et al., intro. by Henry C. Adams (New York: Thomas Y. Crowell, 1893), 1.

2. Ellen Gates Starr to [Mary Blaisdell], 23 February [1889], EGSP.

3. Ellen Gates Starr to [Mary Blaisdell], 23 February [1889], EGSP.

4. Ellen Gates Starr to [Mary Blaisdell], 23 February [1889]; Jane Addams to Ellen Gates Starr, 4 June 1889, EGSP.

5. Kathleen D. McCarthy, *Noblesse Oblige: Charity and Cultural Philanthropy in Chicago, 1849–1929* (Chicago: University of Chicago Press, 1982), 27–50, 75–96.

6. Jane Addams to Anna Haldeman Addams, 9 May 1889, JAMC. See also Jane

Addams to Ellen Gates Starr, 24 January 1889; EGSP; Addams to Mary [Linn?], 13 February 1889, 19 February 1889, 26 February 1889, 1 April 1889, Jane Addams Correspondence (on microfilm), Swarthmore College Peace Collection (hereafter cited as JA-SCPC).

7. Ellen Gates Starr to [Mary E. Allen?], 15 September 1889, EGSP.

8. Jane Addams to Ellen Gates Starr, 3 May [1889], EGSP.

9. Ellen Gates Starr to [Mary Blaisdell], 23 February [1889], EGSP.

10. Jane Addams to Mary [Linn?], 1 April 1889, JA-SCPC; Ellen Gates Starr to [Mary Blaisdell], 23 February [1889], EGSP. Vida Scudder concurred in part of Starr's criticism years later: "We followed the all-too-frequent American method; we began with an Organization, then we established centers, then we sought for people to carry out our ideas." She suggested that Hull-House, by beginning at "the opposite end," with the personality of Jane Addams, was a better seed for an enduring movement. Vida Dutton Scudder, *On Journey* (New York: E. P. Dutton, 1937), 136.

11. *First Annual Report of the College Settlements Association, 1890,* 11; *Second Annual Report of the College Settlements Association, 1891,* 7–8.

12. [William J. Tucker,] "Social Christianity—the Andover House Association," *Andover Review* 17(January 1892): 82–88 (includes appendix reprinting the "personal letter of appeal" from Tucker to potential association members, and the articles of association); Robert A. Woods, "The University Settlement Idea," *Andover Review* 17(January 1892): 98–100; Arthur Mann, *Yankee Reformers in the Urban Age* (Cambridge: Belknap Press of Harvard University Press, 1954), 105–23.

13. A chronological account of the founding of the early American settlements is found in Robert A. Woods and Albert J. Kennedy, *The Settlement Horizon: A National Estimate* (New York: Russell Sage Foundation, 1922), 40–52. The best source for the dates, aims, programs, and workers of the American settlements is the last and most complete listing, Robert A. Woods and Albert J. Kennedy, eds., *Handbook of Settlements* (New York: Russell Sage Foundation, 1911).

14. See Scudder, *On Journey,* 149; Robert A. Woods, "Address before the Seabury Society Conference, Northhampton, July 17," typescript, [n.d.,] 4–5, RWP.

15. Samuel A. Barnett, "The Ways of 'Settlements' and of 'Missions,'" *Nineteenth Century* 42(December 1897): 980.

16. Andover House was unusual in providing fellowships to cover room and board for most of its early residents. The settlement was run on a shoestring in the first years, however, the financial arrangements seem to have been informal, tenuous, and often anxiety provoking. See letters from Robert Woods to William J. Tucker, RWP.

17. Jane Addams to Katharine Coman, 7 December 1891, Denison House Papers, Schlesinger Library, Radcliffe College (hereafter cited as DHP).

18. Ellen Gates Starr to [Mary Blaisdell], 23 February [1889], EGSP; Jane Robbins, "The First Year at the College Settlement," *Survey* 27(24 February 1912): 1801; "Boston Settlement (Denison House)," in *Fourth Annual Report of the CSA, 1892–1893,* 42; Robert A. Woods to W. J. Tucker, fragment, RWP; Eleanor

H. Woods, *Robert A. Woods: Champion of Democracy* (Boston: Houghton Mifflin, 1929), 50.

19. Leo Tolstoy, *What Then Must We Do?* trans. Aylmer Maude, with an introduction by Jane Addams (London: Oxford University Press for the Tolstoy Society, H. Milford, 1934). Addams's introduction, solicited by Tolstoy's English disciple Aylmer Maude, discusses the electrifying effect of the book on English and American reformers. See also Leo Tolstoy, *My Religion,* trans. from the French by Huntington Smith (New York: Thomas Y. Crowell, 1896 [1885]).

20. Jane Addams, *Twenty Years at Hull-House* (New York: Macmillan, 1910), 188.

21. Addams, *Twenty Years at Hull-House,* 191–97; J. Thornton to Jane Addams, [15?] June 1896, JA-SCPC; Aylmer Maude to Jane Addams, 16 October 1896, JA-SCPC: Maude responds to Addams's suggestion that perhaps Tolstoy's stance was too stark and unforgiving of human weaknesses.

22. "Report, Committee of the Residents of Chicago Commons, appointed November 3, 1898," typescript, Chicago Commons Records, Chicago Historical Society.

23. Jane Addams to Anna Haldeman Addams, 3 June 1890, JAMC. A few years later John Dewey's "Aunt Emma" would echo Mrs. Starr's observation with her comment that Hull-House was "a very good thing, but it was a pity they had it in such a bad part of town." John Dewey to Alice Chipman Dewey, 27 October [1894], Dewey Family Letters.

24. Robert A. Woods, "The University Settlement Idea," in Addams, Woods, et al., *Philanthropy and Social Progress,* 65–67, 88. See too the retrospective comments on the movement's early impulses toward asceticism in Woods and Kennedy, *Settlement Horizon,* 56–57.

25. Robert Woods to Anna L. Dawes, 20 December 1893, RWP. Woods also disagreed with Coit, Addams, and Scudder that drafting families into the movement to counterbalance the young, single residents might mitigate the settlements' artificiality. He suggested that a more salutary extension of the movement would be a settlement of "mechanics" on Fifth Avenue. On cooperative living in the settlements, see also Dolores Hayden, *The Grand Domestic Revolution: A History of Feminist Designs for American Homes, Neighborhoods, and Cities* (Cambridge: MIT Press, 1981), 171–74.

26. Robbins, "First Year at College Settlement," 1800; "Records," Denison House, 1892–93, MS, DHP.

27. John Dewey to Alice Chipman Dewey, 10 October 1894, Dewey Family Letters (on microfilm), Center for Dewey Studies, Southern Illinois University.

28. Ellen Gates Starr to parents, 3 November 1889, JA-SCPC; Jane Addams to George Haldeman, 24 November 1889, JAMC; Addams, *Twenty Years at Hull-House,* 83–89.

29. Addams, *Twenty Years at Hull-House,* 81–83.

30. Addams, *Twenty Years at Hull-House,* 83; Jane Addams to Anna Haldeman Addams, 3 June 1890, JAMC.

31. Addams, *Twenty Years at Hull–House,* 86.

32. Robbins, "First Year at the College Settlement," 1800–1801; *First Annual Report of the College Settlements Association, 1890,* 5–6.

33. For example, Jacob Riis, *The Making of an American* (New York: Macmillan, 1901), 289–90.

34. *Fourth Annual Report of the College Settlements Association, 1892–1893,* 11.

35. Florence Cross Kitchelt, AMs journal of a residence in the Rivington Street Settlement, June–July 1900, Florence Ledyard (Cross) Kitchelt Papers, Sophia Smith Collection, Smith College.

36. Report of the residents of Denison House, 1892–93. See esp. entries for December 1892 and 21 March 1893, DHP.

37. See *Fourth Annual Report of the College Settlements Association, 1892–1893,* 41; Mann, *Yankee Reformers,* 25–27.

38. *Epworth League House (University Settlement) . . . A Religious Social Study . . .* (Boston, 1894), 2–4, 7–9, 36–39, 80–81, 112. Several historians contest the notion that most of the settlements followed Hull-House, Denison House, and other major settlements in being nondenominational and culturally pluralistic. In fact, many settlements in the smaller cities actively proselytized for their own denominations: see Raymond A. Mohl and Neil Batten, "Paternalism and Pluralism: Immigrants and Social Welfare in Gary, Indiana, 1906–1940," *American Studies* 15(Spring 1974): 5–26. For an account of a settlement that through its early years blended the usual social and cultural objectives with a specific denominational mission, see Ruth Hutchinson Crocker, "Christamore: An Indiana Settlement House from Private Dream to Public Agency," *Indiana Magazine of History* 83(June 1987): 113–40.

39. Robert A. Woods, "Report of the Work of the House at the End of the First Official Year," TD; Woods, "The Andover House Association Report for the Year 1892–93," Circular 9, 9 December 1893, RWP.

40. Jacob Riis and Jacob Schiff, the Jewish philanthropist, had several misunderstandings over whether Riis was proselytizing Jewish children in his settlement, the Jacob Riis House on Henry Street in New York. Since some of the classes offered New Testament instruction, Schiff thought that Riis should get written permission from Jewish parents for their children to participate in Riis House activities. On another occasion, Riis appealed to Schiff for a donation for a settlement gymnasium with the comment that the gym would benefit many Jewish children. Riis got his donation and a rebuke from Schiff for his sectarian appeal. Riis was thoroughly baffled, and Lillian Wald was called in as an intermediary between the two proud and strong-willed men. Jacob Riis to Lillain Wald, 16 November 1903; Jacob Schiff to Lillian Wald, 26 November 1906, Lillian D. Wald Papers, Columbia University. The Riis House had other problems with religious sensitivities in the neighborhood: in 1908 Father Curry of Saint James Church attacked the settlement for "stealing the souls" of Jewish and Catholic children and even suggested that if the women working in the house truly loved children, they would bear them themselves. (Clipping, "Priest Denounces Riis; Raps Settlement Work," unidentified newspaper, Lea Demarest Taylor Papers, Chicago Historical Society.) This nasty offensive called forth a response from *Charities and the Commons* 20(18 April 1908): 89, suggesting that Saint James Church ought to emulate the settlement in its "practical concern for the physical and educational well-being of the young people rather than fulminate

against its neighbors." On Riis and his Jewish critics, see also Jeffrey S. Gurock, "Jacob A. Riis: Christian Friend or Missionary Foe? Two Jewish Views," *American Jewish History* 71(September 1981): 29–47.

41. Herman Hegner, "Scientific Value of the Social Settlements," *American Journal of Sociology* 3(September 1897): 175.

42. Robert A. Woods, "University Settlements as Laboratories in Social Science" (1893), in *The Neighborhood in Nation-Building* (Boston: Houghton Mifflin, 1923), 31–37.

43. Woods, "University Settlements as Laboratories," 36–37.

44. Woods, "Andover House Association Report . . . 1892–93."

45. The first Charity Organization Society by that name in the United States was founded in Buffalo, New York, in 1877. See Frank Dekker Watson, *The Charity Organization Movement in the United States: A Study in American Philanthropy* (New York: Macmillan, 1922), esp. chap. 6. Also see the tract by the Reverend S. Humphreys Gurteen, the English immigrant founder of the Buffalo Society, *A Handbook of Charity Organization* (Buffalo: the author, 1882).

46. Denison House records, 4 January 1893 (entry by Emily G. Balch), DHP; see also "Andover House Association Report . . . 1892–93."

47. Robert Woods to William J. Tucker, 8 February 1892, RWP; Watson, *Charity Organization Movement,* 178–79, 197–201; Nathan Irvin Huggins, *Protestants against Poverty: Boston's Charities, 1870–1900* (Westport, Conn.: Greenwood, 1971), 60–71, 126–28.

48. W. S. Tryon, "Annie Adams Fields," *Notable American Women,* 1:615–17; Huggins, *Protestants against Poverty,* 58–60, 163–67.

49. Robert Woods to William J. Tucker, 14 February 1892, RWP.

50. Paine proudly but inaccurately claimed credit for generating this slogan when a movement was afoot to change it at the Twenty-fifth Anniversary Conference of the New York COS. "Twenty-five years and After," *Charities and the Commons* 19(30 November 1907): 1131; Daniel Levine, *Poverty and Society: The Growth of the American Welfare State in International Comparison* (New Brunswick, N.J.: Rutgers University Press, 1988), esp. 124–27. Also see Huggins, *Protestants against Poverty,* 69–76; "Opening Charity Conference of New York Women," *Lend a Hand* 1(February 1886): 101–3; "For the Friendly Visitors," *Lend a Hand* 2(May 1887): 291–92; Josephine Shaw Lowell, "The Organization of Charity," *Chautauquan* 9(November 1888): 80–82; D. O. Kellogg, "The Function of Charity Organization," *Lend a Hand* 1(August 1886): 450–54; Robert Treat Paine, Jr., "The Work of Volunteer Visitors of the Associated Charities among the Poor," *Journal of Social Sciences* 12(December 1880): 101–5, 113–14.

51. Quoted in "Charity Organization: Abstract of the Fourth Annual Report of the Central Council of the Charity Organization Society of the City of New York," *Lend a Hand* 1(April 1886): 201.

52. Addams, *Twenty Years at Hull-House,* 159–62; Robert Hunter, "The Relation between Social Settlements and Charity Organization," *Proceedings of the National Conference of Charities and Corrections* (1902), 304–5. On the ideals, methods, personnel, and backers of the Chicago COS, see Kenneth Kusmer, "The Functions of Organized Charity in the Progressive Era: Chicago as a Case Study," *Journal of American History* 60(December 1973): 657–78.

53. Mary Kingsbury Simkhovitch, unpublished speech, 1916, United South
End Settlements Records, Social Welfare History Archives, University of Minnesota (hereafter cited as USES).

54. J. P. Gavit to Mary E. Richmond, 19 March 1898, Letterbook of the Chicago
Commons, 1897–1900, Graham Taylor Papers, Newberry Library. From the beginning the settlers differentiated themselves from the charity organizers, and
the emphasis on environmental determinants of poverty was "imported" with
the rest of the English settlement doctrine. William J. Tucker wrote in 1893 that
charity organization, though itself a needed reform of traditional charitable
practices, still belonged to the "lower philanthropy" in its central concern " 'to
put right what social conditions had put wrong.' " The settlement house had
moved on to a "higher philanthropy," which attempted " 'to put right the social
conditions themselves.' " Tucker, "The Work of the Andover House in Boston,"
in *The Poor in Great Cities,* ed. Robert A. Woods (New York, 1895; reprinted
New York: Arno Press, 1971), 179–80.

55. "Discussion of Settlement Work," *Charities Review* 4(June 1895): 462–66.

56. Hunter, "Relation between Social Settlements and Charity Organization,"
307–8.

57. Mary A. Richmond, "The Settlements and Friendly Visiting" (1899), in
Mary Richmond, *The Long View: Papers and Addresses,* ed. Joanna C. Colcord
(New York: Russell Sage Foundation, 1930), 120–26; see also "Criticism and
Reform in Charity," 50–51.

58. Mary Richmond, "Discussion of Settlement Work," 462–63; Allen Davis,
*Spearheads for Reform: The Social Settlements and the Progressive Movement,
1890–1914* (New York: Oxford University Press, 1967), 17–22.

Chapter Four

1. *Hale House Log* (March 1898), 1. Woods and Kennedy wrote of the early
settlers: "They hoped to establish the principle that voluntary undertakings of
proved public utility might be assumed by municipalities, though they made it
clear that as soon and as far as possible the solidarity, continuity, and compre-
hensiveness of public services at their best should be expressed in private
enterprises for the public good." Robert A. Woods and Albert J. Kennedy, *The
Settlement Horizon: A National Estimate* (New York: Russell Sage Foundation,
1922), 223.

2. Jane Addams, *Twenty Years at Hull-House* (New York: Macmillan, 1910),
130–32. For a full treatment of the development of public kitchens and their
relation to the settlement house movement, see Dolores Hayden, *The Grand
Domestic Revolution: A History of Feminist Designs for American Homes, Neighborhoods, and Cities* (Cambridge: MIT Press, 1981), chap. 8.

3. George Rosen, *A History of Public Health* (New York: MD Publications,
1958), 208–24, 287–90; Stephen Smith, "The History of Public Health, 1871–
1921," in *A Half Century of Public Health: Jubilee Historical Volume of the
American Public Health Association,* ed. Mazyck P. Ravenel (New York: American Public Health Association, 1921), 1–12.

4. In 1845, Dr. John Hoskins Griscom published *The Sanitary Condition of*

the Laboring Population of New York (New York: Harper, 1845), based on his reports as former city director of the New York Board of Health. This work came to the attention of Edwin Chadwick and Southwood Smith in England. By 1846 New York City's Association for Improving the Condition of the Poor was investigating housing in the growing poor districts, and in 1853 it issued a report asserting the connection between overcrowding and poor health. In 1857 a pioneer legislative commission drafted a report on housing that included detailed recommendations for government supervision of tenement maintenance and reform. After the draft riots of 1863, the newly formed Citizens' Association, moved not just by the desire to impose social control but also by reports of a cholera epidemic in Europe, sponsored yet another sanitary survey; this one inspired the legislative acts of 1866 and 1867. See Rosen, *History of Public Health,* 233–45; Lawrence Veiller, *Tenement House Reform in New York, 1834–1900* (New York: Evening Post Job Printing House, 1900), 5–24; Veiller, "Housing as a Factor in Health Progress in the Past Fifty Years," in Ravenel, *A Half Century of Public Health,* 323–34; quotation on 326.

5. Jacob Riis, *How the Other Half Lives* (New York: Charles Scribner's Sons, 1890), and Riis, *The Making of an American* (New York: Macmillan, 1901), 194–200. See also Roy Lubove, *The Progressives and the Slums* (Pittsburgh: University of Pittsburgh Press, 1962), 49–80; Veiller, *Tenement House Reform,* 28–32.

6. Lubove, *Progressives and the Slums,* 81–115; Veiller, *Tenement House Reform,* 32–38. For the significance of the Tenement House Committee in the history of the New York COS, see below, chapter 7.

7. Lubove, *Progressives and the Slums,* 140–47.

8. Riis, *Making of an American,* 188–89, 277–80; on alliances with other settlers, see, e.g., Riis to Lillian Wald, 12 November 1896, soliciting Wald's help in reporting violations of the law requiring lights in tenement hallways to the University Settlement (at this time Riis was, among other things, general agent of the Council of Good Government Clubs), Lillian D. Wald Papers, Columbia University (hereafter cited as LDW-CU).

9. See Lubove, *Progressives and the Slums,* 120; James B. Lane, "Jacob A. Riis and Scientific Philanthropy during the Progressive Era," *Social Service Review* 47(March 1973): 32–48.

10. Woods and Kennedy, *Settlement Horizon,* 243.

11. Woods and Kennedy, *Settlement Horizon,* 243; Graham Taylor, *Chicago Commons through Forty Years* (Chicago: Chicago Commons Association, 1936), 11–13.

12. Ellen Gates Starr to Mary Blaisdell, 25 July 1892, EGSP. True to their rejection of "asceticism" and an artificial emulation of the living conditions of the poor, most of the settlement workers continued to take their accustomed summer vacations. For example, Jane Addams to Anna Haldeman Addams, 11 August 1890, JAMC. Of course, one of the main thrusts of the settlements' special summer programs was to get their neighbors, especially the women and children, out of the city, often for several weeks and at least for one- or two-day trips. A tragic exception to the rule of health was the death of a woman resident

of Greenwich House in New York who contracted measles from a local child; see Mary Simkhovitch, *Neighborhood: My Story of Greenwich House* (New York: W. W. Norton, 1938), 140.

13. R. L. Duffus, *Lillian Wald: Neighbor and Crusader* (New York: Macmillan, 1938), 1–17; Beatrice Siegel, *Lillian Wald of Henry Street* (New York: Macmillan, 1983), 7–9.

14. Copy of a letter from Lillian Wald to George P. Ludlum (New York Hospital School of Nursing), 27 May 1889, Lillian D. Wald Papers (on microfilm), New York Public Library (hereafter cited as LDW-NYPL).

15. Wald to Ludlum, 27 May 1889, LDW-NYPL.

16. Charles E. Rosenberg, *The Care of Strangers: The Rise of America's Hospital System* (New York: Basic Books, 1987), esp. 212–36; Josephine A. Dolan, *Nursing in Society: A Historical Perspective* (Philadelphia: Saunders, 1978), 166–71, 210–11.

17. Duffus, *Lillian Wald*, 20–24, 35.

18. Moses Rischin, *The Promised City: New York's Jews, 1870–1914* (Cambridge: Harvard University Press, 1977 [1962]), esp. 19–33, 95–104. The classic fictional portrait of the "Americanization" of a Russian Jewish immigrant is Abraham Cahan, *The Rise of David Levinsky* (1917). Esther Panitz demonstrates that American Jewish attitudes toward Eastern European Jewish immigration swung from resistance to active support about 1890, when the establishment of the Baron de Hirsch Fund greatly eased the financial strain, and the increased oppression of Jews by the czarist government moved American Jews to lobby against United States restrictionist initiatives. Esther Panitz, "The Polarity of American Jewish Attitudes toward Immigration (1870–1891)," *American Jewish Historical Quarterly* 53(December 1963): 99–130; Panitz, "In Defense of the Jewish Immigrant," *American Jewish Historical Quarterly* 55(September 1965): 57–95. See also Kenneth D. Roseman, "American Jewish Community Institutions in Their Historical Context," *Soviet Jewish Affairs* 4(Spring 1974): 25–38; Deborah Dash Moore, *At Home in America: Second Generation New York Jews* (New York: Columbia University Press, 1981). Also of interest is Edmund J. James, Oscar R. Flynn, Dr. J. R. Paulding, Mrs. Simon N. [Charlotte Kimball] Patton [*sic*], and Walter Scott Andrews, *The Immigrant Jew in America* (New York: B. F. Buck, 1906), 43–49, 62–74, 184–99. This study of Jewish immigrants in New York, Philadelphia, and Chicago was sponsored by the Liberal Immigration League. The authors wrote enthusiastically about the Jewish immigrants' group characteristics and their contribution to American life. Like other pro-immigrant spokesmen, including influential American Jews like Jacob Schiff, they urged the development of sound programs for the resettlement of Jews outside the eastern cities.

19. Years later, Rita Wallach Morgenthau described Mrs. Loeb's arriving at a family luncheon with the report that "an extraordinary young woman has called upon me. I don't know whether she is a genius, or whether she is mad. I prefer to think she is a genius, so I am going to ask your Uncle Jacob [Schiff] to give this young woman her chance." Rita W. Morgenthau, radio talk, 15 October 1953, TD, LDW-NYPL. See also Duffus, *Lillian Wald,* 35–36.

20. Lillian Wald, *The House on Henry Street* (New York: H. Holt, 1915), 26–29, 41–43.

21. By 1980 Jacob Schiff was one of the most powerful financiers in New York and already a philanthropist on a grand scale. Brought up in Frankfurt as an Orthodox Jew, he joined the Reform branch after his emigration to America in 1865. Many though not all of his favorite causes were Jewish: he helped to endow the Jewish Theological Seminary in New York, supported the Hebrew Union College, the Yeshibah of New York, and the Jewish Publication Society, and made substantial gifts to the National Library and to Harvard University to support Semitic studies. He also made more general contributions to higher education, particularly at Columbia. Almost single-handedly he created the Montefiore Home and Hospital in 1885, so it is not surprising that he should take an interest in Lillian Wald's visiting nurse plan. Schiff was able to use his tremendous financial influence with the government to secure the abrogation of the Treaty of 1832 with Russia, to protest the czarist government's policy of discriminating between American Jews and non-Jews in granting visas to Russia. Not surprisingly, Schiff opposed Zionism, particularly in its more doctrinaire forms; he also staunchly opposed American immigration restriction. See Cyrus Adler, *Jacob Henry Schiff: A Biographical Sketch* (New York: American Jewish Committee, 1921); Adler, *Jacob H. Schiff: His Life and Letters,* 2 vols. (Garden City, N.Y.: Doubleday, Doran, 1928), 1:354–98. Typically, his interest in the individual institution extended beyond the original donation to embrace a continuing concern with its day-to-day operations. The correspondence between Wald and Schiff, LDW-CU, is extensive and illuminating.

22. For the history of visiting nursing in England and America, see Dolan, *Nursing in Society,* 224–27; M. Louise Fitzgerald, *The National Organization for Public Health Nursing, 1912–1952: Development of a Practice Field* (New York: National League for Nursing, 1975), 3–6; Amy Hughes, "The Rise of District Nursing in England: The Work, Organization and Extent of the Queen Victoria's Jubilee Institute for Nurses," *Charities and the Commons* 16(7 April 1906): 13–16; Fitzpatrick, *National Organization for Public Health Nursing,* 7; Ysabella Waters, "The Rise, Progress and Extent of Visiting Nursing in the United States," *Charities and the Commons* 16(7 April 1906): 16–17.

23. See Wald's monthly reports to Jacob Schiff and Mrs. Solomon Loeb, particularly those of 2 October 1893, 3 November 1893, and 28 November 1893, LDW-NYPL. The nurses established especially good relations with the New York Hospital, which accepted many of their indigent cases. Wald, *House on Henry Street,* 29–40.

24. Wald, *House on Henry Street,* 81–82.

25. Wald, *House on Henry Street,* 17.

26. *Fifth Annual Report of the College Settlements Association, . . . 1893 . . . to . . . 1894,* 46; Woods and Kennedy, *Settlement Horizon,* 49–50.

27. Jane Addams to Mary Rozet Smith, 26 August 1893, JA-SCPC.

28. *Fifth Annual Report of the CSA,* 20–21.

29. *Fifth Annual Report of the CSA,* 21.

30. *Fifth Annual Report of the CSA,* 44–45.

31. Jane Addams to Mary Rozet Smith, 26 August 1893, JA-SCPC. Lillian Wald

likewise noted the "loveliness of heroism and traits not apparent to the man or woman, who know our neighbors as beggars and intreators [sic]." Wald to Jacob Schiff and Mrs. Solomon Loeb, 2 February 1894, LDW-NYPL.

32. *Fifth Annual Report of the CSA,* 34–35.

33. Vida Dutton Scudder, *On Journey* (New York: E. P. Dutton, 1937), 153–54.

34. Announcement signed by Alfred Hicks, 7 April 1890, Hull-House Scrapbook II, JAMC.

35. "Weekly Programme of Lectures, Clubs, Classes, Etc.," January 1891; "Working People's Social Science Club, Tuesdays, 1893," Hull-House Scrapbook II, JAMC.

36. Addams, *Twenty Years at Hull-House,* 134–39; Taylor, *Chicago Commons through Forty Years,* 139–47. For Taylor's relationship with the *Daily News* and its editor, Victor Lawson, see Taylor, *Pioneering on Social Frontiers* (Chicago: University of Chicago Press, 1930), 207, 327, 330, 430–39; Louise C. Wade, *Graham Taylor: Pioneer for Social Justice, 1851–1938* (Chicago: University of Chicago Press, 1964), 101–2, 127, 135, 207–11. See also Woods and Kennedy, *Settlement Horizon,* 173–74.

37. Jane Addams, "The Settlement as a Factor in the Labor Movement," in *Hull-House Maps and Papers,* by Residents of Hull-House (New York: Thomas Y. Crowell, 1895), 184–85.

38. "Autobiography of Mary Kenney O'Sullivan," TD, Schlesinger Library, Radcliffe College, 1–65; Addams, *Twenty Years at Hull-House,* 156–58.

39. O'Sullivan, "Autobiography," 65–67; Addams, *Twenty Years at Hull-House,* 156–58.

40. Allen F. Davis, "Alzina Parsons Stevens," *Notable American Women,* 3: 368–69; Davis, *American Heroine: The Life and Legend of Jane Addams* (New York: Oxford University Press, 1973), 79–80; Allen F. Davis and Mary Lynn McCree, eds., *Eighty Years at Hull-House* (Chicago: Quadrangle Books, 1969), 46–47. Like Mary Kenney, Stevens grew up a factory laborer and became an AFL organizer. She was coeditor of the *Vanguard* ("Marching toward a Diviner Civilization"), a crusading journal that failed after only a year. On Bisno, see Davis and McCree, *Eighty Years at Hull-House,* 21, 110. On Mary Kenney's additional contribution to Hull-House, the organization of the Jane Club as a cooperative boardinghouse for women workers, see Delores Hayden, *The Grand Domestic Revolution: A History of Feminist Designs for American Homes, Neighborhoods, and Cities* (Cambridge: MIT Press, 1981), 167–70.

41. Lloyd is one of John L. Thomas's three central characters in *Alternative America: Henry George, Edward Bellamy, Henry Demarest Lloyd and the Adversary Tradition* (Cambridge: Harvard University Press, 1983); see 71–82.

42. Thomas, *Alternative America,* 132–51; E. Jay Jernigan, *Henry Demarest Lloyd* (Boston: Twayne, 1976), esp. 17–26. The fullest biography of Lloyd is Caro Lloyd, *Henry Demarest Lloyd, 1847–1903: A Biography,* 2 vols. (New York: G. P. Putnam's Sons, 1912).

43. For example, Jane Addams to H. D. Lloyd, 18 November 1891; Ellen Gates Starr to H. D. Lloyd, 21 March 1893, Henry Demarest. Lloyd Papers, State Historical Society of Wisconsin.

44. Ellen Gates Starr to Mary Allen, 24 December [1890s], EGSP.

45. O'Sullivan, "Autobiography," 89.

46. Denison House Records, entries for 21 November 1893, 27 November 1893, DHP; *Fifth Annual Report of the CSA,* 43–44.

47. *Fifth Annual Report of the CSA,* 43.

48. *Fifth Annual Report of the CSA,* 42.

49. O'Sullivan, "Autobiography," 171–80.

50. Herbert Gutman finds a perfectionist Christianity in the rhetoric of many labor leaders in the Gilded Age. He believes that their development of a religiously fueled model of cooperation and brotherhood had little in common with the middle-class Social Gospel, but I suggest that where middle-class reformers and working-class spokesmen did interact, as in the settlements, their cooperation took on a mutual lucidity in the matrix of their shared social Christianity. See Herbert G. Gutman, "Protestantism and the American Labor Movement: The Christian Spirit in the Gilded Age," *American Historical Review* 72(October 1966): 74–101.

51. Robert Woods, "University Settlements as Laboratories in Social Science," in *The Neighborhood in Nation-Building* (Boston: Houghton Mifflin, 1923), 39.

52. For reports, see clippings from the Chicago *Herald* (21 April and 5 May 1892), the Chicago *News* (29 April 1892), the Chicago *Tribune* (30 April 1892), Hull-House Scrapbook I, JAMC.

53. *Fifth Annual Report of the CSA,* 22.

54. *Sixth Annual Report of the CSA,* 38.

55. *Sixth Annual Report of the CSA,* 43; Robert Woods, "The Andover House Association Report for the year 1892–93"; F. W. S., "The World's Fair Congress of Social Settlements," *Unity* (27 July 1893): 251–52, Hull-House Scrapbook I, JAMC.

56. Addams, "The Settlement as a Factor in the Labor Movement," 183–204.

57. Thomas, *Alternative America,* 211–15.

58. Ellen Gates Starr, "Art and Labor," in *Hull-House Maps and Papers,* 175–79.

59. Addams, *Twenty Years at Hull-House,* 257–61; Allen F. Davis, "Ellen Gates Starr," *Notable American Women,* 3:352–53; Davis and McCree, *Eighty Years at Hull-House,* 83–85. On her relations with labor leaders, see, e.g., Sidney Hillman to Ellen Gates Starr, 22 December 1915; Ellen Gates Starr to Caleb Starr, 9 December 1910, EGSP; and note 65 below.

60. Ellen Gates Starr, "Why I Am a Socialist," [unidentified newspaper clipping, Chicago, 1917?], EGSP.

61. O'Sullivan, "Autobiography," 66.

62. Madeleine Wallin [Sikes] to [?], 22 September 1896, Madeleine Wallin Sikes Papers.

63. Alice Hamilton to Agnes Hamilton, 28 January 1904, Hamilton Family Papers (on microfilm), Schlesinger Library, Radcliffe College (hereafter cited as HFP).

64. For the inception of the relationship between Addams and Mary Smith, see letters from Addams to Mary Rozet Smith from late 1890 to 1891, JA-SCPC.

65. For example, see letter from Starr to her father, Caleb Starr, during the

garment workers strike against Hart, Schaffner, and Marx in 1910: "The *whole* procession passed the house, & I was leaning out of my window all the time, recognizing my friends, waving to them, throwing kisses to the girls I know. The men took off their hats to me, & waved them, & cheered. It was great. I never had such an experience. They cheered the house three or four times, & Jane once, rather feebly. She said to me, afterward 'I am glad they cheered the house.' And I didn't say, 'I suppose you know why,' " Ellen Gates Starr to Caleb Starr, 9 December 1910, EGSP.

A letter from Starr to an unidentified intimate, probably in the mid-1890s, hints at the kinds of conflicts Starr was experiencing in her changing relationship with Addams. She mentions a "bad spell" the previous Sunday: "I had an outward & visible excuse for the bad temper, which was convenient, but it knocked me up, fearfully. All the saintliness which I have been singing to you took flight to the [shades?] & I was of the outward color of a pale lemon; & of about the acidity. What's the use in talking about it? only I don't want you to think well of me when 'my conduct has been *such*.' Well, one swings back, & goes on and most people don't know that one has been off. Miss A. knows. Once I thought she knew some other things, but she doesn't. I sit & smile at my own cleverness & daring, sometimes, & take a dramatic interest in it!" EGSP.

66. On the remarkable Wellesley College faculty community in those years, see Patricia Palmieri, "Here Was Fellowship: A Social Portrait of Academic Women of Wellesley College, 1895–1920," *History of Education Quarterly* 23(Summer 1983): 195–214.

67. Scudder, *On Journey* 154–59, 168–72, 175–79. On Boston's genteel radicals, particularly Bliss, see Howard H. Quint, *The Forging of American Socialism: Origins of the Modern Movement* (Indianapolis: Bobbs-Merrill, 1964 [1953]), 109–26.

68. Scudder, *On Journey,* 162–63.

69. Vida Scudder, *A Listener in Babel* (Boston: Houghton Mifflin, 1903), 296.

70. Scudder, *Listener in Babel,* 100.

71. Denison House records, entry for 7 February [1894], DHP. Also see Scudder, *On Journey,* 163: "Socialism in those days hovered for most people on the horizons of Utopia. In New England, we felt hardly at all the impact of the harder and more aggressive movement on the Continent, or even of that in England." See also Kenneth McNaught, "American Progressives and the Great Society," *Journal of American History* 53(December 1966): 510–12; Arthur Mann, *Yankee Reformers in the Urban Age* (Cambridge: Belknap Press of Harvard University Press, 1954), 76–77.

72. Josephine Shaw Lowell, "Discussion of 'Settlement Work,'" *Charities Review* 4(June 1895): 465.

Chapter Five

1. Lillian W. Betts, *The Leaven in a Great City* (New York: Dodd, Mead, 1902), 165–92; quotation on 190.

2. Tay Hohoff, *A Ministry to Man: The Life of John Lovejoy Elliott* (New York: Harper, 1959), 1–53; [obituary for John Lovejoy Elliott,] *New York Times,* 16

April 1942, National Federation of Settlements Records Social Welfare History Archives, University of Minnesota (hereafter cited as NFSR).

3. Hohoff, *Ministry to Man,* 35, 49–50, 70–71. By the 1920s Elliott was calling the Hudson Guild "a settlement or a neighborhood house." John Elliott, *A Short Story of the Hudson Guild,* [ca. 1922?], 20, NFSR.

4. Quoted in Hohoff, *Ministry to Man,* 78.

5. Elliott, *Short Story of the Hudson Guild,* 7.

6. Allen F. Davis, *Spearheads for Reform: The Social Settlements and the Progressive Movement, 1890–1914* (New York: Oxford University Press, 1967), 33–34.

7. Alice Hamilton to Agnes Hamilton, 9 August 1898, HFP; also see Agnes Hamilton to Phoebe Hamilton: "[Miss Addams] has been away all week, and we miss her terribly. The dinner table in only half filled, and at lunch there are two or three residents only" (4 March 1898, HFP). John Dewey made a similar observation: "Hull-House was rather deserted last night. Miss Addams was in Detroit . . . Miss Lathrop was away; & Miss Starr came in late—It's astonishing how much the social atmosphere depends on Miss Addams' presence." John Dewey to Alice Chipman Dewey, 24 November [1894], Dewey Family Letters.

8. Madeleine Wallin [Sikes] to father, 27 October 1896, Madeleine Wallin Sikes Papers. Agnes Hamilton also served briefly as Addams's secretary, after Addams suggested that she knew Agnes wrote "good letters." Agnes Hamilton to Phoebe Hamilton, 4 March 1898, HFP.

9. Alice Hamilton to Agnes Hamilton, 22 January 1898, HFP.

10. Alice Hamilton to Agnes Hamilton, 18 June 1899, HFP; Barbara Sicherman, *Alice Hamilton: A Life in Letters* (Cambridge: Harvard University Press, 1984), 111–20 ff.

11. John Dewey to Alice Chipman Dewey, 7 October [1894], 19 October [1894], Dewey Family Letters.

12. Louise C. Wade, "Julia Clifford Lathrop," *Notable American Women,* 2: 370–72; Jane Addams, *My Friend Julia Lathrop* (New York: Macmillan, 1935), 32–55. Lathrop wrote a paper, "The Cook County Charities," for *Hull-House Maps and Papers* (New York: Thomas Y. Crowell, 1895), 143–61. See also James Johnson, "The Role of Women in the Founding of the United States Children's Bureau," in *"Remember the Ladies": New Perspectives on Women in American History,* ed. Carol V. R. George (Syracuse: Syracuse University Press, 1975), 183–96; Graham Parker, "The Juvenile Court Movement: The Illinois Experience," *University of Toronto Law Journal* 26(1976): 263–65.

13. See Addams, *Julia Lathrop,* 58–60; Alice Hamilton, *Exploring the Dangerous Trades: The Autobiography of Alice Hamilton, M.D.* (Boston: Little, Brown, 1943), 63–64.

14. Louise C. Wade, "Florence Kelley," *Notable American Women,* 2:316–19. The fullest biography to date is Josephine Goldmark, *Impatient Crusader: Florence Kelley* (Urbana: University of Illinois Press, 1953). A biography treating Kelley's life and career through 1900 is Dorothy Rose Blumberg, *Florence Kelley: The Making of a Social Pioneer* (New York: A. M. Kelley, 1966). See also Kathryn Kish Sklar, "Hull-House in the 1890s: A Community of Women," *Signs* 10(Summer 1985): 658–77. Correspondence between Kelley and Richard T. Ely

is on reel 22 of JA-SCPC (microfilmed from documents at the State Historical Society of Wisconsin); see esp. Florence Kelley to Richard Ely, 11 December 1890. See also Florence Kelley to William D. Kelley, 3 November 1877, 2 December 1878; Florence Kelley to Caroline Bonsall Kelley, 24 February 1891, 24 May 1892; Florence Kelley to Mary Thorn Lewis, 4 January 1885, 12 February 1885, 22 June 1885, in Nicholas Kelley Papers, New York Public Library.

15. Florence Kelley to Caroline Bonsall Kelley, 24 February 1891, 24 Mary 1892, Nicholas Kelley Papers. On the remarkable Lloyd ménage in Winnetka, see Caro Lloyd, *Henry Demarest Lloyd, 1847–1903: A Biography,* 2 vols. (New York: G. P. Putnam's Sons, 1912), 1:166–80. Jane Addams once called the Lloyd home "an annex to Hull House" (174).

16. Florence Kelley to Richard T. Ely, 21 June 1894, JA-SCPC.

17. Goldmark, *Impatient Crusader,* 51–65.

18. Madeleine Wallin [Sikes] to [?], 22 September 1896, Madeleine Wallin Sikes Papers, Chicago Historical Society.

19. Hamilton, *Exploring the Dangerous Trades,* 61–62; James Weber Linn, *Jane Addams: A Biography* (New York: D. Appleton-Century, 1935), 137–40; Allen F. Davis, *American Heroine: The Life and Legend of Jane Addams* (New York: Oxford University Press, 1973), 76–78.

20. Alice Hamilton to Agnes Hamilton, 8 August 1900, HFP.

21. This affectionate appellation is used repeatedly by Wald's correspondents; see LDW-CU.

22. Alice Hamilton to Agnes Hamilton, 25 May [1904?], HFP.

23. Frances Kellor to Lillian Wald, n.d. [letterhead, 190?], LDW-CU. Kellor was then the general director of the Inter-Municipal Committee on Household Research.

24. See Mabel Hyde Kittredge, "Home-making in a Model Flat," *Charities and the Commons* 15(4 November 1905): 176–81.

25. Mabel Hyde Kittredge to Lillian D. Wald, n.d., LDW-CU. The quotations given below are from a series of undated letters. Internal evidence suggests that Kittredge was part of the Henry Street activities from about 1901 on. See too Blanche Wiesen Cook's analysis of this relationship, "Female Support Networks and Political Activism: Lillian Wald, Crystal Eastman, Emma Goldman," in *A Heritage of Her Own: Toward a New Social History of American Women,* ed. Nancy F. Cott and Elizabeth H. Pleck (New York: Simon and Schuster, 1979), 423–27.

26. Kittredge's career may be at least partially reconstructed from the letterheads as well as the content of the letters in the Wald correspondence.

27. Alice Hamilton to Agnes Hamilton, 18 June 1899, HFP.

28. Esther G. Barrows, *Neighbors All: A Settlement Notebook* (Boston: Houghton Mifflin, 1929), 172–74.

29. Alice Hamilton to Agnes Hamilton, 13 June 1897, HFP.

30. See, for example, this letter from Graham Taylor to Chester D. Hartranft on Taylor's long and labored decision to move to Chicago: "I am not unmindful of the present exigency in seminary interests. . . . Your own condition of health, & your love for me, have repeatedly almost overwhelmed my sense of the larger loyalty I owe to the Kingdom. But God help me, I cannot do otherwise":

11 August 1892, Graham Taylor Papers, Newberry Library (hereafter cited as GTP). See also Taylor to O. B. Owen, 27 June 1898, Letterbook, Chicago Commons, 1897–1900, GTP.

31. See comments of Louise C. Wade, *Graham Taylor: Pioneer for Social Justice, 1851–1938* (Chicago: University of Chicago Press, 1964), 98–99, 149–51, 224–25. See also letters solicited from former residents on the occasion of the fortieth anniversary of Chicago Commons, 1934, Chicago Commons Records, Chicago Historical Society (hereafter cited as CCR).

32. [Graham Taylor,] *Chicago Commons: A Social Settlement* (Chicago, 1899), 37.

33. Robert Woods to William J. Tucker, 12 February 1892, RWP.

34. Alice Hamilton to Agnes Hamilton, 26 November 1898, HFP.

35. Florence Cross, journal of her residence in the Rivington Street Settlement, 29 April 1902, 15 May 1902, Florence Ledyard (Cross) Kitchelt Papers, Sophia Smith Collection, Smith College. Note that "migrating" from settlement to settlement for extended periods of residence was already common by 1900. Of 169 residents or former residents questioned by the CSA in 1900, fifty, or 29 percent, had lived in more than one settlement. See Helen Annan Scribner, "Residents of College Settlements," in *Twelfth Annual Report of the College Settlements Association . . . 1900 . . . to . . . 1901* (Boston, 1901), 20.

36. Florence Kelley to Richard Ely, [ca. 1890,] JA-SCPC.

37. Alice Hamilton to Agnes Hamilton, 13 October 1897, HFP.

38. Agnes's story is told more fully in Mina J. Carson, "Agnes Hamilton of Fort Wayne: The Education of a Christian Settlement Worker," *Magazine of Indiana History* 80(March 1984): 1–34. For educational background, see Sicherman, *Alice Hamilton,* 11–23.

39. Florence Cross, journal of her residence at the Rivington Street Settlement, Kitchelt Papers; quotations from entries for 3 August 1900, 5 February 1901.

40. For biographical background on Hunter, see Peter d'A. Jones, introduction to Robert Hunter, *Poverty: Social Conscience in the Progressive Era* (New York: Harper Torchbooks, 1965 [1904]), esp. x–xi; TD copies of newspaper clippings announcing Hunter's appointment as headworker of the University Settlement, Papers of the University Settlement Society of New York City (microfilm edition, 1972), State Historical Society of Wisconsin (hereafter cited as USSP). See also John Hobson to Robert Hunter, 12 July 1899; Keir Hardie to Robert Hunter, 21 July [1899]; Gertrude Toynbee to Robert Hunter, 21 July [1899], USSP.

41. On *Poverty* and its reception, see Daniel Levine, *Poverty and Society: The Growth of the American Welfare State in International Comparison* (New Brunswick, N.J.: Rutgers University Press, 1988), 126–27. On the ascendancy of the Socialist party's center-right coalition and its efforts to recruit just such middle-class liberal reformers as Hunter and Phelps Stokes, see Ira Kipnis, *The American Socialist Movement: 1897–1912* (New York: Columbia University Press, 1952), 171–75, 199–217.

42. In a questionnaire sent by the College Settlements Association to its settlement "veterans" on the occasion of its twenty-fifth anniversary (1914), the

settlement workers were asked whether they could call themselves socialists. Out of 145 who responded to the questionnaire, 40 answered yes, but as the questionnaire's collators reported, most qualified that response with phrases such as " 'very mild and in a broad sense,' 'broadly speaking,' 'theoretic,' 'opportunist and evolutionary,' 'to a limited degree,' 'perhaps Fabian,' 'semi,' 'near,' 'conservative,' 'tolerant,' 'not an enthusiastic supporter,' 'to live poor, not take from rich.' " Only five called themselves party members. "Anniversary Report of the College Settlements Association," in *The New York College Settlement, 1889–1914* (n.p., 1914), 35, 41–42.

43. Alice Hamilton to Agnes Hamilton, 18 June 1899, HFP.

44. Robert Woods to William J. Tucker, 7 December 1892, RWP.

45. Quoted in Davis, *Spearheads for Reform,* 76; also in Kennedy, "Settlement Heritage," TD, NFSR.

46. "Report on the Questions Drawn up by Present Residents in Our College Settlements and Submitted to Past Residents" (reprint from Publications of the Church Social Union, September [1896]), 22. Agnes Hamilton wrote to her mother after a month's visit at Hull-House: "I don't believe I shall run off at a tangent on any brand new scheme. It is amusing to hear people, each one with his own scheme for setting us all straight and so sure that any other scheme would wreck us worse than ever. Looking at them all has quite cured me of any one." Agnes Hamilton to Phoebe Hamilton, 8 February 1898, HFP.

47. "Report on the Questions," 21–24.

Chapter Six

1. Quoted in *Settlements 60th Anniversary, 1886–1946* [New York: National Federation of Settlements, 1946?].

2. Horace Kallen's vision of cultural pluralism—though not the term itself—was first laid out in "Democracy *versus* the Melting Pot," published in the *Nation* in 1915. Kallen pleaded for a national attitude of tolerance and appreciation for the cultural and linguistic forms brought by each ethnic group to the common political nationality—a "multiplicity in a unity, the orchestration of mankind." The essay is reprinted in Horace Kallen, *Culture and Democracy in the United States* (New York: Boni and Liveright, 1924), 67–125; see also 11. See also David Hollinger, "Ethnic Diversity, Cosmopolitanism, and the Emergence of the American Liberal Intelligentsia," in *In the American Province: Studies in the History and Historiography of Ideas* (Bloomington: University of Indiana Press, 1985), esp. 65; Sidney Ratner, ed., *Vision and Action: Essays in Honor of Horace M. Kallen on His Seventieth Birthday* (New Brunswick, N.J.: Rutgers University Press, 1953), 83–111; Milton M. Gordon, *Assimilation in American Life: The Role of Race, Religion, and National Origins* (New York: Oxford University Press, 1964), 140–49.

3. Graham Taylor, *Chicago Commons through Forty Years* (Chicago: Chicago Commons Association, 1936), 89.

4. John Higham, *Strangers in the Land: Patterns of American Nativism, 1860–1925,* 2d ed. (New York: Atheneum, 1974), 87–104.

5. Frederick A. Bushee, "The Invading Host," in *Americans in Process,* ed. Robert A. Woods (Boston: Houghton Mifflin, 1903) 49, 52.

6. There is a large literature on the acculturation of American immigrants, particularly for the period of the "new immigration" in the late nineteenth and early twentieth centuries. First-person narratives relevant to settlement neighborhoods and concerns include Mary Antin, *The Promised Land* (Boston: Houghton Mifflin, 1912); Philip Davis, *And Crown Thy Good* (New York: Philosophical Library, 1952); and Abraham Cahan's powerful novel, *The Rise of David Levinsky* (New York: Harper Brothers, 1917). Certainly the most evocative account of transplantation from Europe to America is Oscar Handlin, *The Uprooted* (Boston: Little, Brown, 1951). These titles barely sample the wealth of material on this subject.

Besides contributing their own interpretations of the human costs of immigration, the settlement workers helped inspire the first great sociological grappling with the experience, that of the "Chicago school," personified by William I. Thomas and his student Robert Ezra Park. Thomas developed an empirical sociology that concentrated on the interactions between social organization and personality. His great work (with Florian Znaniecki) was the five-volume *Polish Peasant in Europe and America* (Chicago: University of Chicago Press, 1918–19). A few years later he collaborated with Park and Herbert A. Miller on *Old World Traits Transplanted* (New York: Harper, 1921). Park had studied with John Dewey and William James and worked with Booker T. Washington at Tuskegee Institute. Park's *Old World Traits* used immigrants' accounts of their adjustment to life in America to explore such issues as loss of status and demoralization in a new environment and to attempt a typology of personalities according to reactions to the acculturation experience. His reading of William James and Charles H. Cooley influenced his later work on "social personality" and his concept of the "marginal man," caught between two cultures and not really rooted in either. Like the settlement workers and John Dewey, Park perceived the growth of an urban economy and social arrangements as exacting a toll in the loss of the kinds of social control and individual gratifications afforded by membership of a "primary group"—the family, community, or neighborhood. On the Chicago school, see Martin Bulmer, *The Chicago School of Sociology: Institutionalization, Diversity, and the Rise of Sociological Research* (Chicago: University of Chicago Press, 1984). Also see Morton White and Lucia White, *The Intellectual versus the City: From Thomas Jefferson to Frank Lloyd Wright* (New York: Oxford University Press, 1977); on Thomas, see Donald Fleming, "Attitude: The History of a Concept," *Perspectives in American History* 1(1967): 322–31, and Mary Jo Deegan and John S. Burger, "W. I. Thomas and Social Reform: His Work and Writings," *Journal of the History of the Behavioral Sciences* 17(January 1981): 114–25.

7. Jane Addams, "Report of the Committee on Immigrants," *Proceedings of the National Conference of Charities and Corrections* (1909), 214.

8. Jessie Fremont Beale and Anne Withington, "Life's Amenities," in Woods, *Americans in Process,* 227.

9. For example, Jane Addams, *Twenty Years at Hull-House* (New York: Macmillan, 1910), 231.

10. Lillian Wald, *The House on Henry Street* (New York: H. Holt, 1915), 303.

11. *Seventh Annual Report of the College Settlements Association, 1895–1896,* 41; Vida Dutton Scudder, *On Journey* (New York: E. P. Dutton, 1937), 256.

12. Scudder, *On Journey,* 253.

13. Vida D. Scudder, "Experiments in Fellowship: Work with Italians in Boston," *Survey* 22(3 April 1909): 48–49.

14. Scudder, *On Journey,* 257; see also Denison House Diary, entries for 4 April [1904], 16 February [1906]; Denison House directors' meeting minutes, esp. 11 January 1905, 8 February 1905, 1 October 1906, 4 March 1906, 1 June 1908, 8 March 1909, DHP.

15. Scudder, "Experiments in Fellowship," 49; also see *Seventeenth Annual Report of the College Settlements Association, 1905–1906,* 86–89.

16. Scudder, *On Journey,* 254.

17. For example, Addams, *Twenty Years at Hull-House,* 21–22. In February 1909, the centennial of Lincoln's birth, Addams reported to Lillian Wald that "Chicago has never been so pulled together as by their common enthusiasm for Lincoln, it has really been quite touching." Addams to Wald, 14 February 1909, LDW-CU.

18. Jane Addams, *Newer Ideals of Peace* (New York: Macmillan, 1907), 77–78.

19. Addams, *Twenty Years at Hull-House,* 231–32; Daniel Levine, *Jane Addams and the Liberal Tradition* (Madison: University of Wisconsin Press, 1971), 154–55.

20. Robert A. Woods, "University Settlements: Their Point and Drift," in *The Neighborhood in Nation-Building* (Boston: Houghton Mifflin, 1923), 53.

21. Addams, *Twenty Years at Hull-House,* 231.

22. Addams, *Twenty Years at Hull-House,* 371–76; James Weber Linn, *Jane Addams: A Biography* (New York: D. Appleton-Century, 1935), 122–23.

23. *Hull-House Bulletin* 3 (November–December 1899): 8–9; *Hull-House Bulletin* (June 1897): 4.

24. Ellen Gates Starr, "Hull-House Bookbindery," *Commons* 47 (30 June 1900): 5–6, reprinted in Allen F. Davis and Mary Lynn McCree, eds., *Eighty Years at Hull-House* (Chicago: Quadrangle Books, 1969), 83–85.

25. See Jane Addams, "A Function of the Social Settlement," *Annals of the American Academy of Political and Social Science* 13(May 1899): 332. Helen Lefkowitz Horowitz places the Hull-House arts programs of the late 1890s to 1900s in the local context of late nineteenth-century Chicago "cultural philanthropy." Although the founders of the city's museums, libraries, and university viewed art mainly as an ideal counteracting the materialism of industrial civilization, Horowitz argues, Addams implicitly criticized this view through her growing determination to connect art to the lives of industrial workers, an enterprise that led her deeper into social criticism than the cultural philanthropists were ready to go. Ultimately Chicago arts administrators responded to this critique by making their offerings more accessible and responsive to working people. See Horowitz, *Culture and the City: Cultural Philanthropy in Chicago from the 1880s to 1917* (Lexington: University of Kentucky Press, 1976), 126–44.

26. Quoted by Addams in "Function of the Social Settlement," 34.

27. Addams, "Function of the Social Settlement," 35–39.

28. Addams, "Function of the Social Settlement," 36.

29. Addams, *Twenty Years at Hull-House,* 237.

30. Jane Addams, "The Humanizing Tendency of Industrial Education," *Chautauquan* 39(May 1904): 26.

31. Addams, *Twenty Years at Hull-House,* 243–44.

32. Addams, *Twenty Years at Hull-House,* 240–41.

33. Adelene Moffat, "The Exhibition of Italian Arts and Crafts in Boston," *Survey* 22(3 April 1909): 51 ff.; Scudder, "Work with Italians in Boston," 50–51.

34. Rita Teresa Wallach, "The Social Value of the Festival," *Charities and the Commons* 16(2 June 1906): 315; see also Lillian Wald, *Windows on Henry Street* (Boston: Little, Brown, 1934), 166.

35. Wallach, "Social Value of the Festival," 317–19.

36. Robert A. Woods and Albert J. Kennedy, *The Settlement Horizon: A National Estimate* (New York: Russell Sage Foundation, 1922), 185.

37. Florence Kelley and Alzina P. Stevens, "Wage-Earning Children," in *Hull-House Maps and Papers* (New York: Thomas Y. Crowell, 1895), 72; see also Florence Kelley, *Some Ethical Gains through Legislation* (New York: Macmillan, 1905), 5–11, 58–60; Addams, *Twenty Years at Hull-House,* 199–200; Adams, *Newer Ideals of Peace,* 161–62.

38. Woods and Kennedy, *Settlement Horizon,* 185–86; Dorothy Blumberg, *Florence Kelley: The Making of a Social Pioneer* (New York: A. M. Kelley, 1966), 134–35; Kelley, *Some Ethical Gains through Legislation,* 38–40.

39. Woods and Kennedy, *Settlement Horizon,* 185–87, 417. The members of the National Child Labor Committee included Felix Adler, Robert W. De Forest, Edward T. Devine of *Charities* and the New York COS, V. Everit Macy, Paul M. Warburg, Florence Kelley, and Lillian Wald: see Devine to Wald, 23 April 1904, LDW-CU. See also Wald, *House on Henry Street,* 137–38; Josephine Goldmark, *Impatient Crusader: Florence Kelley* (Urbana: University of Illinois Press, 1953), 81–92; James Johnson, "The Role of Women in the Founding of the Children's Bureau," in *"Remember the Ladies": New Perspectives on Women in American History,* ed. Carol V. R. George (Syracuse: Syracuse University Press, 1985), 179–82.

40. Lillian Wald to Jacob Schiff, 17 February 1914, LDW-CU.

41. Kelley, *Some Ethical Gains through Legislation,* 2–6.

42. Robert Hunter, *Poverty: Social Conscience in the Progressive Era* (New York: Harper Torchbooks, 1965 [1904]), 229.

43. Kelley, *Some Ethical Gains through Legislation,* 3, 101; Frank J. Bruno, *Trends in Social Work, 1874–1956: A History Based on the Proceedings of the National Conference of Social Work* (New York: Columbia University Press, 1957), 152. In *Children of the City: At Work and at Play* (New York: Oxford University Press, 1985), David Nasaw argues that the movement to regulate the street trades was largely ineffective because the children, less vulnerable and naive than their elders assumed, easily circumvented the statutes; see esp. 138–57.

44. Hunter, *Poverty,* 202–3.

45. Hunter, *Poverty,* 196.

46. Hunter, *Poverty,* 197.

47. Hunter, *Poverty,* 219–20.

48. Hunter, *Poverty,* 196–98.

49. Philip Davis, *Street-Land: Its Little People and Big Problems* (Boston: Small, Maynard, 1915), esp. xvi–xviii; quotations on 227–29.

50. Joseph F. Kett, *Rites of Passage: Adolescence in America 1790 to the Present* (New York: Basic Books, 1977), 133–43.

51. Jane Addams, *The Spirit of Youth and the City Streets* (New York: Macmillan, 1909), 3–4.

52. Addams, *Spirit of Youth,* 16.

53. Addams, *Spirit of Youth,* 6. For an anatomization of this constellation of attitudes toward sexuality in the mid-nineteenth century, see G. J. Barker-Benfield, *The Horrors of the Half-Known Life* (New York: Harper and Row, 1976).

54. Addams, *Spirit of Youth,* 30.

55. Addams, *Spirit of Youth,* 75–85.

56. Fifty years later, television and video games would elicit a similar shudder from educated adults who feared that the sensory overstimulation resulting from these pastimes would cause premature enervation in children and that graphic depictions of sex and violence would rob them of their innocence. Beneath these genuine anxieties lay the critics' conviction that television was "vulgar" and that the child exposed to the "low" culture of the screen would never develop a desire for the "high" culture of print. Parents also feared a loss of moral suasion over their children; they resisted the implications of their accurate if not fully articulated sense that their children were learning to inhabit gracefully a new world to which an older generation had limited access.

57. Addams, *Spirit of Youth,* 91–92.

58. See Kathy Peiss, *Cheap Amusements: Working Women and Leisure in Turn-of-the-Century New York* (Philadelphia: Temple University Press, 1985), 141–43.

59. Vida D. Scudder, *A Listener in Babel* (Boston: Houghton Mifflin, 1903), 90.

60. Addams, *Spirit of Youth,* 15.

61. Addams, *Spirit of Youth,* 101.

62. See, e.g., *Andover House Bulletin,* no. 1, 1893, RWP; Frederick S. Lamb [secretary, National Arts Club] to Dr. Millard Knowlton, 19 June 1911; Millard Knowlton to Jacob Riis, 3 August 1911, Jacob A. Riis Neighborhood Settlement Records, New York Public Library; Woods and Kennedy, *Settlement Horizon,* 146–47.

63. *Eleventh Annual Report of the College Settlement, 95 Rivington Street, 1899–1900,* 14; Woods and Kennedy, Settlement Horizon, 152–56.

64. Woods and Kennedy, *Settlement Horizon,* 156. About 1910, the Hull-House residents participated in a campaign against the use of children on the professional stage; some accused the residents of hypocrisy, and Addams defended the settlement's dramatic activities as scrupulously regulated and fundamentally educational: see Jane Addams, "Stage Children," *Survey* 25(3 December 1910): 342–43. In *Twenty Years at Hull-House* she pointed out that after fifteen years and much success, the Hull-House Players had not spawned a

single professional actor—"contrary to all predictions and despite several offers." Addams, *Twenty Years at Hull-House,* 390.

65. Addams, *Twenty Years at Hull-House,* 390; Elsie F. Weil, "The Hull-House Players," *Theatre Magazine,* September 1913, xix–xxii, reprinted in Davis and McCree, *Eighty Years at Hull-House,* 88–91. For a hostile view of pretensions of the Hull-House Players, see James O'Donnell Bennett, "Tempting Fate," Chicago *Record Herald,* 12 December 1912, clipping, JA-SCPC.

66. See Robert A. Woods and Albert J. Kennedy, eds., *Handbook of Settlements* (New York: Russell Sage Foundation, 1911).

67. Some of course accepted not only Ruskin's aesthetics but also his economics. See Ellen Gates Starr, "Art and Labor," in *Hull-House Maps and Papers,* 172–79.

68. Kennedy, "The Visual Arts in the New York Settlements," TD, Albert J. Kennedy Papers, Social Welfare History Archives, University of Minnesota (hereafter cited as AJKP).

69. For example, the Music School Settlement in Brooklyn, and the Music School Settlement on Third Street in Manhattan, which had separated from the College Settlement in 1903; and in Boston, the Boston Music School Settlement and the South End Music School, an offshoot of South End House.

70. Woods and Kennedy, *Handbook of Settlements,* 131. The Music School Settlement in Manhattan wrote of its aims: "The School . . . appeals to those who, desiring to procure that cultural training which come from well-directed music study, are limited in their opportunity to secure it. . . . The principal aim then is to permit those who love music to find means for self-expression in it, to stimulate love for it, to place it in the home as a cultural investment of the best kind; . . . and to lead no one astray into the profession of music who is not gifted with sufficient talent and industry to accomplish the long-continued necessary work which such a choice of profession imposes." Woods and Kennedy, *Handbook of Settlements,* 219. See also Woods and Kennedy, *Settlement Horizon,* 154–55.

71. See Albert Kennedy's comment on this trend in New York settlements in Kennedy, "Visual Arts in New York Settlements," n.p.

72. Robert A. Woods, "Assimilation: A Two-Edged Sword," in *Americans in Process,* ed. Robert A. Woods (Boston: Houghton Mifflin, 1902), 373–74; see also Woods and Kennedy, *Settlement Horizon,* 274, 140, 309. Woods and Kennedy commented, "Talent of the first order among tenement children is the rare exception. But there is, in most working-class quarters, a considerable number of boys and girls whose modest, though real, promise is lost because unperceived by its possessors or because there is no interested person close at hand to give timely encouragement." *Settlement Horizon,* 309.

73. Woods, "Assimilation, 375. Also see Woods, "University Settlements: Their Point and Drift" (1899), in *Neighborhood in Nation-Building,* 12–13, for an early hint of this idea.

74. John Dewey to Alice Chipman Dewey, [October?] 1894, Dewey Family Letters.

75. Caroline S. Atherton and Elizabeth Y. Rutan, "The Child of the Stranger," in Woods, *Americans in Process,* 294–95, 299–304; Mrs. Vladimir [Mary Kings-

bury] Simkhovitch, "The Enlarged Function of the Public School," *Proceedings of the National Council of Charities and Corrections* (1904), 471–86; Diane Ravitch, *The Great School Wars: New York City, 1805–1973* (New York: Basic Books, 1974), 161–86.

76. See Addams, "Humanizing Tendency of Industrial Education," 266–72, for the relation of the Labor Museum to her ideals of public education. See also Addams, *Democracy and Social Ethics* (Cambridge: Belknap Press of Harvard University Press, 1964 [1902]), 178–220; and Addams, *Spirit of Youth,* 107–35. John Dewey's ideas are clearly laid out in *The School and Society* (Chicago: University of Chicago Press, 1899).

77. See, e.g., Jane Addams, "Neighborhood Work," *Charities and the Commons* 15(20 January 1906): 535–36. On the "two wasted years," see Mary Flexner, "The Case for Vocational Training," *Survey* 22(7 August 1909): 650, 654–55; Albert J. Kennedy, untitled manuscript, folder 15, AJKP.

78. Addams, *Spirit of Youth,* 109–10.

79. Quoted by Lawrence Cremin, *The Transformation of the School: Progressivism in American Education, 1876–1957* (New York: Alfred A. Knopf, 1961), 28–29. See Cremin's account of the manual training movement, chap. 2.

80. Cremin, *Transformation of the School,* 33.

81. Elizabeth Fones-Wolf, "The Politics of Vocationalism: Coalitions and Industrial Education in the Progressive Era," *Historian* 46(November 1893): 40–45.

82. Fones-Wolf, "Politics of Vocationalism," 44–45.

83. Paul U. Kellogg, "The National Society for the Promotion of Industrial Education," *Charities and the Commons* 17(1 December 1906): 363–71.

84. John Dewey, *Democracy and Education: An Introduction to the Philosophy of Education* (New York: Macmillan, 1916), 358–74; quotation on 372. Horace Kallen also spoke disparagingly of "vocational training" that taught the immigrant child "the habit of being a cog in the industrial machine." Kallen, "Democracy versus the Melting Pot" (1915), in *Culture and Democracy in the United States,* 95. See also Steven J. Diner, *A City and Its Universities: Public Policy in Chicago, 1892–1919* (Chapel Hill: University of North Carolina Press, 1980), 92–97.

85. Robert A. Woods, "Industrial Education from the Social Worker's Standpoint," *Charities and the Commons* 19(5 October 1907): 852–55.

86. Woods, "Industrial Education from the Social Worker's Standpoint," 852.

87. *Annual Report of the North Bennet Street Industrial School, 1910,* 14. The writers of the report acknowledged "liberal use" of the thought of Albert Kennedy of South End House, among others.

Chapter 7

1. See M. Katharine Jones, *Bibliography of College, Social and University Settlements* (Chicago, 1893). The second edition appeared in 1896, and the third, compiled by John Palmer Gavit, editor of the *Commons* in Chicago, in 1897.

2. Robert Woods to Jane Addams, 26 June 1893; also Robert Woods to Jane

Addams, 5 May 1893; Charles C. Bonney to Jane Addams, 14 January 1893; James B. Reynolds to Jane Addams, 5 February 1893; Everett Wheeler to Jane Addams, 29 May 1893, JA-SCPC.

3. Jane Addams to Henrietta Barnett, 30 May 1899, JAMC; *Hull-House Bulletin* 3(April–May 1899): 10; Albert Kennedy to Lillian D. Wald, 9 November 1910; LDW-CU; "Events Leading to the Formation of the National Federation of Settlements, Inc.," 1, TD, United Neighborhood Houses of New York City Records, Social Welfare History Archives, University of Minnesota (hereafter cited as UNHR); Robert A. Woods and Albert J. Kennedy, *The Settlement Horizon: A National Estimate* (New York: Russell Sage Foundation, 1922), 399.

4. "Social Settlements and the Labor Question," *Proceedings of the National Conference of Charities and Corrections* (1896), 106–75.

5. See, e.g., Jane Addams, "Child Labor and Pauperism," *Proceedings of the NCCC* (1903), 114–21; Mrs. Vladimir Simkhovitch, "The Enlarged Function of the Public School," *Proceedings of the NCCC* (1904), 471–86; Graham Taylor, "Organized Charity and Organized Labor," *Proceedings of the NCCC* (1905), 458–62.

6. Frank J. Bruno [and Louis Townley], *Trends in Social Work, 1874–1956: A History Based on the Proceedings of the National Conference of Social Work* (New York: Columbia University Press, 1957), 113. Other settlement leaders subsequently elected to the presidency of the NCCC were Graham Taylor, Robert Woods, and Julia Lathrop. Woods and Kennedy, *Settlement Horizon,* 387.

7. For a cogent statement of the "new view" of poverty, see Robert H. Bremner, *From the Depths: The Discovery of Poverty in the United States* (New York: New York University Press, 1956), 123–39. Paul Boyer also recognizes a new "positive environmentalist" approach to poverty; he stresses the continuity with the previous "coercive," individual-oriented philosophy in its primary concern with the moral health of urban dwellers. See Boyer, *Urban Masses and Moral Order in America, 1820–1920* (Cambridge: Harvard University Press, 1978), 179–84.

8. On Lowell, see Robert H. Bremner, "Josephine Shaw Lowell," *Notable American Women,* 2:437–39.

9. Accounts of this campaign against tuberculosis may be found in Edward T. Devine, *When Social Work Was Young* (New York: Macmillan, 1939), 81–101, and in Frank Dekker Watson, *The Charity Organization Movement in the United States: A Study in American Philanthropy* (New York: Macmillan, 1922), 293–97. Devine first asked Alice Hamilton to head the campaign, but she turned him down. See Florence Kelley to Nicholas Kelley, 29 June 1902, Nicholas Kelley Papers.

10. Devine, *When Social Work Was Young,* 10–11; Daniel M. Fox, *The Discovery of Abundance: Simon N. Patten and the Transformation of Social Theory* (Ithaca: Cornell University Press, 1967), 21–26, 36–38.

11. Devine, *When Social Work Was Young,* 12–20.

12. Clarke Chambers summarizes the editorial history of *Charities* and the *Charities Review* in *Paul U. Kellogg and the Survey: Voices for Social Welfare and Social Justice* (Minneapolis: University of Minnesota Press, 1971), 6–11, 18–24.

13. Graham Taylor, *Pioneering on Social Frontiers* (Chicago: University of Chicago Press, 1930), 420–23; Chambers, *Paul U. Kellogg and the Survey*, 24–26; Devine, *When Social Work Was Young*, 110–11.

14. Joseph Lee to Paul U. Kellogg, 18 July 1904, Paul U. Kellogg Papers, Social Welfare History Archives, University of Minnesota.

15. Edward T. Devine, "Efficiency and Relief: A Program of Social Work," *Charities and the Commons* 15(4 November 1905): 150–51.

16. Edward T. Devine, "The Dominant Note of the Modern Philanthropy," *Charities and the Commons* 16(2 June 1906): 340–45.

17. Devine, "Dominant Note," 344.

18. There were several special numbers of *Charities* from 1904 through 1905, including one on ocean beaches and the park movement, *Charities* 12(6 August 1904); several issues on immigrant groups such as the Italians, *Charities* 12(7 May 1904), and the Slavs, *Charities* 13(7 January 1905); the Negro in northern cities, *Charities* 15(7 October 1905); and the "smaller city," *Charities* 14(6 May 1905). Also see "Publisher's Announcements," *Charities and the Commons* 17(6 October 1906): n.p.

19. Chambers, *Paul U. Kellogg and the Survey*, 33–34.

20. Irvin G. Wyllie, "Margaret Olivia Slocum Sage," *Notable American Women*, 3:222–23. On the social workers' reactions to the Sage Foundation, see *Charities and the Commons* 17(23 March 1907): 1071–72, 1079–85; *Charities and the Commons* 18(11 May 1907): 186–91.

21. See the editorial "The Pittsburgh Survey . . . ," probably written by Paul Kellogg, in *Charities and the Commons* 19(7 March 1908): 1665–70.

22. The University Settlement of New York briefly sponsored a quarterly devoted to the social investigations of residents and fellows of the settlement: see *University Settlement Studies Quarterly* 1–3(April 1905–June 1907).

23. Robert Woods, Paul U. Kellogg, Graham Taylor, and Edward T. Devine, in *Proceedings of the Pittsburgh Conference for Good City Government and the Fourteenth Annual Meeting of the National Municipal League* (1908), 22–35, 388–412. See also Chambers, *Paul U. Kellogg and the Survey*, 33–41; Devine, *When Social Work Was Young*, 112–13; Bremner, *From the Depths*, 154–56.

24. William H. Matthews, *Adventures in Giving* (New York: Dodd, Mead, 1939), 68–69; Devine, *When Social Work Was Young*, 113; Eleanor H. Woods, *Robert A. Woods: Champion of Democracy* (Boston: Houghton Mifflin, 1929), 232–35.

25. Allen F. Davis, "Crystal Eastman," *Notable American Women*, 1:543–45.

26. *Survey* 22(3 April 1909): n.p.

27. Chambers, *Paul U. Kellogg and the Survey*, 42–45; Devine, *When Social Work Was Young*, 113–16, 120–22.

28. Fox, *Discovery of Abundance;* see also Fox's introduction to Simon N. Patten, *The New Basis of Civilization* (Cambridge: Belknap Press of Harvard University Press, 1968); on the relationship between Devine and Patten, see esp. xxxi–xxxiv.

29. Patten, *New Basis of Civilization*, 56–57.

30. Patten, *New Basis of Civilization*, 162.

31. Patten, *New Basis of Civilization*, 137–38, 161.

32. Patten, *New Basis of Civilization,* 127.

33. Patten, *New Basis of Civilization,* 132–33.

34. Patten, *New Basis of Civilization,* 142–43.

35. Fox, *Discovery of Abundance,* 77–78, 160–61.

36. Patten, *New Basis of Civilization,* 178.

37. Patten, *New Basis of Civilization,* 181.

38. Patten, *New Basis of Civilization,* 179.

39. Fox, *Discovery of Abundance,* 95–114.

40. Patten, *New Basis of Civilization,* 218.

41. Simon N. Patten, "Who Is the Good Neighbor?" *Charities and the Commons* 19(29 February 1908): 1045. For Devine's attempts to mediate the debate, see [Edward T. Devine,] "Neighborliness and Personal Service vs. Citizenship and Improved Conditions," *Charities and the Commons* 19(29 February 1908): 1635–36; "The Friendly Visitor," *Charities and the Commons* 21(28 November 1908): 321–22; "The Social Worker," *Charities and the Commons* 19(2 November 1907): 947–48. Devine sketched a floppy middle-of-the-road position by suggesting that the "friendly visitor" might play some role *after* essential material needs were provided for. See also Zilpha D. Smith, "The Good Neighbor Again," *Charities and the Commons* 20(16 May 1908): 230–32, for a response to Patten that supported the charity workers' position while pointing out that much of their practice was firmly in line with Patten's recommendations.

Besides Patten, other social scientists interested in the theoretical basis of social work wrote for *Charities and the Commons* and its successor, the *Survey.* Charles A. Ellwood, a sociologist at the University of Missouri, contributed "The Functions of Modern Social Work," *Charities and the Commons* 19(4 January 1908): 1348–53. Ellwood argued along the same lines as Patten that charity must be reconceived to include "the searching out and removing of the causes of dependency, defect, and crime in society." Even more indebted to Patten's ideas was Frank D. Watson, "The Program of Social Work," *Charities and the Commons* 21(3 October 1908): 52–57. This was a chapter from *Economics,* by Watson and Scott Nearing. Both authors were from the University of Pennsylvania. *Charities and the Commons* and the *Survey* also began regularly to report the proceedings of the American Sociological Society (organized in 1907), the American Economic Association, the American Political Science Association, and even occasionally the American Historical Association.

42. Patten, *New Basis of Civilization,* 58–59.

43. Roy Lubove, *The Professional Altruist: The Emergence of Social Work as a Career* (Cambridge: Harvard University Press, 1965), esp. chap. 2. "The core of any profession," he writes, "is a special skill applied to a special function."

44. Mary E. Richmond, "The Need of a Training School in Applied Philanthropy," *Proceedings of the National Society of Charities and Corrections* (1897), 181–86; Richmond, "Need of Training Schools," *Charities* 8(3 May 1902): 431.

45. One significant issue troubled the relations between the settlement leaders and the universities: whether universities and philanthropies ought to accept what was called "tainted money"—the gifts of wealthy industrialists who had profited from exploiting their labor force and cheating consumers. Vida

Scudder, Jane Addams, and Florence Kelley agreed with Washington Gladden, who opposed the ethical compromise of seeming to condone unsavory industrial practices. For the Chicago women, any connection with the University of Chicago, founded by Rockefeller, was suspect. Graham Taylor, with much to gain from an affiliation of the Chicago School of Civics and Philanthropy with the University of Chicago, was less troubled by the dollar that arrived trailing clouds of oppression. Vida Dutton Scudder, *On Journey* (New York: E. P. Dutton, 1937), 181–83; Florence Kelley to Henry Demarest Lloyd, 31 January 1899, Henry Demarest Lloyd Papers (microfilm), State Historical Society of Wisconsin; Taylor, *Pioneering on Social Frontiers,* 422–23. Lilliam Wald also raised this issue with the Henry Street board in 1916; as a pacifist, she objected to the settlement's holding bonds with Bethlehem Steel while the company was profiting from war orders: see Lillian Wald to Felix Warburg, 12 January 1916, 20 January 1916; Felix Warburg to Lillian Wald, 19 January 1916, 21 January 1916, LDW-CU.

46. Robert A. Woods, "Social Work: A New Profession," first published in the *International Journal of Ethics* 16 (October 1905): 25–39, reprinted in *The Neighborhood in Nation-Building* (Boston: Houghton Mifflin, 1923), 88–104.

47. A list of the holders of South End House fellowships in economics and education is included in a circular soliciting funds from Harvard alumni for South End House fellowships, [ca. 1910,] RWP; "Settlement Training," *Charities* 8(3 May 1902): 428–30; "Settlement Ideals," *Charities* 12(12 February 1904): 195.

48. Philip W. Ayres, "The Summer School in Philanthropic Work," *Charities Review* 6(March 1901): 186–87.

49. "Preliminary Program of the Summer School in Philanthropic Work . . . ," pamphlet, Kellogg Papers; "Proposed Two Years' Course of Training in Philanthropic Work," pamphlet, Kellogg Papers; "The Winter Course in Philanthropy," *Charities* 12(23 April 1904): 415–16; "The New York School of Philanthropy," *Charities* 13(8 October 1904). See too Jeffrey R. Brackett, "Present Opportunities for Training in Charitable Work," *Proceedings of the National Conference of Charities and Corrections* (1901), 289–93. See also Edward T. Devine to Lillian Wald, 4 May 1915, LDW-CU; *Journal* [Henry Street Settlement] 7(November 1911): 7; Lubove, *Professional Altruist,* 139–44. Florence Cross (Kitchelt), discussed in chapter 6 above as an early New York settlement worker, moved into the Rivington Street Settlement when she enrolled in the third summer session of the New York school.

50. "Encouraging Opening of the Boston School for Social Workers," *Charities* 13(5 November 1904): 112–13; "The School for Social Workers, Boston," *Charities* 14(3 June 1905): 783–84.

51. "Chicago Institute of Social Science," *Charities and the Commons* 15(9 December 1905): 350–51; "Chicago Institute of Social Science," *Charities and the Commons* 17(10 November 1906): 267.

52. The Sage Foundation gave similar grants to the Boston, New York, and Saint Louis schools, specifically for departments of social investigation. See Sophonisba P. Breckinridge, "Securing and Training Social Workers: Report of the Committee," *Proceedings of the National Conference of Charities and Cor-*

rections (1911), 368; Robert W. De Forest, "The Initial Activities of the Russell Sage Foundation," *Survey* 22(3 April 1909): 74.

53. "The Chicago Institute of Social Science and Arts," *Charities* 14(9 September 1905): 1068; "Chicago School of Civics and Philanthropy," *Charities and the Commons* 20(20 June 1908): 388–89; "Chicago School," *Charities and the Commons* 21(10 October 1908): 83–84; Graham Taylor to Victor F. Lawson, 2 January 1907; Graham Taylor to Washington Gladden, 25 March 1914, GTP; Taylor, *Pioneering on Social Frontiers,* 305–11; Christopher Lasch, "Sophonisba Preston Breckinridge," *Notable American Women,* 1:233–36; Lela B. Costin, "Edith Abbott," *Notable American Women: The Modern Period, 1–3;* E[dith] A[bbott], "Grace Abbott: A Sister's Memories," *Social Service Review* 13(September 1939): 355–58.

Tension seems to have built between Breckinridge and Taylor in the period just before the university's annexation of the School of Civics and Philanthropy. Fund raising had become difficult, and Breckinridge seems to have blamed this "miserable situation" chiefly on Taylor's "educational disqualifications" to lead the school. See Sophonisba Breckinridge to Graham Taylor, 25 November 1919, GTP; Breckinridge to Mrs. Kohn, 15 August 1920, Grace and Edith Abbott Papers, University of Chicago. Breckinridge was one of the most strenuous advocates of professional, university-affiliated education for social work. See Breckinridge, *Social Welfare and Professional Education* (Chicago, 1931), 12–19, 30–43.

54. These advertisements, from *Charities* 14(9 September 1905) and *Charities and the Commons* 15(25 November 1905), are representative of those that mention settlement work as an interest or as a facet of the individual's experience.

55. The papers of Jane Addams and Lillian Wald contain a particularly large number of these letters of inquiry, certainly because of the reputations of Hull-House and the Henry Street Settlement outside their own cities.

56. Richard Henry Dana, Jr., to James B. Reynolds, 14 April 1902, USSP.

57. Entry for 6 February [1903], Denison House Diary, 1900–1908, DHP.

58. Minutes for 8 January 1912, directors' meeting, DHP.

59. Graham Taylor, "Whither the Settlement Movement Tends," *Charities and the Commons* 15(3 March 1906): 840–44.

60. Gaylord S. White, "The Social Settlement after Twenty-five Years," *Harvard Theological Review* 4(January 1911): 47–70.

61. Mary Kingsbury Simkhovitch, "Settlement Organization," *Charities and the Commons* 16(1 September 1906): 566–69. For an earlier statement, see Simkhovitch, "The Function of a Social Settlement," *Charities* 8(31 May 1902): 481–82.

62. Mary K. Simkhovitch, "Is the Settlement an Institution," MS, n.d., Mary K. Simkhovitch Papers, Schlesinger Library, Radcliffe College.

63. Mrs. Vladimir [Mary K.] Simkhovitch, "Standards and Tests of Efficiency in Settlement Work," *Proceedings of the National Conference of Charities and Corrections* (1911), 299. Simkhovitch's choice of Cooley as an authority on the social importance of the neighborhood was particularly appropriate because Cooley, a sociologist at the University of Michigan, had in turn gleaned much

from his reading of Jane Addams. Cooley's most important works from this period are *Human Nature and the Social Order* (New York: Charles Scribner's Sons, 1902), and *Social Organization* (New York: Charles Scribner's Sons, 1909).

64. Samuel Haber, *Efficiency and Uplift: Scientific Management in the Progressive Era, 1890–1920* (Chicago: University of Chicago Press, 1964).

65. Mary E. Richmond, "Of the Art of Beginning in Social Work," *Proceedings of the National Conference of Charities and Corrections* (1911), 376–77.

66. White, "Social Settlement after Twenty-five Years," 49.

67. Simkhovitch, "Standards and Tests of Efficiency," 299–305.

68. Simkhovitch, "Standards and Tests of Efficiency," 305.

69. Jane Addams, "The Call of the Social Field," *Proceedings of the National Conference of Charities and Corrections* (1911), 370–72.

70. John L. Elliott to Lillian Wald, 11 May 1911, LDW-CU. This and the two following citations seem to be responses to a request from Wald for opinions on the ideal qualifications of a child worker in a settlement.

71. Alice P. Gannett to Lillian Wald, 13 May [1911], LDW-CU.

72. M[ary] deG. Trenholm to Lillian Wald, 13 May 1911, LDW-CU. Mary Riis of the Riis Settlement clearly looked for education and gentility in her workers. Of one applicant she lamented that "I was only sorry she is not a woman of broader education, as I should like to see her grow in a position of responsibility" (Mary Riis to Charlotte Waterbury, 6 February 1914); of another she reported that "as soon as she talked I know she would not do for us. . . . She would make an excellent working housekeeper or matron" (Mary Riis to Charlotte Waterbury, [n.d.,] Jacob A. Riis Neighborhood Settlement Records).

73. Woods and Kennedy, *Settlement Horizon,* 375–87.

74. Robert A. Woods, "Settlement Expansion," *Charities and the Commons* 17(3 November 1906): 227.

75. Woods and Kennedy, *Settlement Horizon,* 376–78; see "Suggestions for Work to Be Undertaken by a Federation Including All Settlements and Other Centres for Neighborhood Improvement throughout a Large City," TD, LDW-CU. The Minutes of the Boston Social Union, USES, provide an excellent picture of the BSU's activities and concerns. See also "1900–1950: Fifty Years of Service . . . Outline Story of the United Neighborhood Houses of New York, Inc. . . . ," TD, UNHR.

76. The "committee of ten" included Jane Addams, George A. Bellamy, Anna F. Davies, Flora Dunlap, Frances Ingram, William H. Matthews, Graham Taylor, Lillian Wald, Gaylord S. White, and Robert Woods. Robert A. Woods, "National Settlement Conference," 1 May 1911, TD, LDW-CU. A list of officers and convention agendas from 1911 to 1931 is in "National Federation of Settlements," TD, UNHR; see also "Topical Summary Resolutions Passed by National Federation of Settlements and Neighborhood Centers, 1911–1952," TD, NFSR.

Smaller settlement conferences continued to be held occasionally, such as the "Inter-City Settlement Conferences" held by the New York Association of Neighborhood Workers and the Boston Social Union in 1913 and 1914. See "Inter-City Settlement Conference . . . ," leaflet, 1913, and "Inter-City Conference of Settlements . . . ," leaflet, 1914, LDW-CU.

77. "Address of Edward T. Devine, Director of the School," *Charities* 13(28 January 1905): 405.

Chapter 8

1. Jane Addams, *Twenty Years at Hull-House* (New York: Macmillan, 1910), 281–89; Ray Stannard Baker, "Hull-House and the Ward Boss," *Outlook* 58(26 March 1898): 769–71.

2. Baker, "Hull-House and the Ward Boss," 769; "A Voter" to Jane Addams, 17 January 1898, JA-SCPC; Agnes Hamilton to Phoebe Hamilton, 27 January 1898, 30 January 1898, 4 March 1898, HFP; Jane Addams to Mary Rozet Smith, [March 1898,] JA-SCPC.

3. The speech was reported under the title "Why the Ward Boss Rules," *Outlook* 58(April 1898): 879.

4. Jane Addams, "Ethical Survivals in Municipal Corruption," *International Journal of Ethics* 8(April 1898): 276, 281.

5. Addams, "Ethical Survivals," 279.

6. Addams, "Ethical Survivals," 274–76.

7. In a paper of 1896, James B. Reynolds, head of New York's University Settlement, pointed out the two-tiered influence of machine politics—on the quality of city services and on the morals of the voters. He too argued that "in personal disposition and character" the city bosses were not depraved individuals. Reynolds, "The Settlement and Municipal Reform," *Proceedings of the National Conference of Charities and Corrections* (1898), 138–40.

8. Addams, "Ethical Survivals," 273–74.

9. Jane Addams, *Democracy and Social Ethics,* ed. with an intro. by Anne Firor Scott (Cambridge: Belknap Press of Harvard University Press, 1964), 222–23.

10. Addams, "Ethical Survivals," 290.

11. Robert A. Woods and Albert J. Kennedy, *The Settlement Horizon: A National Estimate* (New York: Russell Sage Foundation, 1922), 223–30; Allen F. Davis, *Spearheads for Reform: The Social Settlements and the Progressive Movement, 1890–1914* (New York: Oxford University Press, 1967), 148–69; Katharine Bement Davis, "Civic Efforts of Social Settlements," *Proceedings of the National Conference of Charities and Corrections* (1896), 131–37.

12. In 1903 Lincoln Steffens hailed Chicago as "Half Free [of political corruption] and Fighting On." Steffens, *The Shame of the Cities* (New York: McClure, Phillips, 1904), 233.

13. Allen Davis, "Raymond Robins: The Settlement Worker as Muncipal Reformer," *Social Service Review* 33(June 1959): 132–36; Davis, *Spearheads for Reform,* 163–69; Graham Taylor, *Pioneering on Social Frontiers* (Chicago: University of Chicago Press, 1930), 298–300; Graham Romeyn Taylor, "Chicago Settlements in Ward Politics," *Charities and the Commons* 16(5 May 1906): 183–85; Woods and Kennedy, *Settlement Horizon,* 224–25, 228n. See also Graham Taylor to E. K. Whicher, 28 October 1915, GTP; *Seventeenth Ward Community Club: Constitution* (Chicago, n.d.) [booklet], CCR.

14. Edwin Burrett Smith, "Council Reform in Chicago: Work of the Municipal

Voters' League," *Municipal Affairs* 4(June 1900): 347–62; Steffens, *Shame of the Cities,* 249–68; Woods and Kennedy, *Settlement Horizon,* 228n; Graham Taylor, *Pioneering on Social Frontiers,* 56–61, 66–75.

15. Quoted in Morrison I. Swift, "The Working Population of Great Cities," *Andover Review* 13(June 1890): 609–10; Woods and Kennedy, *Settlement Horizon,* 223–24.

16. Steffens, *Shame of the Cities,* 279–306.

17. James B. Reynolds to Jane Addams, 21 July 1897, JA-SCPC; Albert J. Kennedy, Notes on J. B. Reynolds, USSP.

18. Mary K. Simkhovitch, *Neighborhood: My Story of Greenwich House* (New York: W. W. Norton, 1938), 80–81.

19. *Tenth Annual Report of the East Side House Settlement, 1901.*

20. Davis, *Spearheads for Reform,* 180–87.

21. See, e.g., Lavinia L. Dock to Lillian Wald, December 1903, 22 May 1904, LDW-CU.

22. Steffens, *Shame of the Cities,* 302–6.

23. Davis, *Spearheads for Reform,* 185.

24. Douglas Webber Dunham, "Bullyboys, Ballots, and Brahmins: The Transformation of the Boston Democratic Party, 1895–1905" (honors thesis, Harvard University, 1983); Davis, *Spearheads for Reform,* 148–51, 174–80.

25. Eleanor H. Woods, *Robert A. Woods: Champion of Democracy* (Boston: Houghton Mifflin, 1929), 118–27; Jane Addams to Mary Rozet Smith, 9 July 1898, JA-SCPC.

26. Robert A. Woods to Jane Addams, 28 April 1898, JA-SCPC; also see minutes of the Lincoln House directors' meeting, 7 April [1897], USES; William Clark to Jane Addams, 18 March 1897, JA-SCPC.

27. Robert Woods, "Settlement Houses and City Politics," *Municipal Affairs* 4(June 1900): 395–98; reprinted in *The Neighborhood in Nation-Building* (Boston: Houghton Mifflin, 1923), 67–71.

28. Robert A. Woods, ed., *Americans in Process* (Boston: Houghton Mifflin, 1903), 177–89; Woods, *Robert A. Woods,* 169.

29. Davis, *Spearheads for Reform,* 176–80; *Sixteenth Annual Report of the South End House, 1908,* 11; *Eighteenth Annual Report of the South End House, 1911,* 6. See also William Howe Tolman, *Municipal Reform Movements in the United States* (New York: Fleming H. Revell, 1895), 52–55.

30. Albert J. Kennedy, untitled manuscript, folder 14, AJKP.

31. *Sixteenth Annual Report of the South End House,* 3.

32. Allen Davis argues that the settlement workers took their reform platform into national politics after becoming frustrated by the vagaries and reverses of municipal politics: *Spearheads for Reform,* 193.

33. Jacob Riis, *The Making of an American* (New York: Macmillan, 1901), 257–60; Jane Addams et al., "Theodore Roosevelt—Social Worker," *Survey* 41(18 January 1919): 524–25; Edmund Morris, *The Rise of Theodore Roosevelt* (New York: Ballantine Books, 1979), 481–88.

34. Addams et al., "Theodore Roosevelt," 523–24; John Morton Blum, *The Republican Roosevelt,* 2d ed. (New York: Atheneum, 1962), 18–21.

35. Henry Street received a gift of a "pair of deer heads with locked antlers"

after one of Wald's reports to the president on New York social issues. "Of course," cautioned Roosevelt's secretary, "do not make this public in any way or it will bring a flood of requests for like donations." William Loeb to Lillian D. Wald, 15 February 1904; see also William Loeb to Lillian Wald, 4 November 1903, LDW-CU. Wald was not always so successful in gaining the president's ear; Jacob Riis responded to one of her pleas for intervention with Roosevelt by protesting that he really did not have any pull in Washington and would hesitate to disturb Roosevelt even if he felt it would do any good. Jacob Riis to Lillian Wald, 4 June 1906, LDW-CU.

36. Addams et al., "Theodore Roosevelt," 523, 525–27; Jane Addams, *the Second Twenty Years at Hull-House* (New York: Macmillan, 1930), 18; Lillian D. Wald, *Windows on Henry Street* (Boston: Little, Brown, 1934), 122–24; Florence Kelley to Nicholas Kelley, [1903,] Nicholas Kelley Papers.

37. Jacob Riis to Lillian D. Wald, 24 December 1904, LDW-CU.

38. [Edward T. Devine,] "The Message," *Charities and the Commons* 17(15 December 1906): 449–50.

39. Davis, *Spearheads for Reform,* 208–13.

40. Davis, *Spearheads for Reform,* 194–201; Allen F. Davis, "The Social Workers and the Progressive Party, 1912–1916," *American Historical Review* 69(April 1964): 671–88. See also Addams, *Second Twenty Years,* 25–31; George E. Mowry, *Theodore Roosevelt and the Progressive Movement* (Madison: University of Wisconsin Press, 1946), 256–66.

41. Mowry, *Theodore Roosevelt and the Progressive Movement, 262–63; Davis, Spearheads for Reform,* 197–98; Addams, *Second Twenty Years,* 32–33.

42. Theodore Roosevelt to Jane Addams, 24 January 1906, JA-SCPC.

43. Dewey wrote to his wife, "I suppose that's the subjective nature of sin; the only reality is unity, but we assume there is antagonism & then it all goes wrong. I can see that I have always been interpreting the dialectic wrong end up—the unity as the conciliation of opposites, instead of the opposites as the unity in its growth, and thus translated physical tension into a moral thing." John Dewey to Alice Chipman Dewey, 10 October [1894], Dewey Family Letters.

44. See, e.g., Charles L. Hutchinson to Jane Addams, 5 August 1912, JA-SCPC. Addams's incoming correspondence in August and throughout the autumn of 1912 was full of mixed reaction to her political activities both from colleagues and from the public. See also Allen F. Davis, *American Heroine: The Life and Legend of Jane Addams* (New York: Oxford University Press, 1973), 184–97.

45. See, e.g., Robert Woods to Jane Addams, 7 August 1912, JA-SCPC. Woods, on the other hand, had little trouble in accepting Roosevelt's conservatism on this issue. See "Can Politics Be Human?" [1912,] TD, RWP; Mowry, *Theodore Roosevelt and the Progressive Party,* 267–69.

46. Jane Addams, "My Experiences as a Progressive Delegate," *McClure's Magazine* 40(November 1912): 14. Other peace workers also had a difficult time with the battleships and found it hard to "swallow" Addams's decision to support Roosevelt, a forthright militarist. See, e.g., Charles E. Beals [secretary, the Chicago Peace Society] to Jane Addams, 2 October 1912, JA-SCPC.

47. Wald had initially leaned toward Wilson and in fact was asked to head Wilson's national women's committee. She went over to Roosevelt partly be-

cause she was excited by his "Confession of Faith," endorsing "almost word for word the things that we all hope and labor for," and also because the Democrats had repudiated a women's suffrage plank. See Jacob Schiff to Lillian Wald, telegram, 9 August 1912, LDW-CU; Lillian Wald to Jane Addams, 12 August [1912], JA-SCPC. Not all suffragists united in this stance for Roosevelt and the Progressives, however. Anna Howard Shaw of the National American Woman Suffrage Association berated Addams for her support of the Progressives because Roosevelt was untrustworthy. Shaw to Jane Addams, 16 August 1912, JA-SCPC.

48. Addams, "My Experiences as a Progressive Delegate," 13. Mary Simkhovitch, another Progressive supporter, argued for enfranchising women on much the same ground as headworker of Greenwich House: "The minute it is made clear to [neighborhood women] that politics is another name for the control of the conditions under which people live, that it is just as practicable a matter as making bread and getting the children ready to go to school, it interests them enormously. . . . As social legislation becomes more important, as the old home-idea gets registered in political life more effectively, the desirability of entrance of women into politics will become more evident." Simkhovitch, "Speech for woman's suffrage at Albany," typescript, n.d., Mary K. Simkhovitch Papers. This brand of argument for women's suffrage was also less culturally threatening than a strident insistence on women's equality with men. One male correspondent wrote to Addams after the convention: "I was afraid you would be influenced to say more than you did about the representation of women in the affairs of government. As a matter of fact, putting the emphasis on the protection of children, relief of the overworked girl, human welfare and juster social conditions, was indirectly the most effective possible influence that could have been exerted for woman suffrage." Seymour Coman to Jane Addams, 8 August 1912, JA-SCPC.

49. See, e.g., "Women Cast Ballots," *Chicago Record,* 7 November 1894, clipping, Hull-House Scrapbook I, JAMC.

50. She often used the example of the Yankee widow who had lived with her two daughters in the Nineteenth Ward since its days of middle-class prosperity. When the Italians began "closing in around her," she stayed "quite aloof" from the life of the community and held on to her property only so that she could afford to send her daughters East to college. When typhoid broke out in the neighborhood and spread owing to faulty plumbing, both of her daughters were infected, and one died. Though clearly not responsible for the typhoid epidemic, the woman was guilty of perpetuating the outworn value of social isolation, and her private tragedy was the price she paid for ignoring the "rest of the community and its interests." Addams, "Woman's Conscience and Social Amelioration," in *The Social Application of Religion,* ed. Charles Stelzle et al. (Cincinnati: Jennings and Graham, 1908), 43–44. See also Addams, *Why Women Should Vote* (New York, 1914), a pamphlet published by the National American Woman Suffrage Association, reprinted from an article for the *Ladies' Home Journal.*

51. Jane Addams, *Newer Ideals of Peace* (New York: Macmillan, 1907), 26–30.

52. Addams acknowledged her debt to William James's concept of the "moral equivalent for war" (*Newer Ideals of Peace,* 24), though it is clear that the

evolution of her thought on this issue grew organically from her previous social and historical thought and was virtually simultaneous with his; her more important debt to James was his concept of "pragmatism," which she transplanted from the religious and philosophical to the social realm under the influence of John Dewey. See chapter 6 above for a discussion of Addams's first major grappling with pragmatism as a philosophical underpinning of social reform.

53. Addams, "My Experiences as a Progressive Delegate," 14.

54. Davis, *Spearheads for Reform,* 199–204; Harold Ickes to Jane Addams, 6 January 1913; Mary McDowell to Jane Addams, 16 August 1912; form letter from Margaret Dreier [of the Illinois Progressive Committee] to [Jane Addams], [1912]; Katharine Coman to Jane Addams, 1 January 1913; John A. Kingsbury to Jane Addams, 17 January 1913, JA-SCPC.

55. Addams, *Twenty Years at Hull-House* 280; Aylmer Maude to Jane Addams, 7 July 1904, JA-SCPC; Lillian D. Wald, *The House on Henry Street* (New York: H. Holt, 1915), 233.

56. See, e.g., Jacob Schiff to Lillian Wald, 21 January 1907, [June 1907?], LDW-CU; John Martin, "Maxim Gorky's Socialism of Culture," *Charities and the Commons* 17(3 November 1906): 193–94; "The Friends of Russian Freedom," *Charities and the Commons* 17(17 November 1906): 284; "Sympathy for Russian Freedom," *Charities and the Commons* 17(9 March 1907): 1031. Richard T. Ely introduced Kropotkin to the Chicago settlers in 1901; the exiled prince also passed through the Henry Street Settlement, and for years a portrait photograph hung on the Henry Street wall. In the 1920s Anna Cobden-Sanderson, one of the Kropotkins' British friends, solicited the American settlers for funds to help preserve Kropotkin's personal library. See Richard T. Ely to Jane Addams, 28 February 1901, 19 April 1901, JA-SCPC; Jane Addams to Richard T. Ely, 21 April 1901, 19 May 1901, JA-SCPC; Anne Cobden-Sanderson to Lillian D. Wald, 12 February [1926]; Graham Romeyn Taylor to Anne Cobden-Sanderson, 17 April 1926, LDW-CU. Paul Avrich has reconstructed Kropotkin's two trips to the United States, in 1897 and 1901; see Avrich, "Kropotkin in America," *International Review of Social History* 25, 1(1980): 1–34. The settlers' relationship with Emma Goldman, Kropotkin's fellow anarchist, was far more troubled and ambivalent on both sides. See chapter 10 below.

57. Ernest Poole, "Katharine Bereshkovsky [*sic*]: A Russian Revolutionist," *Outlook* 79(7 January 1905): 78–88; Wald, *House on Henry Street,* 238–48; Vida Dutton Scudder, *On Journey* (New York: E. P. Dutton, 1937), 157–58; Denison House Diary, 11 November 1904, DHP; George Kennan to James Bronson Reynolds, 6 December 1910 (copy), LDW-CU. There is a thick folder of correspondence with and concerning Breshkovsky in LDW-CU.

58. "Sympathy for Russian Freedom," 1031; "Friends of Russian Freedom," 284; Wald, *House on Henry Street,* 235. The National Committee members in 1910 included Lyman Abbott, Jane Addams, Felix Adler, John Graham Brooks, John Dewey, Franklin H. Giddings, V. Everit Macy, and Everett P. Wheeler. By 1910 the National Committee had added John B. Clark, R. Fulton Cutting, Samuel Gompers, Robert M. La Follette, Joseph Lee, Jacob Riis, Julius Rosenwald, Jacob Schiff, and Oswald Garrison Villard, among others. See the pamphlet by

Vladimir Bourtzeff, *The Czar's Responsibility* (Friends of Russian Freedom, May 1910), LDW-CU.

59. "American Settlement Workers in Russia," *Charities and the Commons* 17(1 December 1906): 361–62. On Kennan, see Christopher Lasch, *The American Liberals and the Russian Revolution* (New York: Columbia University Press, 1962), 7–9.

60. William English Walling, "The Call to the Young Russians," *Charities and the Commons* 17(1 December 1906): 373.

61. Reed wrote an article on the Henry Street Settlement as the "American home of the Russian revolution": "In the remotest prison settlements of Siberia, beyond the cold Lena, the name of the Henry Street Settlement was known, and to its doors came for years a steady stream of revolutionists." Clipping, *Evening Mail,* 11 July 1917, LDW-CU.

62. A. Zelenko, "Russia's First Settlement," *Charities and the Commons* 21(3 October 1908): 61–64.

63. See, e.g., minutes of the residents' meeting, Chicago Commons, 15 October 1914; Graham Taylor, "Warden's Report to the Trustees of Chicago Commons Association for the year ending September 30, 1915," CCR; also see accounts of early war-related activities of South End House in *South End House Annual Report, 1915 and South End House Annual Report, 1918.*

64. Lillian Wald to [William Dean Howells and other] Committee Members on issue of War, 22 September 1914, LDW-CU; Jane Addams, *Peace and Bread in Time of War* (New York: Macmillan, 1922), 2–6. The Henry Street group constituted itself the American Union against Militarism and had a short and turbulent history until it ruptured over aiding conscientious objectors after Congress passed the Selective Service Act in 1917. Wald, Addams, and Kellogg strongly opposed the AUAM's "compromising" its respectability and credibility with influential officials, while Roger Baldwin spearheaded the campaign for the defense of conscientious objection and free speech in wartime. The Civil Liberties Bureau he founded at this time became the American Civil Liberties Union after the war. See Donald Johnson, *The Challenge to American Freedoms: World War I and the Rise of the American Civil Liberties Union* (Lexington: University of Kentucky Press, 1963), 1–24.

65. Mary McDowell to Lillian D. Wald, 28 December 1914, LDW-CU.

66. Mary McDowell to Lillian D. Wald [president of the Association of Neighborhood Workers of New York City], 16 February 1915, LDW-CU; mimeographed announcement to member houses of the Boston Social Union, 23 February 1915, USES.

67. Minutes, meeting of the Boston Social Union, 14 October 1914, USES.

68. Minutes of the executive meeting, Boston Social Union, 13 April 1916, USES.

69. Minutes of the executive meeting, Boston Social Union, 26 April [1915], USES.

70. Other delegates included Carrie Chapman Catt, former president of the National American Woman Suffrage Association, Anna Garlin Spencer, a minister, Ethical Culturist, and charity worker, Mrs. Henry Villard, Lucia Ames Mead,

and Elizabeth Glendower Evans of Boston. See Addams, *Peace and Bread in Time of War,* 6–9.

71. Addams, *Peace and Bread in Time of War,* 10. Some objected from the beginning to Addams's style of argument and dissent. Ellery Sedgwick, editor of the *Atlantic Monthly* and basically sympathetic to American peace agitation, wrote to Lillian Wald about a speech of Addams's in Boston: "I felt that she is as much lacking in judiciousness as she is endowed with spiritual passion." Sedgwick to Wald, 12 March 1915, LDW-CU.

72. Graham Taylor, "Chicago Initiative in the Peace Cause," Chicago *News,* 6 March 1915, clipping, JA-SCPC; minutes of the executive meeting, Boston Social Union, 13 April 1916; circular notice, 18 June 1916, USES.

73. Addams, *Peace and Bread in Time of War,* 12–14; [Alice Hamilton] to Mary Rozet Smith, 2[2?] April [1915], JA-SCPC.

74. Addams, *Peace and Bread in Time of War,* 14–18; Alice Hamilton to [family?], 15 May 1915, Alice Hamilton Papers.

75. Jane Addams, *Peace and Bread in Time of War,* 28–46; Graham Taylor to Louis P. Lochner, 1 December 1915, GTP.

76. See, e.g., Jane Addams to Rosika Schwimmer, 18 February 1916 (copy), JA-SCPC. Victor Lawson, the editor of the Chicago *Daily News* and a strong preparedness advocate, wrote to Graham Taylor about the Peace Ship: "I find myself forced into a feeling of lack of confidence in the sanity of some good people who, once they have attained a measure of success in some good line of social up-lift, apparently lose their heads and imagine themselves directors in general to the American people. Did I mention Jane Addams' name? No, I think not," Lawson to Taylor, 30 November 1915, GTP. Addams protested her continuing support for the Ford mission from afar; certainly she had cause to regret his "abrupt" withdrawal of financial support from the peace forces still trying to arrange a Conference of Neutrals in early 1917: Addams, *Peace and Bread in Time of War,* 45–46.

77. See, e.g., Arthur Gleason, "Social Workers and the War," *Survey* 36(13 May 1916): 185–86; Alice Hamilton, "The Attitude of Social Workers toward the War," *Survey* 36(17 June 1916): 307–8; Clarke Chambers, *Paul U. Kellogg and the Survey Voices for Social Welfare and Social Justice* (Minneapolis: University of Minnesota Press, 1971), 56–57; Graham Taylor to Paul U. Kellogg, 10 April 1916; Graham Taylor to Victor Lawson, 18 April 1916, GTP.

78. Mary K. Simkhovitch, "The Universities and Preparedness," TD, speech at Boston University, 8 June 1916.

79. Addams, *Peace and Bread in Time of War,* 139–40.

80. For Addams's reflections on the significance of "pragmatism" and its limits as a guide to her reactions to the war, see *Peace and Bread in Time of War,* 142–44.

81. David M. Kennedy, *Over Here: The First World War and American Society* (New York: Oxford University Press, 1980), 39–43; Ronald Steel, *Walter Lippmann and the American Century* (Boston: Little, Brown, 1980), 110–15.

82. Minutes of meeting of the Boston Social Union, 14 March 1917, USES.

83. Mary K. Simkhovitch to the editor of the *Evening Post,* 2 April 1917,

clipping, Lea Demarest Taylor Papers, Chicago Historical Society (hereafter cited as LDTP); see also "Social Settlements and the War," *Survey* 38(7 April 1917): 29–30.

84. Mary K. Simkhovitch to Robert Crosby, 24 April 1917 [form letter to NFS members], AJKP; Lillian D. Wald to Mary K. Simkhovitch, 27 April 1917, LDW-CU; Mary K. Simkhovitch, "A Settlement War Program," *Survey* 38(5 May 1917): 111–12; "Social Settlements in War Time," leaflet of the Association of Neighborhood Workers, New York City, n.d., LDW-CU; *Annual Report of the East Side House for 1918,* 1–2.

85. See Woods and Kennedy, *Settlement Horizon,* 297–303; *Annual Report of the South End House, 1918,* 4–5; Samuel Gompers to Lillian D. Wald, 12 June 1917; Lillian D. Wald to Samuel Gompers, 14 June 1917; V. Everit Macy to Lillian Wald, 27 November 1917; Elsbeth J. Merck to Lillian D. Wald, 23 March [1918], LDW-CU; [Jane Addams?] to R. A. Gunn, 2 February 1920, JA-SCPC; Graham Taylor to Victor F. Lawson, 4 October 1917, GTP.

86. *Annual Report of the South End House, 1918,* 4; Graham Taylor to Jane Addams, 9 July 1918, CCR; Graham Taylor, "Warden's Report . . . ending September 30, 1917," TD, CCR.

87. Newton D. Baker, "Invisible Armor," *Survey* 39(November 1917): 159–60.

88. Minutes of the meeting of the Boston Social Union, 8 May 1918, USES; *Annual Report of the South End House, 1918,* 7; Robert A. Woods, "The War Camp Community Service" (1919), in *Neighborhood in Nation-Building,* 220–33.

89. See "House Bill No. 402. A statement by Robert Woods . . . ," TD, n.d., USES; Robert A. Woods, "Winning the Other Half: National Prohibition a Leading Social Issue," *Survey* 40(20 April 1918): 59–62; *Annual Report of the South End House, 1918,* 7–8.

90. Minutes of the meeting of the Boston Social Union, 12 December 1917, USES.

91. Robert A. Woods, "The Regimentation of the Free," *Survey* 40(6 July 1918): 395–99. South End House apparently tried to institute such a "surveillance" system during the war by transforming its "friendly visiting" routine into a mode of checking up on the patriotism of its near neighbors. The *Annual Report* of 1918 boasted that the settlement "had in its possession, after the United States had been in the war a few weeks, a classified report as to the attitude toward the war of a substantial proportion of the people in every one of these fourteen blocks." *Annual Report of the South End House, 1918,* 13.

92. Woods, "Regimentation of the Free," 398. For over a decade Woods (and many of his colleagues) had advocated the "segregation of the unfit," and in his 1918 address he called for the "elimination of the feeble-minded strain from out of our national stock." It is interesting to note that his early political heroes, the Webbs of the Fabian Society, had come to advocate eugenics by 1914. J. M. Winter, "The Webbs and the Non-white World: A Case of Socialist Racialism," *Journal of Contemporary History* 9(January 1974): 100; Edward R. Pease, *The History of the Fabian Society,* 2d ed. (London: Fabian Society, 1925), 160–62.

93. Simkhovith, "The Universities and Preparedness," n.p.

94. Mary McDowell, "The Immigrant American," typescript, synopsis of address given 9 July 1916, Mary McDowell Papers, Chicago Historical Society.

95. See William S. Bernard, "Immigration: History of U.S. Policy," in *Harvard Encyclopedia of Ethnic Groups,* ed. Stephan Thernstrom (Cambridge: Harvard University Press, 1980), 492; John Higham, *Strangers in the Land: Patterns of American Nativism, 1860–1925,* 2d ed. (New York: Atheneum, 1974), 202–7.

96. Statement of policy, National Federation of Settlements, [May 1918,] TD, LDTP; see also "The War-Time Outlook of Social Settlements," *Survey* 40(31 August 1918): 616–17.

97. Mary K. Simkhovitch, president of the NFS, to NFS members, n.d., NFSR.

98. Simkhovitch, "The Universities and Preparedness," n.p.

99. M[ary] de G. Trenholm, "Report of the Headworker," *Annual Report of the East Side House, 1918,* 1.

100. Mary McDowell, "The Foreign Born," TD, n.d., Mary McDowell Papers.

101. Charles Cooper, "The Necessity for Changes in Americanization Methods," *Proceedings of the National Conference of Social Work* (1918), 435–42.

102. Mary McDowell, "Making the Foreign Born One of Us," *Survey* 40(25 May 1918): 213–15.

103. *The New York Settlements in War Time. After One Year of War. June 1918* (New York: Association of Neighborhood Workers, 1918), n.p. Virtually all annual reports and other public relations documents were implicit appeals for funds; for examples of more explicit accountings of the financial burdens of war due to the increased and special activities of the settlements, see "Help Give War Work the Right of Way at Chicago Commons," open letter to contributors, [October 1917,] TD, CCR; "Hold the Home Lines," open letter to contributors from Graham Taylor, [1918,] CCR; Statement for contributors, the Boston Social Union, n.d., USES; *Bulletin of the Association of Neighborhood Workers,* September 1918; *Twenty-Third Annual Report, Hale House* (1918), n.p., USES.

104. Lillian D. Wald, "Influenza: When the City Is a Great Field Hospital," *Survey* 43(14 February 1920): 579–81; Simkhovitch, *Neighborhood,* 195.

105. Robert A. Woods to Frances R. Mores, [1918,] RWP.

Chapter 9

1. Richard Sennett, "Middle-Class Families and Urban Violence: The Experience of a Chicago Community in the Nineteenth Century," in *Nineteenth-Century Cities: Essays in the New Urban History,* ed. Stephan Thernstrom and Richard Sennett (New Haven: Yale University Press, 1969), 386–420; Graham Taylor, *Pioneering on Social Frontiers* (Chicago: University of Chicago Press, 1930), 117–37; Mary McDowell, "Beginnings," TD [1914, 1927]; Percy H. Boynton, "An appreciation of the life and work of Miss Mary McDowell . . . January 20, 1937," TD, Mary McDowell Papers; Wallace A. DeWolf to Mary McDowell, 14 December 1903; Mary McDowell to Wallace A. DeWolf, [n.d.,] Mary McDowell Papers; Wallace A. DeWolf to Jane Addams, 17 July 1916, JA-SCPC.

2. Clarence Darrow to Jane Addams, 11 September [1901]; W. T. Stead to Jane Addams, 12 October 1901, JA-SCPC; Jane Addams, *Twenty Years at Hull-House*

(New York: Macmillan, 1910), 403–9; Louise C. Wade, *Graham Taylor: Pioneer for Social Justice, 1851–1938* (Chicago: University of Chicago Press, 1964), 134–35.

3. Jane Addams, "The Chicago Settlements and Social Unrest," *Charities and the Commons* 20(2 May 1908): 155–66; Addams, *Twenty Years at Hull-House,* 412–18; Taylor, *Pioneering on Social Frontiers,* 205–8.

4. Letters of reaction to Addams's stand on the Averbuch incident are in JA-SCPC (reel 18). For radicals' reactions, see, e.g., W. D. P. Bliss to Addams, 4 May 1908, JA-SCPC. Graham Taylor asserted that "no perceptible effect upon the financial support of Chicago Commons has followed the clamor against the settlements." "Warden's Report," 1908, CCR.

5. Clipping from the *New York World,* 2 June 1914, USSP.

6. It is unclear whether Gilman felt any backlash from his board after his defense of the IWW. The ostensible reason for the board's dissatisfaction was his refusal to engage in fund-raising. He was quickly hired as headworker of the new North East Neighborhood House in Minneapolis. See Robbins Gilman to Thomas J. Debevoise [chairman of the Council of the University Settlement,] [26 June 1914]; Debevoise to Gilman, 17 August 1914; Gilman to [J. Bunyan?], 2 June 1914; numerous letters from supporters, July and August 1914, Gilman Family Papers, Minnesota Historical Society.

7. Theodore Appel to Jane Addams, 28 February 1898; Emma Goldman to Jane Addams, 15 April [1901], JA-SCPC; Jane Addams to Lillian Wald, 17 September 1901; Emma Goldman to Lillian Wald, 22 August 1917, LDW-CU. In 1928 Wald contributed money to Goldman, who had gone to Saint Tropez to write her autobiography. Wald subsequently felt somewhat betrayed by Goldman's ungenerous treatment of the settlement workers and her criticism of settlements as "palliative," "creating snobbery among the very people they were trying to help." Lillian Wald to John Wilkie, 1 December 1931, LDW-CU; see also Emma Goldman, *Living My Life,* 2 vols. (Garden City, N.Y.: Garden City Publishing Company, 1936), 1:160, 362; on Addams, see 1:375. See also John Palmer Gavit to Graham Taylor, 3 September 1927, GTP.

8. Writing to John Graham Brooks in 1913, Florence Kelley joined those who linked immigration and labor radicalism. She was dismayed at the IWW agitation she had witnessed in Portland, Oregon, during a recent visit. "Anarchy has become hereditary from generation to generation among the immigrants and their children! I came home . . . an active restrictionist!" She felt sure that her long record of "intimate contact with the immigrants" would preclude any charge of "race or religious prejudice" in her new acceptance of immigration restriction. Florence Kelley to John Graham Brooks, 13 August [1913], John Graham Brooks Papers, Schlesinger Library, Radcliffe College.

9. Several inquests on Progressivism in the 1920s challenge the notion that reform died after the Great War. See Arthur Link, "What Happened to the Progressive Movement in the 1920's?" *American Historical Review* 64(July 1959): 833–51; Clarke Chambers, *Seedtime of Reform: American Social Service and Social Action, 1918–1933* (Minneapolis: University of Minnesota Press, 1963).

10. Minutes, directors' meeting, 10 February 1919, 5 March 1919, DHP.

Though Robert Woods stepped in to testify to Gordon's public discretion during the war, the days of cooperation and ideological accord between Denison House and South End House were long since over. See Eleanor Woods to Albert J. Kennedy, 2 March 1933, NFSR.

11. Minutes, directors' meeting, 16 February 1920, 15 March 1920, DHP.

12. Quotation from transcript of clipping from the *New York Times,* 15 May 1921, in "The Lusk Committee Attack on U.N.H. and New York Settlements, 1919–1921," TD, UNHR.

13. Quotation from transcript of clipping from the New York Times, 17 May 1921, in "The Lusk Committee Attack."

14. Transcript of clipping from the *New York Sun,* n.d., "The Lusk Committee Attack."

15. Helen H. Jessup to Harriet Righter, 19 October 1920, Jacob A. Riis Neighborhood Settlement Records (hereafter cited as JARR).

16. Graham Taylor, "Warden's Report for the year ending September 30, 1921," CCR.

17. Lillian Wald, *Windows on Henry Street* (Boston: Little, Brown, 1934), 308; also Lillian D. Wald to Jane Addams, 15 January 1925, NFSR.

18. Jane Addams to R. A. Gunn, 2 February 1920; Jane Addams, *The Second Twenty Years at Hull-House* (New York: Macmillan, 1930), 140–44.

19. Jane Addams, *Peace and Bread in Time of War* (New York: Macmillan, 1922), 73–83.

20. Herbert Hoover to Jane Addams, 2 March 1918; Jane Addams to Mrs. Forbes, 23 April 1918, JA-SCPC; Addams, *Second Twenty Years at Hull-House,* 144–46; Allen F. Davis, *American Heroine: The Life and Legend of Jane Addams* (New York: Oxford University Press, 1973), 232–70.

21. Addams, *Peace and Bread in Time of War,* 156–72, 178–82.

22. Addams, *Peace and Bread in Time of War,* 180–87.

23. Clipping, [January 1920,] JA-SCPC; [Jane Addams?] to R. A. Gunn, 2 February 1920; Jane Addams to R. A. Gunn, [February 1920,] JA-SCPC; clipping, ca. January 1920, JA-SCPC.

24. For example, H. Rowland Curtis to Jane Addams, 23 February 1920, JA-SCPC; Jane Addams to Edward Scott Beck, 23 February 1920, JA-SCPC; Mary McDowell to the editor of the *Tribune,* 22 December 1921, JA-SCPC; "The Tribune and Miss Addams," *Survey* 43(21 February 1920): 601. At Addams's English memorial service in 1935, the British feminist Maude Royden commented: "How well I remember, when I spoke in America in 1922 and 1923, the silence that greeted the name of Jane Addams! The few faithful who tried to applaud only made the silence more depressing." Dr. Maude Royden, Address at Memorial Service for Jane Addams, 4 June 1935, Church of St. Martin's-in-the-Fields, NFSR.

25. Addams, *Second Twenty Years at Hull-House,* 181–82; clipping, *New York World,* 8 June 1924, 10 June 1924, JA-SCPC; Davis, *American Heroine,* 263–65. Charles Norman Fay, the chief custodian of the "spider web" chart, was unabashed by protests from the *Boston Herald* and from Addams's associate Louise de Koven Bowen that he was spreading malicious slander. In response, he offered "115 carefully verified citations from Miss Addams' open record" to

support his remark that Addams "stands for everything Bolshevist, except perhaps murder and robbery." See Charles Norman Fay to editor, *Boston Herald*, 17 May 1927 [copy], JA-SCPC; Mrs. Joseph T. Bowen to Charles Norman Fay, 24 January 1927, JA-SCPC.

26. Mrs. J. Ellsworth Gross to Jane Addams, [1923,] JA-SCPC; Elaine [Goodner?] Eastman to Jane Addams, 25 March [1925], JA-SCPC.

27. Evelyn L. Messenger to Jane Addams, 22 December 1931, JA-SCPC; Addams, *Second Twenty Years at Hull-House*, 180–82.

28. See, e.g., the offer to bring suit against Captain Watkins, Edith Abbott to Jane Addams, [November 1926?]; Marie A. Purvin to Jane Addams, 16 December 1926; Forrest Bailey to Jane Addams, 12 June 1926, JA-SCPC. See also Albert J. Kennedy to Jane Addams, 12 November 1926, JA-SCPC. Journals such as the *Progressive*, 1 December 1926, 77, and the *Boston Herald*, 29 May 1926, spoke out against Addams's detractors. Other friends and allies made symbolic gestures of support. In 1922 Herbert Croly of the *New Republic* thanked Addams in the most flattering terms for allowing him to list her as a "contributing editor." Croly to Addams, 3 February 1922, JA-SCPC.

29. Albert J. Kennedy to Lillian D. Wald, 12 January 1927, LDW-CU; letter from Calvin Coolidge, 26 December 1926, JA-SCPC; telegrams, January 1927, JA-SCPC.

30. Addams, *Peace and Bread in Time of War*, 187.

31. Addams, *Second Twenty Years at Hull-House*, 155–56.

32. Charles Cooper to Graham Taylor, 27 January 1921, GTP; Charles Cooper to Paul U. Kellogg, 11 September 1920, Survey Associates Records, Social History Archives, University of Minnesota (hereafter cited as SAR).

33. Chambers, *Seedtime of Reform*, 133–38.

34. Alice Hamilton to Clara Landsberg, [before 26 February 1925,] HFP. On the child labor campaign, see Chambers, *Seedtime of Reform*, 29–51; James Johnson, "The Role of Women in the Founding of the United States Children's Bureau," in *"Remember the Ladies": New Perspectives on Women in American History*, ed. Carol V. R. George (Syracuse: Syracuse University Press, 1975), 181–82; Richard B. Sherman, "The Rejection of the Child Labor Amendment," *Mid-America* 45(January 1963): 3–17.

35. See Paul Boyer, *Urban Masses and Moral Order in America, 1820–1920* (Cambridge: Harvard University Press, 1978), 191–219.

36. Robert A. Woods and Albert J. Kennedy, *The Settlement Horizon: A National Estimate* (New York: Russell Sage Foundation, 1922), 260–64; Robbins Gilman to Frederick H. Whitin [secretary, the Committee of Fourteen, a municipal morals commission], 20 February 1914, USSP. In 1904 a number of settlement residents cooperated to investigate the effectiveness of the "Sunday closing law." They found that even with reasonable attempts at enforcement, it was being flagrantly violated. Their chief concern was the "alarming" impact of this disregard for statute law on the young people of the neighborhoods. "The Sunday Closing Law of New York: A Report on Conditions by a Committee of the Association of Neighborhood Workers," *Charities and the Commons* 12(23 January 1904): 95–102; see also editorial comment, 87. In 1911 Graham Taylor made an extraordinary proposition to his trustees: that they pay an obnoxious local saloonkeeper the extortionate fee that he demanded ($1,400) to give up

his lease before it expired; see Graham Taylor to Trustees of Chicago Commons, 19 April 1911, CCR.

Many temperance reformers recognized that the saloon served an important social function and that any solution to the "liquor problem" must identify a "substitute for the saloon." The Committee of Fifty for the Investigation of the Liquor Problem, organized in 1893, was a stellar collection of genteel reformers and academics; one of the investigative studies they sponsored addressed this question. See Raymond Calkins, *Substitutes for the Saloon* (Boston: Houghton Mifflin, 1901). Another example of this kind of conclusion was the study by a young Chicago Commons resident, "The Social Function of the SALOON, being an embodiment of the results of an investigation of the Chicago saloons by Wm. B. Harrison," July–September 1898, CCR.

37. Eleanor Woods, *Robert A. Woods: Champion of Democracy* (Boston: Houghton Mifflin, 1929), 252–55, 285–98. See also James H. Timberlake, *Prohibition and the Progressive Movement, 1900–1920* (Cambridge: Harvard University Press, 1963), 57–66.

38. Minutes of meeting of Boston Social Union, 31 March 1910; Second Annual Report, Boston Social Union [n.d.], USES; "House Bill No. 402: A statement by Robert A. Woods . . . ," TD, USES.

39. James A. Lowell to Governor Eugene N. Foss, 13 May 1912; Robert A. Woods to Mary Kenney O'Sullivan, 7 January 191[3], RWP; *Annual Report of the South End House, 1914;* Robert A. Woods, "Massachusetts Ratifies," *Survey* 40(20 April 1918): 60.

40. Minutes of annual meeting of the South End Social Union, [1907?], USES.

41. Robert A. Woods, "Drunkenness: Report of the Committee," *Proceedings of the Conference of Charities and Corrections* (1911), 113–19; see also Woods, "Drunkenness," *Harvard Theological Review* 7(1 October 1914): 497–506.

42. Robert A. Woods, "License in Place of Licensing," *Survey* 36(30 September 1916): 635–37; Woods, "Winning the Other Half: National Prohibition a Leading Social Issue," *Survey* 37(30 December 1916): 349–52.

43. *Annual Report of the South End House, 1918,* 16; *Annual Report of the South End House, 1919,* 16.

44. Robert A. Woods, *Prohibition and Social Hygiene,* Publication 171. (n.p.: American Social Hygiene Association, 1919).

45. By 1923 Woods had further elaborated this justification of Prohibition as a test case for an organicist social ethics by examining its implications for the philosophy of law. To John Elliott he wrote regarding the idea that Prohibition did not create, but merely revealed, lawbreakers: "There is here, it seems to me, an enormously important subject for ethical instruction. Is the law merely a traditional doctrine and ritual, or is it a living thing, growing through the total inner metabolism and outer functioning of the body politic? . . . I am not sure [but] that the best result of prohibition will be in giving us all a *new* really human, really scientific, and really democratic conception of the evolutionary legal process." Robert A. Woods to John L. Elliott, 23 February 1923, RWP.

46. Minutes of the meeting of the Boston Social Union, 9 January 1924, USES; "Jane Addams's Sanity," unidentified clipping, [August 1928?], JA-SCPC.

47. Graham Taylor to Mrs. R. W. MacDonald, 23 February 1928, GTP; Alice

Hamilton to Clara Landsberg, 31 May 1925, HFP; minutes of the meeting of the Boston Social Union, 9 January 1924, USES; Arthur Stewart to Lillian D. Wald, 15 December 1926, LDW-CU; "Jane Addams's Sanity."

48. Lillian D. Wald to Henry Bruere, 17 December 1926, LDW-CU; minutes of the meeting of the board, Riis Settlement, 28 April 1927, JARR.

49. *Bulletin of the Association of Neighborhood Workers* (February 1919), 3; H. H. Jessup [headworker of the Riis Settlement] to Miss Eddingfield [Commonwealth Fund, New York City], 25 March 1920, JARR.

50. Bruno Lasker to Paul U. Kellogg, 16 June 1926. For the inception of the study, see also Bruno Lasker to Paul U. Kellogg, 7 June 1926 (and appendix, "National Federation of Settlements: A Study of Prohibition"); Paul U. Kellogg to Bruno Lasker, 15 June 1926, SAR; Jane Addams, Graham Taylor et al. to Mrs. [Emmons (Anita McCormick)] Blaine, 21 December 1926, JA-SCPC; Lillian D. Wald, "Foreword" to Martha Bensley Bruere, *Does Prohibition Work?* (New York: Harper, 1927), n.p.

51. Bruère, *Does Prohibition Work?* 157; Raymond Robins to Jane Addams, 3 October 1928, JA-SCPC.

52. Lillian D. Wald to the editor, *New York Times,* 7 December 1932, clipping, NFSR.

53. Bruere, *Does Prohibition Work?* 301–2.

54. Robbins Gilman, Resolution against prostitution: "We the undersigned, believing in the 'constant and persistent repression of prostitution . . . ,'" MS, USSP, reel 8. Lavinia L. Dock, the national leader in the professionalization of nursing and long associated with the Henry Street Settlement, wrote a tract on venereal disease that combined a medical description of the varieties of infection with a scathing attack on the "double standard" of morality that allowed prostitution to flourish. Predictably, Dock opposed the "regulation" of vice on both moral and medical grounds. She also devoted a chapter to the "white slave trade" and the culpability of the states for this form of abuse owing to their refusal to pass protective legislation for minors. See Lavinia L. Dock, *Hygiene and Morality: A Manual for Nurses and Others, Giving an Outline of the Medical, Social, and Legal Aspects of the Venereal Diseases* (New York: G. P. Putnam's Sons, 1910).

55. Taylor, *Pioneering on Social Frontiers,* 86–95; Wade, *Graham Taylor,* 198–202.

56. "Proceedings of the City Vice Committee, Chicago, Saturday, January 18, 1913," CCR.

57. Taylor, *Pioneering on Social Frontiers,* 84–85.

58. Ruth Rosen, *The Lost Sisterhood: Prostitution in America, 1900–1918* (Baltimore: Johns Hopkins University Press, 1982), 112–35. Rosen estimates that no more than 10 percent of prostitutes during the Progressive period had been "forced" into prostitution by "white slavers," but ample evidence supports the existence of such coercion. Also see, e.g., James B. Reynolds, "War against the White Slave Traffic and Commercialized Vice," *Proceedings of the National Conference of Charities and Corrections* (1914), 211–17. Reynolds was a former headworker of the University Settlement who became counsel to the American Social Hygiene Association in New York City.

59. Jane Addams, *A New Conscience and an Ancient Evil* (New York: Macmillan, 1912), 191–204.

60. See Davis, *American Heroine,* 183.

61. Addams's book was unusual in part because it was *not* a sensational account of prostitution and the white slave trade. An excellent example of the latter genre that in fact traded on Addams's name was by two Chicago authors, H. W. Lytle and John Dillon, *From Dance Hall to White Slavery: The World's Greatest Tragedy* ([Chicago], 1912). The title page promised "thrilling stories of actual experiences of girls who were lured from innocence into lives of degradation by men and women engaged in a regularly organized WHITE SLAVE TRADE."

62. See, e.g., Bruno Lasker, "The New Youth," *Neighborhood: A Settlement Quarterly* 3(March 1930): 48–53.

63. "Probable Objections to Senate Bill #202 . . . ," flyer from Office of Boston Social Union [early 1915?], USES; minutes of the meeting of the Boston Social Union, 11 June 1919, USES; for a contrary assessment, see Jane Addams to Miss Catherine Brown, 19 December 1919, JAMC.

64. See, e.g., minutes of the staff meeting, Chicago Commons, November 1920, GTP; Lary May, *Screening out the Past: The Birth of Mass Culture and the Motion Picture Industry* (New York: Oxford University Press, 1980), 43–55.

65. See Mrs. Charles Israels, "The Dance Problem," *Proceedings of the National Conference of Charities and Corrections* (1912), 141–46; Beulah E. Kennard, "Emotional Life of Girls," *Proceedings of the National Conference of Charities and Corrections* (1912), 146–48.

66. See, e.g., "A Statement. 1924." North Bennet Street Industrial School, TD, North Bennet Street Industrial School Papers; minutes of the meeting of the Boston Social Union, October 1913, USES.

67. *Annual Report of the South End House, 1914,* 13; minutes of the residents' meeting, Chicago Commons, 15 October 1914, 28 October 1915, CCR.

68. Frances Ingram, "The Public Dance Hall," *Proceedings of the National Conference of Social Work* (1919), 507–12.

69. Minutes of girls' workers meeting of the United Neighborhood Houses, 6 March 1925, JARR.

70. "Condensed from the Rules Governing Social Dancing . . . ," flyer distributed by the United Neighborhood Houses of New York, [1921,] UNHR. See also "Dancing Committee Rules," Boston Social Union, [n.d.,] USES; "Report of Summer Work for the Season of 1926," Stuyvesant Neighborhood House, TD, LDW-CU.

71. Kathy Peiss, *Cheap Amusements: Working Women and Leisure in Turn-of-the-Century New York* (Philadelphia: Temple University Press, 1985), 95–104.

72. Minutes of staff meeting, Chicago Commons, 12 April 1924, GTP.

73. On settlement clubs for young people, besides specific works cited below, see Robbins Gilman, "Clubs and Club Work," and "Club Work for Boys and Girls between the Ages of Thirteen and Seventeen: A Symposium," *Neighborhood: A Settlement Quarterly* 1(April 1928): 15–51.

74. C. L. Bowdlear, "Report on the physical department of Chicago Commons Association, 1919–1920," TD, CCR.

75. *The Settlement Journal* [Henry Street Settlement], January 1913, 16, LDW-CU.

76. Emil Erhardt, response to questions on "Individual Record," MS, Chicago Commons, [1923?], CCR.

77. "Annual Report. University of Chicago Settlement. 1926–27," typescript, Mary McDowell Papers.

78. See, e.g., Miriam A. Sanders, responses to questions on "Individual Record," Chicago Commons, 30 November 1923, CCR; A. K. Maynard, report on manual training, Group Work Reports, Chicago Commons, 1918–1919, AMs, CCR; report of "Bretton Club," South Bay Union, [ca. 1920,] NFSR.

79. Alfreda M. Stiffensen, response to questions on "Individual Record," Chicago Commons, 1 December 1923, AMs, CCR.

80. Mary E. McDowell, "The Young Girl in Industry," typescript, n.d., Mary McDowell Papers. See also Stephen Schlossman and Stephanie Wallach, "The Crime of Precocious Sexuality: Female Juvenile Delinquency in the Progressive Era," *Harvard Educational Review* 48(February 1978): 65–94.

81. Robert A. Woods and Albert J. Kennedy, *Young Working Girls: A Summary of Evidence from Two Thousand Social Workers* (Boston: Houghton Mifflin, 1913).

82. Woods and Kennedy, *Young Working Girls,* 133–34, 140–41, 154–55.

83. Woods and Kennedy, *Young Working Girls,* 155–58.

84. "Chicago Commons Report for the Chicago Council of Social Agencies—Study of Agencies in Chicago Doing Work for Girls, 21 January 1922," CCR.

85. Minutes of the meeting of the Girls' Leaders of UNH, 2 April 1924, JARR. See also minutes of the meeting of the Boston Social Union, 10 May 1916, USES; *Annual Report of the South End House, 1919,* 10; "Girls Work Conference, 1916," UNHP; "Annual Report of the University of Chicago Settlement, May 1, 1928 to May 1, 1929," Mary McDowell Papers.

86. "Report of the Work of Chicago Commons for the year ending September 30, 1927," TD, CCR; Graham Taylor to George Bellamy, 25 October 1921, GTP; "Annual Report of the University of Chicago Settlement, May 1, 1928 to May 1, 1929," TD, Mary McDowell Papers; Woods and Kennedy, *Young Working Girls,* 69–83.

87. Lillian D. Wald to members of the Laurel Club, 18 November 1927, LDW-CU.

88. Woods and Kennedy, *Young Working Girls,* 84–100; Robbins Gilman to Mrs. J. Herbert Roach, 14 February 1914, USSP; Robert A. Woods, "All plans of helpful leadership . . . ," speech notes, [1923?], RWP; "Annual, Summary Report . . . October–May 1923–1924," TD, Mary McDowell Papers; Lillian D. Wald to Felix M. Warburg, 4 February 1913, LDW-CU. See also Woods and Kennedy, *Settlement Horizon,* 409–11.

89. Mrs. Max Morgenthau, Jr., "Training of Club Leaders at Henry Street Settlement," in *First Intercity Conference of the New York Association of Neighborhood Workers and the Boston Social Union* (Boston, 1913), n.p., RWP.

90. Karl D. Hesley to Dr. Clarence Linton, 5 December 1930, LDW-CU.

91. Arthur C. Holden, *The Settlement Idea: A Vision of Social Justice* (New York: Macmillan, 1922), 67–70.

92. Henry M. Busch, "Club Programs: Abstract of a Talk . . . 1924," LDTP.

93. See minutes of the executive meeting of the Boston Social Union, 28 April 1913, USES; Gerald Smith to Mrs. Edgar J. Goodspeed, 21 August 1926, Mary McDowell Papers; minutes of the board meeting, Riis Settlement, 14 November 1929, JARR; minutes of Business Meetings [NFS], Toronto, 22–25 June, 1924, LDTP; Graham Taylor to Edward L. Ryerson, 13 March 1919, CCR. Also see David I. Macleod, *Building Character in the American Boy: The Boy Scouts, the YMCA, and Their Forerunners, 1870–1920* (Madison: University of Wisconsin Press, 1983). I would qualify Macleod's emphasis on the "mass" nature of many of the early urban working-class boys' clubs and the consequent skimping of character-building techniques in favor of simple entertainment to get the boys off the streets. This was far less true of the settlement boys' clubs than of many of the mission clubs and so on.

94. Roy Tibbitts, "Report of Boys Director Camp Farr, Summer 1926," Mary McDowell Papers. See also Hamilton House report of progress, [ca. 1921,] LDW-CU.

95. Lillian Wald to Albert Kennedy, 4 March 1919; Albert Kennedy to Lillian Wald, 22 August 1922, LDW-CU; minutes of the meeting of the Boston Social Union executive committee, 12 January 1916, 8 May 1918, 7 July [1920], 7 April 1924, USES; Report of the Boston Social Union for 1921–22, USES. The United Neighborhood Houses of New York sponsored a Volunteer Conference on 20 November 1925. Among the topics discussed were the dearth of male settlement workers and the universal need for better training: NFSR.

96. Holden, *Settlement Idea,* 65–67, 178–79.

97. Charles Cooper to Robert Woods, 4 October 1921, NFSR.

98. See, e.g., comments on various club leaders in H. M. Atkinson, "Notes on Club House Activities, June 1921," [Henry Street Settlement,] LDW-CU; "Conference on Girls' Work," [Boston Social Union? 1920,] NFSR; *Henry News: Camp and Farm Issue* 24(29 May 1926), n.p., LDW-CU; Lydia Banning to Lillian D. Wald, 22 October 1930, LDW-CU; Mary K. Simkhovitch, *Neighborhood: My Story of Greenwich House* (New York: W. W. Norton, 1938), 277–78.

99. For example, Edward W. Bergstrom, "Chicago Commons Game Room Report for period, September to June, 1926," CCR.

100. Clifford Whittingham Beers, *A Mind That Found Itself,* 4th ed. (New York: Longmans, Green, 1920), 319–91; John Chynoweth Burnham, "Psychiatry, Psychology and the Progressive Movement," *American Quarterly* 12(Winter 1960): 457–65; Roy Lubove, *The Professional Altruist: The Emergence of Social Work as a Career, 1880–1930* (Cambridge: Harvard University Press, 1965), 55–84; Walter I. Trattner, *From Poor Law to Welfare State: A History of Social Welfare in America* (New York: Free Press, 1974), 160–65; Amos G. Warner, Stuart Alfred Queen, and Ernest Bouldin Harper, *American Charities and Social Work,* 4th ed. (New York: Thomas Y. Crowell, 1930), 241–60. The authors state flatly: "By 1920 the voice of modern psychiatry began to be heard in every field, and mental hygiene became the dominant note in social work" (241).

101. See Warner, Queen, and Harper, *American Charities and Social Work,* 318–42; Margo Horn, "The Moral Message of Child Guidance, 1925–1945," *Journal of Social History* 18(Fall 1984): 25–27. Sol Cohen discusses the hygien-

ists' focus on childhood as the " 'conditioning period of personality' " in "The Mental Hygiene Movement, the Development of Personality and the School: The Medicalization of American Education," *History of Education Quarterly* 23(Summer 1983): 125–31.

102. Lubove, *Professional Altruist,* 64–66; Jane Addams, *My Friend, Julia Lathrop* (New York: Macmillan, 1935), 158–65. Dummer had a number of connections to the women of Hull-House; the earliest was her teacher at the Kirkland School, Ellen Gates Starr. Robert M. Mennel, "Ethel Sturges Dummer," *Notable American Women: The Modern Period.* On Dummer's role in the institute, the recruitment of Healy, and the subsequent problems in the institute, see Graham Parker, "The Juvenile Court Movement: The Illinois Experience," *University of Toronto Law Journal* 26(1976): 282–91.

103. Lubove, *Professional Altruist,* 89–91; minutes of the meeting of the Boston Social Union, 9 May 1917, USES. The Judge Baker Foundation became a model for four more child guidance clinics sponsored by the Commonwealth Fund in cooperation with the National Committee for Mental Hygiene.

104. Minutes of the meeting of the Boston Social Union, 12 March 1924, USES; Lubove, *Professional Altruist,* 90–95.

105. Robert Woods, speech, *First Intercity Conference of the New York Association of Neighborhood Workers and the Boston Social Union* (Boston, 1913), n.p., RWP; Lubove, *Professional Altruist,* 66–71. The close relations between a movement to remove one category of the mentally "unfit" from the population and a movement to reintegrate another seems paradoxical on its face. As Lubove explains, the sudden popularity of the idea of segregating the retarded drew its energy largely from the eugenics movement, then at high tide. Little wonder that historians have found the attempt to delineate a "progressive mentality" somewhat traumatic.

106. "South End House: Some Phases of Progress in 1922," TD, RWP; Esther G. Barrows, "The Social Worker and Habit Clinics," *Proceedings of the National Conference of Social Work* (1924), 397–401. Barrows was the director of women's and girls' work at South End House. Also see Steven L. Schlossman, "Before Home Start: Notes toward a History of Parent Education in America, 1897–1929," *Harvard Educational Review* 46(August 1976): 458–62.

107. Minutes of the meeting of Girls' Workers Committee, United Neighborhood Houses, 5 January [1928], UNHR. See also minutes of the meeting of Boys' Workers Committee, United Neighborhood Houses, 19 June [1927], UNHR; minutes of the meeting of the Boston Social Union, 14 May 1924, USES.

108. One of the most outspoken advocates of this view was Jessie Taft, director of the Child Study Department of the Children's Aid Society of Philadelphia; see, e.g., "The Social Worker's Opportunity," *Proceedings of the National Conference of Social Work* (1922), 371–75.

A few settlements did hire experts in psychology and child guidance; for two years Greenwich House had its own mental hygiene clinic, but funding ran out and was not renewed. See Simkhovitch, *Neighborhood,* 282–83. See also Viola M. Jones to Lillian D. Wald, 7 September 1929; Karl D. Hesley to Lillian D. Wald, 1 September 1928, LDW-CU; minutes of the board meeting, Riis Settlement, 4 June 1925, JARR; Albert Kennedy to Lillian Wald, 22 August 1922, LDW-CU.

109. Abbie H. Evans, report on Girls' Work [in the Association of Philadelphia Settlements], TD, n.d., NFSR. See also Kenneth E. Reid, *From Character Building to Social Treatment: The History of the Use of Groups in Social Work* (Westport, Conn.: Greenwood Press, 1981), 111–32.

110. In an address of 1926, Paul Kellogg tackled the question whether the "vogue" of psychology in social work was inimical to a continued drive for social justice. So far, he argued, the trend had been toward "readjusting and reconstructing individual lives, rather than in affording new approaches to social justice." He cited Addams's challenge to the psychiatric social workers to "turn on occasion from their individual cases and apply social diagnosis to the mind of the community, to the tendencies and inhibitions that thwart growth and good will." Kellogg himself suggested that the "rediscovery of the individual" might prove a "refreshment for democracy." Kellogg, address before Teachers' Union, Hudson Guild Farm, October 1926, Paul U. Kellogg Papers.

Chapter Ten

1. John L. Elliott, "Charles Cooper and the Settlement Movement," *Kingsley Record* 33(April 1931): n.p.; Paul U. Kellogg, "Charles Cooper: A Great Neighbor," *Survey* 65(15 January, 1931): 436–37, reprinted in *Kingsley Record* 33(April 1931), n.p., NFSR; Edward O. Taber, tribute to Charles Cooper, [1930], NFSR.

2. Charles C. Cooper to Robert Woods, 29 September 1921, NFSR.

3. C. M. Bookman, "The Community Chest Movement—an Interpretation," *Proceedings of the National Conference of Social Work* (1924), 20–21; *Yesterday and Today with Community Chests: A Record of Their History and Growth* (New York, 1937). See also Graham Taylor to Robert W. Kelso, 27 September 1921, GTP.

4. Charles Cooper to Paul U. Kellogg, 29 September 1921, SAR.

5. Charles Cooper to Paul U. Kellogg, 12 January 1922, SAR; see also "Memorandum of Business to Come before the Executive Committee [of the NFS]," 28 October [1920?], LDTP.

6. His allies against the Pittsburgh Chest included forty-two clergymen representing most of the Protestant denominations; see "Clergymen Condemn Community Chest," *Pittsburgh Sun-Telegram,* 9 February [1922?], clipping, SAR.

7. Charles Cooper to Albert J. Kennedy, 15 February 1928, copy, LDTP; see also Charles Cooper to Paul Kellogg, 12 March 1928; Charles Cooper to Arthur Kellogg, 12 March 1928; Charles Cooper to Paul Kellogg, 23 April 1929, SAR.

8. Judith Ann Trolander, *Settlement Houses and the Great Depression* (Detroit: Wayne State University Press, 1975), 9–11, 50–63. In her study of Indianapolis's Christamore House, Ruth Hutchinson Crocker argues that the Community Fund's generous support of the settlement reflected a "congruence between the goals of the settlement and those of elite groups within the society," suggesting that the changing goals of some settlement leaders fit well with the general conservatism of the Chest movement. Crocker, "Christamore: An Indiana Settlement House from Private Dream to Public Agency," *Indiana Magazine of History* 83(June 1987): 138.

9. See, e.g., exchange between Sina Evans, headworker of the Neighborhood House in Lorain, Ohio, and Lillie Peck, secretary of the NFS in 1933; Evans asked for Peck's advice on how to cope with the cutting of Chest funds to the settlement. Peck replied that the best course was to break free of the Chest altogether, as being "a weak reed supporting a still weaker reed, i.e., the ineffective settlement whose board doesn't really understand what the settlement is set to do." Evans was able to bring her board in line, and Lorain's Neighborhood House survived outside the Community Chest. Lillie Peck to Sina Evans, 11 October 1933; Sina Evans to Lillie Peck, 17 October 1933, NFSR.

10. Isabel Taylor, "Problems of the Small Settlements," *Neighborhood: A Settlement Quarterly* 3(March 1930): 21–28.

11. See "National Federation of Settlements: 1911 FF.," typescript, [1932?], NFSR; Cooper to Paul Kellogg, 3 January 1924, SAR; Cooper, "Endowment Funds Held by Settlements," *Neighborhood: A Settlement Quarterly* 2(April 1929): 97–100.

12. See the table compiled by Cooper in "Endowment Funds," 98; see also Robert Woods, "Notes on Settlement Endowments," [n.d.], TD, RWP.

13. "South End House. Twenty-fifth Anniversary Fund of $125,000. To Provide for the Larger work of Its Second Quarter Century," [1923?], TD; William J. Tucker to Robert Woods, August 1923, RWP.

14. Jacob Schiff to Lillian Wald, 26 November 1912, LDW-CU.

15. "Memorandum on Ivy Lee situation," 4 January 1919; see also Charles Stelze to Lillian Wald, 13 July 1921; Lillian Wald to Charles Stelze, 14 July 1921; Charles Stelze to Mrs. Elsa H. Herrman, 14 June 1924; Charles Stelze to Lillian Wald, 30 September 1926; Jacob Schiff to Lillian Wald, 18 May 1914, 29 October 1915, 10 November 1915, 23 December 1915; Lillian Wald to Henry Bruère, 3 December 1926, LDW-CU.

16. Robert Woods to Charles Cooper, 25 July 1921; Charles Cooper to Robert Woods, 9 August 1921, NFSR.

17. [Carnegie Corporation] to Mrs. Janet D. Schenck, 27 May 1926, NFSR.

18. Charles Cooper to Albert J. Kennedy, copy, 2 July 1925, LDTP.

19. Cooper to Kennedy, 2 July 1925, LDTP.

20. Kennedy's curriculum vitae, AJKP.

21. Albert J. Kennedy to Charles Cooper, 6 July 1925, copy, LDTP.

22. Lillian Wald to Albert Kennedy, 21 August 1925; Harriet Vittum to Albert Kennedy, 2 October 1925; S. Max Nelson to Albert Kennedy, 18 August 1925; Lou-Eva Longan to Albert Kennedy, 26 August 1925, all copies, LDTP.

23. Albert J. Kennedy, ed., *Settlement Goals for the Next Third of a Century: A Symposium* (Boston: National Federation of Settlements, 1926).

24. His decision seems to have been precipitated by a letter from Paul Kellogg, the self-appointed gadfly-cum–mentor of the settlement world. Like Cooper three years before, Kellogg feared that the technical emphasis on the arts and activities was draining energy from the settlements' "civic function" and suggested that perhaps a dual secretaryship should be created, to make sure the national headquarters gave equal emphasis to both "lines" of settlement work. Paul Kellogg to Albert J. Kennedy, 17 February 1928, copy for distribution, LDTP.

25. Charles Cooper to Albert Kennedy, 2 April 1928, NFSR.

26. "Policy and Procedure of Secretary" [minutes of executive committee meeting, NFS, 1928], LDTP.

27. Trolander, *Settlement Houses,* 36; on Peck, see Fred and Grace Soule to John MacDowell, 8 March 1957, NFSR; Helen Hall, *Unfinished Business in Neighborhood and Nation* (New York: Macmillan, 1971), 78–80; folder on Ellen Coolidge, NFSR.

28. Hall, *Unfinished Business,* 31, 40–43; Graham Taylor, *Chicago Commons through Forty Years* (Chicago: Chicago Commons Association, 1936), 179–83; Clinch Calkins, *Some Folks Won't Work* (New York: Harcourt, Brace, 1930). Commercially, Calkins's book could not have been better timed. It went through a number of printings in the next few years. See also Trolander, *Settlement Houses,* 36–37. Helen Hall moved from Philadelphia to direct the Henry Street Settlement in 1933; in 1935 she and Paul Kellogg were married. They continued to live at the settlement.

29. "Suggestions for the New Settlement Periodical," n.d., TD, NFSR.

30. Morton Keller, "Anglo-American Politics, 1900–1930: A Case Study in Comparative History," *Comparative Studies in Society and History* 22(July 1980): 458–77. Keller argues that the underlying differences between British and American progressives and liberals were more important than surface similarities before the Great War. See also Kenneth McNaught, "American Progressives and the Great Society," *Journal of American History* 53(December 1966): 512–20.

31. Jane Addams to H. O. Barnett, 30 July 1913, JAMC; Henrietta Barnett to Robert Woods, 16 July 1913; Henrietta Barnett to Jane Addams, 10 July 1913, 25 July 1913, 11 October 1913, 1 December 1913, JA-SCPC; see also other correspondence, clippings, and obituaries for Canon Barnett in folder 18, NFSR.

32. See, David Shannon, ed., *Beatrice Webb's American Diary* (Madison: University of Wisconsin Press, 1963), 60, 62, 107–9. Mrs. Webb reacted comically to Hull-House. She wrote: "In the evening of our arrival we underwent a terrific ordeal. First an uncomfortable dinner, a large party served, higgledepiggledy. Then a stream of persons, labour, municipal, philanthropic, university, all those queer, well-intentioned or cranky individuals, who habitually centre round all settlements" (108). See also Sidney Webb to Jane Addams, 14 March 1906, introducing Wells, JAMC; Graham Wallas to Jane Addams, May 1914, JAMC; Graham Wallas to Jane Addams, 11 August 1921, JA-SCPC. See also Keir Hardie to Lillian Wald, 24 January 1909, LDW-CU; "The Bishop of London at the University Settlement," *Charities and the Commons* 19(26 October 1907): 937–38; "Mrs. Humphry Ward on Play," *Charities and the Commons* 20(11 April 1908): 79–83; "Percy Alden's Work in Parliament," *Charities and the Commons* 21(3 October 1908): 6.

33. London *Evening Standard,* 12 September 1921, clipping, JA-SCPC.

34. [London] *Star,* 13 September 1921, clipping, JA-SCPC. Coming at the nadir of Addams's American popularity, these British press squibs must have been heartening to her. See also Edward B. Butler to Jane Addams, [9 December 1910,] JA-SCPC.

35. A. Maude Royden to Jane Addams, 19 April 1913, JA-SCPC.

36. Graham Wallas to Jane Addams, 14 May 1915; Catherine E. Marshall to

Jane Addams, 24 June [1915]; Jane Addams to "Dear Lady" [Lillian Wald?], 8 August 1916, JA-SCPC.

37. Beatrice Webb to Jane Addams, 10 May 1915; Gertrude Toynbee to Addams, 14 May 1915; Mary Rebecca H. Cheltham to Addams, 12 May 1915; J. St. John Heath to Addams, 10 May 1915, JA-SCPC.

38. Henrietta O. Barnett to Jane Addams, 21 June [1915], JA-SCPC.

39. Robert Woods to Graham Taylor, 16 October 1918, LDTP; Robert Woods to Lillian Wald, 21 October 1918, LDW-CU; H. O. Barnett to Jane Addams, 24–28 January 1919, JA-SCPC.

40. H. O. Barnett to Jane Addams, 24–28 January 1919, [?] 1919, JA-SCPC.

41. H. O. Barnett to Jane Addams, 2 December 1919, JA-SCPC; H. O. Barnett to Albert J. Kennedy, 8 March 1920, NFSR; H. O. Barnett to Mr. Adams and Mr. Buckley, 1 March 1920, copy, JA-SCPC; Jane Addams to Albert J. Kennedy, 26 May 1920, NFSR; Jane Addams to H. O. Barnett, 26 May 1920, JAMC; H. O. Barnett to Jane Addams, 15 April 1920, 15 October 1920, 31 October 1920; George E. Vincent to Jane Addams, 29 October 1920, JA-SCPC. Mrs. Barnett had long been interested in the "garden suburb" idea; she and Canon Barnett had been instrumental in founding the Hampstead Garden Suburb, where Mrs. Barnett lived after Samuel Barnett's death. H. O. Barnett, *Canon Barnett: His Life, Work, and Friends,* 2 vols. (Boston: Houghton Mifflin, 1919), 2:312–24.

Henrietta Barnett had a special and to all appearances overwhelming fondness for Jane Addams, whom she bombarded with long letters full of political opinions, requests for information, and protestations of affection, which Addams characteristically rarely answered. "I have 100 things I am longing to hear about from you," read a typical letter of 9 March 1921, "—the Ireland Commission, the activities of Hull House, your hopes of Mr. Harding, the welfare of prohibition, your action on leading a housing scheme, & above all your *dear* self—but I don't expect I shall get my longings satisfied. . . . I will not write more now, because I feel you may be too busy even to read my letter, but I will add, what you know, that I love you, & revere you, & am grateful to you, & long to hear from you."

42. See extensive correspondence, printed circulars, etc., in folders 19–22, NFSR. See also J. J. Mallon to Jane Addams, 25 October 1923; Albert Kennedy to H. O. Barnett, 26 July 1924, JA-SCPC; H. O. Barnett to Jane Addams, 29 December 1928, JA-SCPC.

43. Henrietta O. Barnett to Robert and Eleanor Woods, 20 November 1920; H. O. Barnett to Robert Woods, 22 August 1921; USES; Jane Addams to H. O. Barnett, 22 April 1921, JAMC; H. O. Barnett to Jane Addams, 18 November 1926, JA-SCPC; H. O. Barnett to Albert Kennedy, 10 December 1926, NFSR; Albert Kennedy to Jane Addams, 5 January 1927, JA-SCPC.

44. "Among Our Exchanges," *Charities Review* 6(July/August 1897): 517.

45. Address of Ellen Coolidge, minutes of the meeting of the Boston Social Union, 8 November 1922, USES.

46. [W. J.] Bassot to Jane Addams, 4 November 1920, JA-SCPC; Lillie Peck to Isabelle Dubroca, 30 July 1954, NFSR; Alfred B. Yeomans to Jane Addams, 17 February [1918], JA-SCPC; minutes of the meeting of the Boston Social Union, 14 April 1920, USES.

47. Marie-Thérèse Vieillot, memorial notes on Ellen Coolidge, 2 November 1954; Marie-Thérèse [Vieillot] to Lillie Peck, 3 December 1954; Ellen Coolidge, "Notes on the International Association of Settlements," n.d., AMs, NFSR.

48. Dr. J. J. Mallon, "Earlier International Conferences," in *The Building of Human Relationships in Our Times: Conference Report of the Sixth International Conference of the International Federation of Settlements . . . 16–20 June 1952* (The Netherlands, 1952), 28; minutes of the executive committee meeting of the NFS, 9 December 1921, LDTP; clipping, *Westminister Gazette,* 16 September 1921, JA-SCPC; clipping, [London] *Daily Telegraph,* 12 September 1921, JA-SCPC.

49. Captain L. F. Ellis to Albert Kennedy, 27 November 1924, LDW-CU.

50. *Building of Human Relationships in Our Times,* 23. The International Federation of Settlements survived World War II and reconvened in 1952 with an ambitious theme, embodied in the title of the pamphlet cited above. See also Helen Morton, "A Summer Conference De Luxe," *Neighborhood: A Settlement Quarterly* 2(April 1929): 112–16; Helen Morton, ed., "The Third International Conference of Settlements," *Neighborhood: A Settlement Quarterly* 2(July 1929): 159–84.

51. Charles Cooper to Helen Hall, 18 January 1928; also Cooper to Albert Kennedy, 18 January 1928, NFSR.

52. John Elliott to Lillian Wald, 7 June 1926, LDW-CU.

53. Lea Taylor to Albert Kennedy, 12 September 1932; Kennedy to Taylor, 26 September 1932, NFSR. By the 1950s, males outnumbered females as head-workers; Judith Trolander tells this sad story, which turns on the emergence of the MSW as the professional degree of choice among settlement workers and the decline of feminism in the broader culture, in *Professionalism and Social Change: From the Settlement House Movement to Neighborhood Centers, 1886 to the Present* (New York: Columbia University Press, 1987), 49–69.

54. All four of the Taylor children remained true to the ideals of their settlement upbringing. The oldest, Helen Demarest Taylor, took kindergarten training at the Commons and worked at the settlement until her marriage. Graham Romeyn Taylor returned to Chicago Commons after graduating from Harvard, then moved onto the staff of *Charities and the Commons.* He worked as an assistant to the ambassador to Russia with special responsibility for relief efforts during the Great War and then returned to Chicago to collaborate with Charles S. Johnson on a state inquiry into the causes of the race riots in 1919. He moved to New York in 1922 to work with the Commonwealth Fund. Katharine Taylor attended Vassar like both of her sisters, was an English instructor there for several years, and then taught at the Francis W. Parker School in Chicago for five years. In 1922 she became director of the Shady Hill School in Cambridge, Massachusetts. See Taylor, *Chicago Commons through Forty Years,* 250–53.

55. Minutes of the staff meeting, Chicago Commons, 21 May 1927, 4 June 1927, GTP.

56. Algernon Black, in "Settlement Faith and Practice: A Symposium by Head-workers Who Have Taken Office since 1915," *Neighborhood: A Settlement Quarterly* 3(September 1930): 101–6.

57. Lillian Wald to Mary McCurley, 4 November 1929, LDW-CU.

58. Anne Geddes to Nan Collier, 11 March 1927; see also Bertha B. Carter to Lena Lillian Crosscup, 14 August 1928, LDW-CU.

59. See, e.g., Lea Taylor to Martha H. Chandler, 11 April 1921, CCR.

60. See Neva Boyd to Josephine Schain [Henry Street Settlement], 24 October 1922, LDW-CU; Edna Winship to "Cartwright," 15 May 1926, North Bennet Street Industrial School Papers, Schlesinger Library, Radcliffe College.

61. Mary M. Phinny to Lillie M. Peck, 5 March 1934, NFSR.

62. "Annual Report," University of Chicago Settlement, 1928–29, TD, Mary McDowell Papers.

63. Robert Hunter to Albert J. Kennedy, 23 November 1936, AJKP.

64. Trolander, *Professionalism and Social Change,* esp. 93–95; Howard Jacob Karger, *The Sentinels of Order: A Study of Social Control and the Minneapolis Settlement House Movement, 1915–1950* (Lanham, Md.: University Press of America, 1987), 103–20; Crocker, "Christamore: An Indiana Settlement House from Private Dream to Public Agency," 133–34.

65. Albert J. Kennedy, untitled TD [produced for the fiftieth anniversary of the University Settlement, 1936?], AJKP.

Index

Abbott, Edith, 130–31, 150
Abbott, Grace, 131, 150
Abbott, Lyman, 15, 35
Adams, Henry C., 124
Addams, Anna Haldeman, 42
Addams, Jane, 73, 99, 124, 127, 192, 196;
    and Henrietta Barnett, 265 n; and
    Catherine Breshkovsky, 152;
    influenced by Thomas Carlyle,
    43–46; and Chicago politics, 140–41;
    on conflict, 148; death of, 195; and
    Depression of 1893, 75, 76; and John
    Dewey, 106–7; on educational
    reform, 119, 120; and English
    reformers, 189; family of, 41–42,
    46–48; as feminist, 148–49, 169; and
    Food Administration, 164; and Ford's
    Peace Ship, 155; on free speech, 77;
    health problems of, 47; and
    Hull-House, founding of, 48, 54–56;
    and Hull-House atmosphere, 228 n;
    on immigrants, 103, 104–5; at
    International Conference of
    Settlements, 191; at International
    Congress of Women, 155; influenced
    by William James, 106–7, 149; and
    labor organization, 77–78, 81;
    leadership of, 88–89; as NCCC
    president, 122; on organized charity,
    66; pacifism of, 58–59, 149, 153; on
    popular culture, 113–15; postwar
    attacks on, 164–66; and pragmatism,
    149; and Progressive party, 147–49,
    150; on Prohibition, 170; on
    prostitution, 171–72; and radicals,
    161–63; religious beliefs of, 43–46;
    at Rockford Female Seminary, 41,
    42–44; and Theodore Roosevelt, 146,
    147–48; on settlement function,
    106–7; on settlement households, 58;
    on social work, 134–35; and Ellen
    Gates Starr, 41–48; on suffrage for
    blacks, 148; influenced by Leo
    Tolstoy, 58–59; at Toynbee Hall, 48;
    as Women's Peace party chair, 154;

and Robert Woods, 139; youth and
    education, 41–48. Works: *Democracy
    and Social Ethics,* 142; *New
    Conscience and an Ancient Evil,*
    171; *Newer Ideals of Peace,* 149;
    Second Twenty Years at Hull-House,
    166; *Spirit of Youth and the City
    Streets,* 113–15
Addams, John Huy, 41–42, 46–47
Addams, Sarah Weber, 41
Adler, Felix, 18, 36, 70, 86, 118
Adolescence, 112–16
Adolescent boy, NFS study of, 172
Adolescent girl, NFS study of, 172
Adolescents, settlements' work with,
    172–77
African-Americans, 195
Aladyin, Alexis, 152
Alcohol, 167. *See also* Drunkenness;
    Prohibition; Saloons
Alcott, May, 38
Alden, Percy, 32, 49
Altgeld, John Peter, 89–90, 91
American Civil Liberties Union (ACLU),
    165, 249 n
American Economic Association, 17, 123
American Federation of Labor (AFL),
    77–78, 161
Americanization, 103, 158–59, 185. *See
    also* Immigrants
American Legion, 165
American Protective League, 165
Americans in Process, 102
American Social Hygiene Association, 169
American Social Science Association
    (ASSA), 16
American Society for the Extension of
    University Teaching, 124
American Union against Militarism
    (AUAM), 249 n
Amherst College, 28–29, 36
Anderson, Sarah, 48
Andover House (Boston), 98; as early
    American settlement, 53, 56; and
    organized charity, 65; and religion,

Webb, Sidney, 130, 188
Welfare history, ix–x
Wellesley College, 40, 83
Wells, H. G., 188
Wells College, 97
Western Reserve University, 21
White, Gaylord, 132, 134
Whitechapel (G.B.), 5
White House Conference on Dependent
  Children, 146
White slave trade, 170–71
Whittier House (New Jersey), 187
Wicksteed, P. H., 35
Williams, Elizabeth, 95, 97
Wilson, Woodrow, 155–56
Wischnewetzky, Florence Kelley. *See*
  Kelley, Florence
Wischnewetzky, Lazare, 90
Wise, Stephen S., 153
Women's colleges, 42, 49, 54. *See also*
  Colleges; Liberal arts; Students,
  college
Women's International League for Peace
  and Freedom, 164–65
Women's Land Army, 157
Women's Peace party, 154, 155
Women's settlements (G.B.), 32
Women's University Settlement (G.B.),
  32
Woods, Robert Archey, 29, 35, 36, 49, 56,
  83, 122, 144, 191, 196; and Jane
  Addams, 106, 139; and British
  settlements, 190; and charity
  organizers, 65; on class differences,
  120; death of, 182; and English labor
  leaders, 80; and Fabians, 30–31; on
  "friendly visiting," 65; and

Handbook of Settlements, 186; and
  immigrants, 105; leadership and
  personality, 94–95; on localism,
  98–99; and mental hygiene
  movement, 179; as NCSW president,
  158; as NFS secretary, 182; and NFS
  study of adolescent girl, 174; and
  Pittsburgh Survey, 125; in
  Progressive Service, 150; and
  prohibition, 168–69, 170; on
  resident neighborhood work, 66;
  and *Settlement Horizon,* 186; on
  settlements in politics, 144, 145; on
  settlement's similarity to Franciscan
  order, 57; on settlement as
  talent-saving station, 118; on social
  science, 64–65; on social work, 129;
  at Toynbee Hall, 27, 29–31; and
  "Traffic in Citizenship," 144; on
  wartime social work, 156, 157–58,
  160; youth and education, 28–29
Woodward, Calvin, 119
Wordsworth, William, 38
Working People's Social Science Club,
  76–77
World War I, 151, 153–60
Wright, Carroll, 91

Yale University, 123
Yerkes, Charles, 140, 142
Young Men's Christian Association
  (YMCA), 177
Young Working Girls, 174
Youth, 112–16, 172–77

Zueblin, Charles, 57
Zurich, University of, 90